002307215

Eva Zeisel: *Life, Design, and Beauty*

Eva Zeisel: LIFE, DESIGN, AND BEAUTY

Edited by Pat Kirkham

Executive Direction by Pat Moore

Concept and Design Direction by Pirco Wolfframm

Photographs by Brent Brolin

CHRONICLE BOOKS

SAN FRANCISCO

I have always made my designs as gifts to others and I invite you to enjoy them in this lovely book.

I know that all those who contributed to this book did so with love and with incredibly hard work, and I accept their generosity gratefully.

—*Eva Zeisel,* *June 2011, Rockland County*

I met Eva Zeisel through her dishes. Her *Tomorrow's Classic* dishes in the Bouquet pattern were our family's Sunday-best dinnerware during most of my growing-up years, and I was given the set when my parents retired. Years later, when I was searching for missing pieces, I checked directory assistance and called Eva's number. I heard a soft voice say, "This is Eva Zeisel." It took me a second to respond—I had learned enough about her by then to be in awe of her—but I introduced myself and began asking about her designs. I soon realized, however, that she was interviewing me. It was so typical of Eva, whose curiosity about the world extended to everyone and everything with which she came in contact. She asked what I did, and when I said I was retired, she asked my age (sixty-eight). "You can't retire; you're just a baby," she replied. I laughed, but soon realized she was serious: one continues to work at what one loves. My new love became collecting all of Eva's designs, and when someone remarked that it was a shame there was no collector's club for Eva's designs, my husband, Gene Grobman, and I started one (in 1998, now the Eva Zeisel forum, EZf). Thus began an expanding circle of friends-with-a-common-interest: Eva.

I met both Eva and Pirco Wolfframm, the first member of the club, at an exhibition about Eva's work in 1999, and we agreed that I would prepare, and she would design, a catalogue of Eva's work. We published the *Eva Zeisel Times* newsletter, each issue focused on a different design line, but stopped when we realized it would take more than newsletters to cover Eva's more than ten thousand designs and more than one person to write it. Members of the EZf joined the effort, and the distinguished design historian Pat Kirkham agreed to come aboard to write an overview of Eva's life and work. The project went beyond a catalogue to become a fully rounded story of Eva's life and accomplishments. We hope it adds to your life, as Eva has added to ours.

Pat Moore

My first encounter with Eva was through "soul contact," as she called it—instant, unabashed love for a pair of salt and pepper shakers at a thrift store on my third day in the United States in 1996. Like many, I hesitated to approach this famous lady only to be disarmed by her kindness the minute we met. I was pierced by her curiosity and hardly was able to satisfy mine. I came to take her remarkably soft, outreaching hands for granted, almost forgetting that the wonder of a long, whimsical life would still eventually be finite.

Our initial bond evolved from my interest in her design, our mutual interests in history, culture, and even mundane aspects of life, and from her keen interest in anybody who brought stories, music, good food, or who would read to her in the five languages she spoke. When equipped with a faculty development grant from Pratt Institute to pursue a small publication, I thoroughly frustrated her with questions rooted in the academic world of cultural criticism that she had little interest in. She turned my quest for her wisdom into an opportunity to tell me what was on her mind, such as her memories from childhood to her arrival in the U.S. Our friendship evolved into an exchange of stories—hers versus mine or the latest interesting news. Though we never discussed design through the academic lens again, I was able to get my answers.

When watching her sketch and seeing her ideas unfold into piles of paper cutouts, models, and prototypes, and watching her touch them repeatedly to confirm or refine them, I understood that what she was doing was not about ideology or heavily theorized design; this process of form giving was indeed her playful search for beauty, her way of being alive, her love of making things, and her desire to give. It is with my various experiences in mind of Eva as a designer and as a friend that I have tried to find an appropriate visual voice to reflect the rich, enriching, and idiosyncratic continuum she lived.

Pirco Wolfframm

I am delighted to be part of this project. In the past, I had turned down offers to write a book about Eva, largely because I did not want anything to interfere with my relationship with her. By the time I joined this project, however, she was nearly 103 years old and I had to face the fact that she might not be with us much longer. To write an overview of her life and work, and edit the book, seemed the least I could do for someone whose designs have given pleasure to so many for so long. It offered me a way of thanking Eva for many things, including her "salon" evenings, talking with my students about her work, and the warmth and affection shown to me, my husband (whom Eva adored and who adored her), and the guests we took along to her apartment and home in the country. It was also an opportunity to think and write about Eva at greater length and to try to articulate some of the many thoughts that had crossed my mind over more than a decade of discussions with her, and others, about her life and work.

I was intrigued by the fact that the project was collector-led, in the sense that Pat Moore, the co-founder of the Eva Zeisel forum, and many of those writing about the individual commissions, are avid collectors of Eva's work. It seemed a marvelous opportunity to transcend barriers between collectors and academics; between amateur and professional historians; between what some might consider old-fashioned connoisseurship, on the one hand, and design history and material culture studies, on the other. So often in the histories of objects, collectors and dealers have kick-started scholarship.

I met Eva in 1998 through the delightful Ron Labaco, who worked as Eva's assistant while writing his MA thesis on her work under my supervision. Eva agreed to be featured in an exhibition I was organizing on women designers working in the U.S. in the twentieth century and I came to know her well. I hope that something of the flavor of how she was as a person comes over in my writing about her.

Pat Kirkham

Life

Jeannie, now that you are old enough I thought you might want to start to figure out how to live right, but how can you if you don't know precisely where and when life is? So I made this poem for your birthday.

It's Life you are living
and life is here.
It's not sometime later,
it's now, Jeannie dear.

It's not a road
with beginning and end.
It leads not anywhere,
it's the time you spend.

It's life when the sun shines,
it's life when it rains,
not where you are going,
but riding the trains.

Life is not a stamp collection
of memories of the past.
Life is in the present tense,
the memory while it lasts.

The cloud that hurries gently by,
the bunnies' funny leaps,
if you hug them with your eye,
belong to you for keeps.

Don't think that once will come a day
when we'll all be rich and smart
and laughter will be here to stay,
and then real life will start.

Between the not yet gilded past
and the time for which we strive
lies, unnoticed and not to last,
the moment which is life.

Eva Zeisel (1950: To Jean on her 10th birthday)

A hugely talented designer with a tremendous life force, Eva Zeisel (born 1906, Hungary; died 2011, United States) was a major figure in the world of twentieth-century design, and both her work and her approach to it inspired, and continue to inspire, younger generations of designers. Eva worked in Hungary, Germany, and the Soviet Union in the 1920s and 1930s and was the pre-eminent designer of mass-produced ceramics for domestic use in the United States in the 1940s, 1950s, and early 1960s. During her extensive career she also worked for companies in Mexico, Italy, Hungary, England, Russia, India, and Japan. She was honored with many prestigious awards, from honorary degrees to two of the highest awards open to civilians in her native Hungary.

Introducing Eva

This chapter introduces Eva's ideas, work, and life in all their varied aspects in the hope that readers will gain a better understanding of her as a person and of the breadth, variety, and quality of her designs. As part of setting these topics within the wider histories of which they were part, and assessing the various influences upon Eva and her formation as a designer, I seek to broaden, and sometimes challenge and revise, current understandings of them. I am interested in telling history in many ways and through many "voices," including oral history, memoirs, images, and anecdotes, as well as through more formally academic and analytical modes, and I have tried to weave Eva's own and very distinctive voice throughout this chapter. I loved hearing her talk, loved talking with her, and hope that something of that experience will resonate with readers.

Her work has been the subject of many exhibitions, as well as the film *Throwing Curves*, a documentary about Eva and her work released in 2002. By the end of this chapter, readers may well feel that a Hollywood biopic or a novel would be more fitting. Indeed, her experiences during her sixteen-month incarceration in a Soviet prison in the 1930s were a source for *Darkness at Noon* (1940), a novel by Arthur Koestler

(1905–1983), a childhood friend of Eva with whom she had a love affair in Paris in the 1920s.[1]

So, too, were the prison experiences of the Austrian physicist Alexander Weissberg (1901–1964) to whom Eva was married (though separated) at the time of her arrest.[2] Weissberg placed himself in considerable danger by trying to help Eva and narrowly avoided death on several occasions, including when, like Eva, he was falsely accused of plotting against Soviet leader Joseph Stalin; when he was handed over to the German Gestapo by the Soviets; and when fighting with the Polish underground during World War II. Eva's departure from Vienna on one of the last trains out of the city in March 1938 as the German army marched in, coming as she did from a family of assimilated Jews, was yet another drama-packed episode of what was, by any estimation, a most remarkable life.

One of the joys of studying a designer who worked in the world of mass production for most of her career is that thousands of pieces made from her designs continue to circulate, some of them still used by those who first bought them, or by their descendents. Some objects found their way into museum collections at the time, and many more have followed. The *Museum* service was created with the intention of producing heirloom-quality pieces and the *Tomorrow's Classic* line was named to suggest such a future. Today many of Eva's other designs have also acquired heirloom status.

As a designer, Eva thought of herself as working in a modern way, but long before she thought about herself as a designer of any sort, she thought of herself as modern. As a child, she was conscious of the modernity of the world into which she had been born.[3] The family, and the circles in which family members moved, believed that the new century would reap all the benefits of the progress made during the previous century while realizing even greater achievements. Children born in the new century were considered more fortunate than those from earlier generations and symbolized the hopes of a better world.[4] She recalled:

When I was about six years old I was read to from a small volume . . . It was the memoir of a doll who started her story as follows, "I am a modern doll who prides herself on having been born at the end of the superb nineteenth

Eva at Brooklyn Botanic Garden, 2006. PWA.

century which one can call the century of miracles, of the triumphs of technology. Evidently it is to the science of technology that I owe the suppleness
of my limbs, my uncertain speech, and the grace of movements unknown to
my forebears." Out of the miracle of technology, this doll, who has shed the
dullness, the passivity of other dolls, and had acquired intelligence and feelings, was able to tell her life story.[5]

Eva liked to describe herself as a "modernist with a small m."[6]
The lower case is enormously important. It marked her distance from
the architecture and design movement in interwar Europe, known
as the Modern Movement. That movement grew out of several over-
lapping progressive and avant-garde trends in Europe, from Russian
Constructivism and De Stijl in Holland to the Bauhaus in Germany and
architect-designers such as the Swiss-born but French-based Le Corbusier,
who famously described a house as a *"machine à habiter"* (machine for
living in). Its adherents (Modernists with a capital *M*) took a rationalist,
functionalist, and problem-solving approach to design, and advocated
new materials, new technologies, and industrial mass production to
produce objects and buildings appropriate for what they thought of as
the new "Machine Age."[7] For the most part, they rejected both decoration and looking to past styles for inspiration (historicism).

Eva, like many others, welcomed the social agenda of bringing
affordable, well-made, and well-designed goods to greater numbers of
people, but felt that few designers or reformers of any worth in the
late 1920s or 1930s would oppose such a notion. She believed that this
should be a *given*, a starting point for any designer rather than a man-
tra unto itself, and was skeptical about the Modern Movement's claim
that style had disappeared. When I told her that British designer
William Lethaby dubbed it the "No-Style style," she chuckled, clapped
her hands with glee, and said she wished that she had coined the
phrase.[8] Eva thought of the world in far broader terms than a "Machine
Age" and considered Modernist designs to be the result of narrow-
minded people obsessed with "so-called functionalism, anti-historicism,
and the ridiculous idea that form followed function."[9] Eva was just
as interested in everyday objects as Modernists but took a much more
open-ended approach to design, while always respecting historicism.

She insisted that "the designer must understand that form does

not follow function, nor does form follow a production process,"
adding, "For every use and for every production process, there are
innumerable equally attractive solutions."[10] Eva sought "soul contact"
with users and found Modernism to be insufficiently cognizant of the
user, too patronizing and didactic, and inherently dangerous, because
its narrow definitions of "good design" radically limited variety and
choice, especially when it came to the vocabulary and outlook of the
designer before he or she had even begun to consider the particular
commission or problem at hand.[11] The role of the designer, as she saw
it, was to go beyond applying rationalism to the task at hand and
evoke the more psychological and aesthetic dimensions of design.[12]
She was not alone in holding such ideas, but her articulation of them
through notions of playfulness and beauty was distinctive. Her
emphasis on "the playful search for beauty" was both modest and
hugely ambitious, as we shall see throughout this book.

Eva's ideas and designs offer an excellent case study for seeing
European modern design of the interwar years through lenses other
than that of the Modern Movement, especially the Bauhaus. The stories of Eva's modernism, and the designs of many others who thought
of themselves as modernists with a small m, need to be told for their
own sakes, but they also need to be told to redress the balance of histories too often written from pro-Modernist points of view.

The disillusionment with Modernism and the greater impact of
postmodern ideas from the mid-1970s and 1980s (in some cases earlier)
underpinned reassessments of several major designers who, each in
their own ways, at some point stood aside from orthodox Modernism,
including Alvar Aalto, Charles and Ray Eames, and Eva. All four were
about the same age: Aalto was eight years older than Eva, while Charles
Eames was just one year younger and Ray Eames six years younger. The
more organic forms of the 1930s and 1940s were central to what Eva
called the "wider aesthetic history" of which she was part, and Russel
Wright, an important figure in bringing the forms of what today is
often referred to as "Organic Modernism" to pottery design in the U.S.,
was only two years older than Eva.

Unlike Aalto, who came to stress the human and humanistic aspects
of design after something of a love affair with orthodox Modernism,
Eva always distanced herself ideologically from it. The Eameses

Eva in front of Monmouth Pottery, c. 1953. EZA. · Eva in front of a kiln (possibly at Monmouth), c. 1953. EZA. · Eva with model maker, Monmouth Pottery, c. 1953. EZA.

engaged with ideas and approaches to design that today are considered postmodern or prototypical of postmodernism, including playfulness, whimsy, and humor, as well as a more humanistic approach to design, objects, and users.[13] Eva was just as engaged with such issues, but she went further than they did by never, at any stage, rejecting past design traditions—an approach that explains, in part at least, the breadth of appeal of her designs.

Starting in the 1970s, Eva felt herself blessed to witness young designers rejecting Modernism while embracing the decorative and embarking upon their own playful searches for beauty. She welcomed the acknowledgment of pluralism, variety, and richness of decoration implied in *The Architecture of the École des Beaux-Arts* exhibition (1975–1976) held at the Museum of Modern Art (MoMA), New York. Always optimistic, Eva felt sure that postmodern approaches to design and visual culture would be the touchstones for the twenty-first century. In the late 1990s, she commented: "We can already sense the mood of the new century; a thirst for beauty, freedom, aesthetic exuberances, elegance, refinement and light-heartedness. The words delight and desire in the names of recent exhibitions might fill us with optimism."[14] Such traits were, of course, characteristic of Eva's own outlook on design and, again, offer clues as to the continuing popularity of her designs.

Shortly after the millennium, the emotion in Eva's voice was as palpable as the tears in her eyes when she spoke to me of the intensity of the emotions and the multitude of memories that surfaced as she watched the countdown to 2000. "It was my century," she said.[15] The comment was not made from a sense of self-importance, but rather from the realization she had lived out her life through almost every single one of those one hundred years.

Within minutes of her telling me about the powerful feelings that had welled up within her as the new millennium was ushered in, however, Eva was back to life in the present as we began rehearsing a "double act" presentation about her work, her thoughts on design, and the importance of living life in the here and now (under the guise of a rehearsal, she was checking to see that I was up to scratch).[16] More than almost anyone else I have known, Eva lived in the moment, a talent she honed to a fine art during her days in a Soviet prison. She often referred to herself as "an outsider looking in," "like a tourist,

looking in on my life from a distance," and told her daughter that she had always felt that way. The "outsider" theme runs through certain of her interviews and her memoirs (a varied assortment of recollections: some handwritten, others typed—some from recordings), but the most poignant recurring theme is aloneness.[17] I knew Eva as a gregarious person from a large extended family who reveled in social intercourse, and so I was somewhat surprised when she first told me, "I think I was more alone in my life than most people; first in the top of the garret at the Schramberg factory, then on long evenings in the hotel room in Leningrad, then in the dreariest of rooms at Dulevo, or in a sequence of little sublets in Moscow . . . and then, of course, came prison."[18] Ironically, when she was finally granted her own "half-room living space" in the USSR, she never got to use it; her new "home" was a prison cell. It is tempting to see Eva's gregariousness, love of company and storytelling, and her desire to make soul contact through her designs as a result of her imprisonment but, while they undoubtedly contributed to that desire, they were all part of her character long before then. Indeed, those very characteristics make her survival of imprisonment all the more impressive.

For someone who focused so intently on the present, Eva had a great love of history. When she stated that "just as there are some people who believe events happen suddenly, there are others who believe events come from somewhere," she saw herself firmly in the latter camp.[19] Her great-grandfather and her mother were both historians. Eva witnessed and applauded her mother's return to academic historical writing in the 1950s, and when there was a dip in her design career, she took up the study of history herself.

That Eva continued designing past the age of 100 is impressive by any standards, especially when problems with sight and hearing occurred which would have led less redoubtable characters to retire. Her standards and enthusiasm remained as high as ever, as her design assistants Olivia Barry and Pirco Wolfframm, and others who helped her in a similar capacity in the last years of her life, can testify (as does the list of undertakings cited in the chronology). Each time we visited, my husband, a sculptor and printmaker who shared her strong three-dimensional sensibility, teasingly asked, "So what did you design today, Eva?" She always pretended to think hard, waited (she had great

12

Eva with assistants at Riverside Drive studio, 1947. EZA. · Eva at Heisey Glass Company, c. 1953. EZA. · Eva at Lomonosov Porcelain Factory, St. Petersburg, Russia, 2000. TPA.

comedic timing), and then smiled impishly as she reached for some-thing, or called for an item to be brought to her. It may not have been designed that day but it was always recent. One night a paper proto-type for a leather handbag hung from the back of a chair by its string "handle"; another time she showed us designs for rugs; and on yet another occasion she presented balsa wood prototypes for cutlery that balanced beautifully in the hand.[20]

Eva's memoirs speak to the gendered and class nature of the work she did in the 1920s and early 1930s. Although she began to think of herself as designing for industry in the late 1920s, she saw herself also as one of a wider group of women designers from respectable middle- or upper-class backgrounds who worked in the Kunstgewerbe (Eva told me to translate this as "applied arts") workshops and small fac-tories."[We] did not consider our job either very important or pushing us into the limelight of art history," she later wrote. "We were just young ladies, not very high employees in our factories. So our job, making things for others, is a generous occupation, an occupation of giving our gifts to our public," and in order to emphasize her point about class and social standing, she pointed out that a niece of the Archbishop of Vienna also belonged to this profession.[21]

Today Eva is so well known as a designer of industrially mass-produced goods that it is easy to forget that when she arrived in the United States from Europe in 1938, there were not many women who worked as industrial designers, or who managed to combine working with CEOs and visiting factories all over the country with marriage and motherhood. Not that it was easy. Even though she had better child care arrangements than many (her mother always lived nearby), the strains of being a working wife and mother were considerable and took their toll. So, too, did the day-to-day grind of housewifery, which she hated—apart from the creative aspects of cooking.

One reason why Eva managed to survive in what were often very tough commercial and work environments dominated by men is that she was extremely tenacious and could be stubborn, indeed obstinate and immoveable, especially when trying to protect her vision of how a piece should look or be manufactured, advertised, or exhibited. Everyone who knew her well saw that side of her. For the most part, however, she was warm, generous, great company, an excellent host

with an engaging disposition and a wry, sometimes risqué, sense of humor as well as an unexpectedly "proper" attitude to certain social conventions (it was often only then that one remembered that she had been born in 1906). She wore her fame lightly, studiously avoiding "name-dropping" in the belief that designers should be realistic about the type of work they do and not think of themselves as superstars. Her daughter commented, "Right until the end she thought of herself as a working woman, not an artist."[22]

Although most of what Eva designed was mass produced by machine or machine-assisted processes, there were usually some hand processes or hand-finishing involved, and the hand played an important role in her work process. Somewhat unusually for someone with such a strong three-dimensional sense, Eva often drew shapes out by hand on paper (i.e., in two dimensions), sometimes cutting them out with scissors, the better to "feel" them. She could "see" profiles in three dimensions, and the process of cutting was somewhat akin to three-dimensional drawing in that it raised the flat, thin pencil line into space. This transformation between two and three dimensions was at the heart of Eva's work process. In many ways, it was a craft process. She recalled her surprise, in 1928, upon first seeing the finished version at the Schramberger factory of something she had visualized purely in two-dimensional terms and for which she had drafted only a front view.[23] At a previous job she had created models by hand from modeling paste or plaster or used a metal template to help form the desired shape on a wheel. She had also cut out shapes from paper since childhood. Thereafter she worked closely with the modelers who translated her designs into three dimensions, placing great emphasis on feeling the prototypes as a means of perfecting form. She liked to carve the pro-totype handles out of plaster herself, and I often thought what a won-derful sculptor she would have been.

"Touchability is very important," she used to say, and a great deal of handling always accompanied the prototyping stages of her projects as she searched to re-create the exact forms that she could "see and feel" in her head.[24] Eva was one of the most tactile people I have known (and I have known many); she was always touching and stroking, be it fabrics, pottery, or the hands of those close to her. Her fantastically strong sense of the tactile was part of a broader human warmth that

Laura Polanyi-Stricker, age 20, c. 1902. EZA. · Laura and Sándor Stricker. EZA. · Laura Stricker with Michael and Eva (R), c. 1909. EZA.

was perhaps best expressed in her closest relationships. As she put it, "My small Red Wing salt-and-pepper shows the way I felt about my daughter at the time I designed them."[25] A related characteristic was her desire as a designer to make soul contact with those who came into contact with her work. In other words, Eva was a communicator.

She often spoke of designing pieces in relation to one another, in *family groups*. "I design in groups. I try to fit everything into a kind of family resemblance," she stated.[26] This, of course, is not at all unusual for designers of lines of crockery or, indeed, many other types of designers, including corporate identity designers, but Eva had a special gift for creating individual yet complementary designs, for riffing brilliantly within a given range of forms and patterns. In my opinion, she ranks alongside Robert Adam, Frank Lloyd Wright, and Saul Bass in terms of her ability to play with difference, similarity, and complementarity within unified, harmonious schemes. Eva lavished attention on the individual piece, but she never lost sight of its relationship to the wider group. Her approach sometimes reminded me of the creativity of jazz improvisation and has been likened to the ways in which she saw people, politics, and history: ways rooted in social democratic views of the relationship of the individual to society which so clearly marked the politics of her mother and the political circles in which her mother's family moved.[27] The various ways in which her individual pieces related to the whole can be seen in the case studies that follow in part two.

Family, Family Circles, and Role Models

Eva Amalia Stricker was born November 13, 1906, the second child of Laura Polanyi Stricker (1882–1959) and Alexander (Sándor) Stricker (1869–1955) in cosmopolitan Budapest, a fast-growing city in a country that had been experiencing a cultural renaissance since the late nineteenth century. In this, the twin capital and second city of the Austro-Hungarian Empire, she was born into a high bourgeois family of assimilated Jews and a life of considerable economic, social, and intellectual privilege. Eva's father owned a textile company; her "progressive" mother, a noted beauty, was a social democratic, feminist intellectual with interests in history, the social sciences, education, and Freudian psychology. These loving and supportive parents, Laura

in particular, encouraged their daughter to develop her creativity and pursue her own path in life.

According to the signs of the zodiac, Eva was a Scorpio, the star sign reputed to produce strong characters and more people likely to be considered a genius than any other. Whether one believes in astrology or not, Eva shared many of the characteristics deemed typical of Scorpios, including being imaginative, unconventional, adventurous, self-confident, tenacious, sensual, intuitive, strong-willed, and sometimes overly demanding. Eva was all of these and more. Her boundless curiosity and determination seem to be traits inherited or learned from her maternal grandmother, Cecile Wohl Pollacsek (1862–1939), who was widowed the year before Eva was born and died when Eva was thirty-three years old. A dashing, witty, cigarette-smoking bohemian with radical views who cared little for worldly goods and social standing, Cecile seemingly was not afraid of anything or anyone. Eva's recollections of her formative years mainly revolve around two strong female role models, her mother and grandmother Cecile, both of whom were articulate and committed feminists and, each in her own way, represented the "new woman."[28]

The Pollacsek (the Magyarized version is Polanyi) family is notable for its prominence in the cultural and intellectual life of early twentieth-century Budapest. Eva's uncles, Karl and Michael Polanyi, later became world-renowned for their contributions to economic history and economic anthropology (Karl), and science, economics, and philosophy (Michael), but when Eva was growing up, the most notable member of the Polanyi clan was grandmother Cecile. Described by Eva as "very much part of the early feminist movement in Central Europe," Cecile was born in Vilna in the Russian Empire (now in Ukraine).[29] Her father, a respected rabbinical scholar and historian of "moderately assimilationist" views, set great store by education. Cecile graduated high school in 1878 and Eva recalled that her grandmother had been trained as a teacher. In about 1880, Cecile and her friend Anna Lvovna were packed off to Vienna to distance them from revolutionary politics, and probably also to continue their education. Ironically, Anna's marriage in Vienna to Samuel (Semyon) Klatschko, a Marxist with close connections to Russian revolutionaries in exile (including Leon Trotsky, who lived in Vienna between 1907 and 1914), only strengthened

Eva with grandmother Cecile, c. 1916. EZA. · Laura, Michael, and Eva (R) c. 1911. EZA.· Laura with brothers Adolph, Karl, and Michael Polanyi (L–R), 1939. EZA.

their link with radical politics.[30] The Polanyi and Klatschko families remained extremely close.

Cecile worked in a jewelry shop at some stage, reputedly as an "apprentice."[31] The extent of her training is not known, but some of Eva's interest in decorative art objects and making things may have come from Cecile, who in 1881 married Mihály Pollacsek (1848–1905). An acculturated cosmopolitan Hungarian Jew then working in Vienna as a railroad construction engineer, he had trained and lived in Switzerland before moving to Vienna. The Pollacseks and their children Laura, Adolf, Karl, and Sophie moved to Budapest (Michael was born there in 1891) in order that Mihály could take advantage of the economic boom in Hungary.[32] He made a great deal of money building railroads, and the family lived in an enormous apartment on the swankiest boulevard in the city and had a summer home on the outskirts.[33]

Mihály, whose family was long-established in Hungary, refused to Magyarize his name, partly because he felt it undignified to have to prove a Hungarian identity in that way and partly to distinguish himself from nouveau riche Hungarian Jews whom he felt were overly eager to be seen to be assimilating.[34] Cecile often went by Pollacsek Polanyi, and the children's last name was altered to Polanyi in the first decade of the century.[35] Laura's biographer notes that Cecile and the children converted to Protestantism of a Calvinist persuasion, but family members believe that this was a category checked off on official documents.[36] Significantly, however, Cecile chose not to identify, officially or otherwise, as Jewish. Family members feel sure that Laura and her siblings were not brought up in any religion, or if they were, they soon abandoned it. The Polanyi siblings, like many intellectual and assimilated Austro-Hungarian Jews, thought of Judaism only as a religion, and one to which they did not belong.[37] The children mainly spoke Hungarian but spoke German with their mother, who did not speak Hungarian with any fluency, although she understood it well.[38]

Determined that her daughter suffer as little as possible from sexist conventions and assumptions, Cecile ensured that Laura attended the best boys' school in Budapest, the Lutheran Boys' Gymnasium, as a "special student" before moving to a new Girls' Gymnasium founded by the National Association of Women's Education in 1898.[39] Mihály lost huge amounts of money in 1899 when months of torrential rain led to

a railway scheme failing and he tried to meet his financial obligations rather than declare bankruptcy. Suddenly, the summer residence and the fancy apartment were gone; as Judith Szapor noted, now the family was "merely middle-class."[40] Cecile, whose bohemian disdain for money and social standing served them well on this occasion, established what became one of the most famous salons in Budapest and presided over it until her death in 1939. She also began taking a keen interest in psychoanalysis.[41]

Recalling her grandmother's Saturday afternoon salons, Eva stated, "All the intellectual people came—journalists, actors, writers, and painters. She was always full of new ideas. . . . My grandmother knew all the Hungarian intellectuals, painters, and also Russian revolutionaries from the 1905 uprising."[42] Asked about Sigmund Freud and her grandmother, she quipped, "I find it amusing that she 'diagnosed' *him* as having a 'mother complex.'"[43] The salon provided an excellent opportunity for Cecile's children, and later grandchildren, to meet all manner of interesting people. Gathering interesting people around her was one of Eva's great pleasures, too.

Laura and Sándor Stricker

After the change in family fortunes, the academically brilliant Laura, who was studying English language and literature as well as Hungarian literature and history at university, worked to subsidize her studies, assisting her cousin and close friend, the economist and social scientist Ervin Szabó, to produce the *Bibliographica Economica Universalis* (1902) and completing the 1904 edition on her own.[44] She was also keenly interested in social welfare, especially in relation to women and children, and like her brothers Karl and Michael helped validate the social sciences as a respectable, socially useful academic discipline and supported the Free School for Social Science. Eva liked to talk about how her mother was well known in social science circles and how Freud referred to Laura as the "beautiful and interesting Dr. Stricker."[45] She remembered her mother as "a combination of Victorian strictness and absolute tolerance," adding "that meant whatever I took into my mind to do, she supported."[46]

Although she later became the first woman to gain a doctorate in

Laura's kindergarten, c.1911 (Arthur Koestler, center front). EZA. · Kindergarten drawing. Arthur Koestler, c. 1911. EZA.

history at the University of Budapest, in 1904, Laura postponed her studies in favor of marriage at the age of twenty-two. Some family members, who expected her to marry someone within their intellectual circle—someone like the philosopher and critic Georg Lukács, for example—found it difficult to reconcile themselves with her choice of an older, wealthy textile merchant who did not share her intellectual interests.[47] Her brother Karl never fully reconciled himself to the loss of the dazzling future his beloved sister might have had if she had chosen a different partner.[48] Eva, who adored her father, had no problem understanding why her mother fell in love with such a good-looking and kindly man, but in later years she acknowledged that Laura also made a deliberate choice about the type of lifestyle she wanted for herself and for her future children.[49]

Sandor offered Laura considerable emotional and financial security, and a great deal of independence to do what she wanted—far more independence than many men who were focused on their own intellectual and political activities would have given. Marriage allowed Laura to return to the neighborhood where her family had formerly lived, to again enjoy a summer residence, and when children came, to hire private nurses and governesses. Thus, Eva was born into a lifestyle almost as privileged as that formerly enjoyed by her mother. Her brother Michael was only fourteen months older than she; Gyorgy Otto (usually known as Otto) was seven years younger. When Eva was just a year old, Laura published an article on "Women of the Intellectual Middle Class," and lectured on "Feminism and Marriage"; and she completed her doctorate (in those days a relatively short document) just before Eva was three.[50] Her family and friends, and Laura herself, had expected her to enter academia when she completed her doctorate, but changes in the university's regulations about that time closed the doors of that institution to women.[51]

Kindergarten

Eva had a nurse and then governesses from whom she learned English and French, but in 1911, Laura opened a progressive kindergarten for her own two children and about ten others.[52] Rooted in Rousseau's notion of the potential of the uncivilized child, the ideas of Froebel

and Pestalozzi, and the example set by Franz Cizak, who ran arts-and-crafts classes for children in Vienna, the kindergarten movement was popular with progressive, liberal-minded educators and parents across Europe and North America.[53] The pervasiveness of play and playfulness in Eva's later work traces back to the huge emphasis on play during her early life. Her mother later considered playfulness to be Eva's most predominant characteristic as a person.[54]

Art, music, and movement were key components of the kindergarten and "new education" movements, and Laura hired a disciple of the famous Swiss musician, composer, and educator Emile Jacques-Dalcroze (1865–1950) to teach eurythmics (the expression of music and sounds through whole body movement); the artist Dezső Czigány (1883–1937) taught drawing.[55] Laura's commitment to Freudian ideas distinguished her preschool from other progressive middle-class kindergartens largely because nudity was encouraged. Photographs show children naked or in gym suits, barefoot and happily dancing, painting, drawing, and enjoying nature.[56] Some people were shocked by the nudity, but Eva loved it. Koestler recalled attending "an experimental, avant-garde, kindergarten in Budapest. It was run by a young lady belonging to a very erudite family . . . [who] had committed an intellectual mésalliance by marrying a successful businessman and, feeling frustrated, had opened the kindergarten for five- and six-year olds, where she put into practice some extremely advanced and, I suspect, somewhat confused pedagogical ideas."[57] Eva shrugged her shoulders and laughed when I re-read this to her in 2000, dismissing his opinions and crude psychoanalysis, but adding that anxieties about naked bodies were so great in the early decades of the century that even her "advanced" mother took baths wearing a slip.[58] She also recalled how, just before a vacation, the children were asked what they would do: Eva said "make pictures" while Koestler, who went on to become a journalist and writer, said "make stories."[59]

Vienna 1912–1918

The kindergarten was short-lived. For business reasons, the family moved in 1912 to Vienna, the capital of the Austro-Hungarian Empire, until just before the end of World War I. There the family mixed

Eva and other pre-teens enjoying outdoor education, c. 1914. EZA. · Kindergarten drawing. Eva, c. 1911. EZA. · Eva, c. 1920. EZA.

frequently with the Klatschkos and spoke German, a language new to Eva (not quite six years old). She continued to be educated at home with a private tutor and may have attended school in Vienna from the age of ten.[60] She already showed promise at art, and as a preteen she soaked up the delights of the city, from Otto Wagner's Secession Building (1897–1898), which she described later as "like a castle in a fairy tale," and art and design exhibitions therein, to the "shapes of the Wiener Werkstätte" (Vienna Workshops, 1903–1932) and "the aggressive geometric ornaments" of architect-designer Josef Hoffmann.[61] She recalled trips to see Baroque churches and monasteries, and family dinner conversations about the controversial Loos House (1909–1912), which she described as "brazenly facing the stately, traditional Imperial Palace"; criticism of its austere aesthetic, steel and concrete construction, and lack of decoration inside and out had brought building to a halt temporarily in 1910.[62] Eva's language, albeit later, suggests that she disapproved of the placement of the building and probably of the building itself.

Eva was extremely well-grounded in the history of art, architecture, and design, especially of the Renaissance and Baroque periods, even as a preteen. Of all the Mid-Century Modern designers in the U.S. after World War II, she probably had the greatest understanding and appreciation of historical styles and movements. The "almost weekly" guided tours she took in the winter months included trips to "the old towns along the Danube" where she absorbed the "spirit and details" of Baroque design.[63] One of her tutors was the young Frederick Antal, also from a wealthy Hungarian Jewish family. A former student of the distinguished German art historian Heinrich Wolfflin, Antal, like fellow art historian Arnold Hauser, proposed that art was closely related to its social and economic contexts, a point of view held thereafter by Eva. The strong Baroque inflections in Eva's work grew out of her deep knowledge of designs from that period, as well as from the pervasiveness and depth of Baroque forms and motifs within Hungarian and Austrian visual and material culture, including folk traditions. The soft curves of many of her later designs owe much to the Baroque, and also to Austro-German and Hungarian Biedermeier designs of the 1820s–1830s. There was a revival of interest in classicism across Europe between about 1900 and 1930 and, for many of Eva's generation, classical influences, including Biedermeier, came in both contemporary and historical forms.

Polanyi Circles

Antal moved in some of the same intellectual circles in Hungary as Eva's uncle Karl Polanyi, a leader of the progressive student movement and a founding member of both the Galileo Society and the Hungarian Radical Party. Both Antal and Polanyi were friendly with Lukács, who was soon to embrace historical materialism and join the Austrian Communist Party, and with the philosopher and sociologist Karl Mannheim. All four men belonged to the Sunday Circle, another forum for young intellectuals that began meeting about 1916, and in 1917 they helped establish the Free School of the Cultural Sciences, which offered classes on various aspects of modern bourgeois culture, from art and literature to politics. Other figures in such circles included Szabó, who became a leading socialist theoretician; Oszkar Jaszi, editor of *Twentieth Century* and leader of the Sociological Society (a long-term Polanyi friend); artist Irma Seidler, another Polanyi cousin and an early girlfriend of Lukács; and Emmi Seidler, who married Emil Lederer, a professor of economics at Heidelberg University (later at the New School, New York). Artist Anna Leznai, composers Béla Bartók and Zoltán Kodály, and the novelist Emma Ritook also moved in these circles.[64] Mannheim and Polanyi's political views were more liberal and social democratic than those of Lukács and Antal, as were those of Karl's siblings Michael and Laura. At that time, the eldest Polanyi brother, Adolf, founder of the first socialist student club at Budapest University in the early years of the century, was the most politically radical Polanyi sibling.

After the Strickers returned to Budapest, Laura became heavily engaged in postwar social democratic politics. Along with brothers Karl and Michael, she supported the bourgeois liberal program of the Hungarian Democratic Republic (October 1918–March 1919) in which Michael was Secretary to the Ministry of Health. When the head of government, Count Karolyi (a neighbor of the Strickers), called an election based on universal suffrage for April 1919, Laura planned to run for parliament on a reformist, social democratic, and feminist ticket under the auspices of the Bourgeois Radical Party. Her position on women, however, differed little from that of the Marxist feminists who insisted that class was a key factor in what was then known as the "woman question."[65] That election did not take place; the Hungarian

Eva (back L), family and friends, Budapest, c. 1920. EZA. · Eva, c. 1921–22. EZA. · Painting by Eva of brother Otto, c. 1924. EZA. · Eva in traditional dress, c. 1923. EZA.

Democratic Republic was replaced by the Hungarian Soviet Republic (March–August 1919). It was too extreme for Laura and her brothers Karl and Michael. By contrast, brother Adolf, Lukács, and Antal took up positions of responsibility.[66] Hopes for building a workers' state in Hungary were smashed after a coup in August 1919, led by Admiral Miklós Horthy, established a right-wing, anti-communist, and anti-Semitic regime. Laura acted as courier between Hungarian social democrats and the exiled Karolyi, an act that could have cost her her life had she been caught. Eva, who was just approaching her teenage years, later recalled little of the details but remembered it as an exciting period, with people constantly coming and going from the house.[67]

Mad about Art

Eva had forgotten much of her native tongue by the time the family moved back to Budapest, but she soon remembered it. Still "mad about art" and keen to become a painter, she studied at home with a tutor and governess until attending gymnasium (high school) between 1921 and 1923.[68] Such were her artistic talents and family "pull" that she was allowed to miss certain classes in order to study on a one-to-one basis with artists such as the talented Gyula Derkovits. A member of the Hungarian Communist Party who had studied under Karoly Kernstock (an uncle by marriage who may also have taught Eva) at the Free Art Studio during the Hungarian Soviet Republic, Derkovits's work was influenced by Cubism, Constructivism, and Expressionism, and often depicted workers and peasants. Eva recalled him coming to the house, but she had to go to the studio of the more commercially successful Ödön Márffy.[69] Her pursuits outside the home were those of a young girl of her class with artistic and modern inclinations. She attended lectures on modern art and exhibitions at museums and leading galleries, and one of her girlfriends was the daughter of the then-president of the Academy of Fine Arts (where Eva would study in 1923). Her closest friend Agnes (Kati) Köveshaczi went on to study modern dance, an area of performance which Eva loved. That friendship brought another independent bohemian woman into Eva's life—Kati's mother, the sculptor and designer Elza Köveshaczi-Kalmar.[70]

Eva loved nature. As a youngster she often slept outdoors in the summer months with her pet dog in the beautiful family garden, which she claimed first inspired her to be an artist, and she loved walking and hiking. She and her friends were part of the "simple life" movement, which Eva referred to as the back-to-nature movement. It was rooted, in part, in British Arts and Crafts ideas and practices, which were hugely influential in continental Europe, including Hungary, in the 1900s and 1910s, and beyond in many cases. The strong Arts and Crafts emphasis on nature and the revalidation of folk culture were central to this simple life ethos that Eva embraced as a young woman.[71] Indeed, her deep reverence for the simplest things of life and her dual concern for dignity in work and beauty in life were commented upon by Franz Baumann at her memorial service. Similar ideals inspired the Gödöllő Arts and Crafts colony (1901–1920), twenty miles northeast of Budapest, where children also ran around naked in the summer months.[72] Around this time Eva also learned about folk pottery from an artistic aunt who, like many middle- and upper-class homemakers and collectors, was passionately interested in native peasant wares that had stood as symbols of Hungarian cultural independence in the years before World War I.[73] To admire such work was to be up-to-date and progressive.

From the autumn of 1923, Eva studied painting for three semesters at the Magyar Képzőművészeti Akadémia (Hungarian Royal Academy of Fine Arts), Budapest. She was fortunate in that her family accepted this. Many young bourgeois and upper-class women of the time faced strong opposition or were forbidden to train as artists or designers. Although the German movement for women's emancipation was one of the strongest in Europe, only five years earlier Maria Kipp (1900–1988), who later worked as a designer and weaver in the United States, had faced considerable opposition from her guardian before she was allowed to train at the extremely well-respected Kunstgewerbeschule (School of Applied Arts) in Munich.[74]

At the Academy, Eva studied with János Vaszary, a distinguished Hungarian painter trained in Paris who veered students towards modern expression.[75] She also gained a good grounding in traditional fine art, including portraiture. Thereafter she continued to draw in nature and paint on her own, sometimes with professional artists brought in at her parents' expense, including Czigány and Márffy, who was

Painting: self-portrait, c. 1925. EZA. · Eva (R), the first Hungarian woman to become a journeyman potter (newspaper May 1, 1926). EZA.

then involved in setting up KUT (1924, New Society of Visual Arts), a broad-based organization for modern artists.[76] According to Eva, these artists came to "discuss art with me; it was not teaching in any formal sense."[77] Representational modes remained strong in Hungary, along with Expressionism and Cubism. Many Hungarian painters studied in Paris in the 1920s, and Eva first visited there in 1925.[78] There she came to admire the work of Marie Laurencin, a French artist who favored "feminine" subject matter and genres and had been a close associate of Cubist artists and critics such as Picasso and Apollinaire. But Eva's paintings from the interwar years were bolder than Laurencin's and more like those of Vaszary or Angel Zárraga.[79] The latter, a Mexican painter living in Paris who was well known for his murals and portraits, "guided" Eva when she was painting the self-portrait illustrated here.[80]

Apprentice Potter

Although Eva planned to be a painter, she knew a lot about architecture and design. She later recalled the kunstgewerbe movement, the objects of the Deutscher Werkbund (German Work Federation), and the famous working-class housing projects in "Red Vienna."[81] Unlike Werkbund designer Henry van de Velde and others who abandoned painting at the turn of the century because they thought design more democratic, Eva's route to design was more ad hoc. A pragmatist as well as a dreamer, she decided to learn pottery because those trade skills could provide her with the means to support herself financially as a fine artist. Her eminently sensible mother, having witnessed firsthand the volatility of capitalism when her father's businesses suffered major losses, suggested that if Eva was going to pursue such a plan, she should do it "properly."

It was not considered socially acceptable for refined middle- and upper-class girls to apprentice as potters or work as artisans. As Eva put it, "'Ladies' didn't pot when I started, but my mother let me do it anyway."[82] In the autumn of 1924, she was apprenticed to master potter Jakob Karapancsik, one of the last members of the Guild of Chimney Sweeps, Oven Makers, Roof Tilers, Well Diggers and Potters, and Eva became the first woman to be trained through that particular guild.

Although she was trained in a traditional manner, guild power had long been diminishing, especially over key matters such as training, quality control, and pricing. Apprenticeships had recently been reduced to six months, whereas in the early modern period, they typically lasted seven years (from age thirteen to twenty-one).[83]

In those six months, Eva learned a considerable amount about making pottery, from what she called "mushing" the clay with bare feet after it was dug out of the hillside to kneading and "mangling" it until it was ready to be worked. She learned to make pots by hand out of wet clay, glaze them, and dry them outdoors (before they went to the kilns), and to make and repair the tiled stoves used across central and eastern Europe for domestic heating.[84]

When working on mass production projects in later years, she greatly enjoyed those commissions where she had the opportunity to feel the type of clay that would give form to her designs. Such a "connection" with the clay was largely symbolic by then, but Eva would often hold a piece of clay between her thumb and forefinger, rubbing away at it while thinking over precisely what sorts of designs she could create out of it.[85] Design and craft historian Tanya Harrod has commented that just as Eva's uncle, Michael Polanyi, later emphasized the importance of tacit (as opposed to explicit) knowledge, Eva's greatness as a designer was based, in part, "on her profound tacit knowledge of clay."[86]

Her Own Pottery Studio

In March 1925, eighteen-year-old Eva established a pottery studio in a former gardener's shed in the garden of her family home and created a traditional-style underground kiln in order to produce her own versions of "black pottery," a well-known type of Hungarian folk pottery.[87] This smoked earthenware was made from molded clay placed in pits covered over with soil to make them airtight; smoke from the pine logs used to heat the pit created a dark surface on the clay (hence the term "black pottery"). Eva liked to point out that this was also a Native American way of making pots. She made her pots by hand, mainly on a wheel, and later described those black pieces as "the results of the luscious, immediate contact of my hands with the wet, soft, fast-moving

Eva with pottery from her own studio, 1926. EZA. · Shapes and patterns by Eva, Kispester-Granit, 1926. EZA. · Lantern by Eva, Hansa Kunstkeramik, Germany, 1927. EZA.

clay, and its plastic, moldable, slick appeal."[88] The only potential sales outlet, apart from family and friends, was a local market. Horrified to learn that a male friend kept Eva company when she sold her wares in public, Laura chaperoned them thereafter "to add propriety to this activity."[89] Art and design historian Martin Eidelberg and others have pointed to the influence of the Wiener Werkstätte on Eva's work at this time, including her black pots with simple patterns cut out of them.[90]

A photograph of Eva in 1926 in her pottery studio shows her wearing a "simple life" polka-dot cotton dress, drawstring Magyar peasant-style blouse, and open-toe leather sandals, all of which marked her as modern, artistic, and bohemian. The stripes and dots on the pots themselves, as well as the simplified flower forms, recall similar vocabularies in studio pottery workshops in other parts of Europe in the 1920s that were also influenced by folk traditions, one of the most notable being the Carter Stabler Adams pottery in Britain.[91] The partners in charge of Carter Stabler Adams pottery had been associated with the Arts and Crafts movement, but joined the Design and Industries Association (DIA, founded 1915), a British association modeled on the Deutscher Werkbund, an organization which Eva admired for its promotion of rational, practical designs that drew upon the best of past and present forms and techniques, and for its championing of mass production.[92]

To further contextualize the work Eva was doing at this time, only one year before that photograph was taken, DIA founding member Harry Peach, after meeting with Werkbund members and visiting the Bauhaus (he, like Eva, had problems with its "Machine Aesthetic"), bought "peasant pottery" rather like that made by Eva, in the market at Jena.[93] Only seven miles away was the Dornberg pottery which served as an annex of the Weimar Bauhaus from 1920 to 1925. That several pieces produced by Bauhaus students in the early 1920s were influenced by vernacular stoneware traditions underlines the point that Eva's work was part of a wider progressive design reform movement that was sensitive to, and drew upon, past traditions while designing objects for the contemporary world. As Eva's work began to garner attention, an as-yet-unidentified piece of hers was shown in the Hungarian section at the 1926 exhibition held in Philadelphia to celebrate the 150th anniversary of the signing of the Declaration of Independence; it won an honorable mention.[94]

The World of Work: Kispester-Granit and Hansa Kunstkeramik

Eva's first "proper" job came in 1926 when she began working as a freelance designer for Kispester-Granit of Budapest. Out of curiosity, she visited what she referred to as the "first mass-production pottery factory in Hungary" (specializing in toilets and other sanitary equipment).[95] After she bombarded the manager with questions, he asked why she was so interested only to have Eva inform him that she, too, ran a pottery.[96] Rather cheekily, she invited him to visit it. You can imagine his surprise when he saw her small studio and kiln. Eva recalled that despite him telling her "that the Industrial Revolution had broken out some time ago" and that she was an anachronism, he offered her a job.[97] So keen was he and the company to break into the decorative arts market that an art department was created especially for Eva. For the most part, she made prototypes by hand for a variety of objects that were then "copied in molds and successfully sold in the United States"; nearly sixty years later, she recalled "ashtrays in the shape of unicorns" among the type of items produced.[98]

Surviving examples of her Kispester work include pieces from a tea service, with faux-naif bird-and-branch decoration, somewhat in the manner of Wiener Werkstätte pottery.[99] Eva later attributed the "rather inarticulate," "disorganized spontaneity" and "haphazard" elements in her other Kispester work as influenced by seeing the haphazardness she then admired in paintings by artists such as Oskar Kokoschka.[100] Eva recalled "several women casting my designs" and referred to molds, indicating also that she designed for mass production.[101] The decoration was executed by hand, sometimes by Eva herself, as were running glazes and applied decoration.[102] Whimsical animal figurines and similar small objects were sculpted by hand, and the surviving examples of whimsical figurines in Eva's studio may have been prototypes. Although employed on a freelance basis, Eva several times spent a whole work-week at the factory, sleeping on the premises on a makeshift bed: an adventurous thing to do for such a well-brought-up, young, high bourgeois woman at that time. Eva, of course, loved such adventures. Sadly, the bank financing the pottery pulled the plug on the new venture after concluding that too much time and resources were being expended on the art department to the detriment of overall profitability. It ordered a return to making toilets.[103]

Eva as machine dancer, Budapest, 1928. EZA. · Eva, 1927 (outfit designed by friend To Bauch). EZA. · Set design by Eva: Layers of the Soul, Budapest, 1928. EZA.

After six months of fun and experimentation, Eva was out of a job.

The next one came after she advertised in a trade journal for a position as a journeyman potter. This decision to actively seek work probably related to the heavy losses sustained by her father's business in 1927 and what Eva called a sad atmosphere at home. The Strickers were far from destitute, however, and Eva claimed that the changed circumstances made little difference to her, stating, "I was never conscious of whether we had money or not, nor cared."[104] When talking to Eva about this period, I always sensed a wanderlust. The tradition of wandering journeymen persisted in Central Europe and Eva was keen to see more of the world. Although (or perhaps because) she was close to her family (especially her mother), she said that, out of three potteries that replied to her, she chose Hamburg because it was "the one farthest from home."[105]

For six months from the summer of 1927, she worked at Hansa Kunstkeramik, a small pottery in Altona, a section of Hamburg.[106] Eva liked to watch people's reactions when she told them that the pottery was close to the red-light district. Unused to women journeymen, Eva's male colleagues placed "a nicely modeled replica of male genitalia" at her workstation.[107] Her nonchalance over the incident helped win over her three or four workmates, but her deficiency in reproducing a given design by hand on a potter's wheel was soon apparent. No longer in an "art department," she was expected to be able to produce relatively uniform items.[108] Realizing that Eva lacked the necessary hand skills and had little interest in acquiring them, her employers allowed her to create prototypes for production. It was not a happy situation, however, and it ended after six months. Had she been more skilled at hand work, her career may have taken a different path. Her social life, by contrast, was more exciting than ever before; Eva recalled attending parties and arts balls that "went on for days at a time," loving the costumes and gaiety of the latter but hating having to step over "copulating couples."[109] She traveled in Belgium and Holland before returning to Budapest.

Dada and Surrealism

Back in Budapest, Eva became re-involved with Dada performances.

The automatism and randomness of Dadaism, as well as the quirkiness, unconventionality, subversion, and irreverence appealed to Eva. She recalled with delight the Green Donkey cabaret, established in 1925 by Ödön Palasovszky, director and theatrical activist, and Alice Madzsar, a choreographer and "art movement" teacher, together with set and graphic designer Sándor Bortnyik, and former Bauhausler Farkas Molnár.

She had worked with the group on a performance based upon *Romeo and Juliet* in 1926 and in 1928 created sets for at least three performances by a similar group, the Unique Theater (*Mechanical Conference Revue*, *Bimini Pantomime*, and *Layers of Soul*), and also performed in some.[110] Eva recalled a "masked machine dance, illustrating machine movements," which was almost certainly part of *Mechanical Conference Revue*, and concerts based on the sounds made by typewriters and sewing machines.[111] Such dances typified the Dadaist fascination with modernity and machines, but this was as far along the path of machine-age modernism that Eva ever went. For *Layers of the Soul* Eva designed a large heart that lit up and "beat" according to the experiences of the main protagonist; behind the backdrop, Eva connected the electrical wires every time the script called for the heart to beat.[112] In Paris in the late 1920s, Eva saw work by artists such as Man Ray (then fascinated by Dadaism and Surrealism) when they were shown for the first time and, together with Koestler, watched avant-garde films in cinema clubs where members earnestly offered psychoanalytical analyses of them. Those films included *Un Chien Andalou* (1929) by the Spanish Surrealists Luis Buñuel and Salvador Dalí, which Eva remembered as "a fascinating form of Dadaism as it added the fluid sequences of dream-like images and convincingly fantastic, without sarcasm."[113]

Schramberg

Eva moved to Schramberg in southern Germany in the fall of 1928 as the sole designer for Schramberger Majolikafabrik, which specialized in mass-produced dinnerware and other household items such as vases and lamp bases.[114] The job was a big step up for Eva, who accepted it without having any of the necessary drafting skills for such work. Rarely daunted, she begged a friend for a day's intensive instruction.[115]

All photographs on this page: Eva in Schramberg, Germany, c. 1929. EZA.

When asked by her new employers whether she wanted to create forms by shaping them on a potter's wheel or by drafting, she said the latter, thinking that was what a "proper" industrial designer would do: "I had to show that I was not a craftsperson but a real industrial designer," she later wrote.[116] But she did not abandon sketching or sculpting models or cutting out shapes from paper, which she had done at Kispester-Granit. As noted earlier, they were key elements of her work process. Although Eva had designed for mass production at Kispester, it was at Schramberger Majolikafabrik that she seems to have first consciously thought of herself as designing for industry, probably because about 350 people worked there.[117]

Schramberg lay at the confluence of five valleys in the picturesque Black Forest area. Eva lived on one of the surrounding mountains, enjoying views over "the valley with its soft green meadows spotted with the ruins of medieval castles."[118] On a nearby mountainside was the world's largest clock and watch company, Junghans. By about 1900, Junghans employed as many as 3,000 workers, housed in buildings designed by the famous German architect-designer Peter Behrens as a series of glass-enclosed units set into hillside terraces, to ensure that every workspace had natural light. When Eva visited, she was amazed by the modern assembly line (one of the first in Germany) and by the "utter dexterity of the automatic machines which put together so many of the single tiny elements of a watch."[119]

Situated in a large old building on a riverbank, the Schramberger factory, where goods were moved around the building by hand cart, looked decidedly old-fashioned in comparison. It was "modern" in that workers clocked in and out, and the main forms of most pieces were mass produced in molds, but there was a great deal of hand application of decorative elements, as well as handles and such, and the painted decoration was also done by hand, as was usual at that time across Europe. Eva resented the traditional two-hour lunch break taken in the local tavern because it prolonged the workday from seven-thirty a.m. to six-thirty p.m.[120]

Eva worked closely with the modeling department where highly skilled workers translated her designs into material form, and also with the decorating department under Obermaler (Chief Painter) King.[121] She helped the painters to work more closely to her specifi-

cations; she had no interest whatsoever in allowing the individual "hand" of the painter to show through.[122] In about a year and a half, she designed more than two hundred pieces that went into production and was involved in presenting the work to sales representatives and the public. Eva being Eva, she updated the style of photography, just as she updated the product lines. She bought a camera with her first earnings and, judging by extant photographs, had a good eye for framing shots and was fairly skilled with the camera by the time the company's advertising shots were taken about a year later.[123] Items made to her designs were exhibited at the twice-yearly Leipzig trade fairs and began to be featured "very prominently" in the trade magazine *Die Schaulade*.[124]

Design Influences

Eva's designs for Schramberger were the most obviously commercial of her career, in the sense of being in tune with mainstream fashionable ceramics of the sort made for the middle-range of the market by consumer-conscious potteries across Europe, especially Britain and France, but without a distinctive style of her own. Geometrical forms, especially circles, straight lines, and zigzags, are apparent in her designs for Schramberger, which often fall within the Art Moderne style that today is usually referred to as "Art Deco".[125] When discussing the geometrical influences, she explained that it was "in the air" through Mondrian and the Cubists, and that in the late 1920s it was fashionable, even for cheap wallpapers and linoleum.[126]

Eva had seen firsthand the Art Moderne forms and patterns on a wide range of objects at the 1925 *Exposition internationale des arts décoratifs et industriels modernes* (International Exposition of Modern Industrial and Decorative Arts) in Paris, which she visited with her mother, and she knew well both the historicist and modern forms upon which they drew. She kept abreast of design magazines while in Schramberg, and the company sent her to Paris and to the Leipzig trade fairs precisely to keep up with the latest ideas circulating in the industry.[127] Eva remembered reading *Die Form*, the monthly magazine of the Werkbund, recalling the images in particular, and she probably also read magazines such as the French *Mobilier et Décoration* and the German *Die Schaulade*.

Eva in Schramberg, Germany, c. 1929. EZA. · Eva and ceramics designed for Schramberger Majolikafabrik, Germany, c. 1929. EZA.

Furthermore, the company almost certainly had copies of brochures and advertisements issued by rival companies.[128]

Like many artists and designers, Eva absorbed new ideas and forms like a sponge if something resonated with her. She seems to have been very up-to-date and quite inventive, within the parameters determined by the leading companies and established designers, and by the Schramberger company's perceived target audience. Features of her work for Schramberger include circular forms, concentric rings, undulations, asymmetry (she placed small shapes or decoration asymmetrically on symmetrical forms), and flattened, truncated, oval, and even streamlined forms. Eva recalled adapting a design by the much-admired French designer Jean Luce to use at Schramberger, but did not specify which.[129] Some of her flat-sided pitchers and teapots, as featured in the company's 1931 catalogue, seem to have been influenced by a much-publicized elegant French silver Art Moderne teapot by the French company *Tétard Frères*, most probably designed by the well-known designer Jean Tétard. Eva may have seen it during one of her trips to Paris. It certainly inspired British designer Clarice Cliff's popular *Stamford* flat-sided pottery forms of 1930, which also seem to have inspired Eva.[130] The skyscraper motif was already an icon of North American Art Moderne design by the time Eva arrived in Schramberg—in the mid-1920s Austrian-American designer Paul Frankl famously translated it into a bookcase—and Eva used it to form a lamp base. Some of the ashtrays she designed for Schramberger were also architectural in form.[131] Eva loved Matisse's "engaging colors" and some of her decorative patterns seem to have been inspired by his bold juxtapositions of color, and possibly also by those by painter-designer Sonia Delaunay, whose work Eva may have seen at the 1925 Paris Exposition.[132]

The optimism that underpinned much of Eva's thinking was rooted in the belief that with sufficient goodwill and rational intelligence, the world could become a better place. This was not significantly different from that which underpinned Modernism. Given the close association, in theory at least, between Modernism, on the one hand, and rationalism and democracy, on the other, and also the close link with mass production, it is even more remarkable that Eva distanced herself from the Modern Movement. It was simply too dogmatic for her, just as Communism was too dogmatic for her mother and her

uncles Michael and Karl Polanyi. That Eva knew Modern Movement design at least fairly well is implied in her confident rejection of the movement, but apart from a few "machine aesthetic" designs in the 1931 Schramberger catalogue which seem to have been inspired by parts for machinery, she stood aside from any designs that directly evoked the so-called Machine Age.[133]

It is difficult to piece together precisely how and when Eva came across and imbibed aspects of Modern Movement design, not least because she always denied any direct influence. We know from later recollections that she admired Mies van der Rohe's Barcelona Chair, Marcel Breuer's "esoteric interiors, where lovely furniture seemed to float in shadowless space," and Le Corbusier's *L'Esprit Nouveau* pavilion at the 1925 Paris Exposition.[134] When describing the latter, a major marker of early Modern Movement design, Eva recalled its "festive, holier-than-though simplicity" (only Eva would juxtapose such words) and noted, "There I saw for the first time the pure, simple lines of Le Corbusier's construction, which seemed so untouched, clean, and elegant that I felt I had entered a realm beyond my everyday untidy ways."[135] Thus, at the same time as she admired it, she seemed to comprehend immediately that it was too purist for her. She also recalled liking some elegant white "sugar-cube" villas on the outskirts of Hamburg.[136] The Bauhaus influence needs some explanation, because the Bauhaus only had a pottery until the mid-1920s, and the ceramics workshops had strong links to both traditional object forms and vernacular traditions. Eva's work for both Schramberger and Carstens (see chapters 1 and 2), especially the latter, suggests that she was influenced by the refined reworkings of traditional forms (especially for tea services) of two designers associated with the Bauhaus pottery in the early 1920s: Otto Lindig and Marguerite Friedländer. Like Eva, both had apprenticed as potters.[137]

Eva remained apart from the Modern Movement, overriding any admiration of individual designs with her view of it as a movement that was essentially anti-historicist and overly concerned with rationality and stylistic and utilitarian functionalism to the detriment of other important considerations. She thought its rejection of sentiment and the S-curve (which she felt was the most communicative of lines) "ludicrous," and in the dozen or so years that I knew her, the other

Three photographs by Eva, Schramberg, 1928–29. EZA.

words she used to describe Modernism ranged from "untouched," "soulless," and "cold" to "highfalutin'" and "dictatorial."[138] Eva felt that it offered neither "amusement nor beauty," and failed to establish emotional links between object and user.[139] Despite its avowed and laudable aim of bringing mass-produced goods to the populace at affordable prices, Eva considered it elitist, quite unlike her own "democratic" work, which she saw as connecting directly with consumers. Eva had no hard evidence of such connections; her belief was based more upon intuition about what her work conveyed. She similarly had no evidence, apart from her own experience and that of a small but growing body of critics, that Modern Movement objects *lacked* such connections. She seems not to have ever considered that Modern Movement designs might also connect with people.

As suggested earlier, Eva saw her modern designs as part of a wider movement, spearheaded by the Werkbund, to improve the design of all products, including those associated with the kunstgewerbe (applied arts) industries.[140] Fears about the effects of machine mass production, uniformity, and standardization—and the loss of individuality and creativity that this might incur—were hotly debated during the interwar years. Eva recalled heated discussions on such topics in the strongly working-class town of Schramberg. By then, it was evident that machines were not innately labor-saving in and of themselves, and many on both the Left and the Right worried about the effects on labor and culture as a whole of the increasingly widespread standardization and mass production of buildings, objects, and entertainment, as well as the alienation associated with acute divisions of labor. The type of work Eva was involved with at Schramberg was central to such debates, but unlike family members who would probably have immersed themselves in those debates, Eva, the "outsider," flagged in her memoirs the importance of such issues for organized labor but did not comment on how *she* felt about them.[141]

Social and Political Life in Schramberg

At the same time, her memoirs reveal a strong moral responsibility to keeping people in work at a time of high unemployment and she commented on shifts in ideas and political allegiances.[142] As a designer,

Eva was classified as a white-collar worker but she refused to join the white-collar organizations in Schramberg, which she characterized as "rather visible small groups . . . self-segregating, belonging mostly to the right wing conservative Deutsch-Nationale Party (German National People's Party), which were not yet Nazi sympathizers."[143] Some of Eva's strongest recollections of her twenty-six months in Schramberg relate to the politics of pre-Hitler Germany; to debates and allegiances (made all the more significant in hindsight given that the National Sozialistische Deutsche Arbeiter Partei [NSDAP or Nazi for short] took power only three years after she left there); and the horrors that Nazism brought. She recalled the energy and vigor of organized labor, noting the many arguments between conservatives and social democrats as well as the infighting on the Left between socialists and communists, a factor that she, like many others, thought seriously weakened the Left and created a vacuum for Nazism.[144]

Eva found irksome the convention that "young ladies of my position" were expected to be the companion of the boss's wife, but she skillfully negotiated the situation by spending time with his family about once a month.[145] The rest of the time she mainly socialized with the family with whom she lodged; the husband was an employee of the Sozialdemokratische Partei Deutschlands (SPD, German Social Democratic Party) and the wife, a strong-minded daughter of a coal miner.[146] Together with their small daughters, they lived a secular Social Democratic lifestyle (the term is Eva's), which fascinated Eva, especially their not celebrating Christmas (one of her favorite festivities).[147] It was largely through these friends that Eva joined the SPD; she pointed out that political and union organizations were the only way to have a congenial social life in that small town.[148] She felt apart from the political involvement of so many of her friends and family members, telling me that, shortly afterwards when she was living in Berlin, her friend the writer Anna Seghers, a committed Communist, would get exasperated with that side of Eva that kept her on the edges of politics.[149] Her life outside work centered around the SPD, its Nature Lovers' Club, and (blue-collar) union activities.[150] Although she took two long vacations in Paris while at Schramberg, it was a fairly lonely existence. Eva began to yearn for life beyond a small town. She also felt that she was not receiving sufficient name recognition and decided to leave.

Eva's studio in Berlin, c. 1930. EZA. · Eva in her studio in Berlin, c. 1930. EZA. · Eva , c. 1930. EZA.

Berlin

Eva's mother rented the spacious Berlin apartment and studio of artist Emil Nolde for Eva and Eva's brother Michael (then working in
Berlin).[151] Eva loved living in Berlin, then one of the most culturally
dynamic and diverse cities in Europe with a thriving artistic, cultural,
and intellectual life. She recalled, "In Berlin there were writers,
physicists, actors, students, professors; it was the center of the world
for me. It was the most elegant, the *only* elegant, time of my life."[152]
There, for the first time since leaving home, she lived "the life of a
well-brought-up young lady," the type of life she had been accustomed
to in Budapest.[153] The city vibrated with energy; contemporaries noted
a heightened intensity of intellectual debate and creative endeavor,
including performances of all kinds. Eva recalled those things and,
always conscious of class divides, also recollected the rich openly
flouting their wealth in a city where there was a huge gulf between
them and blue-collar workers. She remembered Berlin as "buzzing
with contradictions, obsessed with modernity and urgency, . . . [and]
light-hearted permissiveness . . . It was the time of witty political cabaret; of Bertolt Brecht and Kurt Weill's *Threepenny Opera*, which sang
of the desperation of social injustice with hopelessness and nihilism:
'Erst kommt das Fressen und dann kommt die Moral [First comes gob-
bling the food, then comes morality].'"[154]

Vivacious and attractive with dark hair and sparkling eyes, she
dressed in artistic bohemian versions of fashionable attire and caught
the eye of several young men in the progressive, intellectual, artistic,
and political circles in which she and her brother moved, circles that
overlapped with those of their uncle Michael Polanyi, then at Berlin's
Institute of Physical and Electro-Chemistry. Eva told me she had many
flirtations and a few romances.[155] The men she met in Berlin included
the two whom she later married.

She recalled, "Everyone, but everyone, belonged to a political party
or at least expressed political ideologies. The Romanisches Café, half a
block from my studio, was the Forum Romanum for the exchange of
ideas on how best to save the world."[156] There she socialized with a wide
range of progressive, left-leaning intellectuals, many of them Jewish,
including writers such as Koestler and Seghers, the wife of Eva's cousin
László Radványi (the writer, sociologist, and former member of the

Budapest Sunday Circle—along with two of Eva's uncles—who was
then director of the Marxist Workers' School in Berlin).[157] Seghers' *Die
Gefährten*, 1932, warned of the dangers of Fascism, and within a year
of its publication, another regular at the Romanisches, the sculptor,
metalworker, and jeweler Naum Slutzky, was forced to leave Germany.
(His sculpture was included in the infamous 1937 exhibition of so-called
degenerate art in Munich.) Eva also knew scientists such as Leó Szilárd,
Victor Weisskopf, Alex Weissberg, Fritz Houtermans, and Charlotte
Riefenstahl, all friends of her uncle Michael, and sociologists such as
Hans Zeisel and Paul Lazarfeld, who were friends of her uncle Karl.[158]
Eva recalled Weissberg declaiming Shakespeare and Rilke for hours, and
loving to discuss the minutiae of international communist politics.[159]
It was a heady time and conversations often spilled over into the apartment, where sometimes as many as one hundred people crammed in
for parties. Eva was having such a fantastic time in Berlin that even
her bohemian grandmother Cecile worried that she was in danger of
becoming "inebriated on amusements."[160]

But it was not all café society and parties. Eva worked on a freelance basis for the Carstens company (see chapter 2), mainly designing
for its Hirschau factory.[161] She was fortunate that she rarely had to leave
Berlin to fulfill her obligations. For the most part, a Carstens modeler
came to work with her in Berlin; indeed, she rented a room for him in
the building in which she lived so that they could more easily work
together and to save her traveling to the factory. "It seemed like heaven
after Schramberg," she recalled.[162] With one-hundred-and-seventy
workers, it was a smaller factory than Schramberger, but the company
as a whole was larger. Unemployment stood at about 25 percent of the
working population, and Eva again felt an obligation to help keep
workers in jobs. Her designs for Carstens indicate a continued interest
in Art Moderne and softened geometric forms, as well as in tea services
that brought modern expression to traditional object types such as
those by Lindig, and by the elegant mass-production services by
Friedländer and Trudi Petri for KPM (Königliche Porzellan-Manufaktur).[163]

Eva became acquainted with the Hungarian Modernist architect
Fred Forbát (1897–1972), a Communist Party member who had worked
on housing projects with Gropius and lectured at the Weimar Bauhaus.
She occasionally showed him her designs (somewhat tongue-in-cheek,

Eva and Alex Weissberg, USSR, c. 1932. EZA. · Eva, USSR, c. 1932. EZA. · Eva and Petr Leonov (R) with supervisor Gottwald of the Dulevo Factory, USSR, c. 1934–35. EZA.

according to Eva) "to see whether they were acceptable to these self-declared Olympians of modern design." When telling this story, she liked to add in a jokey manner, "I think he usually accepted them into the fold."[164] Eva, however, remained critical of the Bauhaus and Modernism in general. Her own work was attracting attention and when *Die Schaulade* asked for her thoughts on design, she penned "Die Künstlerin hat das Wort" ("The Artist Has Her Say"; sometimes Eva translated it as "The Designer Speaks Her Mind"), including a plea for "soul contact."[165] Her career in Germany looked poised to take off, but by the time the article appeared in early 1932, Eva was already in the USSR.

Despite enjoying her work and social life, Eva was conscious of a jitteriness, fatalism, and lack of confidence in the future among her friends and the feeling that "one can do nothing today but go to Russia; apparently, otherwise one is bound to this fatalistic mood."[166] Already problematic conditions were exacerbated by the worsening world economic situation. By 1930, most of Europe was experiencing a severe recession in the wake of the 1929 stock market collapse in the United States and the consequent Great Depression. This downturn was felt all the more sharply in Germany because of earlier hyperinflation and high unemployment. When Carstens closed its Hirschau plant in late 1931, Eva was forced to consider other options. Besides the gloom about the economy, Nazism and anti-Semitism were growing. Eva recalled: "the political atmosphere in Germany was becoming alarming, although in our circle, the likelihood of a Nazi takeover seemed remote."[167]

Although friends in Hungary, Germany, and Austria were enthusiastic about helping to build a new social order in the USSR, Eva continued to see political engagement as something that other people did. The USSR intrigued her for other reasons. She had grown up with her grandmother's and the Klatschkos' stories of Russia and Russian revolutionaries, and she recalled "a nostalgia for things Russian" as the influx of émigrés grew and Russian performers brought "strange sounds, costumes, and colors to Berlin."[168] She admired the boldly-designed and vibrantly-colored children's books emanating from the Soviet Union, such as those illustrated by Vladimir Lebedev and others, publications she considered emblematic of "a healthy, colorful positive youth culture—different from our own," and she respected the "exquis-

itely chiseled theater performances, as well as the novel imagery of Kandinsky and Tatlin."[169] "All this seemed to originate from a vigorous healthy source, an unknown, faraway country striving towards a utopia where justice would finally reign," she commented.[170] Then one day, Eva decided "to look behind the mountain to see for myself."[171] She was able to visit the USSR because her friend Alex Weissberg—a Polish-Austrian physicist whom Eva described as "a flamboyant, outgoing character, as generous with others as with himself"—had recently taken up a research position at the Ukrainian Physical Technical Institute (UFTI) in Kharkov.[172]

In later years Eva said that she and Weissberg agreed to a fictional engagement so that she could obtain a travel visa, but Koestler recalled that when he first met Weissberg in Berlin in early 1931, Eva introduced him as her "fiancé," and that he wondered what she saw in him before he grasped the power of Weissberg's intellect.[173] It seems odd that Koestler, a former lover, would be mistaken about Eva and Weissberg's relationship, especially since he and Weissberg became close friends. But with Eva's complicated love life, one can never be sure.[174] Eva commented later that she and Weissberg were "not particularly in love," but they lived together in the Soviet Union from January 1932 for a while, married in 1933, and then stayed together until about 1934.[175] They had many friends in common and both had moved to Vienna as children. Five years older, Weissberg had a jolly disposition but was far more politically engaged than Eva. Highly intellectual, he was well versed in history, politics, and Marxism and was a highly-regarded scientist.[176] He was just the type of young man that the Polanyi family had expected Eva's mother to marry. Not surprisingly, he and Laura became firm friends.

The USSR, 1932–1937

Eva arrived in the USSR in January 1932, by which time the attempts to build a genuinely socialist republic had already gone seriously wrong. The first Five Year Plan (1928–1932), with its emphasis on the rationalization of production, collectivized agriculture, and industrial growth, was a calamitous failure, and her first years there coincided with the horrendous famine of 1932–1933, which was especially harsh

Eva (front row) at an exhibition, Moscow, USSR, c. 1934–35. EZA. · Eva (back row) at an exhibition, Moscow, USSR, c. 1934–35. EZA.

in the Ukraine. Harrowing images of starving and dead people stayed with Eva for the remainder of her life. It is not clear exactly when she decided to stay, but one of the reasons she later gave was "the warmth of the Russian people."[177] She never wavered from that estimation, and even during her darkest days in prison never harbored any bitterness to "ordinary Russians."[178]

Weissberg, co-founder and co-editor of the *Soviet Journal of Physics*, was given charge of the construction of a large experimental plant. Eva accepted a job working for the Ukrainian Porcelain and Glass Trust, inspecting ceramics factories in distant places where few Europeans visited, and in more remote spots where few outsiders ventured.[179]

By the summer of 1932, she was working in the Artistic Laboratory at the famous Lomonosov State Porcelain Factory (formerly the Imperial Porcelain Factory) in Leningrad where she learned a great deal about designing for porcelain, a skill that stood her in good stead in later years (see chapter 3). She worked with the two leading artist-designers at the factory: the artistic director Nikolai Suetin, a well-known Suprematist painter, graphic designer, and protégée of the famous artist Kazimir Malevich, and the sculptor Natalia Dan'ko, who became a close friend. The renowned architect-designer Vladimir Tatlin praised Eva's work at a conference on design, and period archives indicate that Yeva Alexandrova Shtriker, or Shtrikker (as she was known in the USSR), was held in such high esteem that the pieces she designed were usually painted by the very best artists in each factory.[180] After her expulsion from the USSR, her designs were either attributed to Suetin or identified only by the name of the painter who had designed the decorative scheme.[181]

Eva's main task in 1932 was to design models for mass production. Her standardized stackable tableware for use in cafeterias did not go into production, but it formed the basis for an *Intourist Tea Service* that stayed in production until World War II.[182] Eva believed that "the clean lines of modern design could be successfully combined with sensuous, classic shapes," and the references to traditional tableware evident in her work in the USSR were enriched by the elegant examples of eighteenth-century Russian porcelain in the factory's collection.[183] A white tea and coffee service designed for Carstens in about 1930 was a forerunner of the white services that she designed in the USSR (see

chapter 3).[184] Her designs continued to show both Art Moderne and geometric influences, and a fascination with giving refined modern expression to traditional forms and services.

During this period, she was commissioned to design a store and she relished telling of how she was asked *not* to include "gynecological furniture," by which the client meant Modernist tubular steel chairs like the 1928 chaise by Le Corbusier, Charlotte Perriand, and Pierre Jeanneret.[185] Eva used to laugh when she told the story (probably slightly exaggerated for greater effect) of Suetin spending a whole day trying out different ways of placing a single dot on one of her forms, but she appreciated a fellow perfectionist. Indeed, in 2002, I witnessed her and a modeler from the Lomonosov factory spend hours contemplating a teapot before shaving off the minutest sliver from a model.[186]

By 1934 (if not earlier), Eva had separated from Weissberg (they remained good friends), resigned from Lomonosov, purportedly after disagreements with managers, and accepted the post of artistic director at the Dulevo Porcelain Manufactory in the small town of Orekhovo-Zuevo outside Moscow. Her contract promised an apartment—a necessity at a time of severe housing shortages—but she had to make do with a series of borrowed rooms. Some had no electricity or water; at least one was rat-infested.[187] Despite or because of this, Eva was very productive during her sixteen months there (about May 1934 to September 1935), designing a range of items from tea services to kindergarten tableware (see chapter 3). Founded in 1832, by 1900 the Dulevo factory was one of the largest ceramics producers in the world.[188] Some of Eva's white tableware was decorated with simple lines and bands or tight bold geometric patterns, while a liqueur set (c. 1933–1935) more obviously drew upon Art Moderne designs.[189] Eva had fond memories of working there, and greatly admired Petr Leonov, as a person and as an artist, who undertook much of the decoration of the forms Eva designed. His rich, expansive, freely drawn patterns in vibrant colors drew upon Russian folk traditions, especially textiles.[190] Having become a close friend, he vouched for Eva after her arrest.[191]

She moved to Moscow in 1935 and became artistic director of the China and Glass Industry, with responsibility for designing objects for mass production, particularly plates, in a country of some 160 million

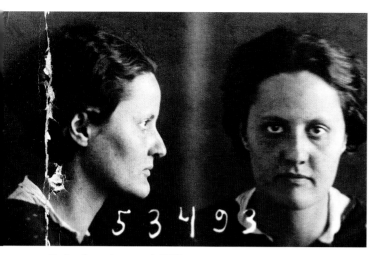

Eva's prison photograph, USSR, 1936. EZA.

people, many of whom had never previously owned plates or anything else made out of pottery. When living in Moscow, Eva took trips abroad and when traveling to or from Paris she met and fell in love with "Jascha" (the pseudonym for Jacob Alexandrovich Ravich). A handsome former member of the Red Army, who was then a high-ranking officer in the NKVD (a precursor to the KGB, it dealt with police matters—public and secret), he was traveling abroad undercover as a business-man. They became lovers and, at some stage in their relationship, Eva had an abortion.[192] About ten years older than Eva and married, Jascha, she told her daughter, was the great love of her life.[193]

Accusations and Incarceration

On May 28, 1936, when Jascha was on a secret mission in Manchuria, Eva was suddenly arrested by the GPU (Stalin's secret security agency). It was only three months before the long-planned show trial of the so-called Trotskyite-Zinovievite Terrorist Center in which leading Party members Zinoviev and Kamenev were accused of treason and terrorism. Today it is commonly accepted that Stalin, who feared those comrades might successfully oppose his policies and his ruthless con-solidation of power, orchestrated both the accusations and the trial, which is often considered as the beginning of "The Purges."[194]

The charges against Eva were grave. Unbeknown to her, Mikhail Bykhovskii, a German-speaking engineer from the Lomonosov factory, had falsely accused her and other German-speaking visiting workers and émigrés (including the German model maker Hermann Fuhlbrügge, who worked with Eva at Lomonosov and Dulevo) of conspiring to assassinate Stalin. She was soon also accused of serving as a courier for Trotsky, the exiled former leading Bolshevik around whom cen-tered much of the opposition to Stalin's dictatorial ambitions.[195] She could hardly have been accused of two worse crimes at the time; the death penalty seemed inevitable. At the time of her arrest, Eva was living in a room in the apartment allocated to her brother Michael (who worked in the Inventions [Patents] Office) and his wife and baby, but earlier she had sublet a room from the Hungarian Communist Gyula Hevesi, who had been an official in the Hungarian Soviet Republic of 1919. When his old pistols were found in the room vacated

by Eva, it gave credence to the claims that Eva had been selected as the assassin.[196]

Given the charges, she was fortunate not to have been executed or "disappeared," as were so many victims of trumped-up accusations during this period. Figures vary, but most scholars estimate that between one and one-and-a-half million of those arrested in 1937 and 1938 were killed. Indeed, most of those accused of the same fictitious conspiracy against Stalin as Eva lost their lives, as did her accuser (who had already been accused of anti-Soviet crimes by someone else and had fabricated charges against others in an effort to save him-self).[197] Weissberg was arrested a few months later, as was his colleague, the physicist Fritz Houtermans, in a wave of accusations against for-eign specialists.[198]

Eva was incarcerated from May 1936 until September of the follow-ing year, spending about ten months in solitary confinement and liv-ing with the daily expectation of execution. "I'm still surprised that I am here today," she used to say. "I was sure to be killed."[199] During the day, she was not allowed to lie down or even to sit on the bench in her cell. "We went to bed at nine p.m., got up at seven a.m.," she recalled, "and when you needed to relieve yourself, they gave you a square of brown paper. . . . We ate mostly black bread. . . . Every three days I was taken for a walk: seven minutes. Every ten days, a shower . . . that was my life for sixteen months."[200] Her memoirs of this period make for harrowing reading, as do the transcriptions of the interrogations of Eva and her supposed accomplices, and the statements of her accus-ers.[201] They also give a glimpse of how she dealt with the situation.

Eva, who turned thirty while in prison, learned to go "inside her-self" to a degree she never imagined possible before, despite thinking that she had perfected this in Schramberg. She devised all manner of ways to live in the present—thought-by-thought, minute-by-minute, hour-by-hour, day-by-day. She exercised "thought control" to blot out the past, as well as hopes or fears for the future: "I did not think of anything in the future. Nothing of loving thoughts, or of Nature, was permitted because it would have made me cry."[202] When not in solitary confinement, she and the people in adjoining cells established contact through a system of knocks; the first she learned was for "who?"

As part of her "very elaborate system of *excluding* certain thoughts" in order to keep focused on the present, she played "mind games," such as imagining how to design and construct a brassiere, or playing chess with herself in her head. She played tic-tac-toe with pieces she made "by rolling bits of bread between my fingers: I imagined it was clay."[203] Writing poetry also helped transport her to a different mental space; the six and a half paces across the cell (corner to corner) provided the basic rhythm.[204] She was determined not to give in to despair—her own or that all around her: someone in a neighboring cell went insane, gnawing at her hands and screaming wildly, while another tried to kill herself. Although Eva tried to set her mind against dark thoughts, living in such circumstances and unable to understand why she had not yet been sentenced to death given the charges brought many moments of utter despair to this formerly formidable and strong-minded woman. At one point she overheard an interrogation in which a man who denied knowing her was told: "Your deposition makes no difference, we will destroy her anyway."[205]

After months of denying the charges and resisting investigators pressing for a "confession," she finally cracked and signed one, fearing that otherwise she could rot in jail without trial for the rest of her life or be summarily executed. When she realized what she had done, she slashed at her wrists with copper wire from the toilet cistern (she described the difficulty of cutting through nerves, veins, and tendons in her memoir).[206] Eva always credited the woman warden who found her with saving her life.[207] When recalling the suicide attempt, Eva wrote in her typical understated way, "For a short time during the winter of 1937, my efforts at keeping sane must have faltered."[208]

Although Eva was eventually cleared of the assassination charge, she still remained accused of being a Trotskyite courier. Such was the relief of being cleared of one charge, however, that her will to fight was renewed. When she later recalled that moment, she stated in that laconic way of hers, "more than dead you cannot be."[209] Then suddenly on September 17, 1937, she was taken out of her cell without any explanation. She thought she was about to be executed but, without pardon or reprieve, was put on a train for Vienna, where family and friends lived.[210] Needless to say, she was extremely fragile, physically and mentally; she used to say that when she was released, she was frigid emotionally.[211]

Stalin, Eva, Orlov, and the FBI

It is not clear precisely why Eva was released, but evidence has come to light indicating that the assassination charge was dropped after Stalin personally sent a senior NKVD officer, now thought to be General Orlov (a pseudonym for Leiba Lazarevich Feldbin, the man responsible for, among other things, masterminding the elimination of the non-Stalinist Left in the Spanish Civil War), to interrogate Eva. In 1938, Orlov, fearing he too was about to perish alongside former colleagues and comrades in the Purges, fled in secret to the United States from a mission in Spain and went into hiding. After Stalin's death, Orlov published *The Secret History of Stalin's Crimes* in 1953. Eva read it, found a reference to her accuser Bykhovskii, and wondered how Orlov knew about him. But at the height of the Cold War, she still feared Soviet reprisals on her and her family and consequently did not follow up that lead, perhaps wisely, given that thereafter Orlov was closely watched by both U.S. and Soviet agents.

Nearly fifty years later, *Alexander Orlov: The FBI's KGB General* was published in 2002, written by Edward Gazur, the FBI special agent who debriefed and ultimately befriended Orlov in the 1970s. Eva's daughter read it but found nothing in it about her mother who, then almost ninety-six years old, had recently been officially rehabilitated in Russia, along with thousands of others wrongfully arrested. Nevertheless, she contacted Gazur, giving him pertinent dates and information that she knew from her mother, including details of Eva's interrogations and interrogators, one of whom had interviewed Eva in an elegant office every night for a week. Eva remembered him as a well-dressed and well-educated man who told her he had come from the Kremlin, informed her that she said too much for her own good, and suggested she keep quiet about her relationship with Jascha.[212]

After consulting his case notes, Gazur came to believe that Orlov was that well-dressed interrogator, but his FBI training led him to be cautious and he asked Eva detailed questions about her interrogators before any further discussions. Just as the accuracy of Eva's recollections about what happened in prison have been verified by documents unearthed in Russia, her replies convinced Gazur that she was the young woman that Orlov had discussed during one of their debriefing sessions and, unusually for Orlov, had continued to talk about when they socialized afterwards.[213] Orlov told Gazur about a young artist—an attractive, well-educated, and rather bohemian and adventurous sort of woman—who had been accused of trying to kill Stalin and whom he had been sent to interrogate. Orlov had mentioned that after being in prison for about a year and a half the woman had been released, and that the interviews were conducted in German (a fact that had led Gazur to assume that the woman was German). Orlov also told Gazur that this woman had told him more than was good for her safety, and he had advised her not to tell anyone else that her lover was a high-ranking NKVD officer.

Eva's family and friends who were interested in her years in the USSR were extremely excited about all this, but Eva seemed to take it in stride, possibly because by then she had been back to Russia, had been feted there, and no longer feared reprisals against her or her family. Perhaps she simply did not want to reopen those painful episodes of her life at a time when she had found ways of coping with them. Besides, she was involved with new projects and always tried to live in the moment. One of many questions remaining is whether Jascha's high position in the NKVD may have played a part in Stalin or Orlov taking Eva's protestations more seriously than may otherwise have been the case. It could just as likely have been that Eva was the liability that cost Jascha his life. Eva never saw him again.[214]

New Beginnings

The first that Weissberg knew of Eva's release was when a letter was delivered to his prison cell asking for him to give his brother right-of-attorney so that Eva could divorce him. Delighted to learn that Eva had survived, he asked if he could write her a note, explaining: "All I want to do is wish her good luck and a happier marriage. She hasn't got a lot of time. She's over thirty, and she has no children, although she always wanted them. . . . She will probably marry a very old friend of mine who loves her very much and has waited for her all this time."[215]

Eva did indeed marry Hans Zeisel (1905–1992), whom she had met in Berlin and with whom she began to build a new relationship in Vienna. Hans, who was a close friend of Eva's uncle Karl Polanyi, seems to have fallen in love with Eva in Berlin, and in 1931 she wrote to him in Vienna from there, but whether as a lover or friend is not certain. Their daughter recalls that Hans, when visiting the USSR, met Eva there at least once after she and Weissberg had separated.[216] To have waited for Eva from 1931 to 1937 suggests that Hans was in love with Eva. Whether Eva was in love with Hans during those years is another matter. That she lived with and loved Jascha suggests not. We may never know. One year older than Eva, Hans, who was quite dashing and very sporty, had doctoral degrees in law and political science. Like Weissberg, he had a formidable intellect and a dogged approach to argument, but he was less jovial than his old friend. Eva and Hans had much in common, from core human values and outlooks on life to a love of skiing and the outdoors. A liberal social democrat, as a young man Hans had been active in socialist groups in "Red Vienna," practiced law, and moved in the same intellectual and political circles in Vienna as Karl Polanyi, Weissberg, and other Stricker family members and friends.[217] He made a name for himself as an up-and-coming sociologist with *Die Arbeitslosen von Marienthal* (1933, *Jobless of Marienthal*), a pioneering study undertaken with Paul Lazarsfeld and Maria Jahoda on the impact of the Depression and unemployment on a small town, and thereafter he specialized in survey research.[218] Like Weissberg, he was the type of man Eva's mother had been expected to marry.

Given Eva's extremely debilitated state, Hans's love and his "take-charge," confident approach to life helped Eva though an extremely difficult time. She told me that she had "something of a breakdown" after her release because she could not adjust to everyday life after prison: "I could not care for myself. I was completely without strength, without confidence, self-assertion or anything for quite a long time. I was put too fast into daily life. An hour seemed like a minute—I had no concept of time. I simply did anything I was told, almost like a robot."[219] When discussing what today would be called posttraumatic stress syndrome, she stated, "Hans took over. . . . When I was asked a question, he answered. I did anything I was told."[220]

Eva recalled Hans as loving during that period but less so after they married.[221] It was not an easy relationship for either of them. Hans found it difficult to back down on any issue, and Eva, although a strong character, hated direct confrontation but also hated being dominated, and became what some have referred to as passive-aggressive in her

Eva, Jean, and Hans, United States, 1941. EZA.

dealings with him.[222] Some friends and family felt that Eva was simply too strong, too bright, and too successful for Hans, who became terribly critical of her while at the same time being very proud of her achievements.[223] Whatever the case, living together peaceably was a problem, and they spent much of the next half century trying to negotiate what one friend called "a collision of force fields."[224]

Meanwhile Weissberg, whose account of the wider witch hunts in which he and Eva found themselves is one of the more politically sophisticated first-hand studies, was held in prison for three years, despite interventions by Albert Einstein and other internationally famous Nobel Prize–winning scientists on his behalf.[225] In a strange twist of history, in the aftermath of the Nazi-Soviet Pact (1939), he was handed over to the German Secret State Police (Gestapo) at the Soviet border of German-occupied Poland. He escaped and went underground when the Nazi extermination of Jews began in 1942, but was caught by the Gestapo in 1943 and sent to a concentration camp. With the help of the Polish Resistance he escaped and, while in hiding in Warsaw, worked with the Resistance and took part in two major insurrections (including the Warsaw Ghetto Uprising) against the German SS. This paramilitary wing of the Nazi Party was then deporting thousands of Jews from the ghetto to extermination camps.[226] His personal losses were great: his second wife, his father, brother, and nearly all his friends perished.[227]

Expulsion, Exile, and Emigration

Eva's journeys up to 1937 had been of her own choosing. Thereafter, however, she experienced expulsion from a country whose people she had grown to love, followed by exile from Vienna (her new home and her home for six years as a young girl) and then emigration. With anti-Semitism growing in Austria, the family decided to move to the United States along with many other Jews, but the announcement on March 12, 1938 of the *Anschluss* by which Nazi Germany annexed Austria disrupted their preparations. Terrified and still traumatized by her arrest and experiences in prison, Eva left immediately for England where her uncles Michael and Karl Polanyi then lived (her British visa had arrived; that for the United States was still pending).

"I felt so vulnerable, physically and in my head, that I would have gone crazy had anything else happened to me," she recalled.[228] On one of the last trains out of Vienna for Switzerland, Eva remembers hearing German airplanes overhead. Eva's mother, an Austrian citizen, and Hans, a Czech citizen, remained to supervise the final stages of Eva's divorce and obtain their visas.[229]

Hans collected his visa in Prague and traveled to England, where he and Eva were married in July 1938. As they awaited their visas for the U.S., Laura, who had been helping secure the release of her sister's husband, a social democratic activist arrested by the Gestapo and sent to Dachau concentration camp, was herself arrested (probably because of her efforts on behalf of her brother-in-law).[230] Eva, who at that time was particularly dependent upon her mother, was frantic with worry, but the family dispatched a top lawyer from Budapest and enlisted the help of British Quaker agencies. Laura was released and was reunited with Eva and Hans in Britain shortly before they left for the United States in October 1938.[231] Laura followed in 1939, and Sándor in 1941.

Early Days in the USA

Eva and Hans settled in New York City, like many other Jewish intellectual and artistic émigrés from Central Europe. Eva found work more quickly than Hans. She immediately tracked down names and addresses of likely contacts from trade publications in the New York Public Library and through Madeline Love, editor of *China, Glass and Lamps*, gained a commission to design small giftware items, the remuneration for which paid charges on household items that arrived from Europe on the same day as the check.[232] Eva saw this as a good sign; her old optimism was returning. Other small design commissions—for watches, china decals, and small china goods—did not reach production, but the fees helped tide the couple over. A line of giftware, including vases, bowls, small boxes, and a lemonade set for Bay Ridge Specialty Company of Trenton, New Jersey, some sixty-six miles from New York City, sold locally. The line indicates Eva's continuing interest in circular forms and the influence of traditional Chinese ceramic forms that are less evident elsewhere in her work.[233]

Eva and John, Silver Point Beach, NY, c. 1948. EZA. · Eva, Jean, and John developing patterns, c. 1949. EZA.

In autumn 1939, Eva began teaching ceramic design at the Pratt Institute in Brooklyn. The job proved to be a lifeline, providing a small but regular income while she and Hans established themselves and started a family. She came about her new position rather by chance, after getting to know a Pratt student while working on a small commission (sculpting plaster Himalayan mountains for a film set at fifty cents an hour). While with him at Pratt one day, she heard about the job vacancy. She had never taught before, but that did not daunt Eva. She proposed teaching ceramics from an industrial point of view as opposed to as a handicraft, at just the time the college was pioneering the teaching of industrial design (under the guidance of Rowena Reed and Alexander Kostellow), the first course in which had begun only five years earlier at the Carnegie Institute of Technology.[234]

Eva's curriculum, together with her later writing on design, shows the same strong emphasis on functionality that abounded in Werkbund-style publications across interwar Europe: teapots had to pour well—drips were not tolerated—and they could not be too heavy when full, while handles had to be both strong and comfortable.[235] There was a clear emphasis on the three-dimensional aspects of design, including modeling, and she argued that links with local manufacturers were essential to the training of designers for industry. At the same time, however—and this is where she differed from many other teachers of industrial design—she sought to train students to design forms expressive of emotions.[236]

Eva understood that designs often had to be changed or refined for mass production, and she recognized that the college could not provide anything near the type of experience offered by industry. On her initiative, therefore, Pratt came to an agreement with Bay Ridge Specialty Company whereby students learned about industrial ceramics as apprentices.[237] As the instructor, Eva was greatly involved with each project. In 1940, this collaboration led to the manufacture of tumblers, pitchers, and tea-and-lemonade sets, and during the academic year (1940–41) whole dinnerware lines.[238]

A major outcome of Eva's approach to teaching was the *Stratoware* line, developed for Sears, Roebuck and Co. and based around a pitcher designed by student Francis Blod, the design of which reflected the vogue for "streamlined" Art Moderne ceramics and plastics in the late 1920s and 1930s (see chapter 4).[239] Another measure of her success was a request by Frederick Rhead, vice president of the Homer Laughlin China Company and famous as the designer of the boldly colored, best-selling *Fiestaware* line (1935), for a group of students to work with him.[240] Rhead also offered Eva a job in 1940. It was a fantastic opportunity to work for a major company and a renowned figure in the field. It would have established her as a major contender, but she was already pregnant with her first child (her daughter, Jean; her son, John, was born in 1944), and Hans refused to move to West Virginia because he was more likely to find work in the New York area.[241] In 1940, it was customary in most circles, including the middle-class intellectual ones in which the Zeisels moved, for the wife's career to be sacrificed for that of the husband.

With a new baby, the family moved to Brooklyn so that Eva could be nearer to Pratt. Either before or shortly after the move, Laura and Eva became members of the First Unitarian Church in Brooklyn Heights, partly because Laura believed that such an institution could help them integrate more successfully into the culture of the new country.[242] Unitarianism, which acknowledges a God but sees Christ only as a prophet, appealed to Laura and Eva because of its strong liberal views and its associations with Hungary; Hans, a hard-line atheist, took no part in the religious aspects of church life but sometimes joined in the social activities.[243] Even after the family moved to a rented apartment on Riverside Drive near Columbia University on Manhattan's Upper West Side, they continued to attend the church.[244] It was there that Eva's memorial service was held in 2012.

The family moved to New Jersey for the academic year 1942–43 when Hans taught at New Jersey State College for Women and Eva, desperate to retain her post at Pratt, commuted back and forth, juggling childcare, housework, her design career, and teaching.[245] Fortunately for her, the family moved to Riverside Drive when the year was up. Eva often remarked that without her mother's assistance, she would not have been able to do all that she did. Laura, who was considered every bit as brilliant as her brothers Michael and Karl, set aside many of her own interests to take over childcare duties whenever Eva needed help. She was pleased to assist her beloved daughter build a career while raising a family.[246] Hans found work in media and market

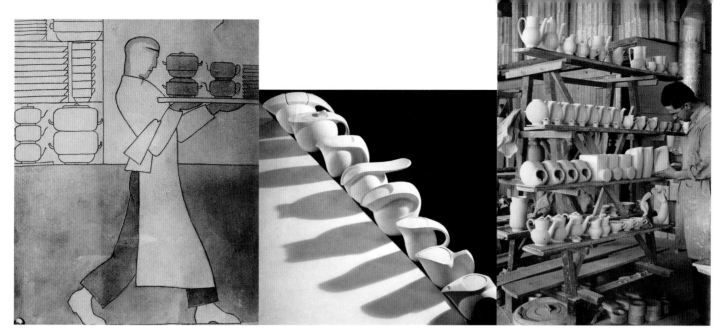

Drawing from Eva's "Some Problems of Dinnerware Design," 1942. EZA. · Student work: pitchers, c. 1941–42. EZA. · Pratt student at Bay Ridge Company, c. 1940. EZA.

research, and Eva continued to teach at Pratt and to design freelance.[247] One of her projects was a series of designs for standardized stacking dishes that saved on both materials and kiln space, which she promoted as part of the war effort (see chapter 26). It was not adopted by the government, but the time and effort invested in thinking about such matters would be repaid many times over during the next twenty years.[248]

Museum of Modern Art, New York

Eva's first major break in the United States as a designer, as opposed to as a teacher, came through Eliot Noyes, director of MoMA's newly formed Department of Industrial Design. Noyes had impeccable Modernist credentials, having worked in the architectural office of Bauhaus teachers Walter Gropius and Marcel Breuer, but was able to see beyond Eva's criticisms of Modernism and appreciate both her industrial experience and her ability to create exciting forms.[249] Noyes and Eva first met when he visited an exhibition of work by Pratt students in 1940, and she invited him to the "Handicraft and Mass Production" lecture that she gave at a meeting of the New York Society of Ceramic Arts held at the Metropolitan Museum of Art in New York in January 1942.[250] There she discussed her vision of industrial design and, conventionally enough by then, stated that "craftwork could become an important influence on mass production, with the industrial designer bridging the gulf between the two."[251] Shortly afterward, Noyes recommended her for a major commission to be undertaken with the museum and Castleton China (see chapter 5) for a well-designed modern line of fine dinnerware acceptable to the museum's design curators, and also to well-to-do consumers.[252] It was to be simple yet sufficiently sophisticated for formal dining and be of such excellent quality that it would be considered an heirloom.

Though not in full production until 1949, prototypes were exhibited at MoMA's *New Shapes in Modern China Designed by Eva Zeisel* (1946), the first MoMA exhibition to feature a single woman designer and the first devoted solely to pottery.[253] It brought Eva a new degree of fame, placing her work on a par with the groundbreaking range of molded plywood furniture designed by Charles and Ray Eames and their small staff team, which had been featured in the MoMA exhibition immediately preceding Eva's.[254] The *Museum* line, in which every item is an essay in fluidity, established Eva's reputation as a leading designer of pottery in the United States. It was Eva's personal favorite.

The MoMA connection led to Eva's inclusion in roundtable discussions during the museum's "Good Design" programs of the 1950s.[255] Typically, Eva's contributions were less orthodox than those of other speakers. In a discussion on ornament and "good design," for example, she stood aside from those who took the position advocated by Adolf Loos in the 1900s that ornament represented a lack of civilization, and when asked what she thought "good design" was, she quipped in that dry way of hers, "Love is a personal matter."[256] In posing love alongside design, Eva, like the Eameses, gave design a human face and helped change the look as well as the ideas underpinning modern design in postwar America.[257] Eva abhorred the concept of "good design," which she found exclusive, moralizing, and all too evocative of missionaries and design police (a phrase that made her chuckle when she first heard it).[258]

The publicity given to the MoMA/Castleton project led to Red Wing Potteries commissioning a line with a "Greenwich Village–type" appeal.[259] What became known as *Town and Country* dinnerware (1946–1947) proved that Eva also excelled at designing inexpensive earthenware that fit well with the more informal postwar lifestyles (see chapter 6). It was more overtly modern in design, more youthful in its appeal, and certainly more colorful than the Castleton line. The forms were more playful: Eva ventured further from conventional object forms, designing unusual plate forms, "thumbprint" handles, and anthropomorphic salt and pepper shakers. As sturdy as it was elegant and affordable, it met the increasing interest in organic, more casual, colorful "contemporary" forms and sold well in the competitive and lucrative postwar U.S. market for informal tableware.[260]

Organic Modernism and Refining Tradition

The 1940s saw the continued influences of prewar and wartime Organic Modernist designs, including those by Finnish architect–designer Alvar Aalto who was strongly influenced by the work of abstract

Eva in claypit, Monmouth Pottery, c. 1953. EZA. · Eva at exhibition of her work, 1951. EZA. · Eva with assistants, Riverside Drive studio, NYC, 1947. EZA.

painters and sculptors, such as Joan Miró and Jean Arp, and U.S. ceramic designer Russel Wright. Leading postwar designers working in the United States in this mode included Charles and Ray Eames, Eero Saarinen, Wright, and Eva. Their influence was enormous, at home and abroad, not least because they paid greater attention to more intuitive, psychological, whimsical, witty, and playful aspects of design as well as to the softer, more organic, curvilinear, and sculptural forms.

Coined in 1949 by designer George Nelson to describe the amoebiclike forms he saw as setting a new trend, Biomorphic was another term given to such forms. The term Humanistic Modernism is also often used about such designs because of the emphasis on what Aalto called "human quality." Eva, with her emphasis on "soul contact" with users, raised the bar in terms of the affectivity of objects more than any other designer.[261] But one needs to be careful not to exaggerate the degree to which Eva's designs fit with the fluid forms generally associated with the formal aspects of Organic/Biomorphic Modernism, with obvious exceptions such as her frequently-illustrated "Schmoo" shakers for Red Wing. Other sources for Eva's refined postwar curving forms ranged from the Baroque forms of her native Hungary, the elegance of Russian porcelains, and her own designs in the USSR to the restrained elegance of designers such as Friedländer and Petri. The case studies that follow give a fuller picture of the parameters within which Eva worked in the postwar period and broaden our understanding of midcentury modern (with a small m) design.

Non-anticommunist

In 1948, Eva severed her long-standing friendship with Arthur Koestler for several years because of his hard-line Cold War anticommunism. Eva declared herself a non-anticommunist and as such, strongly opposed his views. She felt that Koestler had lost all his *joie de vivre* in the 1930s when he became a "holier-than-thou communist" ideologue (she had found him charming and full of fun in the 1920s) and something of "an abyss" developed between them then because, according to Eva, he felt uncomfortable that she was "outside of the fold—a stranger to the common cause"—and he tried to hide from her the obvious shortcomings of daily life in the USSR. She was not sure

exactly how much he saw of the country when he visited (1932–1933) "or how much he wanted to see" as a devoted Party member.[262] Nevertheless, at that time they managed to retain some form of friendship and when he traveled to Samarkand, he brought back trinkets for Eva and together they visited "refugee architect" friends from Berlin then working in the Soviet Union.[263]

She did not see Koestler again until she arrived in Britain in 1938 (the year he left the Communist Party). They exchanged experiences of prison and solitary confinement (he had been imprisoned by Nationalists during the Spanish Civil War).[264] He advised how best to get Laura released when she was arrested in Vienna, and told Eva that had she been detained any longer in the Soviet Union he would have traveled there to help bring about her release.[265] He probably would have done so; their correspondence reveals a closeness that went beyond Eva's intense dislike of his later politics.

After his death, Eva wrote, "People who have shared such experiences [prison and solitary confinement] are forever tied together, and understand each other's thoughts in ways which others cannot." Koestler, in reply to a letter from Eva in 1948 attacking his anticommunism, told her that he still felt nearer to her "than to anybody else, before or after."[266] If Koestler remained a little in love with Eva, she seemed mainly saddened by the changes in this man who seemed to need to cling to one doctrinaire set of beliefs after another: from Zionism to communism and anticommunism. In her generous evenhanded way, however, she always pointed out to his many detractors that he had been a loving and loyal friend to her, while analyzing his behavior in the same objective "outsider" manner that she brought to most situations, including her prison memoirs.

Koestler's *Darkness at Noon* was published in 1940, but Eva did not read it for over forty years "because the memory was too painful."[267] When she did, she commented that although there were many details she recognized as coming from her experiences, including the system for "knocking" messages, "the monologues and dialogues of that book were either Koestler's own soul-searching, or were based upon his long, nightly discussions with Alex [Weissberg]."[268]

When Eva and Koestler next met a decade later, his doubts about the Soviet system had hardened and, at a public meeting held in New

Eva and "aging" cabinet (Tomorrow's Classic), c. 1951–52. EZA. · Eva with fellow designer Russel Wright at the Brooklyn Museum , 1957. EZA. · Eva and Jean, c. 1947. EZA.

York's Carnegie Hall in 1948, he called for war against the USSR to prevent it "from crushing the remnants of western culture."[269] Appalled both by his suggestion that she share the platform with him and people she described as "several dozen of the most outspoken fascist representatives of Yugoslav, Polish, and other organizations of refugees from countries now under the power of Soviet Russia," and at finding herself in an audience filled with "known fascists," she decided to write to him.[270]

His actions nudged Eva out of her typical position of political onlooker. In a precise and clearly argued manner, she spelled out her distaste for his call to arms and told of her fears about the widespread jingoistic warmongering which he and others were fueling, as well as her anxieties about the consequences of atomic war upon the people of the Soviet Union, proposing peaceful coexistence as an alternative. She was concerned with reductions in civil liberties and free speech in the United States as a mood of paranoia and denunciation swept across the country. The House Un-American Activities Committee (HUAC) had been instituted in 1947, and its activities reminded Eva of the USSR in the 1930s.[271] The letter to Koestler reveals Eva's strong intellectual side, her detailed knowledge of contemporary politics, and a willingness to stand up for her beliefs.[272] The difference between Koestler and Eva, she reminded him on several occasions, was that he seemed unable to distinguish the Russian people from the Soviet system he hated.[273] In that outsider way of hers, Eva thought of her positions more in terms of "non"; thinking of herself as a "non-communist" when she lived in the USSR and as a "non-anticommunist" in McCarthyite Cold War America.[274] I have gone into some detail here because this 1948 episode indicates that Eva's later interest in politics and the peace movement was not quite such an abrupt turnaround as some have claimed.

Settling Down

Cold War anxieties aside, things were looking up financially and professionally for the Zeisels in the late 1940s. *Say it with Figures,* Hans's book about cross-tabulation elaboration analysis and questionnaires, was published in 1947, and Eva, who had previously worked from home, designed and created a new four-room studio in the basement of the

Riverside Drive apartment building in which they lived. The design space was fitted out with boldly striped carpeting and the desks (designed by Eva) cantilevered out from the walls.[275] Key features included "aging cabinets," illuminated shadow boxes for looking at prototypes from all possible angles and in different lights, and a fully equipped workshop for making models.[276] Her interns and assistants were mainly former Pratt students.[277]

Few ceramics commissions came Eva's way between 1947 and 1950, but she designed objects in other media, from plastic products (chapter 8) and glass syrup containers to stainless steel wares for General Mills of Minnesota and a chair with a tubular metal frame (chapter 25). In 1949, United China and Glass, an importing and distributing company, commissioned what became the dinner service that was launched to celebrate the company's 100th anniversary in 1950 (chapter 9). The company's New Orleans headquarters suggested the name *Norleans* for its wares, which were produced in Occupied Japan by the Meito company. The line was one of the first U.S.–designed lines made in Japan to be imported into the postwar United States, an early hint that Japanese production would lead to the near demise of the U.S. pottery industry in the next decade.[278]

Commissions came more frequently as the U.S. economy thrived. In 1951, Eva designed a range of rosewood and ceramic items (see chapter 10) and in the following year, pieces from her designs for the Loza Fina company of Mexico were shown in the *Arte en la Vida Diaria* (Arts of Daily Living) exhibition in Mexico City, which organizer Clara Porset envisaged as promoting contemporary Mexican design rather like the MoMA *Good Design* shows (see Select Chronology).[279] Like Eva a hugely talented designer, Porset also knew a little about exile, having been banished in the late 1930s from her native Cuba for participation in the resistance movement.

Meanwhile, the hugely popular *Tomorrow's Classic* line went into production in 1952, followed by a casual-style dinner service for Western Stoneware (chapter 12). Eva now took royalties whenever she could, rather than one-time lump sums (it has been estimated that she enjoyed royalties of at least $600–$700 per month in the early 1950s), and Hans was teaching economics, sociology, and statistics at Rutgers and Columbia Universities.[280] In 1953, they bought a house on South

Eva at Noritake factory, Japan, 1963. EZA. Eva, Chicago, c. 1969. EZA.

Mountain Road in Rockland County, about twenty miles outside of New York City in what, since the interwar years, had been a colony of artists and intellectuals. Composer Kurt Weill had died three years earlier, but his widow, the actress and singer Lotte Lenya, lived there, as did, among others, textile designer Ruth Reeves, artist–potter Henry Varnham Poor, artist Herbert Katzman, art director Cipe Pineles, and graphic designer William Golden. The house provided a haven and workspace for Eva until her death. At her ninety-fifth birthday party in the "country house," as she called it, someone asked what she loved most about the place; she replied without hesitation, "Nature—it still inspires me."[281]

New York, Chicago, and Commissions Abroad

Soon after they took possession of the house, Hans was offered, and accepted, a position in law and sociology at the University of Chicago. Jean was thirteen and John was nine, and in order to keep the family together, Eva agreed to move, albeit reluctantly. When speaking of juggling work and family with Lucie Young, Eva commented, "I don't know how other women managed it. Hans thought my work should be second to his."[282] She resigned from her job at Pratt, closed her studio, and moved the family to Chicago. Once there, Eva was asked to create a line for the Western Stoneware Company's Monmouth (Illinois) division (chapter 12). It necessitated her living near the factory for considerable amounts of time, especially during the development stage. At just over two hundred miles from Chicago, it was too far to commute. Her parents came for long visits and helped out and Eva accepted the job, on the basis that the children would stay in Monmouth with her during school vacations.[283]

Twelve months later, Eva and the children were back in New York, partly because John had not settled in at his new school. With the help of afterschool care and her ever-supportive mother, Eva reopened her studio and worked on a series of commissions, including *Prestige* glassware, Hall China kitchenware, and the highly acclaimed *Century* service, also for Hall China in 1957 (chapters 13, 14, and 24). Hans, a specialist in the application of statistical models from the social sciences to legal matters and an authority on juries, capital punishment,

and survey techniques, continued to research, teach, and reside in Chicago. He had a distinguished career, becoming a fellow of the American Academy of Arts and Sciences and the American Association for the Advancement of Science. He spent some time in New York and Eva spent time in Chicago to keep the marriage together. As Hans's career flourished in the late 1950s and early 1960s, however, Eva's career slowed as tastes changed and the ceramics industry in the United States nearly ground to a halt in the face of foreign competition, mainly from Japan, which offered good quality wares at cheaper prices.

In 1957, when Jean was working as an intern with animal behaviorist Konrad Lorenz and John was in boarding school in Switzerland, Eva accepted a commission that involved spending time in Germany working for the internationally renowned Rosenthal firm (chapter 15). From Germany she traveled to Italy, designing dinnerware, wall coverings, and room dividers for Mancioli (none of which were produced; see chapter 26). She taught once a week at the Rhode Island School of Design for the academic year 1959–60 while Jean was a student there, driving from Manhattan in a battered old yellow DeSoto convertible. When Laura died in December 1959, it was an enormous personal loss for Eva. They had been extraordinarily close.

In 1963, Eva visited Nagoya, Japan, where she worked for several months on two dinnerware lines for the prestigious Noritake pottery. Established as a trading company in Tokyo and New York City in 1876, its wares were mainly aimed at European and North American markets. Once again, Eva's designs did not go into production. Eva moved on to India and designed a few items for Bengal Potteries in Calcutta, yet another project that came to naught, as often happens with freelance designers; a scheme to design for a company in Thailand also failed.[284] In 1964, Eva undertook a commission for the Hyalyn pottery of North Carolina (chapter 16), the founders of which placed great emphasis on design. It was forty years since Eva had trained as an apprentice potter and this proved to be her last ceramics commission for nearly twenty years. Ironically, by the time demand for her work dropped off, Eva no longer needed to juggle child care, family needs, and work in quite the same way as before, because Jean and John were now young adults.

Three photographs by Eva of peace demonstrations, New York City and Washington, D.C., c. 1967–1968. EZA.

Although the changed circumstances in the mass production side of the U.S. pottery industry coincided with, and were partly related to, the growing crafts revival, which brought a greater understanding of the interconnectedness and coexistence of craft and industrial production within modern economies, Eva stood apart from it. Even when pieces by Eva were selected to express the links between the two types of production and were shown alongside work by people who only designed for hand-production in the influential exhibition *Designed for Production* (1964) at the Museum of Contemporary Crafts in New York, Eva never felt any pull to return to craft production. Despite her early involvement with the back-to-nature movement and her continued passion for nature, she never had the urge to turn her back on urban life or mass production and retire to the country to make pots, as did so many potters in the 1960s and 1970s.

Different Times; New and Old Interests

Eva was nearly sixty years old, but there was never ever any question of someone as active as her retiring. It was simply not an option. A major part of her self-identity was that of an active, working woman. She had so many things she wanted to do and so many places she wanted to visit. In her desire never to retire, Eva reminded me of Saul Bass, another designer whom I got to know well, and who always wanted to die with his "boots on."[285] Bass also experienced a dip and shift in his career in the early 1960s when commissions dried up for the aspect of design for which he was most famous, namely film title sequences. Like Eva, he took it in stride, commenting that he hardly noticed at first because he was so deeply immersed in other matters. Similarly, by the time the new realities caused by changes in ceramics production and consumption fully dawned upon Eva, she was already involved in many other things. Between about 1964 and 1984, her "occupations," as she sometimes called them, included learning silk screen printing and using that process to create decorative patterns for pottery (many of which she pitched to Hall China); the researching and writing of history; building a small house; and the antiwar protest movement, especially against U.S. policies in Vietnam and Cambodia.

Protesting for Peace

Eva was passionate about peace. Her pacifist mother had attended women's peace conferences in the late 1910s, and the Unitarian Church, while allowing individual members free choice on such matters as pacifism, preached justice, peace, forgiveness, and reconciliation. This self-styled outsider, who was now middle aged, shifted further from her long-term position of interested and informed spectator than ever before. During our many talks over the years, she showed little interest when I mentioned William Morris (the designer, poet, and socialist) until one day I said that he had written about being aware of pressing socioeconomic and political issues in his youth and of how his passion for art, design, and poetry had got in the way—until one day an antiwar issue propelled him into political activism, when he was middle aged.[286] "Just like me," she exclaimed: "Thank you for bringing a new William Morris to me."[287]

Eva was not the only one of her age group or gender to become more politically active, or even active for the first time, during this period. Large numbers of middle-class women joined the ranks of the peace movement in the 1960s, many of them mothers of sons drafted or draft-eligible. Eva's son, John, was exempt from the draft because he was a student, and Eva would have been against the war whether or not she had a son, but she mentioned in passing once that knowing that it *could* have been her son coming home in a coffin did not escape her.[288]

Eva always became energized when talking about the peace movement of the 1960s, particularly when recounting how she attended a "sit-in" at Columbia University or the ways in which the media sensationalized events and caricatured all protestors as long-haired hippy students. She wanted to show that the movement had a broad class and age base. Eva was not alone in her point of view and several organizations, including Another Mother for Peace (founded 1967), sought to convince those outside the movement of its social breadth. When Eva photographed antiwar demonstrations, she deliberately took images of "ordinary people, respectable people who paid taxes and had good table manners."[289] As might be expected of someone with strong artistic and craft skills, her contributions also included making banners and posters.

Interior, the Little House (designed by Eva c. 1965–1975), Rockland County, c. 1975. EZA.

Little House

From the early 1960s to the late 1970s, Eva created a small house, known as the "Little House," on the South Mountain Road property. She did so without ever putting pencil to paper. The house is both of its time and somewhat quirky. It was, and remained, a work in progress. She enjoyed going with the flow to a degree unknown when working to the extremely precise measurements associated with industrially produced ceramics. Eva knew that she wanted to use local and found materials, especially large rough stones, as much as possible and to create as large and airy a space as possible with a close relationship between indoors and out. She delighted in grappling with new ideas as the form evolved around her and as she acquired and salvaged all manner of materials. The oak that lines the peaked ceilings, for example, began life as several door sills. Wrought-iron railings came from Harlem apartment buildings then being demolished; marble was brought from sites in central Manhattan; and wood from auctions. Some of the stone was "rescued" from building sites in the dead of night. As project manager as well as designer, she worked with two or three local carpenters and a host of volunteers, friends of her children, neighbors, and students, including architectural students. When habitable, Little House provided rental income and a home for a variety of interesting tenants, including the rock group KISS.[290]

Researching and Writing History

Eva, Hans, and the circles in which they moved were resolutely opposed to racism and had long been critical of U.S. policies on such matters.[291] However, while the others tended to study or compile statistical and other evidence to back arguments about the effects of race and class in the United States, Eva tended to be more intuitive—although she, too, loved marshaling facts and arguing her case. I do not mean to imply that Eva was less of an intellectual; design at its best is a highly intellectual activity and her interests outside ceramics were those of an educated cosmopolitan intellectual, but sometimes she approached things rather differently than professional intellectuals such as Hans and many of her friends and family members. As intellectually acute as they were (sometimes more so), she was less worried about following her gut instincts or positioning herself outside academic frameworks. Hans, for example, used statistics to show racial bias in terms of the application of the death penalty (the abolition of which was a cause to which he was deeply committed), whereas Eva became interested in the history of the wider African American experience in the United States, largely because she was both moved by and curious about the life trajectory of a former assistant, an African American gay man named Eddie Freddie. Living in Harlem where he had grown up and alienated from the dominant black male culture, Freddie had become an alcoholic and tipped off the edge of society.[292] Eva's curiosity about how this could happen led her back into history. The focus on a single character, as opposed to broader analyses or statistics, may have been related to her having no formal training in history or to an interest in testing wider theories through case studies, but it also relates to her being an object maker, where focus is trained on the particular and the individual rather than on the abstract, the general, or the theoretical.

Eva's curiosity about African American experiences led her close friend, the Central European–born historian Nicholas Halasz (1895–1985), to write *The Rattling Chains: Slave Unrest and Revolt in the Antebellum South* (1966). The dedication reads, "To Eva Zeisel. Puzzled, she induced me to explore the subject of this book." Encouraged by Halasz, Eva began her own study, and one that was every bit as thorough. Halasz was an ideal companion for Eva. They shared a common Central European intellectual background, and he had written about an individual arrested on false charges of treason. His *Captain Dreyfus: The Story of a Mass Hysteria* (1955) reexamined the 1890s harrowing *cause célèbre* involving a French Jewish army officer, an episode that had powerful reverberations for Eva.[293] Gore Vidal wrote the screenplay from Halasz's book (described as "popularized history at its best") for the movie *I Accuse!* (1958), directed by and starring José Ferrer, who viewed it as a commentary on contemporary American politics.[294]

During her readings on African American history, Eva became fascinated by a series of events that took place in New York City in 1741. Historians differ as to the causes of what some consider a slave or proletarian conspiracy against the ruling white colonial elite.[295] During March and April 1741, there were ten fires in the city. Beatings and harassment led to "confessions" and paranoia spread. A grand jury con-

Eva lending her glasses and a book to an Etruscan sarcophagus, c. 1970. EZA. · Eva having fun at the V&A Museum after Honorary Doctorate, RCA, London, 1988. EZA.

cluded that the fires were the work of black arsonists who planned to burn the city and kill all the white people, and by the end of the year approximately 160 African Americans and 21 European Americans had been arrested. Of the African Americans, about seventeen were hanged, thirteen burned at the stake, and seventy deported; of the European Americans, four were hanged and seven banished. It is not hard to imagine Eva empathizing with these men and women. At the time, some people pointed to similarities with the Salem witch trials of 1692 (recaptured for Cold War audiences by Arthur Miller's play *The Crucible*, 1953), and for Eva the events also evoked comparisons with the 1930s Show Trials in the USSR and her experiences there. Her children recall that Eva was every bit as enthusiastic about her historical research as she was about her ceramics and other design-related commissions, and always eager to share every last research finding. She knew each slave and his or her family by name: "They were not strangers to her," said Jean.[296]

Eva may have begun with a curiosity about someone she knew and the individuals she came to know through her historical research into the lives of the people of New York City in 1741, but she also delved deep into contexts, considering the events from every possible angle and leaving no archival stone unturned (or none that she knew of). As well as the more obvious sources in the city, she visited the British Library; the Lambeth Palace Library; the Bodleian Library; the Library of French Protestantism in Paris; and archives in Spanish Town, Jamaica; Burlington, New Jersey; Philadelphia; and Worcester, Massachusetts in her search for answers to every aspect of the topic, including the trials which were described in a nineteenth-century legal history text as having "no parallel in any civilized community."[297]

Other subjects that she began researching included childhood, an interest she shared with her mother, and earlier movements in architecture and design. She began compiling an anthology of memories of the childhoods of famous and nonfamous people; the former included Gandhi, St. Augustine, and Winston Churchill, while the latter included her friends.[298]

Eva loved the process of research, of finding out more and more about things, turning ideas over in her mind, and discussing them with others. She loved it perhaps more than the process of writing, although she wrote well. Her preferred method was to dictate or speak into a dictating machine and have her thoughts transcribed.

Just as Eva's search for beauty in terms of design was sometimes less about arriving at any given point and more about a deep curiosity and a need to explore, so too was her delving into history. None of Eva's writings on historical subjects were published, but the book on the events around the 1741 trials came close: several suitcases full of her detailed research notes remain in the attic of the Rockland County house. She was still researching and rewriting the events of 1741 in the 1990s. She completed more than one draft but never made the time or found the mental space for that last long rewrite. She tried writing up her research findings as a book and as a play. That nothing was ever published did not seem to bother her unduly, or at least not after she had moved on to other projects. In later years, her main goal in terms of publications was to see that her observations on design were published and available to students.[299]

I have often wondered whether her absorption in history, becoming a historian in the manner of her mother and great-grandfather (and perhaps also Halasz), and spending days and weeks at a time researching in libraries and archives, was, in part at least, related to proving that she could do what they did: she could hold her own in the territory occupied by so many of her friends and relatives. It may have been that, surrounded by intellectuals her whole life, she had no hesitation or hang-up about undertaking painstakingly detailed, sustained, and often laborious work, in her case a major historical project. I have also wondered if Eva's move to the research and writing of history was one way, subconscious or otherwise, of keeping her mother close. She and I once talked about how such things happen when a mother to whom you are close dies. Such considerations aside, however, Eva had a deep love of history and had seen her mother greatly reenergized by resuming historical research in the last decade of her life.[300]

Prison Memoirs

In the late 1970s, partly as a result of writing other histories and partly through the healing process of time, Eva also began writing about her months in a Soviet jail—a harrowing undertaking, especially so for

Eva at Kispester-Granit, Hungary, 1983: with paper cutout and plaster model; working on plaster model; with teapot prototype. EZA.

someone who had schooled herself to live in the present, yet probably a therapeutic one, too. Although Koestler had encouraged her to write her experiences down as early as 1938, there was never any question of publishing them because Eva was still considered guilty of treason in the USSR. She insisted that Koestler continue to protect her identity, as he had done in *Darkness at Noon* (1940), fearing for family members in the United States and especially for her younger brother and his wife who had returned to Communist Hungary. Before his death in 1983, Koestler encouraged her to publish the memoirs and the poems she wrote in prison, but Eva remained uncertain about what to do. Sometime in the 1980s, after Koestler's death, she showed her manuscript to someone recommended by Koestler who, according to Eva and family members, was of the opinion that her recollections did not ring true, largely because they were written with such distance and a distinct lack of bitterness.[301] Indeed, the opening section in which Eva spelled out the difference between a journal, history, memoirs, and memories, is academic in its precision. But as her daughter remarked, "That is Eva; that is how she was."[302] Because Eva so often saw herself as if looking in from the outside, she was able to observe and comment with a degree of distance, and often bemusement too, about truly terrible things. For me, the distance and brevity add to the poignancy while flagging the veracity of the tale.

The matter-of-factness of much of Eva's prison memoirs is rather like documentary reportage. On the occasions we talked about her imprisonment, however, that was less in evidence. The topic clearly raised very strong emotions for her, as it did for me just listening to her relaying events. Her voice became quieter. She had to search far harder than usual for exactly the right word or phrase, and she stopped several times to breathe deeply and hold my hand. She closed her eyes from time to time, explaining that she did so to shut out what she called "the worst parts."[303] Checks against recently available official documents show her recollections of events to be accurate.

Eva spent more time than previously in Chicago in the 1970s and 1980s, especially after Hans retired from teaching in 1973; and he spent more time in New York. An expert on the U.S. jury system, Hans had published widely, from learned books and articles to reviews and opinion pieces for the *Chicago Herald Tribune*. Two of his retirement projects

were writing *The Limits of Law Enforcement* (1982), which posited better education as the only way to reduce crime; and championing the abolition of capital punishment (he argued that capital punishment was *not* a deterrent while pointing to the racial bias within its application). "He felt it didn't belong in a civilized society," recalls his daughter.[304] He lived until 1992, and in the later years, he and Eva managed to live together more harmoniously than in earlier times, although the relationship still had its tumultuous moments.

Full Circle: Directions Old and New

In the early 1980s, Eva effectively rebuilt her ceramics career. A 1983 senior fellowship from the National Endowment of the Arts funded a research and design project in her native Hungary.[305] That year she created objects with stunningly beautiful glazes for the famous Zsolnay company there (chapter 17), proving that the old magic was still within her. She also visited the Kispester-Granit company, where she had worked nearly sixty years earlier, and designed prototypes for a dinner service (see chapter 23). Meanwhile the "buzz" around the forthcoming *Eva Zeisel: Designer for Industry* exhibition (1984), which revealed the consistently high quality of her work across time and materials and reminded people that she was still alive, helped trigger a new interest in Eva's work. Her *Pinnacle* stoneware dinner service was produced in 1984 by Yamaka Shoten, Japan, for the International China Company (chapter 18). The exhibition opened to great acclaim. In 1986, before she had been officially absolved of the accusation against her in the Soviet Union, the Hungarian government ignored its Soviet Bloc overlord and awarded Eva the Middle Cross of the Order of Merit of the Hungarian People's Republic. Two years later came an honorary doctorate from Britain's Royal College of Art, followed by a slew of awards from then until her death (see Select Chronology).

In 1992 Eva finished designing a glass-topped fretwork table with strong Hungarian Baroque and folk influences; it was as bold and decorative as anything in her ceramics. The exhibition *Eva Zeisel: Designer for Industry* was shown at St. Petersburg's State Russian Museum that same year; the accompanying Russian-language catalogue reattributed to her some of her most important Soviet designs of the 1930s and

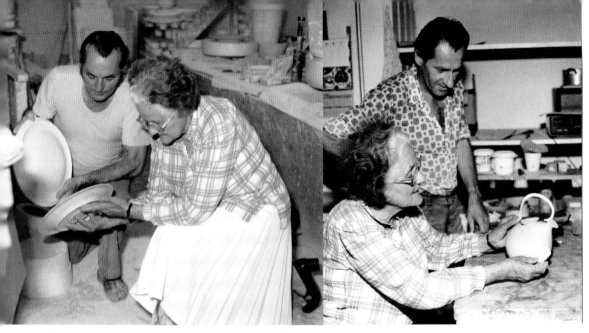

Eva with model makers, Kispester-Granit, Hungary, 1983. EZA.

acknowledged her place in Soviet ceramics history.[306] Meanwhile, Eva spent some of her time preparing new editions of, and finding new outlets for, various past designs; some had been in production, others had not. It proved an exciting, as well as a sometimes frustrating, process for Eva who, as always, insisted on extremely high production values.

A key year was 1999. The original molds made to Eva's designs when working for Hall China were featured in an intriguing exhibition, *Lost Molds and Found Dinnerware: Rediscovering Eva Zeisel's Hallcraft*, and reissues of selected pieces from the *Town and Country* line went on sale at the Metropolitan Museum of Art in New York. But Eva, as ever, was more interested in new challenges; once people realized that her mind and eye were as sharp as ever, new commissions began coming her way. Industrial designer Karim Rashid (whose own work has been greatly inspired by Eva's) recommended her to the Nambé company of Santa Fe, New Mexico (chapter 20).[307] That collaboration led to a range of items in metal alloy, crystal, and porcelain, and its success led to a commission from Chantal (see Select Chronology). The same year saw the first fruits of her collaboration with the young artist–potters James Klein and David Reid, who recall their work with Eva as among the most uplifting experiences of their careers.[308] KleinReid's "nesting vases" (1999) and other work Eva created in collaboration with them are among the most admired of her later designs (see chapter 19).

The new millennium saw Eva in Russia. Such was the recognition of her work there after the 1992 exhibition that the Lomonosov factory invited her to visit and design a new line, later named *Talisman* (after Eva's granddaughter). Composed of wonderfully thin yet delicately balanced pieces, it was one of her most harmonious creations (2000–2004; chapter 21). After touring the factory where she had worked years earlier and participating in a jury critiquing products, Eva sat down with a young model maker, Georgy Bogdevich, to start work on a new tea set. Two years later, he spent several weeks working with Eva in her Rockland Country studio to perfect the forms. When I asked him what he thought of Eva's designs, he told me in halting English, "In any language, Eva is the very best."[309]

Representatives of the Lomonosov works had traveled to New York a few months earlier to present Eva with a bas-relief portrait medallion of her that had been modeled by her old friend at Lomonosov, Natalia Dan'ko. Made either in the late 1930s or the early 1940s, Dan'ko had secretly carved it as part of a series commemorating her friends who had been arrested, expelled, executed, or gone "missing" during the Purges. She hid the medallions for fear that she might lose her own life for creating them. After she died of starvation during the 872-day Siege of Leningrad (1941–1944; more than 600,000 died), nothing was known about the medallions until they were unearthed when the factory was rebuilt in the late 1990s.

That Eva had not lost one ounce of her wit or sense of style was evident in the limited-edition martini glass "Reign" (2000), designed for the Bombay Sapphire company as part of a high-profile advertising campaign for 2001. She seemed unstoppable. Even after falling and breaking a hip, she carried on working from her hospital bed.[310] Designs for Acme, mGlass (a consortium of studios and factories in the Marinha Grande region of Portugal), KleinReid, and Nambé followed (see Select Chronology), and by her one-hundredth birthday in 2006, Eva was the toast of many towns. There were at least three exhibitions—two in New York and one in San Francisco—and many more grand dinners and parties to honor her.[311] She had received the Cooper-Hewitt, National Design Museum Lifetime Achievement award the prior year (the award dinner was held at the White House) and the popular home furnishings company Crate & Barrel, in conjunction with the British company Royal Stafford, had recently released *Classic Century*, reproduced from the original molds for Hall China's *Tomorrow's Classic* and *Century* lines (1951 and 1957–1958 respectively; chapter 22).

By then her sight and hearing were diminishing, but Eva carried on much as before. She was able to do so for two main reasons, aside from guts and determination: firstly, because she had designed in a variety of ways for so many years and was very adaptable; secondly, because of her remarkable ability to translate what she saw in her head directly onto paper or into shapes formed with her hands. Both ways of designing were nicely "low-tech." When asked in 2006, "How do you design these days?" she replied, "Easily. I can still see. I just need to hold things closer. . . . I make sketches in the air," she added, elegantly drawing pictures with her hands, "and I haven't forgotten to draw."[312]

And to see Eva draw was awe-inspiring, so assured was the sweep

Eva inspecting her stackable flowerpots, Schramberger factory, Germany, c. 1988. EZA. · Eva and model maker Gyorgy Bogdevich, 2000. St. Petersburg, Russia. EZA.

of her hand as she made the mark. In Eva's last few years, design assistant Olivia Barry would trace the shapes Eva made. She then cut them out so that Eva could better "feel" them, thus beginning a process of endless refinement until they were exactly what she wanted. "Eva starts with a sketch," said Olivia, "usually a beautifully curved line. But if it's a little shaky, I trace over it and make it smoother. When Eva uses scissors and paper to create new forms, she goes straight from her mind's eye to her hand. This works well for both of us."[313] Sometimes Olivia scanned the forms into a computer before reworking them with Eva and forwarding them to manufacturers.

Once in a while, Eva would refuse to reply to people who asked if she was *still* designing. "Would they ask a younger person that?" she would mutter after they had gone, or else she told them emphatically that she *continued* to design as she had always done. The chronology at the end of this book shows just how very busy she was in the last few years of her life, working with companies such as Design Within Reach, KleinReid, and Gump's. These were important years in terms of her design output and she remained as passionate as ever about everything she did. This was not the case of an old woman trying to keep herself busy. Pirco Wolfframm, who worked with Eva before and during the last six years of Eva's life, said that the levels of intensity and creativity felt no different; she was just as involved with each and every line and about each and every project.[314]

Two designs from her later years, one for a kettle (2005) and the other for a rug (2008), demonstrate her continued involvement with different types of objects, materials, and methods of production. In one instance the company approached Eva, and in the other she approached the company. The "Eva Kettle" for the Chantal company was a relatively low-cost mass-produced object of everyday use, whereas the expensive handmade rug was produced in very small numbers. The kettle involved working with new materials and creating an object type that was new to her as a designer, while the rug grew out of Eva and Olivia playing around with patterns and coming up with the idea of creating one based upon forms Eva had first created in the late 1950s as ceramic space dividers for Mancioli. On spec, Olivia mailed some poster boards of the rescaled pattern to The Rug Company in London. The partners running the company received unsolicited

designs every day, nearly all of which were rejected, but on this occasion they fell in love with the design, even though they did not know who "Eva Zeisel" was.[315] Named *Dimpled Spindle* ("Dimple" comes from Eva's "belly button" shape), it was hand-knotted in Nepal using Tibetan wool; *Fish* and *Lacy X* designs followed.[316]

Several of her designs of the last dozen or so years of her life have both a strong Baroque and a playful sensibility to them. Eva also began designing in plastic again; an acrylic plastic jewelry tree debuted in 2006, and Plexiglas picture frames to her designs came on the market in 2011. She was deeply engrossed in the design of a line of glass lamps for the famous Italian lighting company Leucos; she found it particularly exciting to think around the problem of lighting.

Eva not only carried on working to the end of her life; until the last few months, she often worked seven days a week, stopping only to take short breaks, after which she always had new ideas about solving a particular problem with which she had been grappling, or for a completely new project.[317] When she died at the end of 2011, her lamp designs were being translated into production line items by highly skilled glass workers in Italy, and balsawood prototypes were being translated into stainless-steel flatware.

Conclusion

During one of the longest professional design careers ever, Eva shifted from a craft training and strongly folk-influenced designs to serially- and mass-produced pieces in her native Hungary; and through designing for large-scale industrial production in both Germany and the USSR in the 1930s; to achieving both commercial and aesthetic success in the United States, her home since 1938. In the two decades after World War II, many consumers in the then-most-affluent market ever known consistently selected Eva as their designer of choice. Whether or not they knew her name, they enjoyed the goods that she had designed and bought replacements when pieces broke.

Along with great creative satisfaction, her work gave Eva, an economic independence rare for a married middle-class woman at that time. Her focus on intellectual pursuits and her political activism from the mid-1960s seem less of a disjuncture in terms of her design

Eva with assitant Olivia Barry, c. 2006. EZA. · Eva Zeisel Medallion by Natalia Dan'ko. SVA.

work if one acknowledges that design is both an intellectual and an aesthetic process and acivity. Eva's own intellectuality and the circles in which the Polanyis and Zeisels moved were also factors.

Eva's designs from 1984 onwards garnered considerable popular and critical attention, and deservedly so. Some of her earlier designs sold well when introduced once again, but their production and consumption as reissues took place in very different circumstances from those in which they were first designed or produced. Whether designing a glass for a single advertisement, a limited edition print, or mass production ceramics, many of her new creations proved popular at a time when design and designers were much more widely appreciated than in earlier years. Eva, like several other designers, became a star. The revival of interest in the 1990s of what came to be called "Mid-Century Modern" design was also key to Eva returning to, and remaining in, the limelight and being revered as one of the great designers of the century that was almost coterminous with her life. While flattered and a little bemused by the very large number of fans who delighted in her work, what interested Eva most was continuing her playful search for beauty, and drawing pleasure and satisfaction from creating and refining form. That she did so to the end of her days was, to me, one of the most remarkable aspects of a most remarkable life.

Chapter 1

Schramberger Majolikafabrik

1928

Pat Moore

In the fall of 1928, the ceramics manufacturing company Schramberger Majolikafabrik, located in the Black Forest region of Germany, advertised for a designer in the trade paper *Die Schaulade*. Eva, who was only twenty-one, applied for and was offered the job of sole designer. Before she accepted, however, Eva requested a two-month trial period. Her mother chided her for this audacity, saying, "They should be the ones to ask for a trial period."[1] Whether her request was granted is not known, but despite her boldness or perhaps because of it, Eva was quickly hired.

Her prior experience with mass production (at Kispester-Granit) was short-lived, but Eva was sufficiently savvy to know that she needed to acquire additional skills and asked an architect friend to give her a quick "how-to" course in drafting. Her studio was a small attic room furnished with a potter's wheel, clay, and a table on which she placed the only tools she had brought with her: a ruler and a compass. Her studio was so quiet that she eventually befriended a mouse that shared her office, training it to come to the tip of her pencil.[2]

The factory, which employed somewhere between 320 and 350 people, was the largest for which Eva had worked. Some of her designs took into account the economical use of kiln space. From the design process and the making of molds to the kilns and the glazes that were used, Eva worked closely with the company engineers learning about the materials and production methods. Objects were fired in one of the company's seven kilns, which had capacities ranging from two to forty cubic meters.[3]

The factory used soft clay composed of limestone, quartz, and white-burning clay that was brought in by rail from other areas of Germany and from England, where it was premixed to Schramberger's specific formula.[4] This was a costly process, as was transporting coal from the Saar region, an area then controlled by France but with many German-speaking people and companies.[5] The large German chemical company Degussa and Heraeus supplied the paint department with standard colors and glazes that were specially mixed.[6] The colors sometimes differed slightly from batch to batch depending on variations in the chemicals, the mixing, or kiln heat.[7]

Eva soon realized that two-dimensional drawing limited her ability to express her design ideas adequately. She began, therefore, to supplement her new drafting skills with techniques with which she was familiar: freehand sketches, paper cutout forms, and plaster or clay models. Moving back and forth between these media, she worked on each design until she was satisfied with the results. This was an important practice that she continued throughout her career.[8]

She later wrote, "[The designer] must follow his designs to the place where they can be produced without difficulty in quantity, until they can be mass-produced smoothly and quickly. If the design and mass production clash, the designer has to iron out the difficulty in conjunction with the engineer. There must not be a sixteenth of an inch in the final product which the designer does not control."[9]

Despite her best efforts, however, the production process sometimes led to less-than-satisfactory results. Sometimes the materials reacted unpredictably in the kilns. Most worrisome to Eva, however, were the ways in which some of the workers, carelessly in her opinion, could alter the look of a piece by placing additions to an object at a slightly different angle or location from what Eva intended. As they painted the decorations by hand, china workers would often change the dimensions or flow of a pattern. To counter this, Eva found herself becoming a de facto inspector, checking the work as it progressed in order to help the workers follow her specifications more closely.

Eva always strove to achieve individuality of form while maximizing economy in manufacture to meet the challenge of the marketplace.[10] For example, both her flat-sided pitchers and her upward-reaching jars made economical use of space in the undersized cupboards of small interwar apartments and houses, as well as in the "minimal kitchens" of the period. She partially standardized production by designing parts that served more than one function; the coffee pot, tea-

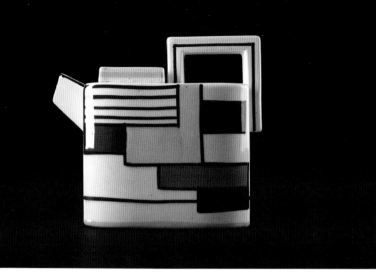

pot, and sugar bowl in the form 3249 tea and coffee service line used the same lid. In other services, coffee pots without their lids became pitchers; plates and saucers fit many cups or became underliners for sauce dishes, pitchers, or pots. Such an approach helped to reduce production costs. Eva was also concerned with the functionality of the pieces produced at Schramberger, making every effort to ensure that coffee pots did not drip and that lids stayed in place, two aspects of her work that made her pieces a pleasure to use.[11]

Whenever possible, Eva liked to be involved in the ways in which her designs were advertised and exhibited. At Schramberger, Eva photographed products for the sales catalogue, documented the manufacturing process, designed graphic displays for publicity, and assembled salesmen's sample kits.[12]

"When I came into the factory, it was a time of great unemployment," she later wrote. "My job was to keep the company going—350 people's jobs depended on me. Our pots were

bought on the basis of design. It was a time of pressure, not options."[13] Her period at Schramberger, from the fall of 1928 to late spring of 1930, was extremely productive. In her efforts to keep herself and others employed, she designed over two hundred pieces that went into production: from tea sets, dinner and luncheon sets to objects such as vases, lamp bases, ashtrays, cigarette and cigar boxes, inkwells and desk trays, flowerpots, wall pockets, kitchen boxes, jars, tea glasses, jugs, brandy decanters and goblets, cookie boxes, butter dishes, candy dishes, serving bowls, compotes, and even a lemon squeezer.[14]

Eva's first designs closely followed the compass-and-ruler aesthetic. Some lamp bases consisted of geometric forms; circles abounded, even on the flat sides of pitchers. Desk sets and smoking sets took on Art Moderne forms of the sort familiar across Europe and in North America by the time Eva had arrived in Schramberg. Circles became concentric rings repeated on vertical slopes of vases and boxes,

and her decorative patterns featured bright colors in geometric patterns that occasionally slipped into softer curves.[15] She later stated, "I played with geometry because this was the fashion; it was accepted in a popular sense and was being used in cheap wallpaper and linoleum designs; the designs of Mondrian could be seen in cheap linoleum and tablecloth designs."[16] Some of her softer lines were reminiscent of her earlier peasant-influenced human and animal forms, and those graceful curves informed the curves that were so central to her signature style of the postwar period. In an article written the year after she left Schramberg and published in *Die Schaulade* early in 1932, Eva explained that her designs were meant to establish a bond with their users and be friendly companions, but they should be restrained enough not to disturb their owners or demand unnecessary attention.[17] Sales figures for Schramberger are not available, but by the time she left, she had raised her profile sufficiently to win a

job at the much larger Carstens company.

From the beginning of her time at Schramberger, Eva had requested that her signature be put on her designs, feeling that she deserved such recognition. The company repeatedly refused to do so, leading Eva to look elsewhere for work during the late spring of 1930.[18]

COLLECTING AND REISSUES

Eva's designs for Schramberger are extremely popular today. It is difficult for collectors to accumulate pristine pieces; although thousands were manufactured, both the soft clay and the glazes were prone to chipping. As a result, "museum-quality" pieces are all but impossible to find.

After she left Schramberger, the factory continued to use Eva's decorative patterns on the shapes designed by others, and some Schramberger pieces are attributed to Eva without any evidence that they were hers. The only positive way to identify a Zeisel shape is by the form number impressed into the bottom of the item; in general, these numbers will be within the range of 3195 to 3463 (see Taxonomy).[19]

Her Schramberger work is in the permanent collections of the British Museum and the Victoria and Albert Museum (both in London); the Bröhan Museum (Berlin); the Museum of Modern Art (MoMA), the Brooklyn Museum, and the Metropolitan Museum of Art (all in New York).

Many of her designs have attracted another generation of collectors. The flat-sided refrigerator jar (form 3287) was reissued in 1996 under Eva's supervision in black and white by World of Ceramics in North Carolina and distributed through the Brooklyn Museum, MoMA, the Orange Chicken gallery (New York), and other retail outlets. In 1997, a number of other colors were added to the range by both World of Ceramics and the Orange Chicken (whose pieces were made by Brett Bortner).

The almond-shaped vase (form 3255) was reissued under Eva's supervision in 1997 by World of Ceramics for the Orange Chicken in white, gunmetal, green, black, yellow, blue, gray, and red. Her flattened, disc-lidded tea set (forms 3432, 3433, 3389) with softly rounded corners was reissued by the Metropolitan Museum of Art in its original multicolored polka-dotted pattern (décor 3669) in 2000. It sold out quickly and has become a collectible item in its own right.

At Eva's ninety-fifth birthday in 2001, it was announced that a street in Schramberg had been named Eva-Zeisel-Straße in her honor.

Left Page

Brandy service (no. 3366 jug, no. 3367 mugs, no. 3387 tray) in Scotland decoration, c. 1930. HUC.

Top Left

No. 3278 teaglass stands in matte beige and pink decorations, no. 3295 tray in matte beige, no. 3239 lidded box in coral-red and matte beige, c. 1930. EZA.

Top Right

No. 3223 lidded box , c. 1929 in decor 3526. MGC.

Bottom Right

No. 3228 vase, in decoration not designed by Eva, c. 1929. HUC.

Chapter 2

Christian Carstens KG, Steingutfabrik

1930

Rolf Achilles and Pat Moore

While still designing for Schramberger during the spring or summer of 1930, Eva was approached by members of the Carstens family, which owned a large and well-known German ceramic manufactory, to create designs for the company. She recalled that they "courted" her over the summer.[1] Later that summer or early fall, Eva had more meetings with Carstens family members.

The company was founded as C. & E. Carstens in 1900 by Christian and Ernst Carstens. In 1914 and following several acquisitions, the company split its holdings. In 1918, C. & E. Cartstens GmbH acquired Ernst Dorfner & Co. Steingutfabrik in Hirschau, Bavaria, which became part of the renamed Christian Carstens Kommandit Gesellschaft in 1930.[2] Joining Hirschau as members of the company were five other ceramic firms: Neuhaldensleben, Rheinsberg, Wallhausen, Gräfenroda, and Georgenthal.[3] The company was well known for its wares in Steingut, a porous earthenware that was normally fired at relatively low temperatures (900–1000 degrees Celsius) and glazed for water tightness. The Carstens group was the second largest producer of ceramics in Germany (after

Villeroy & Boch), with Hirschau alone having 170 employees in 1930.[4] Eva must have been aware that this was a much larger business that was courting her than was Schramberger.[5]

In the 1920s, the Carstens Hirschau factory had mainly produced inexpensive dishes, serving bowls, and coffee and tea sets. Some were decorated with decal patterns, but most were hand-painted, mainly with floral patterns. By the mid-1920s, however, Carstens Hirschau decided to modernize its line by adding affordably priced household articles in matte and glossy finishes designed by recognized artists and designers.[6]

Soon after Eva moved to Berlin in 1930, a Carstens family member took her to see some of their factories. For about fifteen months, she worked for the Carstens Hirschau factory on a freelance basis, but it is not known how many designs she produced, how many were developed to the prototype stage, or how many went into production.

It was not common for a woman designer to work for a factory out of her own studio, as Eva did in Berlin.[7] This practice, especially for a woman, was just beginning in the ceramics industry in Germany. While most prototypes

to Eva's designs were probably fabricated in the Carstens Hirschau factory and then brought to her in Berlin for inspection, sometimes the modelers would come to her studio to make models, and technicians would visit her to consult on the details of production.[8] Eva occasionally made the seven-hour train journey, with three or four transfers, from Berlin to Hirschau to inspect models on-site before production started.[9] While there, Eva often photographed the finished pieces herself.

Die Schaulade featured the Carstens company in its April 1932 issue. In "Der Künstler hat das Wort" ("The Artist Has the Word"), Eva expressed the philosophy that "when designing in the modern style, one must ask what the practical use of the object will be!"[10] She was conscious of cost and space-saving production, and she tried, as is obvious in her pitchers, cups, and pots, not to minimize individuality. Eva produced a wide variety of form and pattern for Hirschau, ranging from extremely refined tea services that gave modern expression to traditional object types to Art Moderne shapes and patterns, a few of which were quite jazzy. Some designs were a continuation of work done for Schramberger (chapter 1), though less quirky, and once in a while she adopted ovoid forms or tried to give her designs "a more harmonious form through a slight swing in the silhouette."[11]

Eva designed several coffee and tea sets (*S, T, R, C, Holland,* and *Ceylon*), the table setting *Nürnberg,*[12] a smoking service, and several table service dishes for Hirschau. The tea services *Holland* and *Ceylon*[13] were presumably designed in 1931[14] (because she left the company at the end of that year) but were not issued until the fall of 1932 or early 1933. *Ceylon* stayed in production until at least 1935 and is documented in at least three or four patterns.[15] The *Jubiläumsservice* tea set has been attributed to Eva, albeit with reservations and based only on the forms.[16] Her 1931 tea service *T,* the

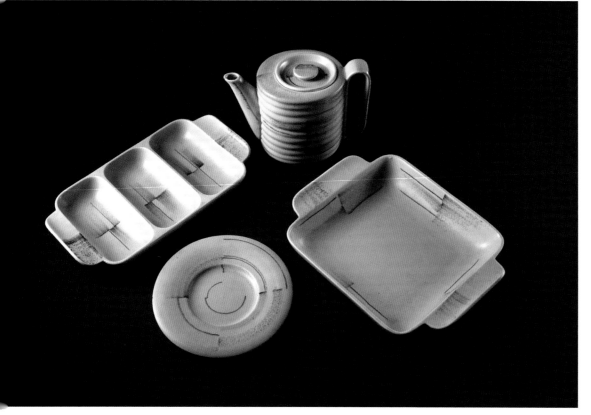

Left

Divided snack tray, coffee pot (from C tea service), rectangular tray, and dessert plate in decoration not designed by Eva, c. 1931. VHC.

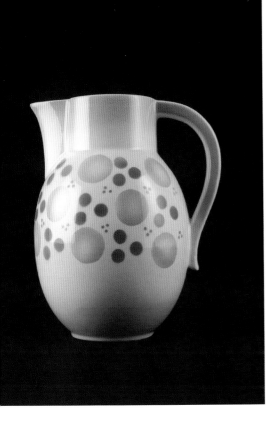

so-called *Kugelservice* (which was exhibited at the spring 1932 Leipzig Trade Fair and illustrated in an article in *Die Schaulade*[17]), was the only one of her tea services to go straight into mass production, remaining in production until 1935–36. The illustration shows clearly that the T form is a sphere. Even its lid supports the teapot's roundness, its knob projecting slightly from its depression to complete the circle. The ear-like handles of this service were more grounded in organic forms than those on other pots.

Eva's first ovoid forms are seen in the C and S tea service designs with their softly rounded shoulders, gently indented middle sections, and broad, sometimes bowed, handles. Their lids are pushed back or are off-center, with wide ribbon-like handles and knob-less lids. Their distinctive elongated flat handles, ribbed bodies, and abstract decoration on a matte turquoise ground represent a high point in what by then was more than a century of Steingut production by Hirschau.[18]

Abstract, geometric Spritzdekor (stenciled, airbrush-applied decoration) patterns, similar to some Eva had introduced at Schramberg, began to appear on Carstens Hirschau products at about the time she began designing for the Carstens company in 1931. She may have suggested these patterns, but various other Carstens facilities were already employing this type of decoration by then. Given her keen interest in how her designs were translated into objects, she may have contributed

some of the patterns for airbrush decoration, especially the earliest ones.

To date, eighteen decorative variations on *Kugelservice T* have been identified.[19] One of the early T decors, in pink and red-brown Spritzdekor, as well as matte turquoise glazes found on several early shapes by Eva, might be her creations.[20]

Another pattern appeared in 1931: Strichdekor, a striped pattern of tight, stencil-lined brushstrokes, line upon line (*strichel*) in staggered and alternating fields in a light and a dark color separated by an overlay of thin lines, either in their own or a neighboring color, and covered with a translucent glaze. To create these lines, the stencil was applied on one side, and the brush or sponge that applied the pigment was manipulated in such a way as to fade the color from dark to light before it met the next stenciled color that repeated the technique. A variety of color choices and placement of fields allowed for many variations. Although the timing and the forms are right, Eva's association with such patterns remains speculative.[21]

With the exception of the *Kugelservice T*, it is not known how long the lines designed by Eva stayed in production. The wide variety of patterns documented on her forms suggests that they were produced for several years after her 1932 departure from Berlin.[22] Designs by her for Hirschau were displayed at the Leipzig Fair in spring 1932, and she completed a design for a butter dish from the USSR.[23]

Chapter 3

Lomonosov State Porcelain Factory; Dulevo Porcelain Factory

1932
Karen L. Kettering

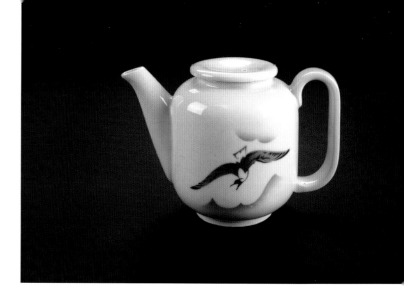

Eva Zeisel's sojourn in the Soviet Union was one of the most productive and creative periods of her long and fruitful career. In just over four years, from February 1932 to late May 1936, she designed dozens, perhaps hundreds, of new ceramic pieces, as well as items new to her such as light fixtures, metal hardware, and other household goods. Her achievements are all the more significant in that she achieved them while simultaneously mastering a new language (particularly the technical vocabulary required for work in a ceramics factory) and the rules, regulations, and practices related to not only individual factories and industries but also the labyrinthine Soviet bureaucracy.

Almost immediately after her arrival in January 1932, she took a job with the central agency overseeing production of all kinds of ceramic and glass in Ukraine.[1] The job, however, was administrative and undoubtedly overburdened the limited Russian she had managed to acquire in the first few weeks in a new country. Nevertheless, it offered a new and prestigious opportunity for this ambitious young designer who had heretofore worked only in earthenware—namely, the possibility to learn about and design porcelain tablewares for mass production. This was an important professional challenge for Eva, who later explained: "Earthenware keeps its form because it isn't fired at very high temperatures, so many shapes can be made easily . . . but porcelain gets soft and close to melting when it is fired, so it is much harder to manipulate."[2]

Her new position required that Eva travel to various porcelain factories to acquaint herself with their production methods. That she chose to stay in this position even after the completion of several difficult journeys underlines how attractive she found her chances for professional advancement in the Soviet Union. She went first to the Budiansk Ceramics Factory, which was located near Kharkov, where she lived. Once part of the technologically advanced M. S. Kuznetsov Ceramics Concern, it was equipped with large tunnel kilns. That this was the first stop on her itinerary suggests that her hosts selected one of the more modernized factories. Budiansk involved only a train ride, but her next trip proved far more difficult: it entailed visiting a factory producing porcelain electrical fixtures in Takarovka, a small village in the region of Berdychev, and the Baranovka Porcelain Factory in Volhynia.

Limited transportation meant that Eva had to travel by a horse-drawn open sleigh; she recalled that the sheepskin covers were teeming with lice that quickly invaded her clothing.[3]

LOMONOSOV STATE PORCELAIN FACTORY

In the summer of 1932, Eva was sent to Leningrad to work at the new Artistic Laboratory that had been established at the Lomonosov State Porcelain Factory in 1930. She was tasked with "rationalizing" Soviet ceramic tablewares, a process that encompassed creating standardized designs for hygienic, sturdy tablewares that were inexpensive to both produce and distribute.[4] One of her earliest designs for Lomonosov also helped to ease the problem of limited storage space (and more efficiently use kiln space) by utilizing stackable forms, a feature later used in her *Utility Ware* of the early 1940s (see chapter 26). The prototypes she designed were intended for production in factories throughout the Soviet Union but to date, no examples of finished pieces, or even

photographs of them, have been found; it is possible that nothing was produced beyond the test pieces recorded in a photograph that survives in Eva's archive. This photograph shows a set with large and small teapots, a lidded sugar bowl, stacking cups, and a covered bowl (perhaps for storage). It is possible that the teapots were sold separately, but the sizes and similarities of the various pieces suggest that they were designed to be used in combination with one another, in accordance with the Russian tea-drinking custom in which the smaller teapot, or *zavarnoi chainik*, held a strong infusion of the beverage, while the larger vessel, the *dolivnoi chainik*, held hot water. Each person could combine proportions of strong tea and boiling water to suit his or her taste.[5]

Many of these innovations were utilized again for her 1933 *Intourist*[6] service. The cylinder-shaped vessels, a form with which she had briefly experimented while at Carstens (see chapter 2), saved fuel because they could be efficiently stacked in kilns for

Overleaf

Tea service, Dulevo Porcelain Factory, c. 1934. EZA.

Left Page

Intourist teapot, with decoration by Aleksei Sotnikov, Lomonosov State Porcelain Factory, c. 1933. EZA.

Biscuit models for a tea and coffee service, Dulevo Porcelain Factory, c. 1935. Photograph: EZA.

Below

S-3 or Mokko coffee service, Dulevo Porcelain Factory, c. 1934. Photograph: EZA.

firing; the sturdy simplified and flattened handles helped extend the life of a piece. The flattened lids were designed to be lifted by means of indented grips rather than by a delicate finial or knob that precluded stacking and was liable to break easily. The service, often with floral and other decorative schemes including those celebrating Soviet achievements such as construction of the Moscow Metro, was often illustrated with a tray. Eva's original scheme for *Intourist* comprised a hot water pot, a teapot, a lidded sugar bowl, a covered milk jug, and cups with saucers. In 1933, it became the first new service to enter production at Lomonosov in nearly a decade.[7] The wide expanse of the cylindrical form was particularly convenient as a backdrop for more dense, sometimes grandiose, decorative schemes. The service remained in production until Germany invaded the USSR in June 1941 and the factory's production was rapidly changed to meet more pressing wartime needs. By the late 1930s, however, the service had been reconfigured to serve as tea sets for important individuals.

Eva also designed a cylinder-shaped teapot that was produced at both Lomonosov and at the Dulevo Porcelain Factory, where she began working in 1934. Surviving examples from Lomonosov are simply decorated, featuring little more than geometric ornament, but unfortunately, only a tiny percentage of Eva's work at Lomonosov has been identified.[8] With the exception of a single, previously unpublished vase (exhibited in London in 2004), a large number of pieces designed by Eva and cited in reviews of a 1934 exhibition still remain to be identified, including a children's service (*detskii serviz*), a coffee service, inkwells, and several different sizes of vases.[9]

In a 1934 newspaper article, Eva described an equally important but largely unknown part of her work at Lomonosov's Artistic Workshop. This included a line of standardized light fixtures for homes and factory buildings and an assortment of objects for daily use made from ceramic bodies (as a replacement for metal), such as door latches, drawer pulls, irons, and electric hot plates.[10] Metal stocks had been reserved for the massive industrialization program begun in 1929; shortages of consumer goods with metal parts were an unintended consequence. Eva used an investigational ceramic body combined with metal slag, designing standardized door handles, drawer handles, and pulls, as well as laundry irons. Photographs of two of the finished lamps, apparently shot in Lomonosov's workshop, used to be in Eva's archive, and she recalled that work on these pieces was done at both Lomonosov and Tokarovka.[11] Any prototypes of the lamps that might have remained at Lomonosov seem to have been lost or destroyed when the factory was evacuated during World War II; examples may remain in Tokarovka or elsewhere in Ukraine.

Eva's relationship with the Lomonosov management was difficult, perhaps partly because her assignments appear to have been dictated by the Central Porcelain and Faience Trust rather than emanating from the Lomonosov managers. She complained that they were slow to test-fire her new designs; her complaints were probably valid, as such activities would have used up valuable staff time and required powering the kilns to produce items not eligible for inclusion in annual audits that determined if each factory had fulfilled its economic plan. The conflict dragged on without resolution until Eva decided that, after seeing to completion certain objects that were going to be exhibited in a national exhibition in Moscow in the spring of 1934, she would quit the job and return to Kharkov.[12]

The exhibition proved to be an unexpected triumph; the press complained that by ignoring Eva's practical and attractive designs, the Lomonosov management was shirking its responsibility to the public.[13] The exhibition also offered a way out of the stalemate at Lomonosov. Petr Leonov, chief artist-designer at the Dulevo Porcelain Factory located in the small town of Orekhovo-Zuevo outside Moscow and then the largest ceramics factory in the Soviet Union, offered her a job overseeing the establishment of a workshop designing for mass production. She was enormously productive during the short time that she worked there (about May 1934 to September 1935), designing four new tea and coffee services, a set for serving water, a liqueur service, special tablewares for kindergartens, eggcups, vases, and a smoker's set.[14]

According to Russian ceramics historian Lidiia Andreeva, Eva's new forms at Dulevo were assigned the names S-1, S-2, S-3, and so on, allowing some sense of the order in which she designed them.[15] The first, the S-1 tea service, which included a hot water pot, a teapot, a covered sugar bowl, a milk jug, and cups and saucers, remained in production until the late 1970s or early 1980s, and its large, spherical teapot was the basis for several others that were put into production after the war.[16] Ironically, both Eva's S-1 service with Petr Leonov's *Krasavitsa* pattern and a profusely decorated version of the *Intourist* service were exhibited at the 1937 Paris International Exposition.[17] Both were awarded a Grand Prix.

The S-1 service was rapidly followed by the S-2 tea service. It was partially based on the *Intourist* service and an earlier teapot form produced at Lomonosov.[18] The S-3 coffee service, called *Mokko*, was produced in relatively large numbers before World War II limited the production of consumer goods. Indeed, it was a favorite of Petr Leonov, who experimented with many of his richest and most complex ornamental patterns on its surfaces. Those familiar with the full range of Eva's career will recognize that her experimentation with gently undulating forms, some of which recall women's waistlines, first appeared in the S-3 set's coffee pot and sugar bowl.

Another tea service departs from this neat chronology. Andreeva described S-4 as a coffee service (which it is not) while Natasha Bam, a Soviet critic who was close to Eva while she was living in the USSR, wrote that Eva completed four new tea services and only a single coffee service.[19] Whether or not Eva's third Dulevo tea service should rightly be called

S-4, the new forms combined the rationalized, flattened lids of the *Intourist* service together with low vessels that form a counterpoint to their high, sweeping handles. The two existing examples in Eva's private collection are decorated with vivid geometric ornament complementing the unusual forms. The design does not appear to have been produced beyond 1940, and to date, there are no editions known with anything other than geometric decoration.

A similar relationship between Eva's forms and a modernizing ornamental scheme can be seen in the 1935 set of a covered water jug, handleless cups, and tray, many examples of which were decorated with patterns Petr Leonov based on decorative textiles, an area of design then flourishing in the Soviet Union.[20] While Eva was working there, designers were under increasing pressure to create a new artistic language that eschewed both the geometric modernism and functionalism of the Modern Movement as well as the floral designs and landscapes negatively associated with bourgeois taste of the late nineteenth and early twentieth century. In the search for a new kind of decoration, many artists tried decorating tea cups or plates with images of collectivized peasants or Soviet workers; others expressed joy through updated floral and other patterns, especially those which resembled peasant designs. Eva, who was no fan of Modern Movement geometric and "functionalist" designs (see Part One), preferred Leonov's solutions.[21] He created decorative schemes based on familiar patterns from Russian printed cottons and peasant textiles and, in doing so, founded what is now recognized as an important school of Russian porcelain painting.[22] By returning to and building upon traditional or classical forms or patterns, designers could create objects that were new, yet familiar and comforting. They would be pleasing to the eye while simultaneously promoting the positive associations that Eva always sought in her work.

Many water services were made to Eva's forms and Leonov's decorations. They were produced (or older, unpainted whiteware was decorated and fired) as late as the early 1950s, but very few examples are in public collections in Russia, Europe, or North America. In 2004, Lidiia Andreeva published one of Eva's smoker's sets designed for Dulevo in 1935 from the collection of Alberto Sandretti.[23] It had

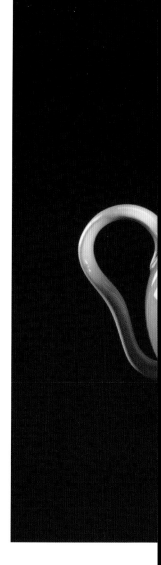

Top
*S-1 tea service, Dulevo Porcelain Factory,
c. 1934. EZA.*

Bottom Left
*Water service with lidded jug and handleless
glasses, Dulevo Porcelain Factory, c. 1934.
Photograph: EZA.*

Bottom Right
*S-1 tea service, Dulevo Porcelain Factory, Blue Net
pattern by Petr Leonov, c. 1934. Photograph: EZA.*

Tea caddies, Dulevo Porcelain Factory, c. 1935.
Photograph: EZA.

previously been known only from a faded
photocopy of a review of Eva's work from the
Deutsche Zentrale-Zeitung, a newspaper published
in Moscow for German-speaking émigrés in
the 1930s.[24] Although the newspaper image
is poor, it is clear that the ashtray pictured
in the foreground differs substantially from
its square counterpart in the Sandretti
Collection. Nevertheless, the appearance
brought to light forms that were previously
assumed to have been lost. An unusual liqueur
set with lustre and metallic glazes also
designed for Dulevo in this period demonstrates the ease with which Eva designed for
such luxurious glazes. In the second half of
the 1930s, precious consumer goods such as
these tea or liqueur sets were reserved for the
Party elite or were awarded to extraordinarily

productive workers. The ball-shaped carafe with its curling handle on one side, the shot glasses, and the small tray recall forms she had designed at Schramberger around 1930.[25] But at Dulevo, Eva took advantage of the sturdier porcelain ceramic body (Schramberger used earthenware) to construct star-shaped feet for the glasses and carafe. The small, luxurious detail harmonizes well with the delicate handle and the rich glazes. Whether these sets were put into production remains unknown; the Museum of the Dulevo Porcelain Factory has no copies and Eva had only a single example of one of the cups and the tray. Similar questions remain about her designs for a tea caddy; her archive contains photographs taken by Eva of an early finished piece, and decorated versions are visible in a photograph of her seated with several colleagues from Dulevo at a 1935 exhibition.[26] No finished versions have, as yet, been located.

At least two of Eva's final designs in the Soviet Union probably never went beyond the preparatory stages. Biscuit models for tea and coffee services were reproduced in a May 1935 article summarizing new directions in Soviet ceramics in *Iskusstvo* (Art), the leading journal of art and design that was published in the Soviet Union, but no finished editions in porcelain have been found. They were almost certainly abandoned when, in late August 1935, she accepted a new position in Moscow as an artistic director overseeing the ceramics industry. Dulevo's management had never provided the apartment promised in her contract, and her brother Michael and his wife were then living in Moscow. Polina Zhemchuzhina

(wife of the chairman of the Council of Ministers, Viacheslav Molotov, who had recently been named to oversee and improve TeZhe, the Soviet trust overseeing the production of soap, perfume, toothpaste, and other cosmetics) invited Eva to design a series of new perfume bottles as part of a radical makeover of the trust's products and shops. The commission was never completed: on May 28, 1936, Eva was arrested and imprisoned.

Chapter 4

Universal Potteries: *STRATOWARE*

1942
Scott Vermillion

In 1942, Sears, Roebuck and Co. commissioned Eva to develop a dinnerware line. Her first design proposal was based on her *Utility Ware* prototypes (chapter 26), but Sears demanded something more streamlined. Eva, who was not a particular fan of streamlined design, proposed developing a line based upon a pitcher designed by one of her students, Francis Blod.[1] When *Stratoware* was introduced by Sears in its 1942 spring and summer catalogue, the line was described as being as much "in key with modern living as the newest TWA Stratoliners."[2] Once the design was approved by Sears, a contract was signed with Universal Potteries for its production. In business since 1934, Universal had manufactured the popular Sears *Cattail* dinnerware line (from 1934 until 1956).

Eva guided Blod through every aspect of the line's development, suggesting what type of pieces and features were necessary to create a commercially viable dinnerware line.[3] She did not design any of the final shapes, but her influence is evident. The covered pitcher, creamer, sugar bowl, and casserole had integrated handles in order to save space, decrease the chance of breakage, and reduce production costs. Stackable cups had down-swept, extended-bridge handles. The five-piece relish set was designed for multiple functions with a large, round platter and four pie-shaped inserts; they could be used together as a buffet serving piece, the inserts could hold four individual food portions, or the platter could be used separately.

Top

Dinner plate, bowl, creamer, sugar, cup and saucer in San Diego Sand with Horizon Blue, Flare Yellow, Wing Brown, and Airport Green accents, 1942. MGC.

Left

Covered vegetable dish and candlesticks in San Diego Sand with Wing Brown accents, 1942. HUC.

Bottom

Salad bowl in San Diego Sand with Flare Yellow interior and spoon in San Diego Sand with Airport Green, 1942. MGC.

The color scheme followed a contemporary trend of muted, earthly pastels with the soft-hued San Diego Sand body set off by accents of Airport Green, Flare Yellow, Horizon Blue, or Wing Brown.[4] Plates, platters, and fruit, soup, and vegetable bowls featured the accent color around the rim while on the sugar bowl, pitchers, salt and pepper shakers, candlestick holders, and casserole, color swept along the integrated lids and handles, with more liberal application of color on the inside of coffee cups and the large salad bowl.

The range initially had sets of four, six, or eight place settings that included a dinner plate, bread-and-butter plate, sauce dish, and cup and saucer. A sugar and creamer set, three-piece salad set, and five-piece salad set were offered along with the other *Stratoware* serving pieces that were sold individually.[5] Later catalogues offered a thirty-five piece set that included a sugar and creamer as well as a new soup plate with rim.[6]

Initially, Sears catalogues credited *Stratoware*'s design to "the Industrial Design Depart. of Pratt Institute," but later catalogues credited "Eva S. Zeisel and associates at the Industrial Design Dept., Pratt Institute, Brooklyn, N.Y.," probably in order to take advantage of Eva's growing reputation. Sears dropped the line after little over a year because of problems related to production. *Stratoware* appeared for the last time in the spring and summer 1943 catalogue.

Castleton China Company: *MUSEUM*

1946
Mary Whitman Davis

In 1942, Castleton China was a new company intent on producing the first modern china dinnerware in the United States. Louis Hellman, the U.S. representative for the high-end German company Rosenthal Porzellan and a co-founder of Castleton China, had attended the 1941 *Organic Design in Home Furnishing* exhibition at New York's Museum of Modern Art (MoMA). His interest was piqued by a display of the winning prototypes for well-designed modern furniture intended for industrial mass production. Hellman asked the curator, Eliot Noyes, to recommend a dinnerware designer capable of creating modern shapes in china worthy of a MoMA exhibition, and Noyes recommended Eva.[1]

Eva had invited Noyes to her lecture "Handicraft and Mass Production" at the Metropolitan Museum of Art in New York in January 1942, where she described her vision of craftwork as an influence on industrial design. She was given the Castleton project, in large part, because she had extensive experience working in factory conditions. It turned out to be a key commission for Eva.[2] She later credited the *Museum* commission with establishing her reputation in the United States, remarking that "it made me an accepted first-class designer, rather than a run-of-the-mill designer."[3] *Museum* remained special to her. When asked in 2004 to choose just one from her many designs, she replied, "Castleton *Museum* Ware. It's the most elegant, pretentious, and I think it's my favorite!"[4]

Museum was designed to "appeal to the elegant, sophisticated rich . . . stately and formal, simple and elegant, fit to become an 'heirloom,'" as Eva described it.[5] Eva consulted the writings of Emily Post, a leading arbiter of manners and etiquette in the United States, in order to better understand what constituted "elegance" at the formal American dinner table.[6] Post recommended individual salt and pepper holders and a demitasse cup and saucer, all of which Eva included in her designs. Post might well have disapproved, though, of Zeisel's salt and pepper holders whose rounded bottoms allowed them to wobble on the table, and Eva's inclusion of tiny china spoons "for people who like to play with things."[7]

Museum was intended to meet two criteria: to be sufficiently "modern" to meet MoMA's standards while appealing to the wealthy sophisticates who could afford to purchase what would be relatively high-priced pieces. Eva designed a "family" of twenty-five pieces whose forms were based on circles, rounded squares, and squared ovals. Their design avoided what Eva regarded as the "monotony of many modern shapes."[8] It also achieved the elegance that Eva thought the commission required.[9] She set out to design pieces that seemed to be "growing up from the table," achieving this most spectacularly with the now-iconic *Museum* coffee pot.[10] *Museum's* handleless creamer was singled out later by art historian Martin Eidelberg as the "most radical . . . for here the spout seems to grow out of the body, the curves are compound, and, especially because the creamer is handleless, there is a sense of organic unity,"[11] qualities that would inform Eva's future work. Further innovation was evident in the scale of *Museum's* bowls. In a gesture that anticipated the changes that were just beginning to occur in the American diet, Eva designed her salad and vegetable bowls to be much larger than was common at the time.

Museum's fluid shapes take advantage of the delicacy of porcelain, with edges that verge on transparency. The heavier bottoms of the pieces added stability, yet the overall effect was one of lightness and delicacy. The set initially was designed in white without decoration, but any suggestion of austerity was offset by the warmth of the slight ivory-toned porcelain visible under the clear glaze. The pieces' smooth shapes and sensuous surfaces invited human contact, encouraging the interaction between human and object that Eva believed defined good design.

The Design Process, 1942–1943

Having agreed to exhibit the china at MoMA if it met its high standards, three curators

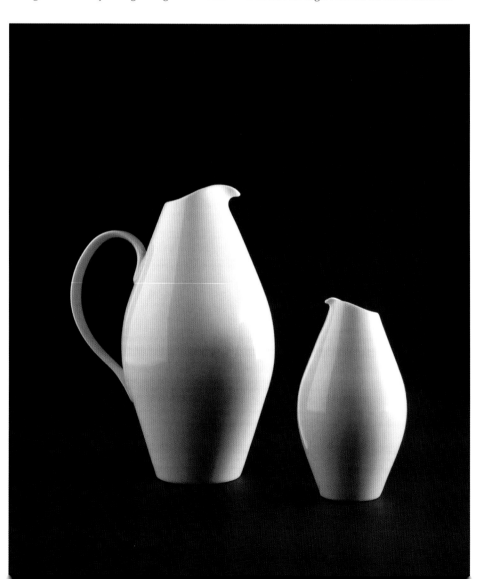

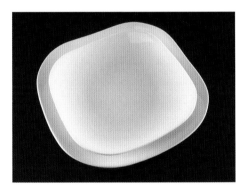

Overleaf
Tea and coffee service, 1946/1949. EZA.

Top
Vegetable bowl, prototype soup (glossy inside, matte outside), covered vegetable dish, 1946. EZA.

Left
Vegetable bowls, 1942–1949. EZA.

Left Page
Hot water pot and creamer without handle, 1946. EZA.

Views of
NEW SHAPES IN MODERN CHINA exhibition
installation at the Museum of Modern Art, 1946.
Photograph: EZA.

played a role in the design process. Eva had initial meetings with associate curator Greta Daniels, followed by more meetings with Noyes and Kaufmann, Noyes's successor at MoMA. Eva recalls the curators controlling "every sixteenth of an inch"[12] and being very puritanical, adding that "they didn't permit decoration and there were certain objects they considered too 'chi-chi,' so they excluded them."[13] Eva made dozens of alterations "that might seem minute and inessential to the average china shopper, but helped to achieve the effect of balanced movement with quietness" that she, the curators, and Castleton sought.[14]

The pieces were tested for ease of production by Castleton during the design process, but in some cases further adjustments were made during full-scale mass production (which began in 1949). The coffee cup, for example, originally featured a downward-turning handle that was attached to an unusually low and flat bowl, but sometime after 1949, a more conventional handle was substituted without Eva's knowledge or permission.[15]

New Shapes in Modern China Designed by Eva Zeisel, APRIL 17–JUNE 9, 1946

The design and prototype process was completed by 1943, but it was not until 1946 that the twenty-five pieces were finally exhibited at MoMA. Designed by Eva in collaboration with curator Greta Daniels, the exhibition *New Shapes in Modern China Designed by Eva Zeisel* was located on the first floor of the museum and overlooked the garden. It featured a custom-built open cupboard containing complete table settings and serving implements for twelve. A table with a reflective surface displayed the *Museum* pieces in multiples to emphasize their interrelationships and the interactions between the shapes and their shadows. Production drawings were displayed to emphasize their importance in the manufacturing process.[16]

Prototypes of Eva's war-time *Utility Ware* had been included in MoMA's 15th Anniversary Exhibition in 1944, but this one-person show conferred an entirely different level of prestige. It was the first MoMA exhibition to exclusively feature work by a woman designer, and the exhibition, accompanied by Eva's engaging comments, received widespread and positive press coverage. *Art News of America* saw a Modernist functionality in the dishes, noting that "unusually formed handles for tea-cups . . . expressly conform to the finger which lifts them."[17] It was more likely that Eva, who had once remarked to Noyes that function followed form,[18] had been considering the pleasure that the cup's user would experience. In Eva's words, "You must imagine how handles feel and how pots balance in your hand before they exist."[19]

In the New York *Herald Tribune*, Eugenia Sheppard singled out Eva's teacup as "outstanding for slightly down-slanted handles that are broad and easy to grasp," noting that "the centers of the saucers are slightly lifted with an indentation to keep cups from the usual sliding."[20] In the *New York Times*, Mary Roche admired the teapot's mahogany handle and the spherical salt and pepper dishes with their tiny china spoons.[21] *Retailing Home*

Furnishings reported that sales were good, but presciently characterized *Museum's* lack of decoration as an "unsolved problem."[22] Castleton had doubts about selling undecorated china, but a Castleton brochure at the time of the exhibition presented the decision positively, claiming that *Museum* had "achieved a form so chaste and lovely that it requires no decoration!"[23]

During the exhibition, the china was available only by special order through a select few department stores: B. Altman & Co., John Wanamaker, Black Starr & Gorham, and Georg Jensen. The delivery time promised was four months, but three years passed before *Museum* went into full production. Decorations were added, a few pieces were deleted, and others were added to the original *Museum* line shown at MoMA.[24]

MARKETING AND DECORATION, 1949
The *Museum* line, plain and decorated, debuted in September 1949 at *Castleton China Collection by Contemporary Artists*, Castleton's exhibition-style presentation at the Galleries of the Associated American Artists in New York.[25] It featured plain *Museum* pieces as well as the newly decorated versions: plates with hand-painted reproductions of original paintings, and mechanically made, hand-applied decals.[26] The dinnerware was now available for direct purchase in department stores. Altman's, for example, stocked the ivory *Museum* plates along with decorated ones.

Anxious about the sales potential of undecorated pieces, Castleton commissioned decorative patterns.[27] Castleton's innovations were not universally appreciated. Eva observed that "the Museum of Modern Art controlled the *Museum* shape, and my contribution ended with the design of the shape itself. . . . Most decorations found on my shapes are not within my control." Further, Eva observed that "I do not value diverse ornamentations very differently. Famous artists' decorations are not necessarily more suitable than other decorations.[28]

The Walker Art Center's *Everyday Art Quarterly: A Guide to Well Designed Products* noted that "at this point we feel impelled to deplore the one-step-forward-two-steps-backward which have been taken by Castleton; this ware is also being manufactured with applied patterns designed by prominent artists, one of whom remarked that he felt that the familiar cliché, 'gilding the lily,' was unusually apt in this case."[29]

MASS PRODUCTION, 1949
Not all original twenty-five pieces displayed by MoMA made it to production. The quirky salt and pepper holders and their tiny spoons, the candle-holder-cum-vase, and the two-handled bouillon bowl and stand were never mass produced. The downward-slanting cup handle had been changed without Eva's authorization. She speculated that "they may have been afraid that the buying public was not ready for the new handle shape, or even for the low cup. Very few with the down-turned handle were produced.[30]

All of the redesigned pieces were added without MoMA's imprimatur, but in some instances Eva was consulted.[31] Although she had patented some of the *Museum* designs at the time of the MoMA exhibition, the rights had reverted to Castleton in 1948, leaving Castleton free to do as it pleased.[32]

The Shenango factory that manufactured Castleton's products was one of the largest ceramics producers in the United States, employing about three thousand people. Producing the *Museum* porcelain required the efforts of many of its most highly skilled workers. Manufacturing began with two-part plaster molds, into which the wet porcelain was poured. When they were dry, the pieces were removed from the molds, cleaned, and fired. *Museum* pieces were fired initially at a very high temperature, then glaze-fired at a lower temperature to produce their clear and reflective surfaces. The firing temperatures had to be extremely precise, as the expansion and contraction of the glaze had to exactly match the expansion and contraction of the forms. Harold Freed, Castleton's firing room manager, recalled that "at first *Museum* gave us all sorts of fits. Her [Eva's] designs were very, very good for forming metal, but they were terrible for forming china. That little creamer (nicknamed the "Zeisel" by the workers) had a high

reject rate because the edge, right where the lip and spout are, would go porous. It was too thin."[33]

Freed recalled that it was difficult to control the amount of shrinkage in the coffee pot's round body; its handles, tops, and spouts were made separately and attached by hand. Every attachment required individual degrees of pressure, and the slightest error could crack and ruin the body. One out of every five handles, spouts, and tops was lost during the firing and assembling processes. According to Freed, one result of these hand processes was that every *Museum* coffee pot looks slightly different.[34]

This labor-intensive process and its high failure rate meant that *Museum* pieces were expensive. Eva was quoted as saying that she certainly could not afford to buy it, noting that at the time, "One coffeepot was $45!"[35] A service for twelve retailed at $300 (the equivalent of $3,000 in 2012 figures), while in 1952 a sixteen-piece white earthenware starter-set of Eva's *Tomorrow's Classic* line cost only $8.95 (see chapter 11).

Epilogue

Two years after *Museum*'s commercial debut, Hellmann sold his Castleton shares back

Prototype trays, not produced, 1946. EZA

to Shenango, and thereafter the company increasingly featured conventional decorations on *Museum* plates.[36] Production of *Museum* or *Museum White*, two of the names under which it was sold, continued into the late 1970s. Blank plates, unmarked as being either Castleton or *Museum*, were distributed by many companies including Saladmaster, American Manor, Interpace, Nancy Prentiss, and Reynolds,[37] and sold at lower prices than Castleton-identified pieces.[38]

Museum was the first modern dinnerware line in fine white china to be produced in the postwar U.S. The elegance Eva sought shines through every one of these "heirlooms," creating pleasurable experiences for those who use them.

Chapter 6

Red Wing Potteries: *TOWN AND COUNTRY*
1947
Meri Villane

Overleaf
Three-pint pitcher in Rust, two-pint pitcher in Peach, and creamer in Sand, 1947. HUC, EZA.

Top
Cup in Metallic Brown with saucer in Sand, cereal bowl in Chartreuse, salad bowl with Metallic Brown interior and Chalk White exterior, 1947. EZA.

Above Left
Salt and pepper shakers in Blue, 1947. EZA.

In 1946, the Minnesota-based Red Wing Potteries, Inc., approached Eva about creating a line of inexpensive "luncheon ware." According to Eva, "In 1946, Mr. Gunshel from Red Wing Potteries came to ask me to design a set of dishes with a distinctive shape, as 'Greenwich Village-y' as possible. These seemed surprising instructions to receive from a Minnesota plant on the banks of the Mississippi. It was so far from Greenwich Village that this distant place seemed almost mythological."[1]

The luncheon ware was to be used for informal dining and entertaining, including buffet-style meals taken both indoors and out, and it was envisioned to have a fairly short life-span because the factory depended on ever-changing designs to maintain its market share. Eva was paid a flat fee of $300 for what turned out to be a very popular range.

Although Eva designed for "delight," she also believed that one must design according to the particular problems to be solved, be they unusual shapes or a desire for either convenience or ease of use.[2] Called *Town and Country* after the popular American lifestyle magazine, the line was presented for sale in January 1947 and sold until the mid-1950s.

Town and Country is more boldly gestural than some of her other designs. The shapes are related yet distinct in their unadorned singularity. "They make love to each other," Eva said, and engage us in their unique interactions.[3]

When introduced in 1947, *Town and Country* consisted of approximately thirty-four pieces,

but by early 1950, the soup tureen and ladle, salad spoons, and coaster had all been discontinued.[4] The brochure introducing the line promoted it as "luncheon ware" that could be mixed and matched.

The colors were informal and representative of the servant-less etiquette of the younger consumer of the 1940s and 1950s. The most youthful colors were specified in a March 1947 article in *China, Glass and Decorative Accessories* as Chalk White, Rust, Sand, Chartreuse, and Metallic Brown. There were thirty-four pieces in twenty-three different color combinations. The line was offered in two glazes, matte and gloss finishes, and with textured or metallic luster, further complementing its versatility.[5] The textured finish might be more appropriately described as "speckled," as can be seen upon close examination of pieces in the Sand and Peach colors.

Eva did not intend an infinite variety of "mixing and matching." She recalled: "I said, let's do two sets of colors. One set was rust, black, and sand. The other color scheme was peach, blue, and also sand and black, I *believe*. However, the minute it got to the market, the colors got all mixed up, and I was not happy about that!"[6]

The walls of the *Town and Country* dishes are thick, some having built-in strong, sturdy handles designed to fit perfectly in the hand. The forms were overtly modern. The plates and bowls were intentionally designed to be off-center, with one side higher than the other. The relish dish and platter are tear-shaped; the pitchers' spout resembles a bird's open beak; and the oil and vinegar cruets snuggle together. The nested shapes of the salt and pepper shakers resemble a pose adopted by Eva and her daughter Jean, in a photograph.[7]

When they were first introduced, *The Pathfinder*, a weekly news magazine, included a comment that "*dishes* with humor make mood" and described the salt and pepper shakers as "modeled after ghosts—gay and usable . . . the trademark of a merry-souled designer."[8] They were thought to have inspired the forms of cartoonist Al Capp's famous "The Shmoo" character that first appeared in his *Li'l Abner* comic strip in 1948. Over the years, "Shmoo" has become a term of endearment for these popular salt and pepper shakers.[9]

Safe to use except for the bronze glaze, which contains lead,[10] many of the items were made with versatility and ease of entertaining in mind, including the coaster/ashtray, and the lazy Susan with seven relish dishes and a condiment server. The mugs and pitcher made a cold drink set while the vegetable dishes, relish dishes, and fruit saucers could be used as cookie, fruit, and nut bowls; the soup tureen could be used to serve fruit punch or cookies. For convenience, the mustard dish had a spoon attached to the lid, and the syrup

Mixing bowl in Sand and syrup jug in Rust, 1947. EZA.

Salad spoons in Chalk White with wood handles, 1947. MGC.

jug and mixing bowl were intended to become a "waffle set" when used together.[11]

The dishes epitomize what designer Russel Wright called "easier living" and, like his designs, helped change the ways in which tableware was used in the United States. Pieces from *Town and Country* were featured on the shelves of the *Idea House*, a full-scale working house designed in June 1947 to demonstrate the advantages of modern living.[12]

The line remains relevant to contemporary living and fits well with an emphasis on casual and "cocooning" lifestyles. Collecting the line can be difficult, as the pieces have no markings beyond their familiar shapes and curves. Working closely with Eva, World of Ceramics, a small pottery in Morganton, North Carolina, reissued select pieces in 1996. They were sold through the Museum of Modern Art in New York, with salt and pepper shakers and cruets produced in black and white, and the batter bowl and syrup pitcher in brown earthenware. That same year, World of Ceramics also manufactured

several items for the Orange Chicken Gallery in New York, with salt and pepper shakers in a variety of colors, and the syrup pitcher and batter bowl in Gunmetal, Caramel, and Red, in addition to Peach, Beige, and Green Sand.[13] The cruets, complete with corks, were made in Black, Chartreuse, White, Gunmetal, and Blue. During this same period, the Brooklyn Museum gift shop carried the salt and pepper shakers and cruets in Black, White, Blue, and Yellow. All reissued pieces created by World of Ceramics were bottom-stamped EZ96 or EZ97 to distinguish them from the originals.[14]

During 1999 and 2000, the Metropolitan Museum of Art acknowledged *Town and Country* as a "design classic" and reproduced nearly the entire line as an "authorized reproduction." Manufactured in Italy, the pieces included a five-piece place setting comprised of a dinner plate, salad plate, soup, and cup and saucer, all of which were made in Matte Black, White, Terracotta, and Lime Green. Also available were a teapot (White with a Black lid), a three-quart pitcher (Lime Green), cream and sugar

dishes (Black/White), salt and pepper shakers (Black/White), a fourteen-inch serving bowl in Black, and a platter in White. These were sold in the museum's gift stores and listed in its 1999 and 2000 catalogues.[15] Additional salt and pepper shakers were manufactured by the Metropolitan Museum of Art, which owns exclusive rights to all future issues. The Swedish design house Formens Hus (House of Design) featured them in Soft Chartreuse as part of its 2005 opening. Both the Hillwood Estate Museum and Gardens, Washington, DC, and the Mingei International Museum, California, had salt and pepper shakers made for exhibitions in 2005 and 2006, respectively. In April 2005, the Hillwood Museum sold them in its gift shops in several colors, but those that were sold at the Mingei in 2006 came only in Mingei Blue, an exclusive color.[16]

Whether originally produced or reissued pieces, Eva understood the job of an industrial designer as one of making lovely things for everyday use. With *Town and Country*, she achieved that goal.

Left Page
Condiment server/mustard in Sand, soup tureen in Metallic Brown, and sugar in Sand with Metallic Brown lid, 1947. EZA.

Above
Oil and vinegar, teapot in Grey, 1947. HUC.

Left
Platter in Rust, baker in Gray, relish in Dusk Blue, sauce dish in Rust, 1947. HUC, EZA.

Chapter 7

Riverside Ceramic Company

1947

Jim Drobka

In 1947, Eva received a commission from a small start-up venture, the Riverside California Ceramic Company, for about fifteen pieces of art ware. The company was the idea of Arthur Krieger, who had moved to Riverside in 1946 and proposed to local businessman Howard Boylan that if Boylan could muster investors to fund a new ceramics company, he would find the ceramists.[1] Boylan, a member of the Chamber of Commerce, persuaded local men to fund this new venture. Boylan became secretary of the board of directors and company treasurer.[2] There was also a family connection: Boylan's daughter, Lois Krieger, was married to Arthur Krieger's son.[3]

The site for the factory was Box Springs Road, then just outside the city limits of Riverside.[4] The local newspaper reported that the factory was expected to be operational by June 1947, with a staff of about fifteen, and that an unusually fine-quality porcelain art ware, the characteristics of which were thinness and translucency as well as fineness of texture and glaze, was to be produced. The company claimed that "artistically designed art ware employing a fine porcelain base" was comparatively rare in California ceramics and announced that "Eva Zeisel, a nationally known New York designer," had been employed to create the designs.[5]

Lois Krieger described her father holding up a dinner plate to the light and demonstrating how the shape of his hand was visible through the thin porcelain.[6] The "family" of shapes that Eva designed included a full dinnerware set and accessories such as candlesticks and small vases. The sugar bowl, creamer, carafe, tumblers, and serving bowls were all designed with rounded bottoms so the pieces could rock gently when touched. Karen Kettering, curator of the 2004 exhibition *Eva Zeisel: The Playful Search for Beauty*, has remarked that this intentional use of movement was unusual, akin to "bringing Alexander Calder and his mobiles to the table!"[7] Eva said that this feature was "just for fun."[8] Most of the pieces consisted of continuous forms: the outline travels down one side, curves under the form, and travels back up as a single, fluid line, with the result that the pieces appear to float upon the table.[9]

At least four ceramic engineers were on staff: company president George Ferdinand, a ceramic consultant and engineer; plant superintendent Ernest Wilson, who brought many years of experience; William Parry, a recent graduate of Alfred University; and John Boyd Cahoon, who was educated at Ohio State University and the University of Utah.[10] Wilson had worked for the Tennessee Valley Authority's Ceramic Research Laboratory program, which had developed ways of using local kaolin clay to produce porcelain wares.[11]

Creamer and teapot, 1947. Photograph: EZA.

Overleaf
Cruet in White and creamers in experimental glazes, 1947. EZA, EMC.

Left
Medium bowl and tumbler in experimental glazes, tumbler in Avocado with Yellow interior, 1947. EMC.

Right
Lidded casserole with metal ring handles in Medium Brown and carafe in Deep Brown, 1947. EZA.

His son, Bruce Wilson, recalled that his father loved to experiment with local clays and mineral ores (for glazes).[12] This interest in research, experimentation, and problem-solving was an important part of the work at Riverside, where the laboratory had to develop methods for casting, firing, and glazing Eva's shapes.[13]

Ernest Wilson arrived in Riverside in April 1947 while the plant was under construction, and he was involved in purchasing the kiln and setting up the operation. His stepdaughter, Mabel Butcher, was hired to do casting. Her husband, Ellery Butcher, prepared the working molds. Wilson's son Bruce began to do the block and casing work for the molds.

Eva sent the designs for the new line by mail from her studio in New York to the plant in California. Bruce Wilson recalled that due to the urgency of the production schedule, some models arrived still damp, having been shipped before they had time to dry properly.[14] Eva recalled a telephone conversation she had with "the man who was making the glazes. He went up in the mountains and found minerals for making beautiful glazes."[15] Bruce Wilson, however, recalled that the clay and glaze materials came from established suppliers "back East."[16] A 1947 letter from Nell Parry (wife of William Parry, whose responsibilities at the Riverside plant included glazing) indicated that the lustre glazes were developed by Charles Harder, head of the ceramics program at Alfred University.[17]

The *Riverside* line included a subtle and sophisticated palette of solid glazes (see Taxo-

nomy). Some pieces swirled with colors; these striking, modulated, iridescent glazes were prepared using minerals that oxidized—and changed color—during the firing.[18] When the amount of oxygen available in the kiln was held back, the glazes would not fully fire to their mature color. The process resulted in colors of extraordinary and unpredictable beauty.

The dinnerware was exhibited in August 1947 in a local department store and at housewares shows on both the East and West Coasts.[19] During the same month, the newspaper *Riverside Enterprise* reported that a national advertising campaign was planned. The dinnerware was featured in magazines such as *House Beautiful*, *House and Garden*, and *American Home* between December 1947 and July 1948.[20] Trade advertisements were placed in *Crockery and Glass Journal* and *Gift and Housewares*, while pieces from the line were exhibited at the Museum of Modern Art in September 1947 as examples of affordable good design[21] and in the Akron Art Institute's *Useful Objects for the Home* in November 1947.[22] By October 1947, however, the investors had come to distrust Ferdinand and the plant closed after operating for only about four months. A last-ditch effort was made by one remaining employee (probably Cahoon) to resolve major production issues, but by the end of the year, experimental pieces and seconds were offered for sale without the line ever going into production.

When interviewed by former student Ed Lebow in the 1990s, William Parry discussed some of the production problems:

These were chiefly copper bearing glazes that fired to maturity. Then, while cooling, they were flash reduced, turning the glazes lustrous and beautiful. Eva Zeisel had seen these and wanted to put them on this line she was doing with Riverside China. I went there for a few months until they folded. The forms she designed were beautiful. They had round bottoms. The plates and tumblers had round bottoms. But since they were china, they couldn't be stacked [in the kiln]. These had to be bisque fired and glaze fired so the round bottoms wouldn't flatten out. They couldn't afford to do it that way. The glazes were also impractical. They were too soft. Knives scored them, so they couldn't hold up to use.[23]

The exact chronology of the company's dissolution remains unknown.[24] One result of this brief venture is that pieces of *Riverside China* are among the rarest of Zeisel objects.

Starting in 1997, Eva authorized and supervised reissues of some of her *Riverside* designs. World of Ceramics produced the teapot, creamer, sugar bowl with lid, carafe, tumbler, cup, nine-inch plate, and seven-inch plate. Gloss glaze colors available were Black, White, Yellow, Blue, Rust, and metallic Gunmetal. Matte glazes included Eggplant, Mustard, Blue, and Green. Marks follow the form of "EZ97" to indicate the year produced.

Chapter 8

Clover Box and Manufacturing Company: *CLOVERWARE*

1947

Antay S. Bilgutay

After World War II, a bevy of new or previously restricted materials, many of which
had been used for military purposes, appeared
on the market. The challenge was to create
products appropriate for peacetime. Many
designers and manufacturers were keen to use
the latest techniques and materials, including
plastics, but many consumers still considered
plastics as cheap, poor-quality substitutes for
other materials.[1]

Monroe Dinell, president of Clover Box
and Manufacturing Company, New York, had
manufactured plastic (Plexiglas) canopies for
wartime fighter planes. He contacted Eva and
thoroughly enjoyed working with her during
a project that added a creative and artistic
aspect to his business.[2]

Fresh from the success of the *Museum* line,
Eva relished the challenge of designing for a

medium new to her. In developing *Cloverware*,
Eva's aims were to render plastic as acceptable
in the modern home as traditional tabletop
accessories and to emphasize "the beauty pecu-
liar to acrylic plastics."[3] She stated at the line's
debut: "I tried to avoid resemblance to other
materials—glass, agate, china, etc., because I
think the disappointment we often feel in handling an item made of plastic (which is light in
weight and tepid to touch, while it looks like
something heavy and cold) is partly the reason for the antipathy we sometimes feel for
this material."[4]

Working closely with Dinell, Eva took a
keen interest in the limitations of the material
as well as its potential, especially its malle-
ability when heated. She described *Cloverware*
as "an attempt to evolve designs from a manufacturing technique and to make free, lively

forms in plastic."[5] These increasingly popular biomorphic shapes were created by using air pressure rather than molds, although in the blowing process, thermoplastic sheets were placed inside closed molds and forced into shape by air or steam pressure.[6] The curved surfaces, hard edges, and variations in thickness of the finished products meant that different effects were created when light struck a piece, creating the illusion of changing color at the rims.[7] These elegant and shatterproof objects helped counter prejudice about the place of plastics in the postwar American home, which had earlier been restricted to the kitchen.

When *Cloverware* debuted in 1947, the first Melamine plastic products were just emerging in the tabletop marketplace.[8] Eva told the *Christian Science Monitor*: "In *Cloverware*, we have tried to open for plastics the way to acceptance among the best and valuable decorative accessories of the dining table and living room. It is our hope that the aesthetic qualities and the elegance inherent in plastics themselves will soon be appreciated, as they now are in a beautiful piece of crystal."[9]

The line included fifteen items in three translucent colors: Deep Emerald Green, Soft Milk White, and Brilliant Orange Amber. A 1948 company catalogue noted *Cloverleaf* bowls in two sizes; a gourd tray; an individual gourd-shaped dish; gourd-shaped bowls in two sizes; trays in two shapes; an undulating bowl; right and left bird-head-shaped salad servers; a salad

bowl; and a rectangular tray with teardrop-shaped recesses. A letter from Dinell to the Akron Art Institute mentioned "long individual serving dishes in the shape of footprints" and "rectangular casual pieces, approximately nine inches by eight-and-a-half inches."[10]

Although boldly modern in style and materials, the company's brochure stated: "Cloverware is happy in any decorative scheme from dining room to boudoir, modern or period."[11] *Riverside Enterprise*, a local newspaper, also noted that *Cloverware* was "designed . . . to complement both traditional and modern service."[12] Modern art and design cognoscenti and institutions embraced the line. Dinell was particularly excited about the Walker Art Center's de facto endorsement of the line when four pieces were included in the 1947 *Useful Gifts* exhibition of "well-designed objects for everyday use selected from Minneapolis Stores."[13] The *Cloverware* items on view were described as a green celery dish (no. 4701); green hors d'oeuvres dish (no. 4703); green salad bowl (no. 4710); and round white dish (no. 4709); and they were displayed alongside items from other designers now well-known for Mid-Century Modern design, including a Russel Wright vase for Bauer.[14]

In the fall of 1947, the Akron Art Institute requested a loan of *Cloverware* objects for the exhibition *Useful Objects for the Home*, as well as four *Cloverware* items for the museum's permanent collection of Industrial Design for exhibition and teaching purposes.[15] In January 1948, James Prestini, on behalf of the Armour

Research Foundation of the Illinois Institute of Technology, asked the company for photographs of "the blown plastic bowls designed for you by Eva Zeisel," adding that he intended to "recommend these designs for the Museum of Modern Art's file of good industrial design."[16] At the same time, the John Herron Art Institute in Indianapolis announced that several *Cloverware* items had been selected for inclusion in its *Useful Objects Designed for Modern Living* exhibition.[17]

Although *Cloverware* pieces had the advantage over china and glass of being shatterproof, they were relatively expensive; the salad bowl, for example, retailed for $12, the round salad bowl for $10, and serving spoons for $7.50 per set. (Russel Wright's ceramic vase for Bauer, by contrast, retailed for $7.50.[18]) Each item came with a label that warned: "IMPORTANT: Cloverware must not be subjected to temperatures of more than 150 degrees. Avoid placing it on a hot stove, or in boiling water. To clean, simply wash with mild soap, warm water and a soft cloth. To polish, use a dab of Simoniz and rub gently with a soft cloth."[19] Plexiglas also has a tendency to scratch, and, as Martin Eidelberg noted, "It is significant that the Cloverware line was only for occasional accessories, such as serving trays, salad bowls, and nut and relish dishes—objects that receive less use than regular dinnerware."[20] Manufactured during 1947 and 1948, the line never became the big seller for which both Dinell and Eva hoped.

Large and small CLOVERLEAF BOWLS, *1947.*
Photograph: EZA.

Chapter 9

United China and Glass Company/Meito: *NORLEANS CHINA*

1950
Antay S. Bilgutay

Overleaf

Fruit bowl, oval vegetable bowl, dinner plate, rimmed soup bowl, sugar, creamer, cup and saucer in El Dorado, 1950. EMC.

Bottom

Covered casserole in El Dorado, 1950. EMC.

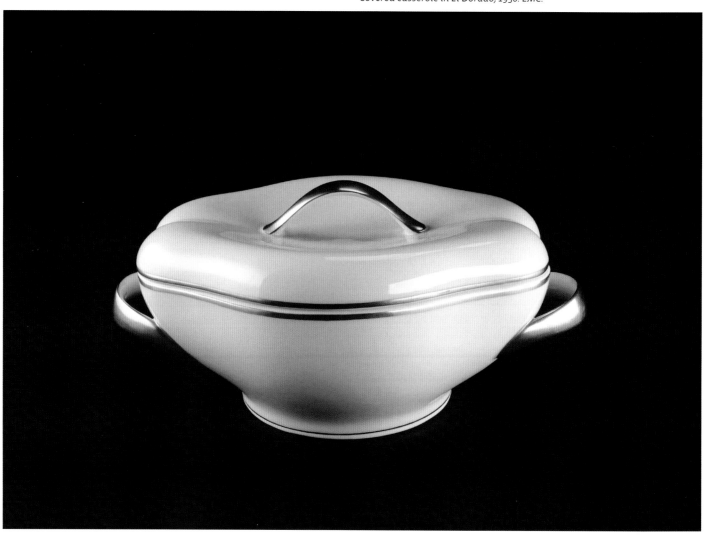

During the first half of the twentieth century, the importing of Japanese ceramics into the United States flourished. As early as 1934, Japan made more than 85 percent of the tableware and kitchenware shipped to the United States.[1] United China and Glass Company (founded in 1850 in New Orleans) began trading with Japan in 1932, but suspended its foreign operations during World War II. In 1947, it "aggressively reentered the Japanese market," becoming the first U.S. company to enter into a contract with the Supreme Command Allied Powers and the Japanese Board of Trade.[2] By the late 1940s, Japanese products comprised 75 percent of the firm's sales.[3]

Company vice president Solomon A. Stolaroff commissioned Eva to design the first new line to emerge from the company's renewed Japanese partnerships. She later recalled the invitation and her inspiration for the design: "A Mr. Stolaroff asked me to design a set for Meito in Japan. . . . He asked me to go to New Orleans. . . . I remember taking a boat down to the tip of the Delta. I photographed many ornamental wrought iron crosses in graveyards."[4]

The resulting line was *Norleans China*. Wrought iron seems an unlikely basis for this delicate line of porcelain dinnerware, but perhaps the connection lies in the graceful curves of the applied handles, which are accented by the fine gilding found on many pieces. The plates and bowls feature a wide rim, a departure from the coupe-shaped plates in the immediately preceding lines (see chapters 5–7). More striking are the surprising forms of the serving pieces, the curves of which Eva playfully likened to "a baby's bottom."[5]

United China and Glass Company announced the introduction of *Norleans China* in trade magazines in late 1949. An article celebrating the company's one-hundredth anniversary reported: "A new line of china dinnerware which will be known as 'Norleans China' will be introduced to the nation in 1950. This new line of dinnerware will incorporate modern and contemporary shapes and patterns."[6]

United China and Glass trumpeted Eva's innovative *Norleans* shapes and the exceptional quality of the porcelain manufactured in Japan by Meito China. A company advertisement declared: "We hate to be trite, but it's out of this world. Nothing like it has ever been made in Japan. . . . Nothing like it in this world at the price."[7] "Created to give you modern, not extreme, styling . . . easily adaptable to contemporary and traditional settings. Soft ivory body; lightest weight and most translucent dinnerware imported from Japan."[8]

Designed for broad appeal, *Norleans China* was commercially successful and company advertisements proclaimed it "the hit of the 1950 shows!" The line was affordably priced. In 1954, one trade journal noted: "Mrs. American Consumer with limited means gets sound value when she settles for Japanese dinnerware."[9] Another journal informed potential customers that *Norleans China*'s new Spring Garden pattern was "priced to retail at $69.95 for a 101-piece set, including six extra teacups and a teapot." At roughly sixty-nine cents per piece, *Norleans China* was a bargain when compared to Bavarian china at $2.15 per piece or the U.S. firm Stangl's new Amber-Glo pattern at ninety-three cents per piece, discussed in the same article.[10]

Today, *Norleans China* holds a remarkably modest place in the pantheon of Eva's designs, perhaps because of the very factors that made it such a success in the first place. The line straddles the aesthetics of tradition and modernism in form and pattern, although as ceramics historian Charles Venable noted, "with subtly undulating walls the forms were especially modern in feel."[11] They were adorned with a host of floral patterns (attributed to Meito china painters) that, today, appear old-fashioned to many.

Chapter 10

Salisbury Artisans

1951

Dan Holden and Colette Morton

In 1951, Eva designed a line of dining accessories in wood and ceramics for Salisbury Artisans, a small company owned by Phil Warner.[1] Richard Parsons was the master turner. The wooden items included candlesticks, nut dishes, and an hors d'oeuvres tray; the ceramic pieces included a tea service, relish tray, and cruets with wooden stoppers.

"The smell of rosewood" is what both Eva and her daughter remember most about their visit to the Salisbury Artisans site in Salisbury, Connecticut.[2] Rosewood, a hardwood with distinctive markings, was popular in the 1950s and was used for some of the pieces; lighter-colored woods were also used. The wooden items were sold directly by Salisbury Artisans, while the ceramic pieces were marketed by Gottschalk Sales Company on Fifth Avenue, retailing from $1 to $30.

The line was introduced at Ohio's Akron Art Institute in a one-woman show entitled *Eva Zeisel—Industrial Designer*, where the Salisbury pieces were exhibited next to her designs for the *Museum* line (see chapter 5).[3] Eva described the Salisbury line as fitting into three distinct forms: bulging, waistline, and geometric. The use of the words *bulging* and *waistline* is indicative of her commitment to the organic form. At first glance, the word *geometric* might seem ill-chosen, but the geometry she refers to is merely a curve coming to fruition. The bulbous shapes of a majority of the ceramic pieces are reminiscent of the *Town and Country* pitchers and creamer (chapter 6), and foreshadowed the sensuous curves of the cruet in Hallcraft's *Tomorrow's Classic* (chapter 11). Like some of the geometric shapes, the waistline objects are hung on brass stands and call to mind the line of a dancing figure. The candlesticks are the exemplar of the waistline, a feminine form evident later in Eva's work for KleinReid (chapter 19) and Nambé (chapter 20).

In 1997, the Orange Chicken released the reissues of two of Eva's Salisbury designs. The candlesticks were issued in six-inch, nine-inch, and twelve-inch sizes (all extrapolated from photographs of the original two sizes) in walnut, cherry, and maple. The six-inch, nine-inch, and twelve-inch fruit bowls were reissued in hardwood with brass legs. Like the originals, few were made and therefore are rare. Eva was fond of these shapes and often used them to illustrate her ideas on design.

Overleaf

Gravy (ceramic), candle holder (wood), footed bowl (wood), and bowl with legs (wood, brass), 1951. EZA.

Below

Candle holders (wood, glass), 1951. Photograph: EZA.

Above

Wood shakers on wood and brass stand, wood and metal corncob holders, 1951. Photograph: EZA.

Right

Teapot, sugar, and creamer on tray, condiment bowls (ceramic) on tray with handle (wood, brass), cruets (ceramic, wood), 1951. Photograph: EZA.

Above
Prototype creamer in green glaze, 1951. RLC.

Top Left
Wood salad bowl, wood muddlers on brass and wood stand, 1951. Photograph: EZA.

Center Left
Lidded wood bowls, 1951. Photograph: EZA.

Bottom Left
Lidded condiment servers (ceramic, wood), small wood bowl and pickle fork, 1951. Photograph: EZA.

Hall China Company: Hallcraft *Tomorrow's Classic*

1952
Earl Martin

Introduced in 1952 and produced until 1962, *Tomorrow's Classic* was a dinnerware line Eva "designed specifically for daily use."[1] It was manufactured by Hall China Company, which drew upon decades of experience in the production of high-quality ceramic ware to create an earthenware material with a "standard uniform texture, purity of body color, and degree of hardness" hitherto unknown in American earthenware.[2] It soon became a bestseller and continued to sell well for a decade, making it Eva's best-selling dinnerware line and one of the most successful of those made in the United States at that time.

When Eva came up with the idea for a line of dinnerware that would utilize a variety of decal decorations, she approached Alfred Duhrssen, president of Commercial Decal, the leading manufacturer of such decoration for the U.S. pottery and glass industries.[3] Duhrssen, who was always open to new ideas, saw the sales potential in utilizing new and interesting decal patterns.[4] He encouraged Hall China Company of East Liverpool, Ohio, to undertake the production.[5] Jonathan Higgins, a close friend of Duhrssen and head of Midhurst Importing Corporation, a New York–based china importer and distributor, handled distribution.[6] Indeed, Hall and Higgins set up a jointly owned entity, Midhurst China, specifically to market and distribute *Tomorrow's Classic* under a newly created Hallcraft brand.[7]

Eva developed the new line between 1950 and 1951 from initial drawings to refined plaster models.[8] Always insisting on exacting standards, she made several trips to Hall's Ohio factory to work with modelers and mold makers. Hall gave Eva fairly free rein, except in a few instances when manufacture proved impossible or too costly. By late 1951, she had created "a happy family of shapes" that shared commonalities, like an oval section and a short foot, but differed in their profiles, curves, handles, and tips,[9] In an article written by Eva and published just before the release of *Tomorrow's Classic*, she identified a trend in dinnerware design toward "gently flowing lines that tend toward the classical" and "lines based on geometric figures, but rounded out and modified"—an apt description of this line.[10]

In 1951, Eva supervised the creation of several of the initial decorative patterns.[11] She stated: "In my new dinnerware, I have attempted to keep the decorations dainty and small but detailed. Through their laciness, the white of the pottery interplays with their warm and expressive colors."[12] This approach is evident in the patterns Frost Flowers and Lyric, created by Irene Haas (Eva's assistant and former student) and in Buckingham, a playful pattern inspired by the iron fence outside Eva's design studio that was designed by Erik Blegvad, working closely with Eva. She also encouraged Charles Seliger, a young staff designer at Commercial Decal, to trust his instincts and "just do something you feel like doing."[13] The result was the patterns Arizona and Dawn. The many other decal patterns subsequently applied to *Tomorrow's Classic* were done without Eva's supervision or approval.

Midhurst hired Katheryn Hait Dorflinger to "take charge of special promotions, exhibitions, advertising and publicity."[14] She traveled to department stores around the country, where she featured *Tomorrow's Classic* in attractive table settings, interacted extensively with customers, and appeared on radio and

Large jug, small jug, and creamer, 1952. HUC.

television programs aimed at women.[15] She told her audiences that "noted designer Eva Zeisel is well-equipped to understand the china needs of women since she is a homemaker with several children."[16]

Tomorrow's Classic received considerable attention in the trade and popular press. The line was previewed in Midhurst's New York showroom (also designed by Eva) on December 19, 1951, followed by its national debut at the major china and glass trade show in Pittsburgh in January 1952.[17] One of its key selling points was its designer. Crockery and Glass Journal characterized Eva as "world famous for her modern dinnerware," while Gift and Art Buyer described her as a "nationally-known designer."[18]

Store buyers and lifestyle journalists were extremely positive about the line. Buyers considered the shapes "strikingly original" but "not bizarre," and having "a sort of classic grace."[19] The New York World-Telegram and Sun noted the dinnerware's "grace and classic simplicity without any of the starkness so often associated with modern design," while the New York Herald Tribune commented that it was "as at home in a traditional as a modern decorating scheme" and had "the serenity of timeless modern rather than exaggerated modern design."[20]

The dinnerware became a favorite of magazine editors. House Beautiful featured it in an informal meal setting within a modern living room and American Home predicted that despite its "thrifty price," the line had "a good chance of becoming an heirloom."[21]

The strong positive response to this modern-but-not-too-modern and inexpensive-yet-elegant dinnerware was reflected in orders. Department stores and shops across the country stocked the line. In large cities, certain patterns were retailed exclusively by a particular department store. In New York, for example, Tomorrow's Classic was stocked by all of the leading stores: Macy's had Bouquet and Dawn, B. Altman's had Mulberry and Buckingham, and Gimbel's had Holiday.[22] By June 1952, it was the most popular contemporary dinnerware design stocked at Barker Brothers in Los Angeles.[23] Three years after its introduction, Midhurst noted that it "Consistently Breaks Sales Records!" and that "the country's fastest selling dinnerware has become an 'American Classic.'"[24]

An early promotional brochure featured undecorated Tomorrow's Classic items in evocative black-and-white photographs (most likely arranged and taken by Eva), as well as outline drawings of the initial line's twenty-

Overleaf
Teapot, cup and saucer, coffee pot, sugar, and creamer in Satin Black with White lids and saucer, 1952. EZA.

Above
Two platters, ashtray, covered dish, and baker, 1952. EZA.

eight shapes (see Taxonomy).[25] Two pieces had slightly different forms from those that went into production: the creamer was without a handle and the after-dinner cup featured U-shaped projections on either side (instead of a loop handle) so that it could be gripped between the fingers of one hand. These shapes were made more conventional before the items went into full production.[26]

Undecorated White pieces were the cheapest; a sixteen-piece "starter set" (four each of dinner plates, bread and butter plates, teacups and saucers) sold for $8.95. Of the fourteen patterns mentioned in the brochure, only eight went into full production: Arizona, Bouquet, Buckingham, Dawn, Frost Flowers, Holiday, Lyric, and Mulberry.[27] The decorated wares fell into two price groups: Arizona, Bouquet, Frost Flowers, and Holiday starter sets retailed at $9.95; Buckingham, Dawn, Lyric, and Mulberry sets sold for $12.95. The most expensive serving piece was the covered dish (which retailed at $5.25 undecorated and $5.50 or $6.95 with a pattern).

Additional serving pieces were introduced in the second half of 1952, including a new coffee pot shape and variations on existing shapes (a smaller casserole, two additional platter sizes, and a large jug).[28] Coordinated glassware, known as *Silhouette*, was also introduced (see chapter 24). Eva believed it was the first time that the shapes of glassware and dinnerware had been coordinated.[29] In 1953, new serving and accent pieces were added, and by the end of the year, the line had grown to its full complement of forty-one shapes.[30] Additions in 1953 included salt and pepper shakers; a footed serving bowl; short and tall candlesticks; a vase; a covered butter dish; and a double egg cup. A matte Satin Black solid glaze treatment was also offered from 1953 and was available on serving pieces to "mix-match with decorated and plain white patterns."[31]

MODERN CRAFT: *TOMORROW'S CLASSIC* IN CANADA
Hallcraft *Tomorrow's Classic* was distributed in Canada from 1953 under the Modern Craft brand. The Robinson Clay Product Company, a Canadian distributor, offered the line in Pinehurst (known as Pinecone in the United States) and Snowglaze (Undecorated White).[32] The *Gift Buyer*, the leading Canadian china and glass trade magazine, featured "a new line of dinnerware by Modern Craft," distributed by the Canadian China & Glass Company.[33] It illustrated a jug in Queen's Rose, a large tea rose decoration, and a coffee pot in Bittersweet, a floral-and-bittersweet-vine motif. The marketing and promotion were similar to that in the U.S., but the designer and manufacturer were not mentioned. Nor did Eva's name, or that of Hall, appear as part of the mark on Modern Craft pieces.[34]

Seconds from Hall were probably used for many Modern Craft pieces. Selling second-quality production to outside decorators and distributors was a common practice among U.S. pottery manufacturers, including Hall. Limiting the release to Canada also limited potential damage to the company's reputation.[35] Modern Craft also employed decorative patterns that had previously been used by other U.S. pottery companies to decorate their wares.[36]

Tomorrow's Classic in its Modern Craft guise proved popular in Canada. New decal decorations were introduced in late 1954 (Cloverdale) and spring of 1956 (Sweet Grass).[37] In 1956, Modern Craft was included in a model home, for a young married couple at the Canadian National Exhibition.[38]

The line was discontinued in Canada in or about 1959.[39]

Later Years and Reissues

In the U.S., *Tomorrow's Classic* continued to sell well. Its prominence in the marketplace began to wane by 1955, partly because Dorflinger left Midhurst and partly because of the changing fashions in home furnishings.[40] New patterns or surface decorations were occasionally introduced to stimulate interest, and the most popular patterns, such as Fantasy (introduced 1953), continued to sell well. Indeed, in 1958 Fantasy was one of the top ten dinnerware patterns registered by brides in the United States.[41] Two years later, a trade journal noted the "proven appeal" of the *Tomorrow's Classic* Fantasy pattern, in a feature on tried-and-true sellers, as a pattern that a customer "expects always to be able to find on your shelves for refill purchases in years to come."[42] Such expectations were dashed in 1962, however, when Hall discontinued all of its earthenware dinnerware production, including *Tomorrow's Classic*.[43]

Since it was Eva's best-selling line and survives in large quantities, *Tomorrow's Classic* is often collectors' first introduction to Eva and remains a favorite of Zeisel enthusiasts to this day. In 1998, the molds for *Tomorrow's Classic* and the *Century* line were rediscovered at the Hall China factory, leading to a 1999 exhibition at Alfred College that featured the molds alongside finished dinnerware.[44] Since the molds belonged to Eva under the terms of her contract, she was able to utilize them to develop a new line released in 2005. The U.S. retailer Crate and Barrel, in partnership with the English pottery Royal Stafford and under Eva's tight supervision, reproduced some of the *Tomorrow's Classic* shapes together with some of the *Century* shapes in a new dinnerware line dubbed *Classic Century*.[45] This line was partially discontinued in 2012.

Chapter 12

Eva Zeisel Stoneware and Ironstone
1953–1964
Scott Vermillion

Western Stoneware Company: *Eva Zeisel Fine Stoneware,* 1953

Of all Eva's dinnerware lines, none better exemplified her design philosophy of linking past and present, or better displayed her virtuosity, than the *Eva Zeisel Fine Stoneware* line from Monmouth Pottery. A division of the Western Stoneware Company, which was founded in 1906 with a merger of seven pottery companies, Monmouth Pottery was situated halfway between Chicago and St. Louis in Monmouth, Illinois, fifteen miles east of the Mississippi River. Consisting of fifty-one pieces, Eva's line was organized into basic dinnerware, a complete kitchenware line, and a group of bird-shaped dishes, all available in fifteen patterns and three solid glazes.[1] The dinnerware, easily her most comprehensive, was sufficiently modern and simple to earn a place in the Museum of Modern Art's 1954 *Good Design* exhibit, but the material, the hand-printed patterns, and the bird-shaped dishes spoke to more "folksy" pottery traditions. As Eva commented, "The bird dishes are entertaining. For thousands of years, potters have used bird shapes for humorous expression, as relief from routine and severe functional design."[2] By designing historical bird-shaped dishes with a modern flair, Eva harmoniously linked past and present, creating something fresh and new in the process.

Western Illinois is rich in clay deposits, and stoneware made from this clay requires the addition of no other minerals. It is fired together with the glaze to a very high temperature (2290°F) and therefore is practically vitreous (nonporous) and very durable. Stoneware products are oven heat-resistant and lead-free, making them suitable for oven-to-table ware.[3] Western Stoneware owned its own clay mines, and its products enjoyed an excellent reputation at the time when Eva was commissioned.

By the early 1950s, the company employed three hundred workers and had three large tunnel kilns in modern buildings covering more than two acres, but just like many other pottery manufacturers, its orders were falling because of increased foreign competition. Hoping to bolster sales, company president Addis Hull, whose brother headed Hull Pottery Company in Zanesville, Ohio (for which Eva had designed a small line of decorative wares), invited her to design a line of dinnerware and some other items. Eva, who was then living in Chicago, accepted the assignment.[4]

Eva had never made dinnerware out of stoneware but was familiar with it from Central and Eastern Europe. In this instance, she envisioned elegant, informal pieces made out of lighter, finer stoneware. Fine stoneware incorporates all of the technical qualities of crude stoneware, but is created with the care and skill usually reserved for fine china. It was both unusual and challenging to use fine stoneware for large-scale dinnerware production because it is thinner and more fragile than regular stoneware. It took Eva and Monmouth over a year of experimentation, introducing new equipment and amplifying the company's engineering skills in order to assure troublefree production of this technically fine product.

Eva was given considerable freedom to do whatever was necessary to create the new line.[5] At Monmouth's Baird Mine in Colchester, Illinois, Eva went into the clay pit, dug into the mountainside, and selected the strata of clay that was best suited for the types of products she envisioned. From there, the clay was shipped by rail to Monmouth, where it was mixed and extruded to her specifications.[6]

Her hotel room doubled as a design office. Templates were made from the drawings and were used by Eva and the model makers as they worked in the factory with a throwing wheel to adjust and perfect the thin walls of the plates, bowls, and other concentric shapes to be produced on a jigger. Pieces produced in plaster molds—the bird bowls, pitchers, and handles—were developed with a combination of precision hand-sculpting and turning.

Eva also designed patterns and developed a technique for their application.[7] Some of the patterns were playful and abstract; for example, Eva described the dancing creatures in her Pals pattern as "turnip people!"[8] Designs and names already in use at Western Stoneware, together with Eva's passion for folk art, inspired the Pennsylvania Dutch and Colonial patterns. Western Stoneware's Mar-crest Pennsylvania Dutch pattern (also known as Daisy Dot) may have inspired the daisy shapes used in Chintz and other *Fine Stoneware* patterns. The scroll design, found in many *Fine Stoneware* patterns and used again by Eva in her later design work, probably drew

Overleaf
Eva Zeisel Fine Stoneware Vegetable bowl, salt and pepper in Colonial, Schmid Ironstone bowl with ladle in Stratford; Eva Zeisel Fine Stoneware sugar and marmite lid in a test pattern; marmite bowl in Chintz with lid in a test pattern, 1953. EZA.

Above
Large jug/pitcher in Colonial; small soup pot in a test pattern; mug, creamer, and prototype bottle in Pennsylvania Dutch, 1953. EZA.

Left
Sugar, handled bean pot, gravy bowl, cup and saucer, all in Pals, 1953. EZA.

upon Western Stoneware's own Colonial pattern as well as traditional European decoration.[9]

Gerald Gulotta, one of Eva's students, traveled to Monmouth to collaborate with her on developing patterns from potato stamps that included fish, birds, horses, stars, and the rosettes used, along with the scroll markings.[10] Gulotta stayed for several weeks and also worked with Eva on models and sample plaster molds. When the designs were developed, rubber stamps were made and used to hand-print the patterns onto the pottery.[11] Patterns to be applied with decals were prototyped by Commercial Decal but never produced. During a time her children were visiting, Eva allowed her son, John, to work on some of the experimental pattern designs.[12]

Although inspired by traditional stoneware, Eva put her own spin on this line, using a modern Cloud Gray glaze rather than the light tan color of traditional salt-glazed stoneware. Eva worked with factory engineers to set up a new kiln capable of firing the delicate stoneware and assembled and trained a team of young women to apply the glaze and decorate the dinnerware; she felt younger workers were less set in their ways and thus easier to train.

Eva Zeisel Fine Stoneware was unlike any other dinnerware or pottery available at that time. It offered both conventional and unconventional object types (the unconventional ones being the bird variations—see Taxonomy). It was priced for the middle market.[13] The bird-shaped dishes made a fine line of gift and decorative accessories. A beverage set, tea set, relish set, and the coffee set were also marketed separately as gifts.[14]

Basic casseroles had lids that allowed for easy stacking or nesting, and they could be turned upside-down and used for serving dishes or hot plates. The heads on the bird-shaped dishes formed handles or became ladles. The wings on the bird-shaped teapot formed the lid. Eva's penchant for familial relationships led to the fledgling creamer and sugar being designed in relation to the mother-bird teapot.[15]

As was customary at Western Stoneware, Eva probably paid for the tooling and retained ownership of the general design and slip cast molds, while the company retained the rights to the patterns and the production.[16] Possibly since she had a stake in *Fine Stoneware's* success, Eva's own design studio, Eva Zeisel Associates, distributed the line. Presented at trade shows and in magazines in 1953, reviewers praised this vitrified stoneware for a thinness and ring not previously produced in the United States.[17] Neiman Marcus, Marshall Field's, and J. C. Penney placed substantial orders.

Success seemed imminent for the new dinnerware line, but faced with a general production downturn, Western Stoneware laid off workers. As was customary with labor union rules, part-time workers and those with the least seniority were the first to go. At a union meeting, Eva pleaded unsuccessfully that the part-time, younger workers she had trained be retained over older workers so the factory could produce what promised to be a successful line. A display of *Fine Stoneware* was arranged in the downtown Monmouth drugstore in order to encourage the factory managers to continue production of the line, to no avail. A labor strike and staff layoffs ensued, and the factory closed. The remaining products were sold at the factory outlet store.[18] By the time the fac-

tory reopened with new owners, a devastating fire had destroyed the only kiln used to produce Eva's dinnerware line.[19]

Eva's designs for *Eva Zeisel Fine Stoneware* linked the folk traditions of her native Hungary and those of the United States to modern design sensibilities. Her carefully planned combination of simple dinnerware shapes and familial bird dishes, with a surprising array of hand-printed traditional and abstract patterns, turned the line into items that were functional, decorative, and unique.

Above
Test pieces (Hollydale): Bowl, cup and saucers, creamer, sugar, dinner and bread plates, platter, casserole, vegetable dish, and Bird dish (not produced), 1957. Photograph: EZA.

Left
Eva at home, pointing out folk and folk-inspired patterns, ca. 1953. Front left plate in Pals pattern. EZA.

Right
Large jug/pitcher in Allegro; lid and interior in Yellow, 1957. EMC.

Hollydale Pottery: *Eva Zeisel Fine Stoneware/Hi-Fi Stoneware, 1957*

After spending over a year developing *Fine Stoneware* for Monmouth, Eva had nothing to show for her hard work but believed that the product had the potential to become a sales success. She needed to find another company. Hollydale Pottery in Harbor City, California, had the clay and technology necessary to manufacture stoneware, and kilns that could fire it at extremely high temperatures.[20] In 1955, the company had developed a harder, tougher vitreous body and higher-silica, lower-lead glazes which were used in the production of all of its dinnerware lines. These improved production processes gave Hollydale the ability to manufacture stoneware and to nearly double its production capacity.[21]

Wally L. Blodgett had been the sales representative in the western part of the United States for Monmouth's *Eva Zeisel Fine Stoneware*; by 1957, he represented Hollydale Pottery in South Gate, California.[22] Blodgett brought together Eva and his new employer. Eva had the original *Fine Stoneware* slip-cast molds transferred from Monmouth to Hollydale Pottery. Hollydale probably had to create new molds for the plates and other flat items formed on a jigger. Western Stoneware (Monmouth) retained the rights to the patterns and glazes.

In the manner of the Monmouth line, the Hollydale line was marked *Eva Zeisel Fine Stoneware* with the addition of "from Hollydale of California." *Eva Zeisel Hi-Fi Stoneware* was used as a tagline. *Hi-Fi* stood for *high-fired*, the process used to vitrify lightweight stoneware; *Hi-Fi* also carried connotations of the new high-fidelity sound of the 1950s. The stoneware was made with local clay mined within fifty miles of the Hollydale factory.[23]

Eva helped to develop four new glaze colors (see Taxonomy).[24] To give the line a fresh look, the undersides of the plates and the interior on some of the pieces were left in the natural terra cotta of the clay under a clear matte glaze.[25] Three patterns were listed in the original promotional materials (probably never produced): Chintz, Penn Dutch, and Provincial.[26]

In March 1957, the eight Broadway department stores in the Los Angeles area introduced *Hi-Fi Stoneware* ninety days in advance of its appearance in other California stores. Eva made a guest appearance at each of the stores, where publicity posters with Eva's photograph were displayed.[27] Her informative and entertaining demonstration *Concert in Color* featured the line, along with brightly colored tablecloths and bits of greenery.[28] Eva hoped that her talks would create new interest in table settings among homemakers.[29]

A sixteen-piece *Hi-Fi Stoneware* starter set—with four dinner plates, salad plates, cups and saucers—sold for $9.95, a mid-market price point. Patterned starter sets sold for $14.95.[30] After the department store promotion was over, *Hi-Fi* started appearing in other stores throughout California, including Gump's in San Francisco, where an impressive window display featured the new stoneware line.[31]

Despite a good product and extensive promotion, competition from cheap imports and an economic recession that began in August 1957 led to Hollydale ending all dinnerware production, including *Hi-Fi Stoneware*. Thus, Eva's second attempt to see this delightful line into production ground to a halt.

But there would be one more chance . . .

Nihon Koshitsu Toki Company: *SCHMID IRONSTONE, 1964*

In 1964, Schmid International, a Massachusetts-based importer and distributor of decorative wares with an office in Japan, commissioned Eva to work with one of its dinnerware manufacturers. The company already worked with other respected U.S. designers, such as Russel Wright and La Gardo Tackett, and had its pottery produced in Japan for import into the U.S. market.

The company, Nihon Koshitsu Toki Co., Ltd. (NKT, established in 1908), was located in Kanazawa, Japan, and specialized in manufacturing high-fired, heat-insulating ironstone (earthenwares).[32] The quality of the material matched or exceeded the requirements necessary to manufacture Eva's stoneware, dinnerware, and bird-inspired accessory line.

Eva traveled to Japan in 1964 and spent more than a month working on prototypes and patterns.[33] By this time, the original designs for Monmouth dinnerware and bird-shaped accessories were over ten years old. Although most of the pieces in the Monmouth and Hollydale dinnerware lines were still considered sufficiently up-to-date to be used,

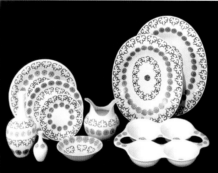

Dinner, salad, and bread plates, oil/vinegar, salt/pepper, soup bowl, gravy, platters, and relish dish, all in Stratford, 1964. Photograph: EZA.

Above
Vegetable dish in Lyric, oil/vinegar in Stratford, vegetable bowl and relish dish both undecorated, creamer and bowl with ladle in Lyric, 1964. EZA.

Salad plate, salt/pepper, gravy, covered casserole, bowl, fruit bowl, dinner plate, soup bowl, cup, saucer, creamer, coffee pot, and sugar, all in Lyric, 1964. Photograph: EZA.

Where space allowed, Schmid pieces were marked "ironstone, design *Eva Zeisel*, schmid NKT, OVEN PROOF, JAPAN." Smaller pieces were marked "JAPAN."

During the design and prototyping process Eva considered retaining the handled bean pots from the original Monmouth stoneware line, but they did not make it into the final line, despite interesting prototypes with a playful circle-and-dot pattern. There is some question about a four-compartment relish dish in the dinnerware group. Eva did not recall designing the piece, but it appears in photographs along with the other prototypes that she was working on at the time. Even if she did not design it, she seems to have sanctioned its inclusion in the line.

Schmid Ironstone was distributed nationally by Raymor (Richards Morgenthau & Company), notable for bringing contemporary design to home furnishings. Announcements for the dinnerware appeared in late 1964. It was sold as open stock or in sets, with a sixteen-piece starter set priced at $12.95 and a forty-five-piece service priced at $39.95.[37]

Schmid Ironstone did not resonate with potential buyers and was not a commercial success. Schmid and NKT discontinued the line in 1965, soon after its launch. In 1996, World of Ceramics in North Carolina worked with Eva to reintroduce some of her most iconic designs, including the *Schmid Ironstone* bird-style oil-and-vinegar and the rocking bird-style salt-and-pepper set. Both reissued designs were sold through the Orange Chicken gallery in New York City. The Brooklyn Museum also sold the bird-style oil-and-vinegar set. In 2010, the salt-and-pepper set was offered by Eva Zeisel Originals, and in 2012, the same company began selling the bird-style oil-and-vinegar and bird-style open bowl.

changing dining habits and NKT's production processes necessitated so many revisions, additions, and deletions that a completely new set of molds was needed.

Whereas the Monmouth and Hollydale dinnerware sets were casual and "folksy," this line was designed for family use and formal entertaining. Eva created new designs for plates, bowls, cups, and saucers—any piece formed on a jigger. Mugs were becoming more popular, so she designed the coffee cup with more of a vertical stance and a pronounced foot, and added a ten-ounce handled mug. The non-bird teapots, coffee pots, and pitcher were given a sophisticated redesign with thinner elongated necks and elegantly curved handles, spouts, and finials. The sugar bowl and creamer were elongated; a handle was added to the creamer. Several dual-purpose pieces were added that could be used as oil and vinegar containers, a vase, or for serving wine. An elegant gravy boat and a pair of non-bird salt and pepper shakers were added. The lids on the covered casseroles were revised to make the bottom edges less susceptible to damage,

and a contemporary product brochure showed them stacked and nested to indicate how the inverted lid could be used as a compote.[34]

Many of the earlier bird-shaped pieces carried over to the new Schmid line with subtle revisions. The open head vegetable dish was elongated and given a wider base.[35] The bird-inspired tableware items were designed to highlight and coordinate with the regular dinnerware and for dual purpose: the relish bowl could be used as a planter and the vegetable bowl could hold a floral centerpiece. Each bird-shaped object was individually boxed and described as making a "charming gift."[36]

Schmid Ironstone was offered in two patterns—Stratford, a blue abstract scroll pattern, and Lyric, a linear black pattern—both on warm white. Stratford was similar to the Colonial pattern; Lyric was unique to the Schmid line. Unlike the Monmouth and Hollydale dinnerware, there were no solid-color glazes. The warm white glaze on the Schmid line was bright, smooth, and more refined in comparison to the rustic Cloud Grey glaze from the original Monmouth line.

Chapter 13

Hall China Company: Kitchenware

1955
Earl Martin

Eva's kitchenware line for the Hall China Company followed the huge success of her *Tomorrow's Classic* dinnerware for the same company (see chapter 11).[1] The line of fireproof cooking and kitchen accessories was introduced in 1955 with brown-glazed bodies and contrasting linings and lids in stark white, accented by a "modern, abstract design in shades of brown, mauve, and blue."[2] The line retailed from $2 to $6.95 per item and became part of Hall's well-known range of durable kitchenwares.[3]

In the early twentieth century, the company developed a ceramic body and glazes which could be fired together simultaneously at very high temperatures (approximately 2400°F). This single-fire process, which closely bonded the glaze and the body, produced a dense, vitrified ceramic ware that was impervious to liquids, resistant to cracking and chipping, and did not craze. Hall used this process to produce large amounts of kitchenware for hotels and restaurants and, starting in 1920, for domestic use as well.[4]

The initial glaze decoration was dubbed Casual Living after a phrase popularized in the postwar period to denote the trend toward more casual lifestyles.[5] In china and glass, the movement resulted in dinnerware and serving accessories with multiple purposes—ware that could be transferred from stove to table and then to refrigerator or cupboard, thus removing the need for separate serving and storage dishes.

Promoted as a "Buffet—Table—Oven Service," Eva created twenty-three items for Hall, five of which were designed as oven-to-table ware.[6] Those designed for table use included serving ware and items for individual use (see Taxonomy).

The overtly utilitarian nature of the cooking, serving, and storage items, such as the bean pot, left-over dish, and various casserole dishes, was belied by the subtle elegance and playful charm of their forms. Although made from a thick, heavy ceramic body, they possess curves as graceful as those on thinner materials. Handles in this line invite the user to touch, and bring to mind ears or perhaps cupped hands. One shape that Eva displayed prominently among her personal collection, and which was reissued twice in later years, was the refrigerator pitcher. Slim in profile, its pinched sides and undulating cover place it among Eva's most organic and beautiful shapes.

According to her, the design seemed an obvious solution to the problem of a lack of storage space in small apartments and in the relatively small refrigerators of the time.[7] The idea for the Casual Living glaze decoration—a subtle satin-smooth Seal Brown glaze with the semi matte white glaze, adorned with abstract swipes and round dots of color—was also hers.[8] The silky feel of the brown glaze adds to the sensual experience of handling these objects.

The company marketed and distributed the line itself, because kitchenware was a field in which it was already well established.[9] Like the company's previous lines of kitchenware, it went directly into shops and department stores across the U.S. The household goods departments in major stores and other outlets, such as Ace Hardware (a regular Hall

Cookie jar: color not selected by Eva, 1955. HUC.

Overleaf
Sugar, round side-handle tureen casserole, salt and pepper, all in Tri-Tone: shapes 1955, decoration 1956. EZA.

Left
Teapot and mug in Tri-Tone: shapes 1955, decoration 1956. HUC.

client), probably sold the majority of the kitchenware items, although some were sold by more design-conscious retailers.[10] Those retailers were more likely to promote the line as designed by Eva Zeisel, even though her name did not appear as part of the mark on the bottom of each piece. The absence of Eva's name in the mark reflected the fact that she was offered a single design fee for the line, as opposed to royalties.[11]

In early 1956, Hall introduced a new decoration for the kitchenware line: Tri-Tone. It featured the white ceramic body under four glossy glazes: clear, pink, blue, and gray.[12] The pink and blue overlapped diagonally toward the bottom of each piece, creating a bluish-gray that was close to, but different from, the gray glaze used on the tops of lids and covers. In later years, Eva did not recall being involved with the development of this decoration, but John Thompson, then a young employee of Hall China and the son of the company president, remembered that the idea came from her.[13] The company also made other changes and additions: the cookie jar in Tri-Tone was substantially smaller in size, making it and the bean jar larger, close in height.[14] Five new bowls (which formed a graduated mixing bowl set) were also added. When asked about these bowls in 2008, Eva characterized them as "unremarkable" and did not recall designing them. It seems likely that a Hall staff designer created the bowls and that the company added them to the line in order to extend its appeal.[15]

In 1957, Midhurst China announced that it was introducing a new line of Hallcraft *Hostessware*, "an ovenproof china service designed for all-season use, indoors and outdoors."[16] Featuring three decorative patterns—Exotic Bird, Flight, and Gold and White—on a milky white matte glaze, *Hostessware* consisted of some of Eva's kitchenware shapes together with several of Hall's standard kitchenware shapes not designed by her.[17]

Exotic Bird is the only *Hostessware* pattern found with any frequency on the secondary market and it is likely that it was the only one to go into full production. It features stylized birds, eggs, mushrooms, and peppers rendered in a colorful design with a Central European flavor.[18] At the base of the bird motif is the signature "Elena," which is likely that of the decal designer.[19] It is almost certain that Eva had nothing to do with this decoration or the others used on *Hostessware*. A limited amount of *Hostessware* was produced with Flight and Gold and White decorations, possibly only enough for display at trade shows.[20]

Hostessware was not terribly successful commercially, but Hall continued to produce selected shapes from Eva's kitchenware line (decorated in glazes and patterns with which Eva was not involved) and sold them in large quantities. From 1957 onward, Hall included her cookie jar in its new kitchenware lines.[21] One of the most popular versions of the cookie jar came in pastel glazes, including pink, blue, yellow, and green, overlaid with intricate gold decoration. Eva's bean pot was reissued

as a cookie jar in the *Autumn Leaf* line made for Jewel Tea Company; the only change was the removal of the small ventilation hole in the cover. Her kitchenware designs faded from Hall's offerings in the 1960s.

In the late 1990s, the Orange Chicken, a New York gallery, worked with Eva to reissue the refrigerator pitcher. The limited edition was manufactured by World of Ceramics, North Carolina, and made in White, Black, Dark Green, Yellow, Gunmetal, Beige, Peach, Green Sand, and Red, with lids in the same color or in Black or White.[22] In 2008, Eva again reissued the pitcher design in collaboration with the Neue Galerie in New York. Made in porcelain, this version is available in Lacquer Red, Ink Blue, and Pure White glazes.[23]

Chapter 14

Hall China Company: Hallcraft *CENTURY*

1956
Earl Martin

The huge success of Hallcraft *Tomorrow's Classic* (see chapter 11) encouraged executives at Hall China Company and its marketer and distributor, Midhurst China, to envisage another earthenware dinnerware line designed by Eva. They waited more than four years, however, before introducing the new dinnerware to minimize any adverse effect on sales of *Tomorrow's Classic*.[1] Hallcraft *Century* debuted to the trade in July 1956. At the preview that was held at New York's Savoy Plaza Hotel, the line was featured in chic table settings created by the staff of Georg Jensen, an upscale retailer noted for artistic and well-designed goods.[2]

For *Century*, Eva created yet another new and elegant family of shapes. *Retailing Daily* noted, "According to Mrs. Zeisel, the flowing, three-dimensional lines are adapted from nature, suggested by the harmonious curves of petals and fruits. Vegetable dishes, pitchers, sugar bowl and coffee pot are done in oval or melon shapes . . . Salt and pepper shakers shaped to resemble pendant fruit. . . ."[3] A distinctive "petal tip" transformed simple round plates into elegant teardrop forms and served as a built-in handle as it rose up and away from the rim. On bowls and platters, Eva placed these petal tips opposite each other to create graceful handles. Inspiration from

nature is also evident when *Century* platters and serving bowls are stacked together, evoking a blossoming flower.[4]

Century shared certain commonalities with its Hallcraft predecessor. Both lines were manufactured from bright white durable earthenware that was resistant to chipping and cracking. Both were available in plain white as well as a choice of decorative patterns supplied by Commercial Decal.[5] There were fewer patterns in the *Century* line, however—only three at first—and it was initially composed of only twenty-four items, significantly fewer than *Tomorrow's Classic*.[6] Those omitted from the new line included covered soup bowls and after-dinner coffee cups and saucers. In addition, the *Tomorrow's Classic* butter dish and ladle were reused for the *Century* line. *Century* included some new items and shapes, such as a relish dish with four sections and a snack plate with a well to hold the cup.[7]

The line was introduced with three decal decorations in addition to the undecorated Century White. Two patterns, both of them stock decorations from Commercial Decal, were created without Eva's involvement: Fern and Sunglow.[8] Both patterns were coordinated with solid-colored accent glazes (blue and yellow, respectively) on the interiors of the cups, creamer, and jug, as well as the covers

of the sugar bowl, teapot, and casserole.[9] Commercial Decal staff continually created stock patterns that were available to all potential clients, but once selected by a client such as Hall/Midhurst, they became exclusive.[10] A client could also commission a pattern from the in-house designers. This was the case with the third *Century* pattern, Garden of Eden, which was created at Eva's suggestion by Charles Seliger, head of design at Commercial Decal; Seliger recalled Eva supplying him with photographs of "Javanese" carvings for inspiration. Described as "an Oriental fantasy of exotic foliage and tropical birds in warm shades of grey," the pattern did not have a coordinating accent glaze.[11]

Prospects for sales seemed good, given the success of Eva's previous line for the company, the reasonable prices (a starter set for four—sixteen pieces—was $11.95 in white and $12.95 decorated), and Midhurst's aggressive marketing. But *Century* was not the runaway success of its predecessor.[12]

Given the sluggish sales, Midhurst and Hall asked Eva to modify the petal tips on the plates, which had proven difficult to manufacture and were often broken during shipping. The modified, round plates were announced in the summer of 1957, but greater orders were not forthcoming and they were not put

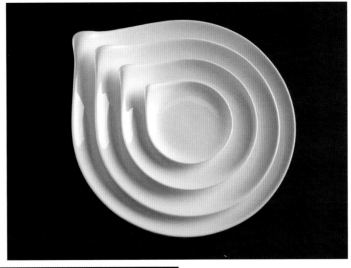

Overleaf
*Salt and pepper in Garden of Eden; covered dish,
fruit bowl, 1956. EZA.*

Left
*Large and medium platters, salad bowl, and gravy
boat, 1956. EZA.*

Right
Dinner, salad, and bread plates, ashtray, 1956. EZA.

Below
Teapot and pitcher, 1956. EZA.

Double vegetable, 1956. EZA.

into full production.[13] Flight, an abstract leaf pattern, was introduced at the same time, but that did not substantially boost sales and likely did not go to full production.[14]

Slow sales probably had less to do with Eva's designs than with changing trends in the tableware industry, rising labor costs, and greater domestic and foreign competition.[15] By 1956–1957, dinnerware in interesting, modern shapes was much more widely available than it had been when *Tomorrow's Classic* debuted in 1952.[16] Pottery industries in Europe and Japan had returned to more-or-less full capacity after several years of postwar recovery. Japanese manufacturers had not only the benefit of lower labor costs, but also considerable experience at producing high-quality dinnerware in porcelain—a harder, more durable, and in the opinion of many, more prestigious ware. Thus, they were able sell more durable porcelain dinnerware at prices only slightly higher than those for American-made earthenwares

such as *Century*. Domestic-made "casual china"—featuring heavier, vitrified ceramic bodies that were more resistant to cracking, chipping, and breakage—by manufacturers such as Iroquois China Company; Syracuse China; and Gladding, McBean, and Company (Franciscan) had also increased exponentially in popularity.[17]

Hall China continued to manufacture *Century* until 1962, when it stopped production of all its earthenware lines because of decreasing profitability.[18] In the mid-1980s, *Century* became one of Eva's best known lines, not least because a beautiful photograph of a stack of *Century* platters and bowls graced the cover of *Eva Zeisel: Designer for Industry* (1984).[19] Thereafter, *Century* took on iconic status for Zeisel enthusiasts. The rediscovery of the original Hall molds led to the *Lost Molds and Found Dinnerware* exhibition at Alfred College in 1999, and a limited edition reissue in a variety of colors of Eva's *Century* jug was undertaken under her supervision in 1997 by the Orange Chicken, a New York design shop and distributor (see Select Chronology).[20] From 2005 to 2012, several *Century* shapes produced by Royal Stafford Pottery, England, as part of the *Classic Century* line, retailed exclusively in the United States by the home furnishings company Crate & Barrel. A platter, a serving bowl, and the salt and pepper shakers from the *Century* line, in addition to many other pieces from the *Tomorrow's Classic* line, were available to consumers across the world through this new production until 2012.[21]

Rosenthal AG: *Eva*

1958
Horst Ullrich

Eva's passion for beauty was equally a passion for life.[1] Her parties, from Berlin in the 1930s to New York in the 1950s and 1960s, were gatherings of "friends bringing in new friends, all involved, devoted, explicit, concerned."[2] Inge Schönthal, a young photo-journalist, was first a guest of the Zeisels' during the winter of 1952–1953. She was introduced by Leo Frischauer, their dear friend.[3] He worked at the Stanford Greenburger literary agency that represented European writers and publishers in the U.S., including Heinrich M. Ledig-Rowohlt, the publisher of Hemingway's novels in Germany, and wanted Schönthal to meet someone "very special," meaning Eva.[4] Rowohlt had entrusted Schönthal with the task of convincing Hemingway to change translators, and she left New York for Cuba in February 1953. Hemingway invited her to stay for a couple of weeks at his beloved Finca Vigía, where she took the photograph of him that "made" her career.[5] Upon her return from Havana, she lived with Eva at the Riverside Drive apartment for several months and they became close friends.

In 1955, when Schönthal and Rowohlt introduced French artist-illustrator Raymond Peynet to Philip Rosenthal Jr., of the renowned German porcelain manufactory Rosenthal AG, Schönthal praised Eva so highly that Rosenthal was intrigued.[6] The stage was set for Eva's return to Germany.

Rosenthal joined the family firm in 1950, working in advertising, marketing, and sales. By 1958, he was the head of the company and within a few years had "set the firm on a course of aggressively avant-garde tableware.[7] When Schöenthal met him, he had just introduced *Form 2000* (1954), the final of four designs by Raymond Loewy Associates, a leading international design studio with headquarters in New York.[8] *Form E* was produced from 1952 to 1962; the next design by Loewy Associates for Rosenthal was distributed in the U.S. by Joseph Block.[9] *Form 95 Exquisit* (1953) appeared on the American market as "Continental China"; Richard Latham, a lead designer at Loewy Associates, remembered it as being "very popular with young people, modern minded, but with small wallets."[10]

In 1957, Eva was commissioned to work with company technicians on designs for dinner-table coffee and tea services. The line selected, *Eva*, was produced under Rosenthal's *Thomas* and *Johann Haviland* label.

Eva, like most of Rosenthal's lines, was manufactured with key pieces in different sizes (see Taxonomy). The number was incised at the bottom of the item, but was not always easy to read. The number three–size cup for hot chocolate and the number five–size cup for bouillon and milk coffee disappeared from Rosenthal's price lists in the 1960s and 1970s.[11] "Starter sets" for two or four, primarily designed for export to the U.S., were sold to the domestic market in the 1960s with moderate success.[12]

A few design changes were made. The rather unique design of interlocking ovals for securing the lid to the top of the coffee pot was abandoned in favor of the traditional round opening, which better fitted standard coffee filters.[13] The creamer was widened at the mouth for easier cleaning, terrines were altered to double as salad bowls, and the bottom of the sauce boat was remodeled to better match *Exquisit* plates and platters.[14] This suggests that the plates and platters—oval and round, with and without handles—likely were not designed by Eva, but were supplements from the *Exquisit* service. The same plates were also used in Tappio Wirkkala's *Finlandia* (1957).[15] The *Eva* eggcup also appeared with *Exquisit*, *Finlandia*, and Richard Scharrer's *Medallion* (1962), and is still in production as part of the *Vario* line. The design should be attributed to

Eva rather than Wirkkala or Latham, as the shape echoes that of her coffee cup, just as the salt and pepper shakers follow the shape of her coffee pot. The butter dish, however, should be considered another supplement from *Exquisit* rather than an original design by Eva.[16] Before royalties were introduced at the Rosenthal AG in 1961, designers were paid a fee based on the number of items designed. By accepting the fee, the designer waived all rights.

To be considered lucrative by the Rosenthal AG, a line had to run at least seven to eight years; and it would not be abandoned until all décor options were exhausted.[17] The company usually started a line with four décors and added one to three new decorations annually,

depending on how well a line was doing.[18] Applying this formula, *Eva*, which was in production for fourteen years, should have appeared with more than forty different surface patterns. More than that are documented, but their names and numbers have not all been identified (see Taxonomy).

The *Eva* line ran from 1958 to 1972. By the late 1950s and early 1960s, the Rosenthal AG's production was booming. *Eva* was in good company; the Raymond Loewy Associates lines were going strong.[19] Elsa Fisher-Treyden's *Fortuna* was in production (1956–1966) and Wirkkala's *Finlandia* had been launched in 1957.[20] Hans Theo Baumann's twelve years with the Rosenthal AG were just beginning (*Berlin* and *Bettina White* were first produced in 1959); Graf

Bernadotte's *Constanze* (1959) and Wiinblad's *Romanze* (1959–60) were at the beginning of very successful runs.[21]

Within this rather impressive gathering, Eva once again found herself in the very best of companies. Another suggested design for the Rosenthal AG (see chapter 26) never made it past the prototype stage.[22] Many decades later during her collaboration with James Klein and David Reid, however, Eva gave them a pitcher from the rejected Rosenthal commission to better understand how she liked to model spouts and handles (see chapter 19). In her collaboration with KleinReid, Eva took the beauty, vigor, and elegance of her Rosenthal designs into the twenty-first century.

Chapter 16

Hyalyn Porcelain Company: *HIGH FASHION*

1964

Debbie Deaver Townley

Hyalyn Porcelain, Inc., began manufacturing fine porcelain ware in 1946 in Hickory, North Carolina, under the ownership of H. Leslie Moody and his wife, Fran. The Moodys had the idea for a nationwide company that would produce fine porcelain at a time when the domestic market for well designed, serviceable dinnerware was picking up after World War II. The pottery produced at the Hyalyn works was a vitreous, nonporous ware containing silica, fired at 2700 degrees (a higher temperature than earthenware), making it oven-proof and chip resistant.[1]

When introduced in 1964, Eva's new line of dinnerware was named *High Fashion* (but was soon given the nickname *Z-Ware* because the bottom stamp read only "Z-[form number] USA" without the name of the manufacturer or of Eva). It was distributed by New York–based Richards Morgenthau and Company, also known as Raymor.[2] At the time, Eva was an established designer and Hyalyn was able to produce tableware that matched her exacting production standards. The twenty-five-piece line made references to hand-thrown studio pottery, the wavy edges of her 1926 vases, and to turned wooden wares.[3] The line featured standard place settings and a group of elegant serving pieces, such as a wine decanter; compotes; and large tureens, as well as tall, shapely salt and pepper shakers and a pepper mill. This array of serving pieces was expanded

when Eva, as she had done for certain other lines, designed some of the lids to serve double-duty as small serving plates when turned upside-down on their flat handles (see chapter 12). The pieces were produced in high-gloss glazes in four colors: Olive, Oxblood, Gold, and Mottled Taupe.[4] Pieces in matte glazes were also produced in Black and White, possibly without Eva's knowledge.[5]

Eva reworked elements from several earlier designs. The "waisted" designs of the wine bottle and peppermill, for instance, were reminiscent of the candlesticks she designed for Salisbury Artisans (see chapter 10). The pitchers and coffee pots were similar to forms designed, but not produced, for Mancioli (Italy) in 1958 (see chapter 26), and the dinner plates had an "amusing, navel-like depression at the center" similar to the Mancioli space-divider elements.[6]

At some point, the size of the dimple on the plates was adjusted and a larger, flatter center surface was created, making for a more abrupt transition between the flat center and edge of the plate so the plates stacked more easily. Both the original and redesigned plates were marked Z29, but only the redesigned ones had an additional Eva Zeisel signature mark.[7] Curvaceous and sturdy finials topped some of the pieces. Eva, who took great care with such details, later stated: "You must imagine how handles feel and how pots bal-

ance in your hand before they exist, and the shape of the flow of the fluid continuing the line of the spout, and the shape of the plate or handle so that it does not slip out of your hand when you pick it up."[8] The plates and accompanying serving pieces, with their reflective glazes, meld together in tone as well as in form, encouraging one to create a table setting that captures the joie de vivre of Eva's designs. It is easy to imagine the young moderns of the era using it for entertaining at casual buffet dinners—high fashion, indeed!

Reissues

In 1997, some of the most interesting of the Hyalyn designs were re-created for the Orange Chicken gallery in New York by Brett Bortner: the footed bowl/compote, Z2B (eight-and-a-half inches high, nine inches in diameter) and the wavy bowl, a smaller version of Z6 (three inches high, eight-and-a-half inches in diameter), in all black or in black with a red or white interior. These same items were made by World of Ceramics, North Carolina, in black, blue, and white (bottom stamped EZ97) and sold at the Brooklyn Museum gift shop. In 1997, a signed version of the seven-and-a-half-inch plate was created in wood by Universal Woodwork for the Orange Chicken.

Overleaf
Vegetable bowl and wine bottle/vase in Oxblood, 1964. EZA.

Top Left
Tureen in Oxblood, footed tureen in Gold, footed dish in Olive, 1964. EZA.

Top Right
Pepper and salt in Gold, pitcher in Oxblood, 1964. EZA, HUC.

Chapter 17

Zsolnay Porcelain Manufactory

1984
Tom Tredway

In 1983, Eva returned to the Hungarian People's Republic at a time of "liberalization" within the Eastern Bloc countries. As a senior fellow funded by the U.S. government's National Endowment for the Arts, she received a $15,000 grant to "design and research architectural decorative elements and execute original designs for dinnerware, china, and other consumer goods in preparation for an exhibition."[1] She hoped to use the grant to return to the cities and factories where she had worked during the interwar years, giving her the opportunity to revisit her homeland for the first time in over half a century.[2] Although she had not worked for the famous Zsolnay Porcelain Manufactory in Pécs, Eva had such a distinguished reputation that the Fine Art Executive Company (Artex), the Hungarian state-controlled body that oversaw artistic commercial production, put her in contact with the factory.[3]

Founded in 1853, Zsolnay enjoyed a considerable international reputation by 1900. Eva recalled the company's products as "seen everywhere in Budapest" when she was a child.[4] The company was nationalized in 1948 and became part of the National Company for Fine Ceramics under the name Pécs Porcelain Manufactory between 1963 and 1974. It reclaimed the right to use the Zsolnay name in 1974, and in 1982, it regained its independence as part of a larger effort to combat economic stagnation and isolation by expanding market forces within the wider planned economy of Hungary.[5] The factory increased production of decorative wares; created retail distribution networks to supply goods to the provinces; and developed export markets in Europe, Asia, and the Middle East.[6] A parallel loosening of artistic restrictions, along with a renewed interest at Zsolnay in rejuvenating past techniques and forms led by chief technician István Kovács, brought about a new creative energy at the company.[7]

Eva's designs for Zsolnay reveal a mix of retrospection and new ideas. The latter are particularly evident in the iridescent eosin glazes she developed with Peter Hesz, a master glazer at the Zsolnay factory, based on the famous glazes first produced by the company in 1893.[8] The technology was new to Eva, but she learned quickly from her excellent teacher and collaborator, producing glazes that created beautiful, abstract, and fluid surfaces to complement the forms they adorned. It often took several different, complex glazes to achieve the rich visual effects and textures Eva wanted.

The process began with a glossy, high-fired ground glaze with airbrushed or painted eosin glaze applied over it, resulting in a glossy finish; acid etching produced surfaces with a more satin-like finish.[9] In some cases, further layers of trickling glazes were applied over the first eosin glaze to produce multicolored, often mottled, iridescent surfaces.[10] Such layered glazes involved not just multiple firings but also the technically challenging reduction firings needed to activate the glazes. Among the most admired glazes are those that included colors such as gold or a wonderfully deep lapis lazuli.

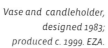

Vase and candleholder, designed 1983; produced c. 1999. EZA.

Overleaf
Small and large fig vases, designed 1983; produced 1984. EZA.

Left
Apples and gourd jar, designed 1983; produced c. 1999. EZA.

The Zsolnay forms that related most closely to Eva's earlier work included the flask-form vases with circular impressions in the center, which were partially derived from the prototypes made in 1958 for modular room dividers for Mancioli Pottery (see chapter 26), the finials of a dinnerware prototype for Rosenthal in 1958 (see chapter 26), and her plates for Hyalyn in 1964 (see chapter 16).

Another example of Eva's retrospective mood can be found in the squat vases which, with their scalloped edges and pinched indentations, are reminiscent of Eva's refrigerator pitchers for Hall (see chapter 13) and some of her early handmade and home-fired "Crinkle" planters and dishes from around 1926. The low, rounded candlesticks recalled several of Eva's dinnerware designs, most evocatively the teapot, creamer, and sugar bowl for Riverside (see chapter 7), a key difference being that Eva abandoned the fully rounded bottoms of the earlier pieces, which could rock on their bases without tipping, because the candlesticks demanded a flat bottom for obvious safety reasons.

After her work at Zsolnay, she continued to return to round, pillowy forms, as in her designs for KleinReid's Nesting Pillow Vases (see chapter 19). Eva's love of fruits and fruit forms, evident throughout her career, can be seen in a group of boxes designed for Zsolnay in the form of apples and pears. One of the most strikingly original pieces she designed while at the Zsolnay factory was a thrown and hand-shaped fig vase; its abstract, organic form with deep scallops harkened back in a

general way to the curvilinear Art Nouveau forms popular in Europe at the turn of the twentieth century, forms closely associated with Zsolnay at the height of its fame.

In 1984, Zsolnay produced some of Eva's designs and offered them for sale, but it is notknown how many objects were produced. It is likely that only a few were made.[11] Eva retained ownership of her designs and kept several pieces, some of which she donated to museum collections.[12]

Always keen to find manufacturers for pieces made from her designs, in 1998 Eva took several Zsolnay prototypes to Totem Design, a gallery in Tribeca, lower Manhattan, that had been established a year earlier by David Shearer.[13] Totem offered a variety of Eva's Zsolnay designs for sale, including the flask vase (sometimes referred to as the belly button vase). The vase caught the eye of Don Joint of the Orange Chicken, another Tribeca gallery. Joint, familiar with Eva's earlier work, was thrilled to learn that she was alive and working.[14] He agreed to manufacture and market her Zsolnay designs, which remained unchanged and were manufactured using the original molds.[15]

Joint and Eva carefully reviewed the prototypes and decided that two were unsuitable for contemporary production: the tall pitcher, due to concerns over the strength and stability of the handle, and the apple box, because of its poorly fitting lid and questionable sales potential.[16] Zsolnay agreed to begin producing Eva's designs again only after Joint offered to pay the factory in cash upfront, which he

did on his first of six visits beginning in 1998; thereafter, funds were wired to Zsolnay in advance of any orders.[17]

Production issues plagued the project from the beginning, with the larger pieces proving particularly troublesome. Zsolnay estimated that it had only a one-in-six success rate with those due to the thinness of the clay body and, more importantly, difficulty with the evenness of the glazes, likely due to the complex and intricate reduction firings needed for the eosin overglaze to achieve its luster. The fig vases proved particularly daunting to execute. After an initial order of twelve, only ten of which arrived at the gallery intact, the factory claimed it could no longer produce the fig vase.[18] This initial order indicates the small size of the production runs; less than forty examples of each piece were made, with the exception of the candlesticks, which had slightly higher runs in the 100–200 range.[19]

Production of Eva's designs for Zsolnay was well underway by early 1999 and in April of that year, the Orange Chicken opened its new fifteen-hundred-square-foot Eva Zeisel showroom.[20] By the end of 2000, however, Eva severed her relationship with the Orange Chicken and reestablished sole control of her Zsolnay designs, although the gallery retained its stock of Zsolnay pieces. The events of September 11, 2001, forced the gallery to close and to put much of its stock into storage. These stored items later formed the core of an exhibition, *Eva Zeisel: The Shape of Life*, at the Erie Art Museum in 2009.[21]

Chapter 18

International China Company: *PINNACLE*

1985

Pat Moore

The idea that Eva might design a line of dinnerware in vitreous stoneware (hard, shiny, nonporous) for the International China Company began with a golf-course conversation in 1985 between Charles LaReau, the company's executive vice president, and Eva's lawyer, Lee Epstein.[1] International China was the U.S. marketing arm for stoneware and bone china dinnerware produced in Japan at the Yamaka Shoten factory in Toki City, a center for stoneware production for over thirteen hundred years.[2]

By 1985, International China was well-known for marketing fashionable stoneware dinnerware that was sold in the United States to the housewares departments of large stores and to discount stores at mid-market prices, generally as decorated twenty-piece boxed sets and completer sets. Few accessories, if any, accompanied the sets unless the line was a high-volume top seller.[3]

LaReau had great respect for Eva's work and was enthusiastic about the possibility of her working for the company. While International China had commissioned several well-known designers to create patterns for their dishes, this was the first (and possibly only) commission to an outside designer for a shape.[4] This was also the first time that International China produced and marketed a design in small quantities and retailed it exclusively through one store, namely Bloomingdale's, a leading department store in New York City.[5]

Eva visited the company's New York showroom and offices at 41 Madison Avenue, where she met with Maureen Manton (now O'Gorman), the senior vice president of new product marketing planning and development.[6] Eva was excited to be working in vitreous semi-porcelain stoneware, a popular material for ceramic housewares at that time. It is fired at a high temperature until hard, dense, and nonporous. Rather gray in color, it does not chip easily, therefore allowing straight edges to be used in production, as they will survive shipping and heavy use. When fired with a clear glaze, vitreous stoneware's light grayish-cream color takes on a softer, more delicate appearance.

The designs for what became known as *Pinnacle* successfully blended curves and straight edges, achieving elegant forms in the process. This blending is most pronounced in the cross-section of the covered casserole

and the rounded teapot. These sturdy designs demonstrate Eva's understanding of, and respect for, the qualities of the material and the shapes of the individual pieces.

Three decal patterns were shown when the line was presented to store representatives by International China, but only an undecorated set in a white glaze was offered to the public. The main set was a twenty-piece starter service, with the salt and pepper shakers sold separately as a set and other accessory items also sold individually.[7]

Pinnacle debuted to considerable fanfare at Bloomingdale's, nestled in colorful boxes that highlighted the elegance of the shapes. Although the line sold fairly well, it was discontinued after less than a year because it had not attained the volume of sales the company deemed necessary for profitability.[8]

In 2006, a *Pinnacle* tea set (consisting of mugs redesigned by Eva to complement the teapot, sugar bowl, and creamer from the original line) was reissued in black and white by Chantal of Texas. In 2009 and 2010, colored versions of the mugs were released (see Taxonomy).[9]

Left Page
Sugar, teapot, cup , saucer, and creamer, 1985. EZA.

Above
Vegetable bowl, covered casserole, salt and pepper, soup/cereal bowl, and dinner plate, 1985. EZA.

Chapter 19

KleinReid

1999
Horst Ullrich

One of Eva's most productive relationships of the 1990s and 2000s was with KleinReid, a company established by James Klein and David Reid. Like Eva, the two men had studied fine art (at the University of Akron) before focusing on ceramics.[1] In 1993, they moved to New York City and established their studio workshop in Williamsburg, Brooklyn. By 1999, they produced approximately two thousand handmade pieces of pottery each month, which were sold in two hundred stores worldwide.[2] As William Hamilton wrote in the *New York Times*, "KleinReid's modern-limbed, matte-glazed pottery business, with a net income (1999) of $240,000, represents a hairline crack in the $8 billion ceramic housewares industry. But as an artist-run indie alternative, it is helping to introduce new options to the standard model for commercial manufacture, thanks also to a young, new audience developing for contemporary domestic design."[3]

They met Eva through Margaret Carney, then director of the International Museum of Ceramic Art at Alfred University and curator of the *Lost Molds and Found Dinnerware* exhibit.[4] Remembering that Klein was a huge fan of Eva's work, she asked if he wanted to meet her. What began as an excuse for the two men to spend time with Eva turned into a lifelong friendship. In early May of 1999, they had lunch with Eva and took a few pieces of their work to show her. "This is very serious," she would comment from time to time, feeling the shapes, materials, and finishes. Recognizing that these young men were running their studio as a small factory, she was delighted when they proposed collaborating. Although some of her earlier designs were then being reissued by several companies, KleinReid wanted to create something entirely new with their idol.

A few days later, they telephoned to set up an appointment. Eva said, "What are you doing now? Come over!" They got to her house that night by eight and were still there at one-thirty in the morning. "It was a magical night," Klein stated: "It was the spike of my life. . . . It was very, very special."[5] As they left, Eva said: "I'm going to the country tomorrow morning, why don't you come up?" They accompanied her to New City, and the three spent much of the day cutting paper silhouettes. The partners wanted to create vases and asked Eva to add some "femininity" to the design. They picked one of the paper

shapes and, in order to create "a little family," they cut out what would be the negative space next to it, and then the negative space next to that.[6] These eventually became the tall vase, the medium vase, and the bud vase.

They played with the scale and retraced the shapes on paper. Eva then reworked the shapes so that each would look beautiful on its own. She spent a long time considering the footprints of the three vases and how they clustered next to each other. The second set of vases, the *Pillow Stack Vases*, began with the large one at the bottom, followed by the "baby" on top; the pillow in the middle was last. Glazes were developed for the vases in matte Ivory and a glossy Three Tone Sepia, but only a few were made before the Three Tone Sepia glaze was discontinued. Cobalt blue was suggested but dismissed because of its high production cost. In subsequent years, mouth-blown crystal versions of the *Upright Vases* were added in various vibrant colors.[7] Once the main decisions were made, things moved fast: shapes were turned in May, models were made in June and approved by Eva at the end of the month, and the *Eva Collection* of six vessels premiered in August. It was a great success.

In 2002, after three years of careful promotion and continuing work on their own lines, Klein and Reid decided to do another project with Eva. They knew Eva loved to design dinnerware and suggested a tea set and a pair of pitchers as their next endeavor. Eva gave them two prototypes she had in her studio—a Rosenthal pitcher from 1957 and a small Mancioli pitcher from 1958—so they could study them and understand how to model the

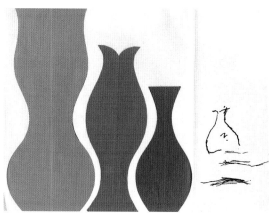

spout and handle. They worked on the pitchers in the spring and on the tea set in the fall. According to Reid, "It was so easy doing the pitcher and the tea set. It was like everybody knew how it should be."[8] Eva fractured her hip the week the models were finished but insisted they be brought to the hospital.

In 2005, the three collaborators embarked on yet another adventure. KleinReid was introducing a series of screen prints and the partners wanted to do one with Eva. They had noted the Baroque references in Eva's work, especially in her table designs and her letterhead. "I always thought of her as the big Modernist. She is, of course, in a way, but people know her dinnerware, and it looks the way it does because it has to function. That's important to her. I never realized she has this Baroque free premodern love for decoration," said Klein.[9]

Eva designed the pattern by cutting out paper shapes: a background color, and then a first shape, and then two successive shapes.[10] Changing one layer slightly meant they had to cut it out again and change all the other layers as well. It took a very long time to get it right. They worked on four prints simultaneously, chose one, but finally selected two. "Does someone need this?" Eva would ask. "Who is going to buy them? Where would you sell them?" She need not have worried; the prints sold well.[11] A second set of four prints, *Lovers' Suite*, came in an edition of fifty and sold out in ten days.[12] The third series was an edition of three hundred prints, called *Lovers' Suite II*. Eva signed them all.

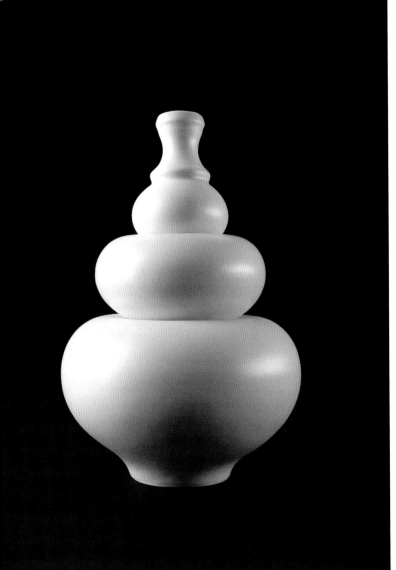

Chapter 20

Nambé

1999

Jim Corlett

Left Page
Accent lamps, 2006. EZA.

Above Left
PEEK-A-BOO VASE and *PEEK-A-BOO ROSE BOWL, 1999.*
EZA.

Left
*EDEN creamer, sugar, pasta bowl, plate, salt and
pepper, 2008; and wine glass, 2004. EZA.*

The Nambé company was founded in 1953
when Pauline Platt Cable and Peter Cable of
Winkler Mills Craftsmen, a metalwork company producing cookware and giftware in the
village of Nambé, near Santa Fe, formed a
partnership with Martin Eden, the metallur-
gist who invented a thermal-retentive eight-
metal alloy named Nambé.[1] When sand-cast,
cooled, and polished (using up to seventeen
different processes), the material takes on a
high luster and the reflective qualities of silver, but does not tarnish.

In 1995, Bob Borden, the company's vice
president of creative design, introduced the
Nambé Studio line (featuring a group of objects
by industrial designer Karim Rashid) in order
to promote a new process: the vertical tooling of pieces made from aluminum blocks.[2]
Rashid, who referred to Eva as his "surrogate
design mother and idol of sensual form,"[3]
was influenced by her biomorphic forms
when creating what he called technomorphic
forms.[4] Borden contacted Eva in 1998, having learned about her from Rashid. When
they met, he gave Eva some of the Nambé
alloy so that she could feel the material. Eva
was intrigued, and trusting both Rashid and
Borden, she agreed to work for the company.[5]

The items produced were close interpreta-
tions of Eva's ceramic platter and coupe bowls
from the *Tomorrow's Classic* line (see chapter
11).[6] In 1999, Nambé produced a sand-cast
mini-series of four bowls and two platters
marked with Eva's name, with proportions
close to those of the originals. Nambé also
produced the curvaceous salt and pepper
shakers in 1999, followed in 2000 by an eight-
inch vase known as the *Double Globe* and other
items that resembled Eva's 1964 gourd shape
for Hyalyn (chapter 16).

A trio of vases that went into production
in 2000—*Freedom, Unity,* and *Harmony*—epito-

mized Eva's observation that "beauty, harmony,
loveliness, elegance and usefulness. . . should
be what designers strive for today in the
twenty-first century."[7] A candlestick/vase was
also produced that year; the KIeinReid *Eva* series of *Upright Vases* that was to come later featured an extension of this shape (see chapter
19). Nambé introduced the *Eden* dinnerware in
2008, featuring designs by Eva in both metal
and ceramic, which included candlesticks
and metal serving trays (see Taxonomy).

Partly because Nambé was a subsidiary of
the Hillenbrand/Batesville Casket Company,
Eva also designed a twelve-inch funerary urn
called *Bloom.* A variation on the *Double Globe*
design, it featured a compartment in the bottom half with a screw-lid on the bottom.

Finally and fittingly, Eva designed the
Essence urn and selected it as the final resting
place for her own remains.

Above Left
HARMONY Vase, 1999.
EZA.

Above Center
UNITY VASE, 1999. EZA.

Above Right
FREEDOM VASE, 1999.
EZA.

Left
ESSENCE URN, 2007. EZA.

Chapter 21

Lomonosov Porcelain Factory: *TALISMAN*

2004
Karen L. Kettering

The post-Soviet period was a tumultuous one for the former Lomonosov State Porcelain Factory (see Part One), which had since its foundation in 1744 fulfilled orders either for the imperial court or the Soviet government.[1] When the factory was privatized in 2000, a group of U.S. investors, including the firm Kohlberg, Kravis, and Roberts, acquired a large stake in the factory. When contacted by one of their representatives, I suggested that they speak with Eva, the only living designer who had not only worked at the factory but was also familiar with the challenges facing designers and craftspeople suddenly forced to compete on the international market. The American investors underwrote the cost of sending a group of eleven of the factory's most senior designers and artists to visit collections and designers in New York, including Eva, who, with family members, hosted them at her studio and home in New City.[2] Members of that group invited Eva and her family to travel to St. Petersburg in July 2000 so that she could participate in the factory's annual "Artistic Council" (*Khudozhestvennyi sovet*) in which the previous year's designs were considered and critiqued.

During this trip, she met an extraordinarily talented young model maker, Georgy Bogdevich, with whom she began work on a teacup that was to serve as the basis for a new service to be called *Talisman*, in honor of her granddaughter who had accompanied her on the trip to Russia. Raised in a family of naval and ship designers who had made major contributions to the development of Soviet naval design, Bogdevich dropped out of Leningrad's prestigious Naval Architecture Institute before finding his way to the Lomonosov factory. Eva considered Bogdevich to be the most talented model maker with whom she had ever worked (see Part One), and it was decided they would collaborate on a new set of dinnerware in Lomonosov's distinctive bone china (an unusually thin and translucent porcelain introduced at the factory in 1969 and a material with which Eva had never worked).[3] At first they collaborated via mail, but it was eventually decided that Bogdevich would spend the summer of 2002 at Eva's home and studio, slowly perfecting the plaster models for the new service.[4]

Eva's design takes full advantage of the bone china's unique characteristics: the "arms" of the sugar bowl shoot upwards in a joyful fashion that demonstrates their startling translucence. Celebrants at her ninety-seventh birthday party gasped in astonishment when the designer held the prototypes up to a strong light and they became almost transparent. The material also allows for details to be rendered with an unparalleled delicacy: the top of the lid is a small, perfectly rendered belly button form recalling her designs at Mancioli and Zsolnay (see chapters 26 and 17). This delicacy and perfection might seem cold were it not for the inclusion of a particular Russian clay in the formula that gives the porcelain a warm, sunny tone. The material can easily sag during firing, so the participation of Bogdevich, who had worked with the factory's formula for this material for several years, was essential to creating a design that could be successfully fired.

The tea service is a compendium of some of the most distinctive elements of Eva's earlier designs and important influences throughout her career. The teapot's ovoid body, and the swelling forms of the creamer and sugar bowl, are reminiscent of the familiar form of the feminine midriff used in her earlier designs for Zsolnay and Mancioli. The handle is molded as a continuation of the body and, like the teacup, arches high above the lid in a manner reminiscent of Empire and Biedermeier period ceramics and closely related to her Hyalyn design (see chapter 16). The handle's high arc ends in a soft tip that is molded to appear to lie against the body of the teapot rather than disappearing or being reintegrated into it. At the top of the teapot opposite the handle, the edge has been extended and curves outward in a manner that echoes the curved lip of the cup and the extended, uplifted "arms" of the sugar bowl.

The service's three oval plates (for bread and butter, salad, and dinner), as well as the saucer, repeat the same basic design in increasingly larger sizes: the relatively heavy body of the base and foot narrow into thin walls that curl under slightly at the left and right ends. This allows the plates to be stacked to form a sculptural design, a feature of Eva's serving pieces for the *Century* line for Hall China (see chapter 14). Unfortunately, the plates proved difficult to pack for commercial shipping, and it was ultimately decided that the design would be produced as a tea and coffee service rather than as a full dinner service. After four years of work, the *Talisman*

service was released in 2004. The expense of producing such delicate and difficult forms was reflected in the price, originally set at $10,000 for the service. As of 2012, it was still in production and could be purchased in the factory's shops in the newly fashionable districts of Moscow and St. Petersburg, where luxury goods are sold.[5] While *Talisman* is important as an example of Eva's continuing design practice, as well as her first foray into working with bone china, its joyful forms, developed in the city in which she had long been imprisoned, seem to symbolize the healing of an old wound. It is fitting that it is named for one of her grandchildren—another of her creative legacies—the existence of whom must have seemed unimaginable as she sat in her prison cell, only a few miles from the factory to which she would return in 2000.

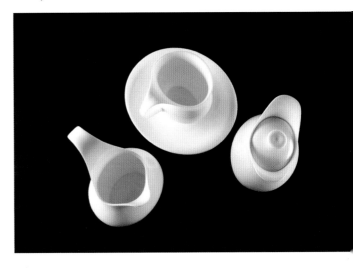

Left Page
Sugar, creamer, dessert plate, teapot, cup and saucer, 2004. EZA.

Above
Creamer, cup, saucer, and sugar, 2004. EZA.

Chapter 22

Royal Stafford: *One-O-One*

2008

Mary Whitman Davis

The first design for the *One-O-One* dinnerware set was drawn by Eva in the early spring of 2005. It is the only dinnerware set that Eva designed without a commission in hand. She had become an industrial designer instead of a painter at least partially to avoid the fate of the starving artist. Olivia Barry, Eva's longtime assistant, recalls that she and Eva were sitting in the garden of Eva's Rockland County house on an extraordinarily beautiful spring day. They were discussing Eva's work and realized that there was no new commission in the pipeline. Eva thought for a moment, turned to Olivia, and said, "Let's design a new set of dinnerware!"[1] Eva began designing the new line that day.

The first piece was a teapot. "Once she got the teapot's shape—with a new line, a new curve," recalled Olivia, "so many other things could be created from it."[2] A teacup, saucer, creamer, and covered sugar bowl followed. The teapot's characteristic high swooping handle and its swollen midsection recur throughout the line. Although there was no commission, Eva hoped that Royal Stafford would be interested, not least because everyone involved with her previous project for the company had been so pleased with *Classic Century* (chapter 14). Furthermore, Bloomingdale's department store had been pressing Norman Tempest, the managing director of Royal Stafford, for an Eva Zeisel "exclusive."

After seeing the finished drawings, Tempest agreed to manufacture the line and a contract was signed in April 2006. The line was to be called "Centennial" to coincide with Eva's upcoming hundredth birthday.

According to the production log kept by Royal Stafford, the drawings for "Centennial" were completed in July.[3] Eva had hired her favorite model maker, Georgy Bogdevich (with whom she had worked at Lomonosov), to execute the plaster-of-paris models that were required for production, and exchanges continued back and forth between Rockland County, New York and Stoke-on-Trent in England through the summer and into the fall. Some changes were made during the production process. Bloomingdale's requested that the oval plates be redesigned as round ones.[4] This may have been intended to further differentiate them from *Classic Century*'s oval plates, as both lines of dishes were made using the identical clay body.[5] Tempest suggested that a large bowl be added, naming it the *Rockland*

bowl after the site of Eva's inspiration in Rockland County.

Tempest suggested a gravy boat, which Eva drew as a curve executed in three dimensions. It became Eva's favorite piece in that line.[6] The curves of the cereal bowl had to be adjusted many times to match Eva's intentions. Eva wanted a huge teapot, far larger than any standard size, but Tempest insisted that it be remodeled as a standard thirty-ounce vessel.[7] Eva retained the "giant" version and displayed it at her country house.[8]

When Eva turned one hundred years old in November 2006, "Centennial" was not yet in production. As revisions continued over the course of the following year, the line was rechristened *One-O-One* in anticipation of Eva's 101st birthday. The dishes that Tempest described as "gorgeous shapes" debuted at Bloomingdale's in January of 2008. Photographs of the smooth, creamy off-white dishes appeared in *bHome*, Bloomingdale's home-fashion catalogue, and in a full-page four-color advertisement in the *New York Times*.[9] Six of the soon-to-be iconic *Rockland Bowl*, signed by Eva, were made available to special customers through Bloomingdale's *Little Brown Book*.[10]

The original line comprised a dinner plate, salad plate, large cup and saucer, serving plate, gravy boat, cream and sugar containers, salt and pepper shakers, the teapot, and the *Rockland* bowl. At Bloomingdale's' request, Eva designed two additional pieces in late 2008— a pair of vases, one of which Eva referred to as "the vase with two exits."[11]

When they are seen together, Eva's concept of individual dishes as "family members" could not be clearer. The curves on one piece echo the curves on the others; the teapot, sugar

bowl, creamer, cup, and salt and pepper shakers resemble one another like siblings, all of whom possess similarly rounded midsections. The forms are varied yet similar, snuggle sensuously together, and engage in lively dialogue. The *One-O-One* dishes are the spectacular and tangible result of Eva's exclamation on that glorious spring day in her ninety-ninth year: "Let's design a new set of dinnerware!"

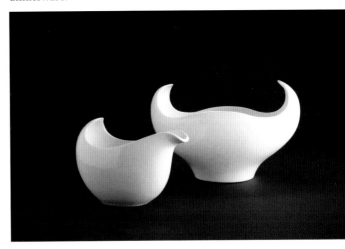

Left Page
Bud vase and vase with two exits, 2008. EZA.

Above
Gravy boat and Rockland Bowl, *2008. EZA.*

Bottom
Salt and pepper, sugar, teapot, cup, saucer, large prototype teapot, and creamer, 2008. EZA.

Chapter 23

Design Within Reach: *GRANIT COLLECTION*

2009
Tom Tredway

While working at Zsolnay in 1983, Eva received an invitation from the director of the Kispester-Granit Pottery to work there, thus giving her the opportunity to revisit the first manufactory to serially- and mass-produce her designs.[1] Working in the factory in the summer of 1983, she designed tableware, known as the *Ufo* line at Kispester-Granit, along with table fountains and other giftware. Photographs taken at the time indicate that Eva followed her familiar work process, from sketches to refining three-dimensional models. One photograph shows the progression as Eva works with a cut paper model and a model of the body of the teapot, presumably in plaster or plastiscene, in order to determine, or at least experiment with, the optimum placement of the handle.[2] Another shows Eva and a member of the Kispester-Granit staff using three-dimensional prototypes to further refine the relationship between the teapot body and the handle.

Eva discussed her return to the factory in almost romantic terms, noting in 1984: "One of the pleasures of pottery is the sound of the fired piece. Walking through the Kispester-Granit factory last summer, I noticed the musical sound of its fired clay, sounding like church bells combined with the tinkling of small chimes."[3] Her return may have been tinged with nostalgia, yet she continued to experiment. Her design thinking on this project was in line with her other work in the 1980s, which often involved creatively rethinking and reworking forms and technical problems that had engaged her in earlier years. Eva's sketches, together with the photographs and her comments on this project, indicate that she was playing with familiar forms such as circles, spheres, and other simple curved geometric shapes, by distorting and elongating them to great effect, as in the quirky teapot.

Eva described her techniques for developing form as similar to blowing up a balloon and then manipulating it; punching it down as in the teapot form for Riverside Ceramic (see chapter 7) or squeezing the air out of the middle to form a waistline, as in her candlesticks for Salisbury Artisans (see chapter 10) and her ochre and green vase for Kispester-Granit in 1926.[4] This approach is evident in the *Ufo* line, especially the teapot, sugar and creamer, and salt and pepper shakers. In all of these objects, Eva appears to be starting

Overleaf
Cup, saucer, creamer, teapot, and sugar, 2009. EZA.

Right Page
Salt & pepper, 2009. EZA.

Below Left
Prototype teapot, pitcher, creamer, sugar, demitasse, cup, saucer, and mug, Kispester-Granit, c. 1983. Photograph from EZA.

Bottom
Prototype teapot, pitcher, creamer, sugar, demitasse cups and saucers, Kispester-Granit, c. 1983. Photograph from EZA.

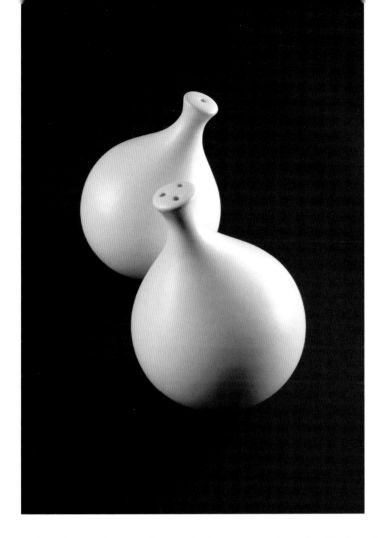

with a sphere and then pulling on the form to create an elongated drop, like an inflated balloon pulled from its neck. The latter form is then placed on its side to create the teapot, with the narrow point forming the spout (not altogether unlike her 1951 teapot for Salisbury Artisans; see chapter 10).

The influence of her earliest work, including her designs for Kispester around 1926, is subtly evident in this line in both the forms and glazes. A vase with fish decoration designed by Eva for Kispester in the 1920s has curves similar to the bowl of the teacup, but the form of the latter is more squat. The looped handle could be a reference to the handles of her 1926 tea service with birds and flora.[5]

For many of the pieces in this line, Eva also drew upon forms which had occupied her thoughts in the 1950s and 1960s. The knobs on the lids of the teapot and sugar bowl recall designs for Rosenthal (see chapter 26) and Hyalyn (see chapter 16), as well as the Mancioli room divider (see chapter 26). The creamer is similar to one she designed for Hyalyn and the salt and pepper shakers were designed to rest on the table at a slight

angle, rather like her salt and pepper shakers for the *Town and Country* line (see chapter 6). Features of the salad plate, dinner plate, and bowl include the lack of a shoulder, a deep well, and a slight depression in the center with a hint of her belly button form that echoes the knobs found on this line.

Though widely exhibited as prototypes (particularly through the *Designer for Industry* exhibition of 1984), Kispester-Granit never put this line into production, at least in part because Eva felt the pieces did not meet her high-quality standards.[6] A letter in Eva's archive suggests that in 1996, Mancioli offered to produce some of the designs that Eva had created for Kispester-Granit; she discussed transferring the models and molds from Hungary to Italy, and seemed excited by the possibility of applying Mancioli glazes to these forms.[7] The letter also mentioned that she had shown samples of the line to an interested buyer at the Museum of Modern Art Store. Given that Eva described the samples as of "unequal and sloppy quality," she was most likely referring to the original prototypes from 1983.[8] Although nothing came of these discussions, it demonstrates Eva's

desire to see her 1983 work at Kispester-Granit produced to high standards for the contemporary market, as well as the growing commercial interest in her earlier work in the 1990s.

In 2009, the Design Within Reach (DWR) company launched the *Granit Collection* dinnerware, reviving some of Eva's 1983 designs for Kispester-Granit. Eva's daughter contacted the founder of the company to discuss the possibility of DWR producing Eva's tubular metal chair.[9] Instead, Eva began working closely with the DWR Design Studio to refine the *Ufo* line, paying particular attention to the quality of the models, which took some time to perfect.[10] The shapes and forms of the *Granit* line remained very similar to their earlier prototypes, but some of the proportions were slightly altered: the bowls of the new sugar and creamer seem to be slightly more full and squat than their predecessors, for example, and the angle of the spout on the creamer is much lower in the DWR version than in the Kispester-Granit prototypes. The overall effect of the forms remains largely unchanged and they maintain their coherence as a group. As Eva noted, "I like the way the very thin, hard edges of the plates change into a soft, inviting belly button . . . All the pieces together make a very nice family."[11] The most striking difference between the pieces exhibited in 1984 and those produced beginning in 2009 is in the glaze. DWR replaced the 1983 dark, mottled semi-matte glaze with a matte white finish; Eva was interested in using colored glazes, but DWR insisted that the line was produced ony in white.[12]

DWR featured images of Eva prominently in advertisements, including photographs of her at Kispester-Granit in 1983 and recent photographs of her interacting with the *Granit* line (beautifully shot by Jim Bastardo).[13] The company has had some trouble keeping the line in production—their Chinese manufacturer went bankrupt—but is planning to continue to produce the *Granit Collection*.[14]

Glass

Rey Ledda

Although Eva's legacy will primarily be considered in terms of her tremendous output as a ceramic designer, her designs for wood, metal, plastic, and glass illustrate the singularity of her vision. They underscore not only her sensitivity to the nuances of different media, but also her disciplined approach to the challenges of mass production and her entrepreneurial eye for the marketing of such products.

Eva had no formal training in glassmaking.[1] Her first foray into designing for glass seems to have been in the USSR in the mid-1930s, where she designed some perfume bottles that never went into production (see chapter 3). About a decade later, Eva again designed perfume bottles when commissioned by two of the leading beauty products companies in the U.S., Richard Hudnut and Charles of the Ritz.[2] They were also not produced.

Eva's main glass commissions in the U.S. were for the Federal Tool Corporation, Bryce Brothers, A. H. Heisey, and Federal Glass Company, but she also created designs for glass for other companies between 1995 and 2012.

FEDERAL TOOL CORPORATION: GLASS JUGS (1947)

A letter dated May 9, 1947, from the Federal Tool Corporation (Chicago) to Eva acknowledged the successful preview of a new product: "It looks very fine, and you will be happy to know that the buyers . . . were very complimentary on it."[3]

The comments refer to a family of pressed glass jugs. The glass parts were manufactured by the Hazel Atlas Company, and the plastic tops that functioned as dispensers, shakers, or grinders were produced by the Federal Tool Corporation. Eva later recalled, "At Federal Glass, a huge machine made one glass per second." She was sent to the factory to learn how the machine worked: "It turned around, put molten glass into the form, the next machine pressed it into the form, still molten, and other steps of production, until finally the glass was cold."[4]

The jugs thus produced are distinguished by a bulbous body encircled by a pressed ribbon pattern (or "ski tracks"). They came in three different sizes (eight, fourteen, and thirty-two ounces) and were marked on the bottom.[5]

Although quite ubiquitous in midcentury homes and restaurants, these glass jugs are some of Eva's lesser known designs.

BRYCE BROTHERS: *Silhouette* (1952)

In the midst of the hectic publicity campaign introducing the Hallcraft *Tomorrow's Classic* line in 1952, Eva took time to introduce a new set of glassware that she had designed for Bryce Brothers Company of Mount Pleasant, Pennsylvania. In a feat of cross-marketing genius, she declared the *Silhouette* range had developed out of her *Tomorrow's Classic* designs (see chapter 11).[6]

The china and glassware lines share a common rhythmic curve that rises from a rounded base and swoops upwards to a gentle flared rim. *Silhouette* was handblown in one piece from full lead crystal. Eva's close collaboration with company staff is evident in the way she was able to achieve tonal variations within each piece; each color graduates from the deepest tones to the lightest suggestion of each shade. Distributed exclusively by Sun Glo Studios and sold at a dollar a glass, the four *Silhouette* glass shapes in seven different colors were meant to be mixed and matched, or used in matched single-color sets.[7]

A. H. HEISEY (1953–1954)

In December 1953, Eva was appointed artistic director at A. H. Heisey & Co., a respected glassmaking business based in Newark, Ohio. Her arrival was heralded by an advertising campaign announcing "New Horizons at Heisey" with promises of "fresh, sparkling ideas . . . designed to set a series of brand new trends in the hand-made glassware industry."[8] Although founded in 1896 and credited as one of the leading glassmakers in the U.S., by the mid-1950s Heisey was on shaky ground financially. Eva's appointment was probably an attempt to boost the company's profile and stimulate sales by capitalizing on her reputation as a successful industrial designer, and by introducing more fashionable designs.[9]

At Heisey, Eva worked closely with the blowers in a two-story glass-blowing studio while designing four distinctive lines of glassware—*Town and Country, Hourglass, Crystal Buds,* and *Roundelay.*[10] Eva also developed several designs for etchings and cuttings that

were used on other popular Heisey glass barware, including one that she designed and introduced as Dawn, a smoky gray glass color with purplish highlights. Although added to the company's line of colored glass, Dawn was used almost exclusively for pieces made to Eva's designs.

Despite the high hopes of both Eva and the company, the lines were not commercially successful; Eva's tenure at Heisey lasted only a few months. The company closed in 1957 and its assets transferred to Imperial Glass Company. Heisey glassware items made to Eva's designs are among the rarest of all those produced to her designs.

Town and Country (1954)

Writing in 1954, Eva attributed *Town and Country's* "snob appeal" to the weight, both visual and actual, of its clear, heavy glass.[11] *Town and Country* was a pressed glass line consisting of twelve shapes, identified in the January 1954 Heisey catalogue.[12] Most pieces flare upward, using the Dawn color (see previous section) to add heft to the thick base and softness to the smooth, rounded rims. *Town and Country* won a "Good Design" award from the Museum of Modern Art in New York in 1955, and several pieces continued to be made by Imperial Glass after Heisey went out of business.[13]

Hourglass (1954)

The *Hourglass* line of blown-glass barware was named after its distinctive hourglass shape.[14] Eva's design plays with the tension achieved by contrasting the thin walls and sheer edges of the bowl with the unusually heavy sham bottoms. The hollow indentation in the base mimics the conical mound of sand that would form at the base of an hourglass.

Crystal Buds (1954)

Described as having a "fleshy roundness," the *Crystal Buds* glass barware was a line of "classic acid-etched drinkware . . . designed by Eva Zeisel to match dinnerware in the same pattern. . . . This followed Eva's previous successful pairing of *Silhouette* glassware and *Tomorrow's Classic* wares."[15] Indeed, the names of decorations used for Western Stoneware are the same as those for the etchings developed by Eva for Heisey glassware (see overleaf and chapter 12). Thin-edged and dainty, each shape in the lines progresses to the next, like a flower in different stages of bloom.

Top right
CRYSTAL BUDS *sherbet and tumbler in Crystal, A. H. Heisey, 1954. EZA.*

Left
HOURGLASS *goblet in Crystal, A. H. Heisey, 1954. EZA.*

Roundelay (1954)

Roundelay was an appropriate name for this line of blown glassware whose shapes were all derived from circles or spheres.[16] As in some of Eva's designs for Castleton and Riverside, several pieces in this line have no defined base and seem to dance when touched.

Etchings and Cuttings (1954)

Eight etching patterns are known to have been developed by Eva for Heisey. These were given descriptive names and assigned catalogue numbers with a B suffix; only a few of the designs have been illustrated.[17] They were probably similar to the eponymous patterns on the Western Stoneware line (chapter 12).

Eva described Leaf as a "reproduction of actual pressed leaves reduced in size and arranged concentrically on the blank," with leaves including "a purple maple leaf, parsley, and various types of weeds. . . ."[18]

Scroll, with its swirling thick and thin calligraphic lines, is similar to the pattern found on Schmid Ironstone.[19] This etching seems to have been used mostly on Heisey's *Country Club* barware.

The Cocktail Party pattern illustrated groups of people rendered in "New York magazine style" line drawings.[20] Zeisel described the groups as "three wives . . . gossiping a bit more animatedly than if they had been drinking only tea. Their husbands are . . . bored, talking business. There is also a little man with a tall wife, each not pleased with the other; he is more interested in the blonde on the other side of the bottle. . . ."[21] Different groupings were meant to appear in different pieces.

There are no documented names given to known glass cuttings designed by Eva, and only three examples are known: a group of stylized arrows, a pattern resembling butterflies, and a stylized duck (used on *Country Club* and *Roundelay* pieces).[22]

Top

Roundelay cruets, individual salad bowl, salad bowl, salt and pepper, A. H. Heisey, c. 1953–1954. Photograph: EZA.

Above

Roundelay open sugar, creamer without handle, pitcher, and ice lip pitcher, A. H. Heisey, c. 1953–1954. Photograph: EZA.

FEDERAL GLASS COMPANY (1954 & 1959)
Prestige BARWARE (1954)

Made of brilliant, clear glass featuring a "sheer rim" and solid, bulbous bottoms that provide the glasses "with extraordinary reflections," the *Prestige* barware line was designed to be made simply and economically; millions of *Prestige* glasses were produced and shipped worldwide. Each type of glass was sold by the dozen in prepackaged sets, or in a sixteen-piece "tumbler set" that contained four each of the cocktail, juice, "Old Fashioned," and highball sizes. In its time, *Prestige* was a best-selling line in the United States.

Eva designed the "plain-bodied" version of the *Prestige* line in the color Crystal. Despite Eva's stipulation, the company introduced pieces in a variety of colors, including Ice Blue, Pink, Amber, and Smoke. A "swirled" variation, with undulating lines around the body was later introduced by the company.[23] The line was also available with special-order decorations such as etched monograms and logos.

STOCKHOLM (1959)

The name Stockholm evoked the high reputation then enjoyed by Scandinavian design. With its narrow solid base, it featured the company's "sheer rim" effect. Mass-produced to sell at twenty to twenty-five cents each, the glasses were often sold in twenty-four-piece sets.

URBAN GLASS ATELIER (1995)

Eva designed heavy-bottomed glass items in 1995 for Urban Glass Atelier of New York. It was founded in 1977 by Richard Yelle and Erik Erikson as the New York Experimental Glass Workshop, and was "an interface between the New York visual art, sculpture, design and architecture communities and glass artists."[24] Her designs for hand-blown crystal candlesticks and bowls, with their distinctive "baby bottom" shapes, later became part of a limited edition collection by the Orange Chicken of Eva's work.

THE ORANGE CHICKEN (1998)

In 1998, Eva collaborated with the the Orange Chicken, with the aim of producing new limited editions and bringing to market earlier designs that had not gone into production. The glassware included four-inch handblown crystal bowls, available with or without an engraving of the 1952 Dawn decoration by Charles Seliger; two handblown crystal vases; handblown breadstick bowls; handblown crystal candlesticks; five-inch handblown crystal bowls; a handblown crystal baby vase; and tall and medium vases in handblown crystal (by Pauly and Co.).

NAMBÉ (1999–2008)

Beginning in 1999, Eva designed several metal alloy pieces, a line of porcelain dinnerware, and three lines of new crystal designs for Nambé (see chapter 20). The glassware lines were *Venus*, a cut Czech crystal glass in a graceful flaring shape with bowls in three sizes, vases in two sizes, a table lamp with a polished metal base, crystal body, and a silk shade; the *Ohana* ("family" in Hawaiian) vases, a set of nesting blue glass vases released in a limited edition of six hundred; and *Eden Stemware*, consisting of a wine glass, water goblet, and champagne flute.

CENTENNIAL GOBLETS (2001)

In 2001, Eva designed monumental handblown glass goblets marketed exclusively through Adam Zeisel's online retail shop featuring designs by his grandmother. The six shapes for the eleven-inch goblets were *Classic*, *Tulip*, *Chalice*, *Modern*, *Cage*, and *Flower*. A seventh goblet shape, named *Reign*, was used for a Bombay Sapphire promotional campaign but was never commercially produced.

Below
KleinReid UPRIGHT VASES in Amber: small, medium, and large, 2005. EZA, KRC.

Below
U VASE, mglass, 2004. EZA.

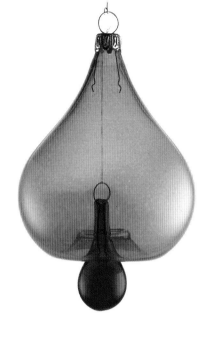
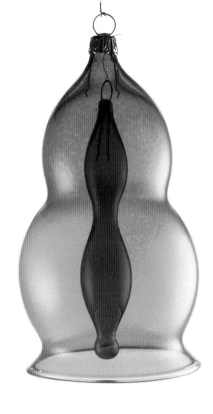

Christmas ornaments, Museum of Modern Art Store, 2009. GNA.

Women in Glass COLLECTION: MGLASS (2004)
Eva designed three lines of glassware for marinha grande mglass' brand: the *U* collection (flared bowls), the *V* collection (vases and bowls), and the *Z* collection (bottles with stoppers). Keen to promote work by women, the company introduced a *"Women in Glass: Three Women, Three Generations, Three Cultures"* collection with work by Eva, the Portuguese designer Paula Lomelino, and the Danish glass-artist-designer Marianne Buus.[25] An eponymous exhibition (sponsored by mglass) featuring their work was held at the United Nations headquarters in New York in 2005.

KLEINREID (2004)
Eva designed glass variations of the *Upright Vases* that were part of an extensive *Eva* line, which Eva designed in collaboration with James Klein and David Reid and which KleinReid produced (see chapter 19).

GUMP'S (2009)
On a visit to San Francisco's famous department store Gump's, Eva was inspired by the glasswork that she saw in the store's Artist Gallery. That visit led to a collection of three handblown vessels that were produced by Lynn Read at Vitrelux Glass Works in Oregon and sold exclusively at Gump's: *Small Golden Vase, Aqua Pedestal Bowl,* and *Lampere Vase.*[26]

MoMA STORE HOLIDAY ORNAMENTS (2009)
Working in collaboration with Olivia Barry, Eva designed a beautiful set of holiday ornaments for the Museum of Modern Art Store in New York, each of which featured a multi-piece glass bell that was mouth-blown in Italy. The ornaments, which were marketed through the MoMA Store, inspired a series of glass lamps for Leucos USA, an importer of high-end Italian lighting.

Furniture
Ted Wells

Eva's desire to create practical, useful, and modern objects extended beyond ceramics to furniture and other decorative arts items. Although playful and experimental in her furniture designs, Eva was also practical, aiming for pieces that could be mass manufactured, efficiently shipped, and easily home-assembled. Like her ceramics, Eva's other decorative art pieces speak to consumers on a personal level as they combine emotional with rational, as well as traditional with modern, elements—and even subtly allude to the mythical.

Her ceramics were intended to be embraced by the user. By contrast, Eva's first furniture design, the *Resilient Chair* (1949), was meant to be "mutually embracing."[1] Although the *Resilient Chair* was original in design, it was similar in context to the 1938 *BKF Chair* (named for its designers Antonio Bonet, Juan Kurchan, and Jorge Ferrari Hardoy and more commonly known as the "Butterfly Chair"). Despite the fact that its low-slung leather seat sometimes made moving around and getting out of the chair difficult, the look and convenience of the *BKF*'s folding wrought-iron frame and removable one-piece cover made it one of the most popular chair types of the 1950s. Countless copies of the *BKF Chair* flooded the market—some with canvas covers selling for only a few dollars each.

Eva wanted the frame of her *Resilient Chair* to contract and expand in response to the movements of the sitter: to embrace and interact with the sitter in a dynamic, adjustable manner. "Eva Zeisel's chair is an original. It has no precedent," explained William Katavalos, the co-director of the Center for Experimental Structures at the Pratt Institute. "It is a series of continuous cantilevers connected at its base that flex and wobble under the weight of the sitter. It is the first chair to be held together by the fabric itself."[2] Like many postwar chairs, the *Resilient Chair*'s sculptural form was meant to be seen in the round and became a complete design when it was carrying the weight of a person. Eva was always thinking about the personal use of her designs, so much so that her son, John Zeisel, insisted, "You can look at everything she does as unfinished until the user touches it and uses it."[3]

Eva Zeisel designed the *Resilient Chair* with a series of curving, connected tubes that could be easily folded, efficiently transported, and quickly reassembled. Katavalos recalled bending the metal tubes for the original chair on the floor of Eva's studio alongside Ross Littell and Douglas Kelley, the three of whom collaborated on midcentury furniture currently held in the permanent collection of New York's Museum of Modern Art (MoMA). Because Eva's chair, which is also in MoMA's collection, was a series of two-dimensional curves that had to become three-dimensional when connected by a pivot joint, Katavalos explained that it first seemed "to have no constructional rationale or means of support." But, he recalled,

"when the fabric was finally slipped over the tubes, it suddenly became a classic."[4]

This idea of transitioning from two dimensions to three dimensions in furniture was born directly out of Eva's work in ceramics, where she would cut a two-dimensional profile in paper to create a three-dimensional plaster prototype. Jonathan Thayer, a professor of Industrial Design at Pratt Institute and a former intern of Eva's, explained: "The transition from 2-D to 3-D was inherent in the process." To this day, the *Resilient Chair* remains one of a kind. Thayer remarked, "Find me another fold-to-ship-flat, in-a-box 'butterfly' chair. I've never seen one."[5] Eva was awarded a mechanical patent for the invention of the *Resilient Chair*. Other than Castleton, this was the design she was most proud of in her life.

Thirty years after developing the *Resilient Chair*, Eva once again began designing furniture in the late 1970s and early 1980s. With the vision of flat-shipping, easy-to-assemble pieces like the *Resilient Chair* in mind, she worked on designs for a line of portable, easily stored wood furniture dubbed *Closet Furniture*, which she believed would be ideal for studio apartment dwellers and students who moved frequently. The various pieces, such as her playful and engaging *Seahorse Wood Table* and the portable, practical *Recycler Wood Table*, included repeating shapes that formed a solid frame. One could store the flat component parts under a bed or inside a closet and easily assemble them when needed. Although never produced, Eva's *Closet Furniture* line contained some of the same ornamental cues—sensuous curves, decorative openings, and traditionally inspired naturalistic motifs—that she later incorporated into her mass-marketed furniture.

Eva was living in Hyde Park, Illinois, in 1989 when she contacted Steve Slusarski, a general contractor and woodworker, to make some items for her apartment. The first pieces were simple, rectangular end tables and a drawing table that she could use while seated in a comfortable easy chair. She did not draw the designs for these items on paper, but simply gave Slusarski the overall dimensions and asked him to go to work.

Even though Eva was not yet fully versed in the process of building wood furniture, her curiosity led her to ask Slusarski numerous questions about the woodworking process, most of which concerned technological limitations and types of machinery, as well as how multiple copies of her designs might be made by a carpenter. Thayer remembered Eva's energy and willingness to work freely without editing her ideas, commenting, "She always exclaimed that there's a possibility that 'we could do something magnificent by accident.'"[6] As she developed her furniture designs, Eva continued to be involved in the process of developing prototypes organically. Her final designs were often an aesthetic and technical evolution from her earliest concepts.

The first piece for which Eva provided a design to Slusarski was a large, round dining table to be used for meetings in her home, such as the upcoming meeting she was to have with a producer of her ceramic pieces. She wanted a surface on which she could display past and present work and working drawings, as well as entertain either business or personal guests. Slusarski recalled:

She was very clever, having worked with tradespeople her entire career, in that she gave me a deadline two weeks earlier than she needed for her meeting, assuming I would be late. It took me a couple of days past the deadline to finish the table, but I didn't know at the time that it was a few days ahead of the actual meeting.[7]

The design of this one-of-a-kind table made for Eva's personal use harked back to her days learning kiln construction in Hungary in the 1920s, where she practiced setting flues (assembling the upper part of a kiln). The table's seven-and-a-half-foot-diameter wood top rested on three legs made of rectangular sections of stacked ceramic flue liners; each liner segment measured fourteen-by-eighteen inches and concealed wooden inserts in the flue liners that connected the legs and tabletop.

In 1992, Eva gave Slusarski four full-scale drawings for a wood-based oval coffee table. As instructed, he glued the drawings to plywood sheets and cut out the patterns directly; however, Slusarski cleverly combined the pairs of drawings to make just two pieces that could be slotted together at ninety-degree angles. This interlocking technique whereby the two pieces visually centered the furniture and facilitated its assembly, became a key feature of many of Eva's furniture designs. They included the *Eva Zeisel Coffee Table* and *Folding Occasional Table* that she later marketed with a New York gallery called the Orange Chicken. According to Jean Richards, when her father

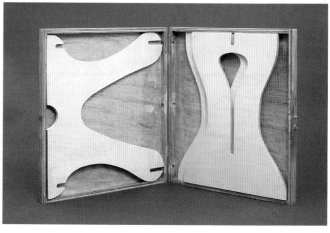

was ill and near death, the prototype of the *Eva Zeisel Coffee Table* was the last design Eva showed him. Jean stated: "My father was dying, and my mother's reaction besides caring for him was to continue to make beautiful things."[8]

The idea of taking planes—be they cutout pieces of paper, bent steel rods, plastic sheeting, pieces of plywood, or curved forms of solid wood—and intersecting them like interwoven fingers to create fluid-looking, three-dimensional shapes was an integral part of Eva's work. Whether it was for dinnerware, decorative objects, or furniture, her concept was consistent. Eva believed that two simple outlines, intersected and relating, create a more complex visual relationship that moves beyond the flat, static geometry of the planes to create a third dimension of evocative form.

Despite the outward simplicity of Eva's furniture forms, her aims remained as ambitious as for her other designs, especially in terms of connecting with users. "I see her using shape and form to communicate complexity versus complex design," said John Zeisel. "She would work at something over and over again.

Those simple curves were worked and worked, sort of like editing when you write." He also noted: "Once you put a half-dozen pure, simple forms together, they form a complex family. I don't see it as simple; I see it as being refined and very modern."[9]

When creating the prototype for her first wood-based oval coffee table with Slusarski in 1992, Eva was unsure if the tabletop should be wood or glass. But as with her *Trestle Table* (1994–1996), *Rectangular Dining Table/Desk* (1994–1996), *Table with Vase Underneath* (1997), *Folding Occasional Table* (1997), *Round Dining Table* (1997), and *Eva Zeisel Coffee Table* (1997), she ultimately chose glass because she believed it would best reveal the clarity of the support beneath it. The design of the table harked back to the bird forms and naturalistic patterns used in her pottery and to the traditional Central and Eastern European designs she had known since her youth. For the rest of Eva's life, she sat at her *Trestle Table*, with its evocative imagery of a mother bird feeding her hungry nestling, when having dinner or tea in her New York City apartment. She entertained countless guests at this table, sharing meals

Screen, c. 1995.
Photograph: EZA.

TABLE WITH VASE
UNDERNEATH, 1997.
Photograph: EZA.

Top
EVA ZEISEL COFFEE TABLE, designed c. 1993. EZO.

Above
TRESTLE TABLE, designed 1994–1996. Photograph: EZA.

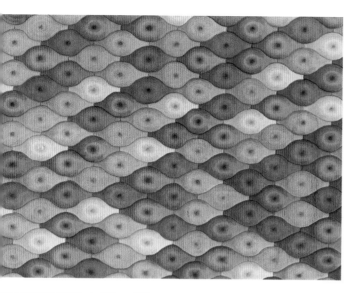

and intimate conversations throughout the years.

Eva's designs for other decorative objects for the home in the 1990s and 2000s were as expressive as her furniture designs. Examples include her ceramic Space Dividers (originally designed in 1957; chapter 26), repetitive molded components that interrelate to create vertical planes of variety and depth. Three rugs (2008) cleverly made use of patterns originally intended for her ceramic work. Two table lamps, two wall sconces, and two pendant lamps were handblown in Murano glass (2012). The light fixtures' internally lit glass shades evoke the sensuous line of upright vases Eva designed for KleinReid in 1999, but with stronger and more voluptuous curves. They are some of the most sensual and expressive shapes she ever produced.

By creating lamps, rugs, and room dividers that shared a common aesthetic, she found yet another way to emotionally and aesthetically affect the rooms in which they were placed. John Zeisel, an expert in the neuroscience of architecture and the built-environment (the human-made surroundings that provide settings for activities), explained how he thought his mother's designs managed to touch on certain innate feelings and themes:

The family is a group of people who protect and nurture each other. . . . In the broadest sense, it is a hardwired and universal concept within our minds. . . . When people touch each other, the neurotransmitter oxytocin [the hormone of love and cuddling] is released in our body and causes a bonding feeling that makes us feel comfortable. Her objects evoked feelings of hunger, love, trust, perhaps passion, and a desire for touch. I think that's how her work had this profound impact.[10]

Although Eva is often included within the group of Modernist designers of the mid-twentieth century, her work does not exhibit the restrictive and constraining rigidity of form often associated with the Modern Movement (see Part One). The graphic flatness of her furniture forms, when combined with the fluidity of her lines, represent her love of archetypal avian imagery as well as her enjoyment of working with wood. Eva's designs also evoke aspects of ancient furniture. For example, her *Trestle Table* (1994–1996) and *Rectangular Dining Table/Desk* (1994–1996) include Roman-style, lyre-like legs. Austro-Hungarian, Baroque, and Biedermeier influences are strong but Eva, always true to her own character, added a playful quality.

Eva's chairs, tables, lamps, and rugs are as tactile in character as her ceramics and equally enliven a room. Her chairs can embrace and support us; her tables can anchor and serve. Their sensual curves engage our eyes and thoughts in deeply personal and subconscious ways. Like Eva's other designs, they ask only to be well used, enjoyed, and—it is hoped—to be loved.

Top
Dimpled Spindle rug, hand-knotted and hand-carved Tibetan wool, 2008. Photograph: The Rug Company.

Center
Lacy X rug, hand-knotted Tibetan wool and silk, 2008. Photograph: The Rug Company.

Bottom
Fish rug, hand-knotted Tibetan wool, 2008. Photograph: The Rug Company.

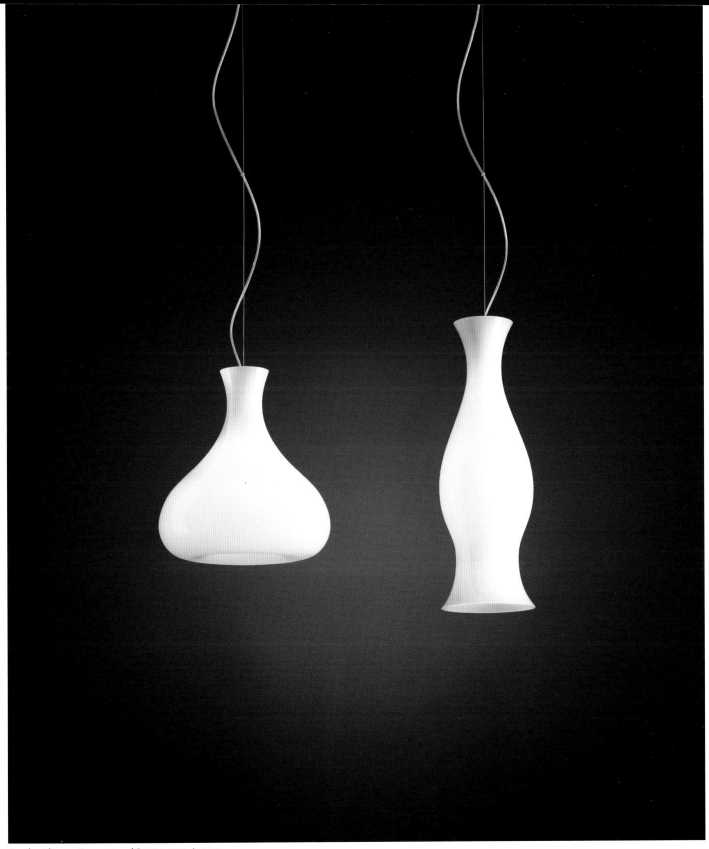

Pendant lamps: SUMMER and SPRING, 2012. Leucos
USA, Inc. Archive.

Chapter 26

Prototypes and Special Projects
Pirco Wolfframm

Among Eva's work, some of the so-called rejects and prototypes that did not reach fruition display noteworthy design explorations. One of the tenets of her design philosophy was "variety, not novelty."[1] Eva described her desire to explore variety as a positive impulse, as opposed to novelty—which she saw as a forced, limiting, and negative motivation to create. This positive impulse fed both the engine of what she called her "project-itis" and her interests in object types, project types, and form-giving.[2] The following examples reveal how Eva's repertoire of forms or concepts that we know only from produced designs began, evolved, or recurred in these prototype designs and how they influenced the development of her idiosyncratic form-giving.

Right
UTILITY WARE variability chart, 1942–1943.
Photograph: EZA.

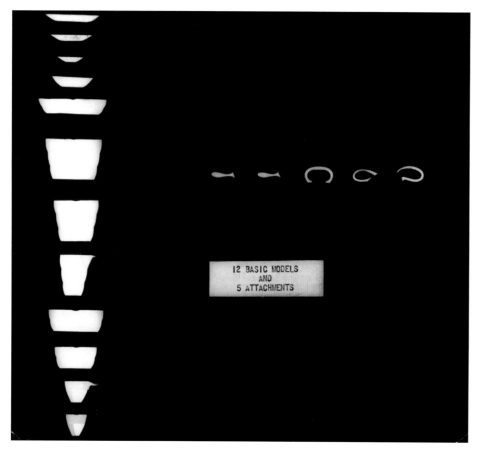

Overleaf
Stacked UTILITY WARE, 1942–1943. Photograph: EZA.

Above
Eva's own pottery, c. 1926. Photograph: EZA.

Left
UTILITY WARE chart, models and attachments, 1942–1943. Photograph: EZA.

162

Utility Ware, 1942–1943

This proposal, inspired by the need to save materials, fuel, and labor during wartime, was a major accomplishment even though it was not produced. With this line, Eva focused on multiuse objects, optimized the advantages of the production process, minimized materials and labor, and standardized heights to maximize the use of kiln space and reduce shipping costs. Using standardized diameters for pots and lids, forty items were designed to be made out of only twelve molds and five attachments, and jiggered-on handles could be converted into spouts. Lids could also be used as plates, providing an advantage in production and saving space in the kitchen (see chapters 12 and 16, respectively). The pieces were stackable, another plus for people with limited storage space.

While picking up on the wavy body previously explored in her own pottery in Hungary, as well as at Kispester-Granit, Schramberger, and Carstens, *Utility Ware* featured organic shapes that later translated into the language of the *Town and Country* line (such as casserole handles—see chapter 6) and certain early pieces of the *Museum* line (such as downward-sloped handles—see chapter 5). Unlike the bodies of these pieces, which have a firm geometric basis, the handles of *Utility Ware* pieces have far greater fluidity.

In March 1943, Eva proposed her designs to the War Production Board in Washington, DC, as a standardization project. Though considered interesting, the project was not recognized as relevant because the production of ceramics did not require the use of any materials considered critical to the war effort.[3] Despite this rejection, Eva gave a presentation on the line at the Pittsburgh meeting of the American Ceramic Society; it was noted in numerous magazines and included in the fifteenth anniversary exhibition, *Art in Progress*, in 1944 at MoMA.[4]

Top
UTILITY WARE, glazed models, 1942–1943. Photograph: EZA.

Above
UTILITY WARE, plaster models, 1942–1943. Photograph: EZA.

GENERAL MILLS, 1948

Long before Eva designed a teakettle for Chantal (2006), she designed in metal for cookware for General Mills. She created a pot, a pan, a water kettle, and an iron, all with handles that provide a solid grip. The handles on the pot allow the wide part to be embraced by the palm of the hand, while the bottom part is twisted to stop the hand from sliding. These grips are an inspiration to any ergonomic study of handles (even though they are unsuitable for a left-handed user). The bodies of the pan and pot "speak" the Zeisel-language of design: the lids curve and a beak-like spout facilitates the easy pouring of liquids as much as it serves as a lock between lid and body. The fluid quality of these pieces is reminiscent of computer-generated design objects in housewares and architecture (*blobjects*), like Philippe Starck's famous weightlifting dumbbells from 1999. While General Mills expressed its satisfaction with her designs, none of the items were produced because of a fire that consumed the plant in which they were to be manufactured.[5]

Top
General Mills prototype iron, 1948.
Photograph: EZA.

Center
General Mills prototype pan, 1948.
Photograph: EZA.

Bottom
General Mills prototype kettle, 1948.
Photograph: EZA.

Below
General Mills prototype pan, 1948.
Photograph: EZA.

Rosenthal AG, 1957

Although the Rosenthal AG produced the *Eva* line in 1958 (see chapter 15), it is worth mentioning one of Eva's design proposals that was shelved. It is remarkable because it is so typical of Eva's ability to bring elegance to modern form.

The concept featured clear, round shapes that end sharply with elevated, flat knob-like handles. The thinness of the porcelain, the white color, and the floating knob handles all contributed to a sense of lightness. Handles were added in the same formal language as the dimpled tops except in the teapot, where wicker was used. Glimpses of earlier designs by Eva can be seen in the pitcher (see *Museum* and *Century*; chapters 5 and 14), but the small straight line at the bottom of the spout exemplifies Eva's ability to control this specific formal concept combined with her "family member" approach.[6] This proposal was a more accomplished expression of modern elegance than the design that was produced. It is somewhat surprising that Rosenthal chose the safer (in terms of marketability) proposal; under Philip Rosenthal Jr.'s leadership, the company had already begun to leverage its brand toward the upscale market by offering exciting new designs by leading designers. (This proposal would have articulated the company's direction more distinctly. At the same time, West Germany was experiencing its "Wirtschaftswunder" [economic miracle]—a period of considerable economic recovery and optimism following the war. Hence the risk of introducing daring designs was not exactly high, given that a vast range of consumer aspirations were longing to be satisfied.) A piece of copy entitled "Advice for a Happy Marriage" in the *Eva* sales brochure for the Travemünde pattern design indicates that the choice was deliberately made to generate greater sales through the mass market.[7]

Rosenthal prototype marmalade jar, sugar, cup, saucer, covered vegetable bowl, creamer, and teapot, 1957. Photograph: EZA.

MANCIOLI, 1958

When Eva agreed to work on a project for Manifatturi Mancioli in Montelupe, Italy, the company had recently changed production methods so that it could make more delicate objects in ovenproof porcelain. Delicacy is a key feature of Eva's designs for Mancioli. While exploring an expressive S-curve, the bodies of the items appear as light shapes, with an upward motion culminating in a whimsical loop handle on top. Embracing playfulness, Eva added loops on items that did not demand a handle, such as the salt and paper shakers and the gravy boat, simply to delight the eye and create harmonious relationships with the rest of the group. Familiar shapes were revisited, such as the gravy boat (which drew upon *Tomorrow's Classic*; see chapter 11) and the neck of the pitcher (Rosenthal; see chapter 15), but these references were part of a distinctly new familial repertoire of designs. Some of her designs for the company have been displayed at the Mancioli Museum in Montelupe and at the British Museum, London. The line never reached the production stage. According to Eva, Luciano Mancioli had hoped to see more austere shapes and decided not to produce it. "I wanted curves; he wanted straight lines," Eva told me.[8] This notwithstanding, the company issued a luxuriously printed brochure in 1995 praising "La Zeisel" and her work at Mancioli, as well as a sales catalogue of glazes that includes Eva's experimental designs.[9]

She also undertook a very different project for Mancioli, namely the design for architectural modules that, if stacked, functioned as space dividers. Eva used a rustic enameled ceramic material and designed several shapes in a variety of colorings, the belly button form being the best known today. Some of the modules are reminiscent of an American football or a honeycomb. (The hexagonal shape has a round hole to provide for a lightbulb to be inserted.) They varied in size and weight and did not always lend themselves easily to three-dimensional pattern making.

Sadly, the pieces chipped easily and their weight would have resulted in high shipping costs, so the company did not pursue the project. Three of these pieces were later produced in a small edition by the Orange Chicken, namely the belly button (which made its way into the lobby of the Standard Hotel in Los Angeles), the hexagonal shape, and the cross shape.

Above
Mancioli prototype chart: bell, pitcher, cruets, covered vegetable bowl, salt and pepper, plates, fruit bowl, sauce dish, footed bowl, cup, saucer, creamer, sugar, coffee pot, teapot, serving bowl, covered marmite, platter, handled bowl, sauce boat, and platter, 1958. Photograph: EZA.

Top Left
Mancioli prototypes: coffee pot, covered vegetable bowl, bell, salt, pitcher, and sauce boat, 1958. Photograph: EZA.

Top Right
Mancioli prototype plate, creamer, and coffee pot, 1958. Photograph: EZA.

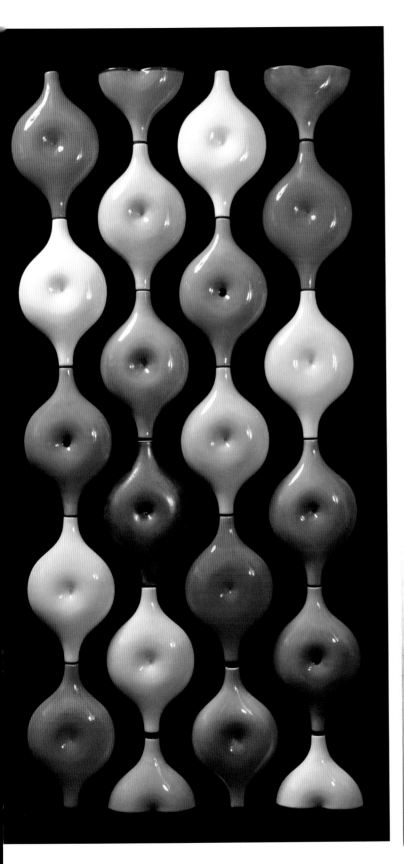

All photographs on this page: Mancioli prototype room divider modules, 1958. Photograph: EZA.

SCHRAMBERGER MAJOLIKAFABRIK
Schramberg, Germany | Earthenware

fig. 1
Vase 3228
dia. 4¾", *h.* 8¼"

fig. 2
Vase 3229
h. 8½"

fig. 3
Vase 3222
h. 8½"

fig. 4
Lidded Box 3223
h. 4", *w.* 4½"

fig. 5
Vase 3254
h. 8¼"

fig. 1
Vase 3369
h. 12"

fig. 2
Vase 3370
h. 11½"

fig. 3
Vase 3383
h. 8¼"

fig. 4
Vase 3372
h. 7½"

fig. 5
Vase 3373
h. 6½"

fig. 6
Vase 3376
h. 5"

fig. 7
Vase 3381
h. 4"

fig. 8
Vase 3378
h. 4¼"

fig. 9
Vase 3379
h. 4¼"

fig. 10
Vase 3380
h. 4¾"

fig. 11
Vase 3377
h. 4¾"

fig. 12
Vase 3375
h. 4¾"

fig. 13
Vase 3374
dia. 4", *h.* 5"

fig. 14
Vase 3371
h. 10"

Items without numbers were not designed by Eva Zeisel.

fig. 1
Vase 3382
h. 9"

fig. 2
Vase 3368
h. 24½"

fig. 3
Ashtray 3384
dia. 4¾"

fig. 4
Vase 3393
h. 6"

fig. 5
Vase 3226
h. 8"

fig. 6
Vase 3297
h. 9"

fig. 7
Vase 3309
h. 10½"

fig. 8
Vase 3315
h. 12"

fig. 1
Vase 3310
h. 11½"

fig. 2
Vase 3313
h. 8¾"

fig. 3
Cactus Pot 3299
dia. 3", *h.* 2½"

fig. 4
Lidded Box 3245
h. 3⅛", *w.* 4"

fig. 5
Wall Pocket 3247
h. 8", *w.* 4¼"

fig. 6
Wall Pocket 3277
h. 7", *w.* 4¼"

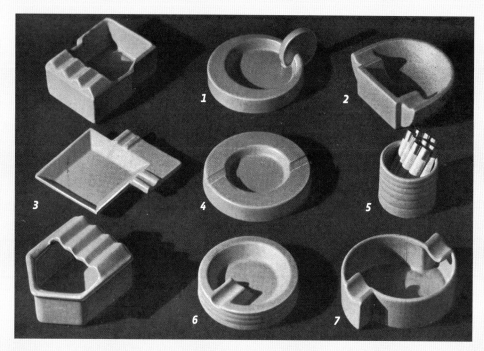

fig. 1
Ashtray 3221
dia. 4", h. 2½"

fig. 2
Ashtray 3238
h. 1½", w. 4¾"

fig. 3
Ashtray 3304
h. ¾", w. 4¼"

fig. 4
Ashtray 3303
dia. 4¾", h. ¾"

fig. 5
Cigarette Box 3321
dia. 2", h. 2½"

fig. 6
Ashtray 3323
dia. 4", h. ¾"

fig. 7
Ashtray 3242
h. 1½", w. 5"

fig. 1
Hanging Basket 3318
dia. 7¾", h. 6½"

fig. 2
Hanging Basket 3288
dia. 7¼", h. 4¼"

Items without numbers were not designed by Eva Zeisel.

fig. 1
Jug 3208
dia. 4½", h. 6", w. 7"

fig. 2
Mug 3209
dimensions unknown

fig. 3
Jug 3366
dia. 9½"

fig. 4
Mug 3367
h. 1¾"

fig. 5
Tray 3387
dia. 8½"

fig. 1
Jug 3391, 1 qt.
dimensions unknown

fig. 2
**Jug 3296,
1 qt./1½ qt.**
dimensions unknown

fig.3
**Jug 3390,
1½ cup/1½ qt.**
*6 sizes,
dimensions unknown*

fig. 4
Goblet 3381, ¾ cup
dimensions unknown

fig. 5
Tray 3387
dia. 8½"

fig. 6
Goblet 3339, 1 cup
dimensions unknown

fig. 7
Goblet 3398, ¾ cup
dimensions unknown

fig. 8
Jug 3397, 1¼ qt.
dimensions unknown

fig. 1
Tobacco Box 3319
dia. 4¾", h. 4"

fig. 2
Tray 3337
dia. 13½", h. 5½"

fig. 3
Cigar Box 3320
dia. 3½", h. 2½"

fig. 4
Cigarette Box 3321
dia. 2½", h. 2"

fig. 5
Match Box 3322
dia. 1½", h. 1½"

fig. 6
Ashtray 3323
dia. 4", h. ¾"

fig. 7
Tray 3295
l. 11", w. 8"

fig. 8
Teaglass Stand 3278
dia. 3", h. 2"

fig. 9
Cactus Pot 3298
h. 2½", w. 4"

fig. 10
Napkin Stand 3338
h. 6", w. 4¾"

fig. 1
Plate 3362
dia. 7½"

fig. 2
Plate 3388
dia. 7½"

fig. 3
Plate 3360
dia. 7½"

fig. 4
Fruit Bowl 3361
dia. 10¾"

fig. 5
Fruit Bowl 3359
dia. 11¾"

fig. 6
Plate 3314
dia. 12", h. 2½"

fig. 7
Covered Bowl 3363
dia. 6¾", h. 3"

Items without numbers were not designed by Eva Zeisel.

fig. 1
Tray 3300
dia. 11¾"

fig. 2
Tray 3332
dia. 10½"

fig.3
Tray 3295
l. 11", w. 8"

fig. 4
Flower Bowl 3308
dia. 10½"

fig. 1
**Cup & Saucer 3252,
¾ cup**
dimensions unknown

fig. 2
Sugar 3251, 1½ cup
dimensions unknown

fig. 3
**Creamer 3250,
¾ cup**
dimensions unknown

fig. 4
Teapot 3249, 1 qt.
dimensions unknown

fig. 5
Plate 3253
dia. 8"

fig. 1
Teapot 3356, 1 qt.
dia. 5½", h. 6", w. 7½"

fig. 2
Sugar 3357, 1½ cup
dia. 4", h. 4"

fig. 3
Cup 3389, ¾ cup
dimensions unknown
Saucer 3389
dia. 6½"

fig. 4
**Creamer 3358,
¾ cup**
dia. 3¼", h. 3", w. 4½"

fig. 1
Cup 3335, ¾ cup
dimensions unknown
Saucer 3335
dia. 6"

fig. 2
Teapot 3301, 3 cup
h. 5¼", l. 8¾", w. 3½"

fig. 3
Sugar 3334, 1½ cup
h. 3½", l. 4", w. 2¾"

fig. 4
**Creamer 3333,
¾ cup**
dimensions unknown

Items without numbers were not designed by Eva Zeisel.

fig. 1
Teapot 3266, 1 pt.
dimensions unknown

fig. 2
Cup 3214, ¾ cup
dia. 4"
Saucer 3214
dia. 6½"

fig. 3
Creamer 3267,
½ cup
dia. 3", h. 2"

fig. 4
Sugar 3268, ½ cup
dia. 3¾", h. 2"

fig. 5
Jug 3287/1, 1 qt.
dimensions unknown

fig. 6
Jug 3287/2, 1½ cup
dimensions unknown

fig. 1
Teapot 3211, 1 qt.
dia. 6½", h. 4½",
w. 10"

fig. 2
Sugar 3213, ¾ cup
dia. 6", h. 3 ½"

fig. 3
Cup 3214, ¾ cup
dia. 4"
Saucer 3214
dia. 6½"

fig. 4
Creamer 3212,
¾ cup
dia. 3¾", h. 2¾",
w. 5½"

fig. 1
Vase 3463
h. 7"

fig. 2
Cup 3389, ¾ cup
dia. 4"
Saucer 3389
dia. 6½"

fig. 3
Sugar 3432, 1 cup
dimensions unknown

fig. 4
Creamer 3433, 1 cup
dimensions unknown

fig. 5
Teapot 3431, 1¼ qt.
dimensions unknown

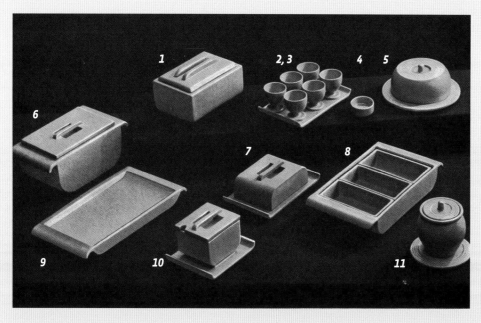

fig. 1
Cake Box 3440
h. 4", l. 6¾", w. 4¾"

fig. 2
Egg Cup 3419
dia. 2", h. 2"

fig. 3
Tray 3436
l. 7¾", w. 4¾"

fig. 4
Salt 3437
dia. 1¼"

fig. 5
Butter Dish 3452
dia. 7"

fig. 6
Tureen for Eggs 3418
h. 5¼", l. 9½", w. 5"

fig. 7
Butter Dish 3416
l. 7¼", w. 5"

fig. 8
Hors D'Oeuvres 3422
l. 11"

fig. 9
Bread Basket 3421
l. 11"

fig. 10
Marmalade Jar 3417
h. 3¾", l. 5½", w. 4¾"

fig. 11
Marmalade Jar 3451
dia. 4¾"

Items without numbers were not designed by Eva Zeisel.

fig. 1
Cup 3331, ½ cup
dimensions unknown
Saucer 3331
dimensions unknown

fig. 2
**Coffee Pot 3329,
1¼ qt.**
dimensions unknown

fig. 3
**Covered Sugar
3251, 1½ cup**
dimensions unknown

fig. 4
**Creamer 3330,
1½ cup**
dimensions unknown

fig. 5
**Honey Pot 3275,
1 cup**
dimensions unknown

fig. 6
Plate 3253
dia. 7½"

fig. 1
**Flower Pot 3426,
4 sizes**
dia. 8¼", 7", 6", 4¾"

fig. 2
Vase 3454
h. 8½"

fig. 3
Vase 3455
h. 8"

fig. 4
Vase 3458
h. 7"

fig. 5
Cigarette Box 3449
h. 2", l. 4½", w. 3¼"

fig. 6
Ashtray 3438
dia. 5¾"

fig. 7
Cactus Pot 3427
dia. 3"

fig. 8
Cactus Pot 3428
dia. 3"

fig. 9
Hanging Pot 3429
l. 7"

fig. 10
Ashtray 3442
l. 5½"

fig. 11
Ashtray 3443
dia. 4½"

fig. 12
Ashtray 3439
dia. 5¾"

fig. 13
Ink Stand 3446
l. 7¼"

fig. 14
Ink Stand 3441
l. 7½"

fig. 1
Tall Compote 3353
dia. 9", h. 3½"

fig. 2
Soup Tureen 3349, 3 qt.
dia. 11½", h. 6½", l. 11½"

fig. 3
Vegetable Bowl 3351
dia. 9¼"

fig. 4
Covered Vegetable Dish 3350, 1½ qt.
dimensions unknown

fig. 5
Salad Bowl 3352
dia. 10¼", h. 3"

fig. 6
Sauce Boat 3406, 1½ cup
dimensions unknown

fig. 7
Low Compote 3354
dia. 8¾", h. 1"

fig. 1
Fruit Dish 3457
dia. 10½"

fig. 2
Fruit Dish 3453
dia. 9½"

fig. 3
Fruit Bowl 3447
dia. 8"
Underplate 3447
dia. 8½"

fig. 4
Fruit Bowl 3435
dia. 7"
Underplate 3435
dia. 8½"

fig. 5
Fruit Plate 3430 x 3
(only two shown)
dia. 10½", 7½", 6"

fig. 6
Citrus Press 3415
dia. 3¾"

fig. 7
Sweet Dish 3444 x 2
dia. 6¾", 3"

fig. 8
Biscuit Jar 3448
dia. 6¾", h. 4¼"

fig. 9
Biscuit Jar 3450
dia. 5¼", h. 4¾"

fig. 10
Lidded Box 3461
dia. 4", h. 2¾"

fig. 11
Lidded Box 3460
dia. 4¼", h. 2¾"

fig. 12
Lidded Box 3459
dia. 4", h. 2¾"

fig. 13
Lidded Box 3462
dia. 4", h. 4¾"

Items without numbers were not designed by Eva Zeisel.

fig. 1
Covered Jug
3348, 6 sizes
1, 2, 3, 4, 5, 6 cup
dimensions unknown
(sold with or without lid)

not pictured:

Lamp Stand 3195/1
Lamp Stand 3195/2
Lamp Stand 3196
Lamp Stand 3207
Lamp Stand 3230
Lamp Stand 3231
Lamp Stand 3232
Lidded Box 3239
Lidded Box 3240
Lidded Box 3241
Vase 3243
Lidded Box 3251
Vase 3255
Vase 3256
Lamp Stand 3260
Triangular Ashtray 3261
Lamp Stand 3262
Lamp Stand 3263
Coffee Pot 3269
Cigarette Box 3270
Lidded Box 3273
Ink Stand 3274
Lidded Box 3275
Bookends 3276
Egg Cup 3285

Salt & Pepper 3286
Creamer 3290
Teapot 3302
Lidded Box 3305
Lidded Box 3306
Lidded Box 3307
Jardiniere 3316
Jardiniere 3317
Lidded Box 3319
Egg Cup 3344
Fruit Dish 3362
Lamp Stand 3365
Lidded Pitcher 3385
Tray 3387
Lidded Box 3399
Lidded Box 3400
Deep Plate 3401
Flat Plate 3407

Patterns
(by Eva Zeisel)

Matte Blue
Matte Rose
Matte Beige
Matte Green
Matte Turquoise
Matte Light Blue
Coral-Red
Black
Gobelin 8
Gobelin 12
Gobelin 13
Decor 3420
Decor 3465-1
Decor 3465-2
Decor 3525
Decor 3526
Decor 3574
Decor 3669
Otto
Rustic
Harp
Gold Spritzdecor
Scotland

UNIVERSAL POTTERIES, *STRATOWARE*
Cambridge, Ohio, USA | Earthenware

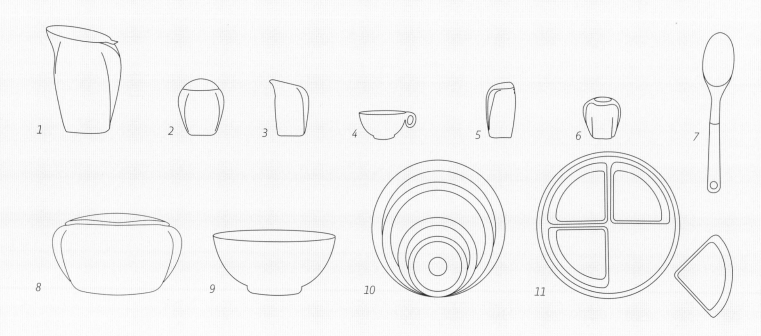

fig. 1
Covered Pitcher
h. 8¼"

fig. 2
Sugar
h. 4¾"

fig. 3
Creamer
h. 4¾"

fig. 4
Tea Cup
dia. 4", h. 2¼"

fig. 5
Salt & Pepper
h. 3¾"

fig. 6
Candle Holder
h. 3¼"

fig. 7
Salad Spoon
l. 10¼"

fig. 8
Covered Vegetable Dish, 2 qt.
h. 5¼"

fig. 9
Salad Bowl
dia. 9¾"

fig. 10
Medium Platter
dia. 11½"
Dinner Plate
dia. 9½"
Rim Soup Plate
dia. 8¼"
Vegetable Bowl
dia. 8¾"
Bread Plate
dia. 6¾"
Sauce Dish
dia. 5½"
Saucer
dia. 6½"

fig. 11
5-Piece Relish Set Platter
dia. 14¾"
Quarter Plate
w. 8¾"

not pictured:
Salad Fork
l. 10¼"

Colors
(not designed by Eva)

TRIM
Horizon Blue
Flare Yellow
Wing Brown
Airport Green

BODY
San Diego Sand

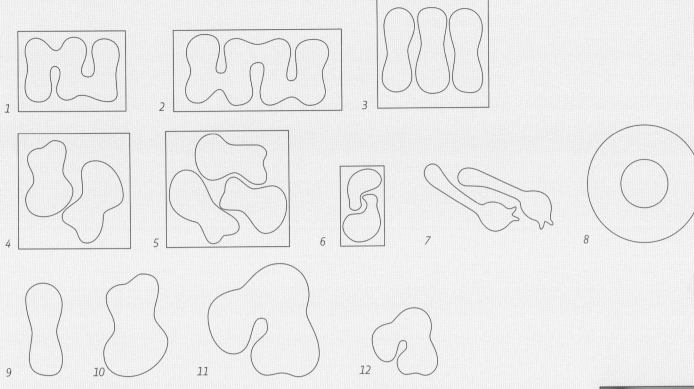

fig. 1
Rectangular Tray
l. 8⅞", w. 6¼"

fig. 7
Salad Servers, Birds
l. 10", w. 3"

fig. 2
Vine Tray
h. 1", l. 3¹⁵⁄₁₆", w. 6⅝"

fig. 8
Salad Bowl
dimensions unknown

fig. 3
**Square Tray,
Gourds**
l. 14", w. 14"

fig. 9
Small Gourd Bowl
l. 4", w. 5¾"

fig. 10
Large Gourd Bowl
l. 10½", w. 4"

fig. 4
Square Tray
dimensions unknown

fig. 11
Cloverleaf Bowl
l. 12", w. 12"

fig. 5
Gourd Tray
dimensions unknown

fig. 12
**Small Cloverleaf
Bowl**
dimensions unknown

fig. 6
**Rectangular Tray,
Comma**
h. 1", l. 7½", w. 3⅞"

Colors
*(it is not known if Eva
selected all three colors)*

*Soft Milk White
Deep Emerald
  Green
Brilliant Orange
  Amber*

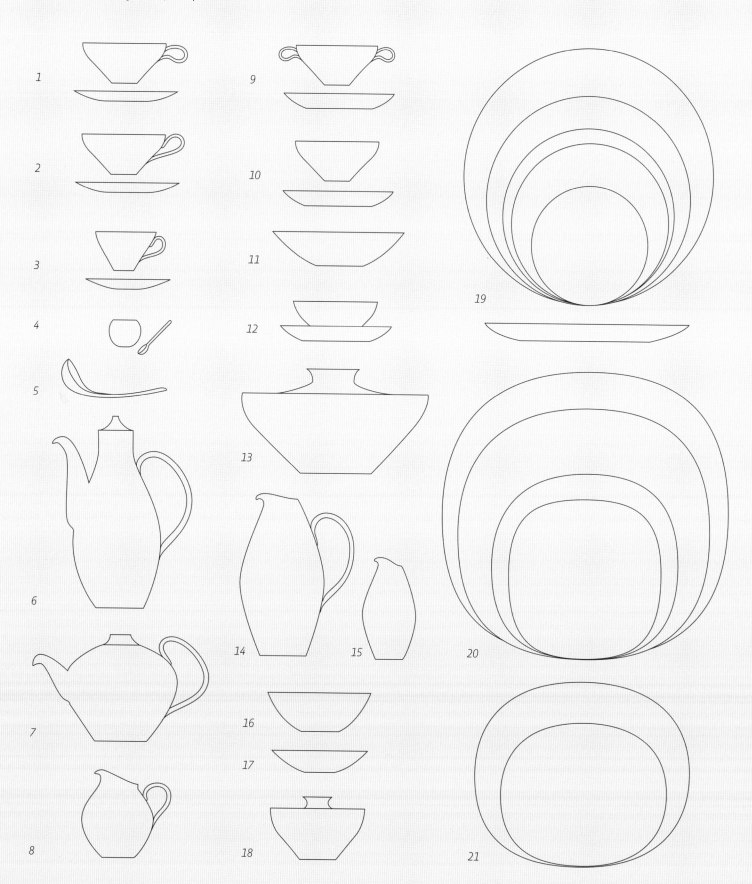

1

2

3

4

5

6

7

8

9

10

11

12

13

14

15

16

17

18

19

20

21

fig. 1
Tea Cup
dia. 4½", h. 2"
Saucer
dia. 6½"

fig. 2
Tea Cup
dia. 4½", h. 2"
Saucer
dia. 6½"

fig. 3
After-Dinner Coffee Cup
dia. 2¾", h. 2"
Saucer
dia. 5⅜"

fig. 4
Salt Cellar
dia. 1¾", h. 1½"
Salt Spoon
l. 2⅝"

fig. 5
Ladle
l. 6½"

fig. 6
Coffee Pot
h. 10½"

fig. 7
Teapot
h. 5¾"

fig. 8
Creamer with Handle
h. 4½"

fig. 9
Bouillon Cup
dia. 4½", h. 2"
Saucer
dia. 6⅝"

fig. 10
Cream Soup Bowl
dia. 4¾", h. 2"
Saucer
dia. 7½"

fig. 11
Cream Soup Bowl
dia. 7⅞", h. 2¼"

fig. 12
Sauce Boat
dia. 5½", h. 3¼"
Stand
dia. 7½"

fig. 13
Covered Vegetable Dish
dia. 9⅞", h. 5½"

fig. 14
Hot Water Pot
h. 8¾"

fig. 15
Creamer without Handle
dia. 2¾", h. 5½"

fig. 16
Cereal Bowl
dia. 5½", h. 2⅝"

fig. 17
Fruit Bowl
dia. 5¼"

fig. 18
Sugar
dia. 4¾", h. 2"
Lid
dia. 4", h. 1⅜"

fig. 19
Platter, Buffet
dia. 13⅛"
Dinner Plate
dia. 10½"
Luncheon Plate
dia. 9⅛"
Salad Plate
dia. 8⅜"
Bread Plate
dia. 6⅛"

fig. 20
Platter
h. 2⅜", l. 15¾", w. 11¾"

Bowl
h. 3⅝", l. 13", w. 13"
Bowl
h. 2½", l. 9⅜", w. 9⅜"
Salad Plate
h. 1", l. 8⅛", w. 8⅛"

fig. 21
Vegetable Dish
h. 3", l. 11", w. 9⅝"
Vegetable Dish
h. 2½", l. 9", w. 7"

not pictured:
Candle Holder
dia. 4¾", h. 2½"
Cup
dia. 3¾", h. 2½"
Cup
dia. 3¾", h. unknown
Saucer
dia. 6⅜"

Patterns
(not designed by Eva Zeisel)

Light Blue
Mandalay
Lyana
French Garden
Tropical Waters
The Farm Plenty -
Early Americana
Thistle
Golden Meadow
Wisteria
Green Thumb
Constellation
Symmetra
Persian Brocade
Royal Baroness
Midnight Halo
Dawn Rose
Classic Scroll
Cellini
Rhythm
Native American
Heroes
Amelia Earhart
Year of the Child
Fiat Stanquelini

Individually hand-painted, 1949

Flowering Maidens
(after Salvador Dalí)
Vin Rose
(after Pablo Picasso)
Arabesque
(after Julio de Diego)
Town with Boats (after Stuart Davis)
Still Life
(after Georges Braque)
Caryatid
(after Amedeo Modigliani)

1

2

3

4

5

6

7

8

9

10

11

12

13

14

15

16

17

18

19

20

21

22

23

fig. 1
Salt
h. 3½"
Pepper
h. 4½"

fig. 2
Sugar
dia. 4", h. 4"

fig. 3
Creamer
dia. 3½", h. 4½"

fig. 4
Pitcher, 2 pt.
dia. 5¾", h. 6½"

fig. 5
Pitcher, 3 pt.
dia. 6¾", h. 8"

fig. 6
Syrup Jug
dia. 3¼", h. 5¾"

fig. 7
Mixing Bowl
h. 5", l. 9½", w. 8¼"

fig. 8
Soup Bowl
dia. 7", h. 1½"

fig. 9
Soup Ladle
l. 14½"

fig. 10
Soup Tureen
dia. 9", h. 8"

fig. 11
Teapot
h. 4¾", l. 11½", w. 7"

fig. 12
Cup
dia. 3⅜", h. 2¾"

fig. 13
Oil/Vinegar
h. 5¼", l. 5", w. 3½"

fig. 14
Coaster
l. 5¼", w. 3½"

fig. 15
Sauce Dish
l. 7", w. 5"

fig. 16
Covered Casserole
h. 4¾", l. 14", w. 9½"

fig. 17
Covered Marmite
h. 3", l. 7½", w. 5½"

fig. 18
Salad Spoon, Left
l. 14¼", w. 2¾"

fig. 19
Cereal Bowl
dia. 6"
Salad Bowl
dia. 8½"
Salad Bowl
dia. 13"

fig. 20
Platter
l. 15", w. 11½"
Baker
l. 10¾", w. 7¾"
Relish
l. 8¾", w. 6"

fig. 21
Dinner Plate
dia. 10½"
Salad Plate
dia. 8"
Bread Plate
dia. 6½"

fig. 22
Saucer
dia. 6½"

fig. 23
Lazy Susan
Relish Dish
l. 7", w. 5"
Condiment/
Mustard Jar
dia. 4¼", h. 5¾"
Lazy Susan Tray
dia. 18½"

not pictured:
Mug
dia. 3½", h. 3½"

Colors
(authorized by Eva)

1947
Chalk White
Dusk Blue
Sand
Metallic Brown Char-
treuse
Rust
Peach

1950
Forest Green
Gray

1951
(not authorized by
Eva)
Mulberry
Ming Green
Copper Glow
Lime Green

1

2

3

4

5

6

7

8

9

10

11

12

13

14

15

16

17

18

19

20

21

22

23

24

25

26

27

28

29

fig. 1
Cup
dia. 4¼", h. 2½"
Saucer
dia. 7¼"

fig. 2
Creamer
dia. 4¼", h. 2½"

fig. 3
Sugar
dia. 4⅜", h. 2⅞"

fig. 4
Mustard Bowl
dia. 3¾"
Spoon
l. 3¾"

fig. 5
Teapot
h. 8¾", l. 7¾", w. 7"

fig. 6
Lidded Bowl
dia. 5½"

fig. 7
Cereal Bowl
dia. 5⅛", h. 2"

fig. 8
Fruit Bowl
dia. 4½", h. 1½"

fig. 9
Cigarette Holder
l. 9"

fig. 10
Large Bowl Fishtail
h. 4⅛", l. 14¾, w. 7⅜"

fig. 11
Medium Bowl
h. 3", l. 9½", w. 4¾"

fig. 12
Nut Dish
h. 1⅝", l. 5", w. 2¾"

fig. 13
Serving Spoons
l. 14"

fig. 14
Lidded Casserole
dia. 8¾", h. 4"

fig. 15
Low Serving Bowl
dia. 18"

fig. 16
Lidded Casserole
dia. 8¾", h. 4"

fig. 17
Serving Bowl
dia. 8¾", h. 4⅛"

fig. 18
Carafe
dia. 7¼", h. 8"

fig. 19
Tumbler
dia. 3½", h. 4⅛"

fig. 20
Cruet
h. 7"

fig. 21
Large Pinched Vase
h. 7"

fig. 22
Small Pinched Vase
h. 3⅞"

fig. 23
Large Upright Vase
h. 12"

fig. 24
Small Upright Vase
h. 6"

fig. 25
Platter
l. 14⅛", w. 10⅛"

fig. 26
Dinner Plate
dia. 9⅜"
Salad Plate
dia. 7½"
Bread Plate
dia. 6⅛"

fig. 27
Divided Relish
l. 6½", w. 11⅜"
Serving Spoon
l. 7⅜"

fig. 28
Small Candlestick
h. 2½"

fig. 29
Candlestick Fishtail
h. 2", l. 5¾", w. 4⅛"

Colors
(authorized by Eva)

SOLID
White
Light Blue
Light Yellow
Bright Yellow
Medium Blue
Avocado Green
Medium Brown
Deep Brown
Gray
Rust Red
Orange Red

TWO-TONE
Avocado Green (outside),
Yellow (inside)

Brown (outside), Light Blue (inside)

EXPERIMENTAL
Lustre (white with iridescent sheen, and varying amounts of yellow, orange, ochre)

"Apple" combination (streaks of green and red)

Mottled/spotted brown with purples and yellows

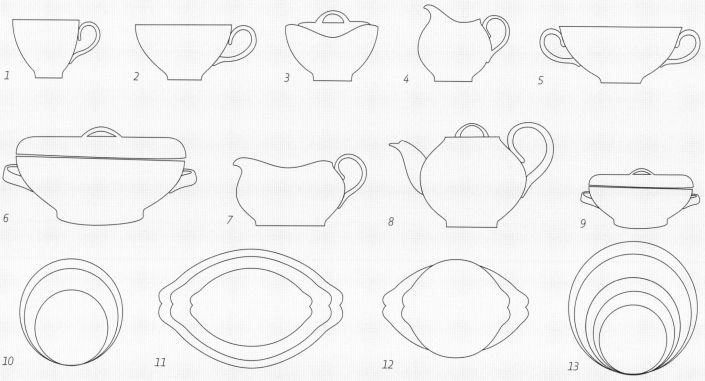

fig. 1
Demitasse Cup
dia. 2⅝", h. 2½"

fig. 2
Cup
dia. 4", h. 2½"

fig. 3
Sugar
h. 4", l. 5", w. 3¾"

fig. 4
Creamer
h. 4½", l. 5½",
w. 3½"

fig. 5
Handled Soup Bowl
h. 2⅛", l. 6½", w. 4¾"

fig. 6
Covered Casserole
h. 5½", l. 12", w. 8"

fig. 7
Gravy
h. 4", l. 7½", w. 4"
Saucer
(not pictured)
l. 9½", w. 5½"

fig. 8
Teapot
h. 6", l. 10", w. 5"

fig. 9
**Commemorative
Dish**
h. 3¼", l. 6½", w. 4"

fig. 10
Saucer, Soup Bowl
dia. 7¼"
Saucer, Tea Cup
dia. 6½"
Saucer, Demitasse
dimensions unknown

fig. 11
Large Platter
l. 18", w. 11½"

Medium Platter
l. 16", w. 10¼"
Small Platter
l. 13¼", w. 8½"

fig. 12
**Round Vegetable
Bowl**
dia. 10", h. 2¾"
**Oval Vegetable
Bowl**
l. 12¼", w. 8"

fig. 13
Dinner Plate
dia. 10½"
Rimmed Soup Bowl
dia. 8¾"
Salad Plate
dia. 7½"
Bread Plate
dia. 6½"
Fruit Bowl
dia. 5¾"

not pictured:
Small Dish
l. 4⅜", w. 2⅜"
**Vegetable Bowl,
Round, Covered**
dimensions unknown

Patterns
(not authorized by Eva
Zeisel)

Adele
Brilliance
Caresse
Chatham
Coronet
Courtley
Desert Rose
Dream of Hawaii
El Dorado
Fairfield
Flora
Fragrance
Garden Rose
Goldrose
Grayson

Livonia
Mayfield
Midas
Pecos
Pink Radiance
Princess
Riviera
Roseanne
Royal Oak
Silhouette
Spring Garden
Sun Glory
Trend
Victoria

SALISBURY ARTISANS
Salisbury, Connecticut, USA | Rosewood, Porcelain, Brass

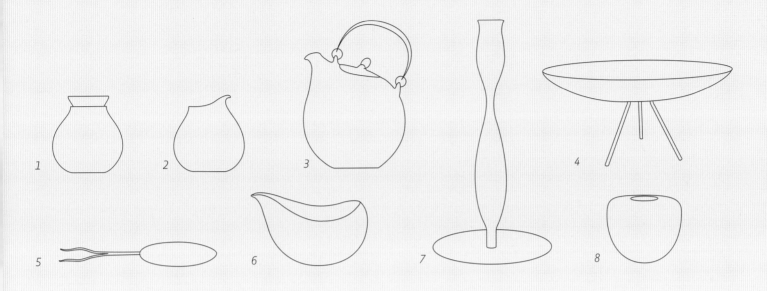

fig. 1
Sugar
h. 4¼", l. 4¼"

fig. 2
Creamer
h. 4¼", l. 4¼"

fig. 3
Teapot
h. 4¾", w. 5"

fig. 4
Bowl
dia. 7", h. 3½"

fig. 5
Fork
l. 4½"

fig. 6
Gravy
h. 2½", l. 6", w. 4½"

fig. 7
**Candle Holder,
Small**
dia. 5", h. 9¾"

not pictured:
**Candle Holder,
Large**
dia. 5", h. 13½"

fig. 8
Candle Holder
dia. 2¾", h. 2⅛"

not pictured:
*It is estimated that
about 50–60 shapes
were designed.
Among them were:*
Wooden Bowls
Wooden Trays
**Bowls on Metal
Stand**
**Tiered Hors
D'Oeuvre Trays**
Ceramic Jars

Match Holder
Candle Holders
Footed Bowls
**Covered Cheese
Board**
Cheese Knife
Pickle Fork
Olive Fork
Salad Spoon
Muddlers
Salt & Pepper
Corncob Holders
Sauce Boat
Ladle
Teapot
Cruets
Lazy Susan
Pepper Mill
Pencil Holder
Cigarette Holder

fig. 1
Coffee Pot
h. 9¼", l. 7¾", w. 4½"

fig. 2
Teapot
h. 6", l. 9", w. 5½"

fig. 3
Jug, Large, 3 qt.
h. 8½", l. 9½", w. 6½"

fig. 4
Jug, Small, 1¼ qt.
h. 6½", l. 7¼", w. 5"

fig. 5
Mug
(Classic Century)
dia. 3¼", h. 4", l. 4½"

fig. 6
After Dinner Cup
dia. 2¾", h. 2¼"
Saucer
dia. 5"

fig.7
Cup
dia. 4", h. 2½"
Saucer
dia. 5½"

fig. 8
Sugar
h. 3¾", l. 4¼", w. 3¾"

fig. 9
Creamer
h. 4½", l. 5¼", w. 3¾"

fig. 10
After Dinner Sugar
h. 4", l. 5¼", w. 3"

fig. 11
After Dinner Creamer
h. 4", l. 6", w. 3"

fig. 12
Dinner Plate
l. 11", w. 10"
Salad Plate
l. 8½", w. 7½"
Bread Plate
l. 6½", w. 5½"

fig. 13
Platter
l. 17", w. 11"
Platter
l. 15", w. 10"
Platter
l. 12¾", w. 8"

fig. 14
Ashtray
h. 2", l. 5½", w. 4"

fig. 15
Covered Onion Soup
h. 4", l. 5¾", w. 4¾"

fig. 16
Oatmeal
h. 2½", l. 6", w. 5½"

fig. 17
Coupe Soup
h. 2¾", l. 9", w. 6¾"
Baker
h. 3¼", l. 11½", w. 8½"
Salad, Large
h. 4¼", l. 14½", w. 10¾"

fig. 18
Covered Dish, Large
h. 5½", l. 11¾", w. 9"
Covered Dish, Medium
h. 5", l. 10", w. 7¾"

fig. 19
Marmite
h. 3½", l. 7½", w. 5½"

fig. 20
Covered Butter Dish
h. 3¼", l. 8½", w. 4½"

fig. 21
Celery Dish
h. 2¾", l. 12", w. 5¾"

fig. 22
Open Vegetable Dish
h. 2", l. 8¾", w. 8¾"

fig. 23
Fruit Bowl
h. 4¾", l. 11½", w. 9¼"

fig. 24
Fruit
h. 2", l. 5¾", w. 4¾"

fig. 25
Double Egg Cup
h. 4¼", l. 3", w. 2½"

fig. 26
Tall Candle Stick
dia. 3¾", h. 8¼"

fig. 27
Vinegar
h. 7¾", l. 4", w. 3"

fig. 28
Vase
h. 8¾", l. 4¾", w. 3¾"

fig. 29
Salt & Pepper
h. 4", l. 2½", w. 2"

fig. 30
Short Candlestick
h. 4½", l. 4½", w. 3½"

fig. 31
Gravy Boat
h. 6¼", l. 6½", w. 5½"

not pictured:
Ladle
h. 4", l. 4¾", w. 2"

Patterns
(authorized by Eva Zeisel)

White
Frost Flowers, 1952, by Irene Haas
Lyric, 1952, by Irene Haas
Buckingham, 1952, by Erik Blegvad
Arizona, 1952, by Charles Seliger
Dawn, 1952, by Charles Seliger

Patterns
(not authorized by Eva Zeisel)

Bouquet, 1952
Holiday, 1952
Mulberry, 1952
Fantasy, 1953
Peach Blossom, 1953
Caprice, 1953
Satin Black, 1953
Satin Grey, 1956
Pincone, 1953
Palo Duro, 1954
Studio 10, 1954
Harlequin (Domino), 1955
Flair, 1956
Metalcraft, 1956
Prairie Grass, 1956
Du Barry, 1958
Raintree, 1958
Romance (date unknown)

(Canada) Patterns
(not authorized by Eva Zeisel)

Queen's Rose, 1953
Bittersweet, 1953
Cloverdale, 1954
Sweet Grass, 1956

WESTERN STONEWARE COMPANY, *EVA ZEISEL FINE STONEWARE*
Monmouth, Illinois, USA | Stoneware

HOLLYDALE POTTERY, *EVA ZEISEL FINE STONEWARE/HI-FI STONEWARE*
Hollydale, California, USA | Stoneware

Same forms and measurements as
Western Stoneware Company

Colors + Patterns
(designed by Eva)

SOLID GLAZE
Allegro Yellow
Largo Brown
Andante White
Bright Blue

PATTERNS
(probably not fully
produced)
Chintz
Pennsylvania Dutch

fig. 1
Sugar
dia. 4½", h. 5⅛"

fig. 2
Creamer
dia. 4¼", h. 5⅛"

fig. 3
Bowl
h. 4½", l. 7⅝"
Ladle
l. 11"

fig. 4
Vegetable Dish
h. 6⅛", l. 12¼"

fig. 5
Large Salt
dia. 3½", h. 6¼"

fig. 6
Marmite
dia. 6⅛", h. 5¼"

fig. 7
Casserole, 2 qt.
dia. 7¾", h. 7½"

fig. 8
Teapot
h. 7", l. 8½"

fig. 9
Salt
dia. 2¾", h. 3¼"
Pepper
dia. 2¾", h. 2⅜"

fig. 10
Basket Gravy Boat
h. 7¾"

fig. 11
Cruet
dia. 3½", h. 7¾"

fig. 12
Cruet with Cork
dia. 3⅝", h. 7¼"

fig. 13
Vase/Candleholder
dia. 3⅝", h. 7¼"

fig. 14
**Large French
Casserole**
dia. 9½", h. 4½"
**Medium French
Casserole**
dia. 7½", h. 3⅝"
**Small French
Casserole**
dia. 5¾", h. 3¼"
Gravy Bowl
dia. 5½", h. 3"

fig. 15
**Small Casserole,
Cover**
dia. 5¾", h. 3¼"
**Medium Casserole,
Cover**
dia. 7½", h. 3⅝"
**Large Casserole,
Cover**
dia. 9½", h. 4½"
**Extra Large
Casserole, Cover**
dia. 11¼", h. 4⅝"

fig. 16
Bowl
dia. 11⅛", h. 4"
Bowl
dia. 9½", h. 3⅝"
Bowl
dia. 7", h. 3¼"
Bowl
dia. 5½", h. 3"

fig. 17
**Tall Casserole,
Handled**
dia. 7¾", h. 7¾"
Bean Pot, Handled
dia. 6¾", h. 7"
**Small Soup Pot,
Handled**
dia. 6⅜", h. 5⅜"

fig. 18
**Ice Bucket with
Insert, 2 Covers**
dia. 7¾", h. 7¾"
**Tall Casserole,
Cover**
dia. 7¾", h. 7¾"
Bean Pot, Cover
dia. 6¾", h. 7"
Small Soup, Cover
dia. 6⅜", h. 5⅜"

fig. 19
Platter
dia. 13"
Dinner Plate
dia. 11"
Luncheon Plate
dia. 9½"
Salad Plate
dia. 8"
Bread Plate
dia. 7"
Coaster
dia. 4"

fig. 20
Mug
dia. 3¼", h. 5½"

fig. 21
Teapot
dia. 5¾", h. 5"

fig. 22
Cup
dia. 3¾", h. 2⅜"
Saucer
dia. 6⅛"

fig. 23
Creamer
dia. 4¾", h. 4⅜"

fig. 24
Sugar
dia. 4¼", h. 4⅛"

fig. 25
Large Jug/Pitcher
dia. 5¾", h. 7½"

fig. 26
**Large Jug/ Pitcher,
Cover**
dia. 5¾", h. 7½"

fig. 27
All-Purpose Bowl
dia. 6⅜", h. 1⅞"

Eva Zeisel
Fine
STONEWARE
from
MONMOUTH

Colors + Patterns
(designed by Eva)

SOLID GLAZE
Cloud Grey
Rust
Blueberry

PATTERNS
(printed in blue, rose,
or multiple colors)

Pennsylvania Dutch
Colonial
Chintz
Commas
Lacey Wings
Pals
Xs
Horses
additional patterns (of-
ficial names unknown)

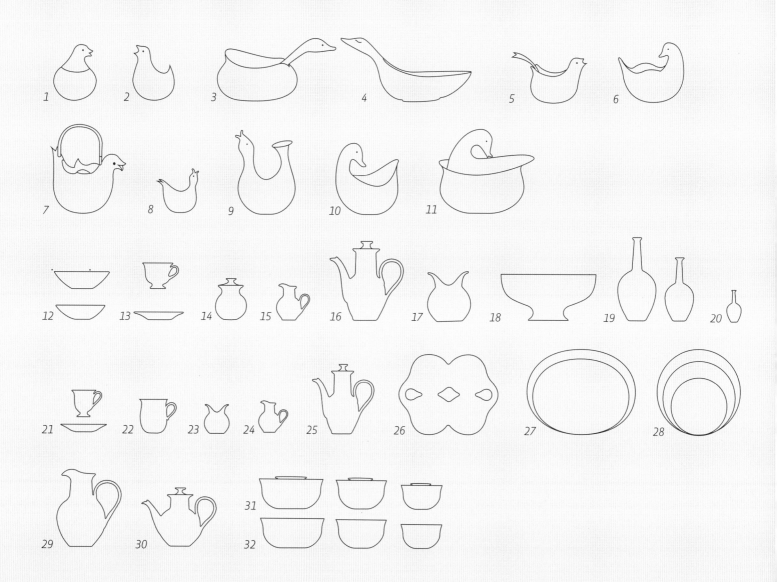

fig. 1
Sugar
dia. 4½", *h.* 5¾"

fig. 2
Creamer
dia. 3½", *h.* 4½"

fig. 3
Bowl
h. 4½", *l.* 8"
Ladle
l. 11½"

fig. 4
Vegetable Dish
h. 5¾", *l.* 13"

fig. 5
Gravy Boat
h. 5", *l.* 7"
Gravy Ladle
l. 6¼"

fig. 6
Relish Dish
h. 6¾", *l.* 6¼"

fig. 7
Teapot, 6 cup
h. 6½", *l.* 8"

fig. 8
Salt & Pepper
h. 4¼", *l.* 4⅜"

fig. 9
Oil/Vinegar
h. 8¼", *l.* 5¾"

fig. 10
**Vegetable Bowl,
1 pt.**
h. 7", *l.* 6¼"

fig. 11
Casserole, 2 qt.
h. 8", *l.* 9½"

fig. 12
Soup Bowl
dia. 7¼"
Fruit Bowl
dia. 6¼"

fig. 13
Cup
h. 3¼"
Saucer
dia. 4"

fig. 14
Sugar
dia. 4", *h.* 5¼"

fig. 15
Creamer
dia. 3½", *h.* 4¾"

fig. 16
Coffee Pot, 8 cup
h. 9⅝", *l.* 9"

fig. 17
Gravy
dia. 5⅜", *h.* 6"

fig. 18
Fruit Bowl
dia. 12½", *h.* 6"

fig. 19
Bottle
dia. 4½", *h.* 10"
Oil/Vinegar
dia. 3⅝", *h.* 7⅝"

fig. 20
Salt & Pepper
h. 3½"

fig. 21
After-Dinner Cup
dia. 5½", *h.* 3¼"
Saucer
l. 3½"

fig. 22
Mug, 10 oz.
h. 4"

fig. 23
After-Dinner Sugar
dia. 3¼", *h.* 3⅝"

fig. 24
**After-Dinner
Creamer**
dia. 3½", *h.* 8¾"

fig. 25
**After-Dinner Coffee
Pot**
h. 9", *l.* 8"

fig. 26
Relish Dish
h. 2", *l.* 13", *w.* 9½"

fig. 27
Platter
l. 16"
Platter
l. 14"

fig. 28
Dinner Plate
dia. 10½"
Salad Plate
dia. 8½"
Bread Plate
dia. 6½"

fig. 29
Pitcher
dia. 5¾", *h.* 9¼"

fig. 30
Teapot
h. 7½", *l.* 9½"

fig. 31
**Covered Casserole,
3 qt.**
dia. 11⅜", *h.* 7"
**Covered Casserole,
2 qt.**
dia. 9⅜", *h.* 5½"
**Covered Casserole,
1 qt.**
dia. 7¾", *h.* 4¾"

fig. 32
Bowl
l. 11½"
Bowl
l. 9½"
Bowl
l. 7"

ironstone
design
Eva Zeisel
schmid NKT
OVEN PROOF
JAPAN

Patterns
(designed by Eva)

*Lyric
(black print on warm
white)*
*Stratford
(blue print on warm
white)*

fig. 1
Cookie Jar
(only one shown)
Item no. 1576
dia. 8", h. 9½", l. 9¼"
Item no. 1566
dia. 7", h. 8½", l. 8¼"

fig. 2
Bean Jar, 3½ pt.
(only one shown)
Item no. 1575/1565
dia. 6½", h. 7¼",
l. 8½"

fig. 3
Pitcher, 5 pt.
Item no. 1580
dia. 7", h. 8½", l. 8½"

fig. 4
Teapot
Item no. 1582
h. 5¼", l. 8¼", w. 5¼"

fig. 5
Oval Casserole
Item no. 1578
h. 5¼", l. 13¾", w. 8¾"

fig. 6
Oval Casserole
Item no. 1577
h. 5½", l. 10¾", w. 6½"

fig. 7
Salad, Large
Item no. 1572
dia. 11¾", h. 4"

fig. 8
Salad
Item no. 1571
dia. 6¼", h. 2¾"

fig. 9
**Round Side Handle
Tureen Casserole**
Item no. 1589
h. 6½", l. 16", w. 10¼"

fig. 10
**Round Side Handle
Tureen Casserole**
Item no. 1579
h. 5¾", l. 14¾",
w. 8¾"

fig. 11
**Individual
Casserole**
Item no. 1585
h. 4½", l. 7", w. 5"

fig. 12
Leftover Dish
Item no. 1568
dia. 4", h. 4"

fig. 13
Covered Soup
Item no. 1567
h. 3", l. 6¼", w. 4¼"

fig. 14
Handled Relish
Item no. 1570
h. 1", l. 6¾", w. 5¼"

fig. 15
Mug
Item no. 1574
h. 3½", l. 4½", w. 3½"

fig. 16
**Refrigerator
Pitcher**
Item no. 1569
h. 8½", l. 4¼", w. 3¾"

fig. 17
Side Handle Teapot
Item no. 1581
h. 4", l. 6¾", w. 6¼"

fig. 18
Creamer
Item no. 1583
h. 3¼", l. 5¾", w. 4"

fig. 19
Sugar
Item no. 1584
dia. 4", h. 3¾"

fig. 20
Jam Jar
Item no. 1573
dia. 3¼", h. 4¼"

fig. 21
Salt & Pepper
Item no. 1586/1587
dia. 3¼", h. 3¼"

Patterns
(designed by Eva)

Casual Living, 1955
Tri-Tone, 1956

(not authorized by
Eva)

Hostessware, 1957
(Kitchenware
    shapes with stan-
    dard Hall shapes
    in patterns:
    Exotic Bird
    Flight
    Gold and White)

1

2

3

4

5

6

7

8

9

10

11

12

13

14

15

fig. 1
Fruit Bowl
h. 2¼", l. 6½", w. 5"
Soup Bowl
h. 3", l. 8¼", w. 6 ¼"
Vegetable Bowl
h. 3½", l. 10½", w. 8¾"
Salad Bowl
dia. 11¾"

fig. 2
Double Vegetable
*h. 3½", l. 11½",
w. 8¼"*

fig. 3
Relish
*h. 1½", l. 14½",
w. 8½"*

fig. 4
Covered Dish, 2 qt.
h. 7½", l. 10½", w. 8¾"

fig. 5
Butter Dish
h. 3¼", l. 8½", w. 4½"

fig. 6
Salt & Pepper
h. 4¼", l. 2½", w. 2"

fig. 7
Gravy Boat
h. 5", l. 6¼", w. 4¾"
Ladle
h. 4", l. 4¾", w. 2"

fig. 8
Sugar
h. 4½", l. 4", w. 3¾"

fig. 9
Creamer
h. 4¼", l. 4", w. 3¾"

fig. 10
Teapot
h. 7", l. 9½"

fig. 11
Pitcher, 1¼ qt.
h. 7½", l. 6", w. 6"

fig. 12
Dinner Plate
*h. 1¾", l. 11½",
w. 10¼"*
Salad Plate
h. ½", l. 9½", w. 8¼"
Bread Plate
h. ½", l. 7", w. 6"

fig. 13
Large Platter
h. 2½", l. 15", w. 12¾"
Medium Platter
h. 2¾", l. 14", w. 11"

fig. 14
Ashtray
dia. 3¾", l. 4½"

fig. 15
Tea Cup
h. 2¾", l. 5¼", w. 4"
Saucer
dia. 6½", h. 1"

Patterns
(not designed by Eva)

Fern, 1956
Sunglow, 1956
Garden of Eden, 1956
Flight, 1957

fig. 1
Tea Cup
h. 2", l. 4¾", w. 4"
Saucer
dia. 5¾"

fig. 2
Tea Cup
h. 2¼", l. 5", w. 4¼"
Saucer
dia. 6⅜"

fig. 3
Mocha Cup
h. 2", l. 3¼", w. 2½"
Saucer
dia. 5⅛"

fig. 4
Hot Chocolate Cup
h. 2½", l. 4", w. 3"
Saucer
dia. 5½"

fig. 5
Coffee Cup
h. 2¾", l. 4¼", w. 3¼"
Saucer
dia. 5¾"

fig. 6
Soup
dia. 4½", h. 2"
Saucer
dia. 6¾"

fig. 7
Coffee Pot
h. 6⅛", l. 7¼", w. 4"
Coffee Pot
dimensions unknown
Coffee Pot
h. 7", l. 8¾", w. 4¾"
Coffee Pot
h. 7½", l. 9¼", w. 5"

fig. 8
Teapot
h. 5¼", l. 8¾", w. 5⅜"
Teapot
h. 6", l. 9¾", w. 5⅞"

fig. 9
Pitcher
h. 6½", l. 7", w. 4½"

fig. 10
Creamer
h. 2¼", l. 2½", w. 2½"
Creamer
h. 2¾", l. 4", w. 3"
Creamer
h. 3", l. 4¾", w. 3¼"
Creamer
h. 3¾", l. 5¼", w. 4¼"

fig. 11
Sugar
dia. 3", h. 2¾"
Sugar
dia. 3¼", h. 3"
Sugar
dia. 3½", h. 3½"
Sugar
dia. 4", h. 3¾"

fig. 12
Jam Jar
dia. 4", h. 3¾"

fig. 13
Salt & Pepper
dia. 1⅝", h. 2"

fig. 14
Egg Cup
dia. 1¾", h. 2"

fig. 15
Butter Sauciere
h. 2½", l. 4⅝", w. 2¼"

fig. 16
Covered Butter Dish
l. 6½", h. 4¾"

fig. 17
Fruit Bowl
dia. 4¾", h. 1¾"

fig. 18
Sauce Boat
h. 2¾", l. 6½"

fig. 19
Flat Round Platter
dia. 12⅛"
Deep Round Platter
dia. 12⅛"

fig. 20
Oval Platter
l. 16½"
Oval Platter
l. 15"
Oval Platter
l. 13"
Oval Platter
l. 11"
Oval Platter
l. 9½"

fig. 21
Cake Platter
l. 11⅜", w. 10¾"

fig. 22
Cake Platter
l. 14½", w. 6¾"

fig. 23
Plate
dia. 10¼"
Plate
dia. 9½"
Plate
dia. 8¼"
Plate
dia. 7½"
Plate
dia. 6⅝"
Plate
dia. 5¾"
Soup Plate
dia. 8⅝"
Soup Plate
dia. 7½"

fig. 24
Salad Bowl
dia. 7", h. 3"
Salad Bowl
dia. 7½", h. 3¼"
Salad Bowl
dia. 8¼", h. 3⅝"

fig. 25
Covered Vegetable Dish
h. 5½", l. 9", w. 6½"

fig. 26
Soup Tureen
h. 6½", l. 10¾", w. 8"

Patterns
(not designed by Eva except White)

0001 White
102 Ruedesheim
109 Lindau
121 Salzburg
126 Nauheim
135 Marburg
401 Wiesbaden
402 Bad Ems
405 Glanzgoldrand 406 Glanzplatinrand
501 Rügen
502 Helgoland
505 Cuxhaven
508 Linz
512 Stuttgart
610 Mainau
611 Fulda
617 Mainz
902 Baden Baden 911 Travemünde
914 Bremen
922 Trier
also 125, 138, 237
(names unknown)

fig. 1
Pepper [Z 26]
h. 8"

fig. 2
Salt [Z 25]
h. 8"

fig. 3
Cup [SZ 31]
h. 4"
Saucer [SZ 32]
dia. 6"

fig. 4
Sugar [Z 15]
dia. 4", h. 5"

fig. 5
Creamer [Z 14]
h. 4¾"

fig. 6
Coffee Pot [Z 13]
h. 8½"

fig. 7
Pitcher [Z 22]
h. 8½"

fig. 8
**Footed Tureen
[Z 1B]**
dia. 15", h. 16½"

fig. 9
**Footed Tureen
[Z 2B]**
dia. 8¾", h. 8¾"

fig. 10
Footed Dish [Z 5]
dia. 5¾", h. 5"

fig. 11
Footed Bowl [Z 4]
dia. 10½", h. 9"

fig. 12
**Footed Soup Bowl
[Z 33]**
dia. 6¼", h. 3½"

fig. 13
Small Salt [Z 23]
h. 3½"
Small Pepper [Z 24]
h. 4"

fig. 14
Tureen [Z 1]
dia. 15", h. 11¾"

fig. 15
Tureen [Z 2]
dia. 8¾", h. 9"

fig. 16
**Wine Bottle/Vase
[Z 20]**
h. 17"

fig. 17
Dinner Plate [Z 35]
dia. 12¼"
Dinner Plate [Z 28]
dia. 10½"
Salad Plate [Z 29]
dia. 8"

fig. 18
Ice Bucket [Z 18]
h. 9"

fig. 19
Casserole [Z 16]
dia. 10"

fig. 20
Bowl [Z 34]
dia. 6"

fig. 21
Bowl [Z 8]
dia. 6½"

fig. 22
**Vegetable Bowl
[Z 11]**
l. 12", w. 6¾"

fig. 23
Platter [Z 9]
l. 20", w. 12½"

fig. 24
Platter [Z 3]
dia. 16"

fig. 25
Wave Bowl [Z 6]
dia. 10"

fig. 26
Footed Bowl [Z 12]
h. 6", w. 6½"

Colors
*(authorized by Eva
Zeisel)*

*Olive
Oxblood
Gold
Mottled Taupe*

ZSOLNAY PORCELAIN MANUFACTORY
Pécs, Hungary | Porcelain

1   2   3   4   5

6   7   8   9

10   11   12   13   14

fig. 1
Gourd Jar
h. 9½"

fig. 2
Apple
dia. 6½", h. 5½"

fig. 3
Apple
dia. 5½", h. 6½"

fig. 4
Candle Holder
dia. 5¾", h. 4"
Candle Holder
dia. 4", h. 3"

Candle Holder
dia. 3¼", h. 2"

fig. 5
Vase
h. 4"

fig. 6
Fig Vase, Large
dia. 8½", h. 8½"
Fig Vase, Small
dia. 7", h. 7½"

fig. 7
Bottle Vase
h. 6½", w. 3¼"

fig. 8
Vase
h. 6½", l. 3½", w. 2¾"

fig. 9
Dimple Vase
h. 7½"
Dimple Vase
h. 9"

fig. 10
Candle Holder
dia. 7½", h. 8½"

fig. 11
Candle Holder
h. 9"

fig. 12
Vase
h. 11"
Vase
dia. 7½", h. 15"

fig. 13
Vase
dia. 6", h. 18½"

fig. 14
Vase
dia. 6", h. 18½"

UNITED CHINA AND GLASS INTERNATIONAL, *PINNACLE*
Toki City, Japan | Semi-Porcelain (Earthenware)

fig. 1
Teapot
h. 8", l. 9½"

fig. 2
Creamer
h. 4¾", l. 5½", w. 3½"

fig. 3
Sugar
dia. 4", h. 5½"

fig. 4
Tea Cup
h. 3", l. 5", w. 3¾"
Saucer
dia. 6¼"

fig. 5
Dinner Plate
dia. 10¾"
Dessert/Salad Plate
dia. 7"

fig. 6
Vegetable Bowl
dia. 9½", h. 2½"

fig. 7
Salt & Pepper
h. 3¼", w. 2½"

fig. 8
Covered Casserole
dia. 12", h. 7⅞"

fig. 9
Mug
(Chantal only)
dia. 3½", h. 5"

fig. 10
Gravy
h. 5", l. 7", w. 5"

fig. 11
Platter
h. 1½", l. 14", w. 10¾"

not pictured:
Buffet Platter
dia. 12", h. 1¼"

Chantal Mug Colors

Black (2006)
White (2006)
Indigo Blue (2009)
Garden Green (2009)
Red (2009)
Lime Green (2010)
Apple Red (2010)
Pure (2010)

KLEINREID
Brooklyn, New York, USA | Porcelain, Glass, Paper

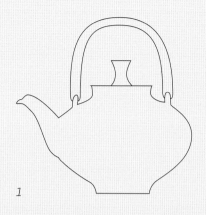 1
 2
 3
 4
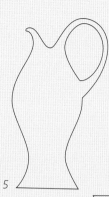 5

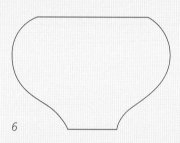 6
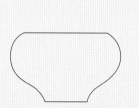
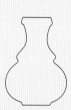
 7
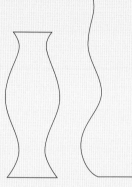

fig. 1
Teapot
h. 8½", l. 7", w. 6½"

fig. 2
Sugar
dia. 3½", h. 6½"

fig. 3
Creamer
dia. 4", h. 3½"

fig. 4
Small Pitcher
h. 8½", l. 7", w. 5½"

fig. 5
Large Pitcher
h. 11½", l. 6½", w. 5"

fig. 6
**Pillow Stack Vases,
3 sizes**
dia. 8½", h. 5½"
dia. 6", h. 3¾"
dia. 4½", h. 3¼"

fig. 7
**Upright Vases,
3 sizes**
dia. 5", h. 12"
dia. 3½", h. 9½"
dia. 3", h. 7½"

not pictured:
Silk screens
Magic Language 1
l. 22", w. 30"
Magic Language 2
l. 22", w. 30"
Lover's Suite 1
[1st + 2nd edition]
l. 21½", w. 14½"
Lover's Suite 2
l. 22", w. 22"

**Colors
in porcelain**
(not designed by Eva)

Ivory
Three Tone Sepia

**Colors
fig. 7 in glass**
(not designed by Eva)

Clear
Blue
Amber
Ruby
Black

LOMONOSOV PORCELAIN FACTORY, *TALISMAN*
St. Petersburg, Russia | Bone China

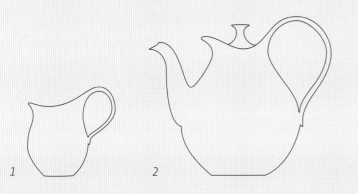

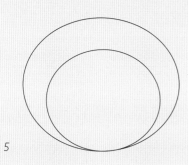

fig. 1
Cup
h. 4"

fig. 2
Teapot
h. 8"

fig. 3
Creamer
h. 6"

fig. 4
Sugar
h. 5"

fig. 5
Dessert Plate
l. 9", w. 7¾"
Saucer
l. 6½", w. 6"

NAMBÉ, *EDEN*
Nambé, New Mexico, USA/Thailand | Metal Alloy, Porcelain, Glass

fig. 1
Sugar
h. 4½"

fig. 2
Creamer
h. 4½"

fig. 3
Mug
dia. 3⅜", h. 4½"

fig. 4
Salt & Pepper
h. 4"

fig. 5
Salad Plate
dia. 9"
Pasta Bowl
dia. 8½", h. 1½"

Dinner Plate
porcelain
dia. 11¾"
metal
dia. 14¾"
Serving Bowl
dia. 10"

fig. 6
Platter
porcelain
l. 15", w. 12"
metal
l. 17", w. 15"

fig. 7
Wine Glass
h. 7"
Goblet
h. 8¼"
Champagne Flute
h. 8½"

NAMBÉ, DIVERSE DESIGNS
Nambé, New Mexico, USA/Thailand | Metal Alloy, Porcelain, Glass

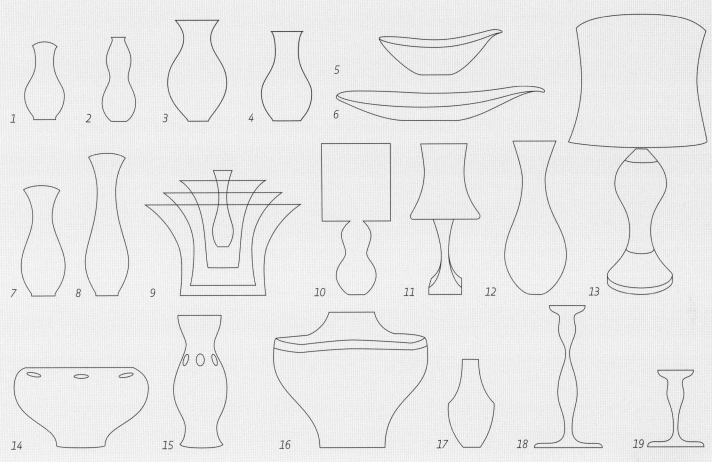

1   2   3   4   5   6
7   8   9   10   11   12   13
14   15   16   17   18   19

fig. 1
Salt & Pepper
h. 4½"

fig. 2
Unity Vase
h. 5"

fig. 3
Harmony Vase
h. 8"

fig. 4
Freedom Vase
h. 6"

fig. 5
Lug Bowl, 3 sizes
l. 8½", w. 6½"
l. 11½", w. 6⅝"
l. 14⅝", w. 11"

fig. 6
Platter, 2 sizes
l. 15", w. 8⅝"
l. 17", w. 10⅝"

fig. 7
Candle Holder
dia. 2", h. 6"

fig. 8
Candle Holder
dia. 2½", h. 8"

fig. 9
Ohana 4 pc. Vase Set
dia. 10", h. 9"

fig. 10
Accent Lamp
dia. 3", h. 5"

fig. 11
Accent Lamp
h. 6", w. 2"

fig. 12
Venus Vase, 2 sizes
h. 16½", h. 10½"

fig. 13
Venus Lamp
h. 25½"

fig. 14
Peek-A-Boo Rose Bowl
dia. 9", h. 5"

fig. 15
Peek-A-Boo Vase
h. 10"

fig. 16
Essence Urn
h. 11½", l. 11", w. 7"

fig. 17
Keepsake Urn
h. 8"

fig. 18
Candle Holder
h. 11"

fig. 19
Eden Candle Holder
h. 6½"

not pictured:
Venus Bowl, 3 sizes
dia. 10"
dia. 9"
dia. 7¼"

Bloom Urn
h. 8"
Double Globe Vase
h. 8"

ROYAL STAFFORD, *ONE-O-ONE*
Stoke-on-Trent, England | Earthenware

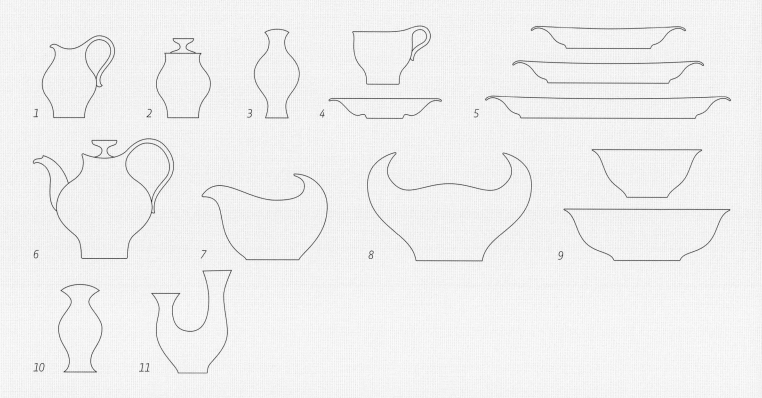

fig. 1
Creamer
h. 6", *l.* 4½", *w.* 3½"

fig. 2
Sugar
h. 6", *l.* 4½", *w.* 3½"

fig. 3
Salt & Pepper
h. 5"

fig. 4
Cup
dia. 4", *h.* 3½"
Saucer
dia. 6¾"

fig. 5
Platter
l. 13½", *w.* 10½"
Dinner Plate
dia. 11"
Salad Plate
dia. 8¼"

fig. 6
Teapot
h. 8½", *w.* 9"

fig. 7
Gravy Boat
h. 3½", *l.* 7", *w.* 3½"

fig. 8
Rockland Bowl
h. 7", *l.* 10", *w.* 7"

fig. 9
Soup/Cereal Bowl
dia. 6½"
Vegetable Bowl
dia. 10"

fig. 10
Vase
h. 7½"

fig. 11
Vase
h. 6½", 8"

DESIGN WITHIN REACH, *GRANIT COLLECTION*
Hong Kong, China | Stoneware

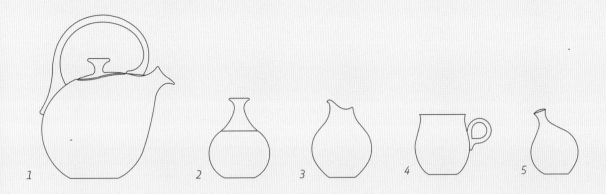

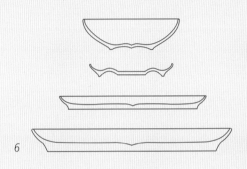

fig. 1
Teapot
h. 7", l. 8", w. 5½"

fig. 2
Sugar
h. 6"

fig. 3
Creamer
h. 4¼"

fig. 4
Cup
h. 3", w. 3½"

fig. 5
Salt & Pepper
dia. 3", h. 4"

fig. 6
Cereal Bowl
dia. 6¼", h. 2"
Saucer
dia. 6¼"
Salad Plate
dia. 8½", h. 1½"
Dinner Plate
dia. 10½", h. 1½"

Eva Zeisel™
Made in China

NEUE GALERIE DESIGN SHOP, BABY FEEDER
Tangshan, China | Bone China

fig. 1
Baby Feeder
h. 2", l. 3", w. 2"

fig. 2
Spoon
l. 3½", w. ½"

EVA ZEISEL ORIGINALS, *EVA ZEISEL CANDLESTICKS*
Moradabad, India | Bronze

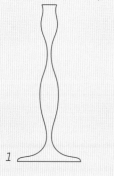
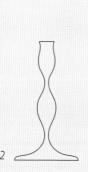

fig. 1
Candle Holder
dia. 4⅝", h. 11"

fig. 2
Candle Holder
dia. 4⅝", h. 8"

fig. 3
Candle Holder
dia. 4⅝", h. 6"

fig. 4
Candle Holder
dia. 6¼", h. 4"

not pictured:
Mark (Engraving)

YAMAZAKI TABLEWARE, EVA FLATWARE
Qindao, China | Stainless Steel

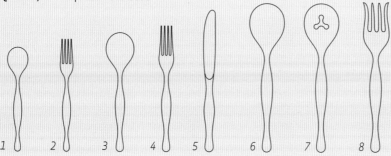

fig. 1
Teaspoon
l. 7"

fig. 2
Salad Fork
l. 7½"

fig. 3
Dinner Spoon
l. 8"

fig. 4
Dinner Fork
l. 7½"

fig. 5
Dinner Knife
l. 9¼"

fig. 6
Serving Spoon
l. 9½"

fig. 7
Slotted Serving Spoon
l. 9½"

fig. 8
Serving Fork
l. 9¾"

NEUE GALERIE NEW YORK

LEUCOS USA, EVA ZEISEL COLLECTION
Murano, Italy | Murano Glass

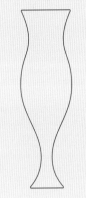  

1   2   3

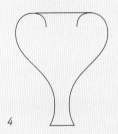 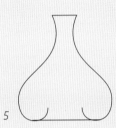 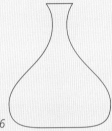

4   5   6

fig.1
Wall Sconce, Spring
h. 19⅝", l. 5½",
w. 6¾"

fig. 2
**Pendant Lamp,
Spring**
dia. 6¾", h. 18½"

fig.3
Table Lamp, Spring
dia. 6¾", h. 19⅝"

fig. 4
**Wall Sconce,
Summer**
h. 13", l. 5", w. 11"

fig. 5
**Pendant Lamp,
Summer**
dia. 11", h. 12¼"

fig. 6
**Table Lamp,
Summer**
dia. 11", h. 13⅜"

Colors
(not designed by Eva)

White
Honey

MUSEUM OF MODERN ART STORE , CHRISTMAS ORNAMENTS
Murano, Italy | Murano Glass

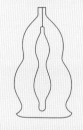 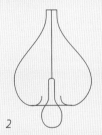 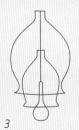

1   2   3

fig. 1
Blue
dia. 3", h. 6"

fig. 2
Orange
dia. 3", h. 5"

fig. 3
Pink
dia. 3½", h. 6"

Colors
*(designed by Eva and
Olivia Barry)*

VITRELUXE FOR GUMP'S
Portland, Oregon, USA | Glass

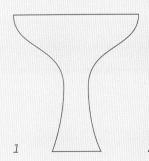 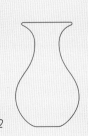 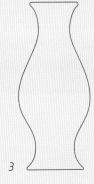

1   2   3

fig. 1
Pedestal Bowl
dia. 9½", h. 8¼"

fig. 2
Small Golden Vase
dia. 2¾", h. 6½"

fig. 3
Lampere Vase
dia. 2¾", h. 12½"

not pictured:
Bulb Vase
h. 7"
Contour Vase
h. 12½"
Curve Vase
h. 12¼"
Vase
h. 10"
Mark (Incision)

Colors
*(gradients designed
by Eva and Olivia
Barry)*

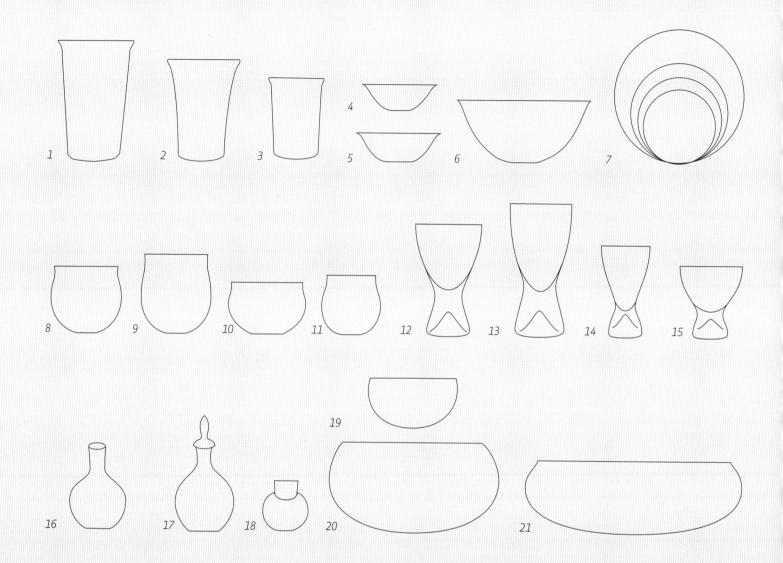

Town and Country

fig. 1
Iced Tea
dia. 3³⁄₈", h. 5¼"

fig. 2
Tumbler
dia. 4¼", h. 4¼"

fig. 3
Juice, 5 oz.
dimensions unknown

fig.4
Flared Nappy
dia. 6", h. 2¼"

fig.5
Flared Nappy
dia. 8", h. 2¹⁄₃"

fig. 6
Salad Bowl
dia. 11½", h. 4¼"

fig. 7
Sandwich Plate
dia. 14"
Service Plate
dia. 10"
Luncheon Plate
dia. 8"
Salad Plate
dia. 6"

not pictured:
Dessert Dish, *dia. 5"*
Relish Dish, *dia. 8"*
Nappy, *dia. 4"*
Ice Lip Pitcher, 54 oz.
dimensions unknown

Crystal Buds

fig. 8
Tumbler
dimensions unknown

fig. 9
Iced Tea, 15 oz.
dimensions unknown

fig. 10
Sherbet, 9 oz.
dimensions unknown

fig. 11
Juice, 7 oz.
dimensions unknown

Hourglass
fig. 12
Goblet, 10 oz.
dia. 3½", h. 5½"

fig. 13
Iced Tea, 12 oz.
dimensions unknown

fig. 14
Claret, 5 oz.
dimensions unknown

fig. 15
Cocktail, 5 oz.
dimensions unknown

Roundelay
fig. 16
Bud Vase
dimensions unknown

fig. 17
Oil Bottle, Stopper, 8 oz.
dimensions unknown

fig. 18
Salt & Pepper
h. 2¼"

fig. 19
Individual Salad Bowl
dia. 4½"

fig. 20
Salad Bowl
dia. 8"

fig. 21
Gardenia Bowl
dia. 10"

not pictured:
Open Sugar
dia. 3"
Mayonaise
dia. 4"
Ashtray
dia. 3"
Candle Centerpiece
dia. 6"
Salad Bowl
dia. 8"
dimensions unknown:
Pitcher, 16 oz.
Ice Lip Pitcher, 54 oz.
Cocktail Shaker, 54 oz.
Bitters, 6 oz.
Cocktail, 5 oz.
Goblet, 8 oz.
Saucer Champagne, 6 oz.
Footed Soda, 5 oz.
Footed Soda, 12 oz.
Creamer, no handle
Decanter, Stopper
Finger Bowl
Marmalade
Water Bottle

Patterns
(designed by Eva)

ETCHINGS
520B Leaf
521B Scroll
522B Cocktail Party
523B Steed
524B Classic
525B Chintz
526B Pennsylvania Dutch
527B Ponies

CUTTINGS
3 patterns
(official names unknown)

FEDERAL GLASS COMPANY, *STOCKHOLM*
Columbus, Ohio, USA | Glass

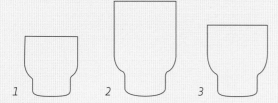

fig. 1
Cocktail
dia. 2¾", h. 2¾"

fig. 2
Highball
dia. 3⅛", h. 4¼"

fig. 3
Old Fashioned
dia. 3", h. 3¼"

FEDERAL GLASS COMPANY, *PRESTIGE*
Columbus, Ohio, USA | Glass

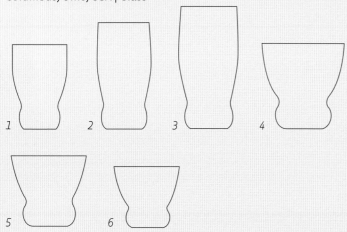

fig. 1
Juice
dia. 2½", h. 3⅞"

fig. 2
Tumbler
dia. 2¾", h. 4¾"

fig. 3
Iced Tea
dia. 2¾", h. 5⅝"

fig. 4
**Double Old
Fashioned**
dia. 4", h. 3¾"

fig. 5
Old Fashioned
dia. 3⅛", h. 3¼"

fig. 6
Cocktail
dia. 3", h. 2½"

BRYCE BROTHERS, *SILHOUETTE*
Mt. Pleasant, Pennsylvania, USA | Glass

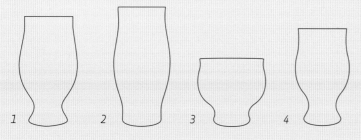

Colors
(authorized by Eva)

*Amethyst (purple)
Cerulean (blue)Green
Amber (gold)
Smoke (brown) Char-
treuse (yellow)Crystal
(clear)*

fig. 1
Water Goblet
dia. 3", h. 5⅜"

fig. 2
Iced Tea
dia. 3", h. 5¾"

fig. 3
Sherbet
dia. 3½", h. 3¼"

fig. 4
Juice
dia. 2½", h. 4⅜"

CHRISTIAN CARSTENS KG, STEINGUTFABRIK
Hirschau, Germany | Stoneware

DULEVO PORCELAIN FACTORY
Orekhovo-Zuevo (Moscow region), USSR | Porcelain

LOMONOSOV STATE PORCELAIN FACTORY
Leningrad (St. Petersburg), USSR | Porcelain

FEDERAL TOOL CORPORATION
Chicago, Illinois, USA | Glass, Plastic

GOSS CHINA COMPANY, *WEE MODERN*
Location unknown, USA | Stoneware

WATT POTTERY, *SOUTH MOUNTAIN STONEWARE*
Crooksville, Ohio, USA | Stoneware

MGLASS
Marinha Grande, Portugal | Glass

SELECT CHRONOLOGY
Pat Moore

Short contributions by:

Jim Drobka, JD
Pat Moore, PM
Dennis Thompson, DT
Debbie Deaver Townley, DDT
Raymond Calvet Vlach, RV

The following abbreviations are used:
   LP: Limited production
   NP: Not produced
   NYC: New York City

*Bay Ridge Specialty
bowl, vase, and
ashtray, 1939. EZA.*

*Federal Tool
Corporation glass jug,
1947. EZA.*

1906	Eva Amalia Stricker born Budapest, Hungary.
1923	Studies at Hungarian Royal Academy of Fine Arts, Budapest.
1924	Apprentice potter, Budapest.
	First woman member, Guild of Chimney Sweeps, Oven Makers, Roof Tilers, Well Diggers, and Potters, Budapest.
1925	Establishes her own pottery studio, Budapest.
	Visits 1925 Paris Exposition, France.
1926	Honorable Mention, Sesquicentennial Exposition, Philadelphia, Pennsylvania, U.S.
	Freelance designer, Kispester-Granit, Budapest.
1927	Designer, Hansa Kunstkeramik, Hamburg, Germany.
1928	Designs stage sets, continues painting, Budapest.
1928–30	Designer, Schramberger Majolikafabrik, Schramberg, Germany.
1930–31	Designer, Christian Carstens KG, Steingutfabrik, Germany.
	Lives in Berlin, Germany.
1932–37	Lives and works in USSR.
1932	Consultant, Ukraine Central Glass and Porcelain Trust.
	Designer, Artistic Laboratory, Lomonosov State Porcelain Factory, Leningrad, USSR.
1933	Marries Alex Weissberg.
1934	Designer, Dulevo Porcelain Factory, Orekhovo-Zuevo, USSR.
1935	Artistic Director of China and Glass Industry, USSR.
1936–37	Imprisoned, Moscow, USSR.
1937	Joins family members in Vienna, Austria.
1938	Divorces Weissberg, Vienna.
	Flees Vienna for England.
	Marries Hans Zeisel, England.
	Emigrates to U.S. with Hans Zeisel.
1939	Miniature tea set, Simon Slobodkin, NYC (probably NP).
	Watches, Hamilton Watch Co., Lancaster, Pennsylvania (NP).
	Giftware, Bay Ridge Specialty Corporation, Trenton, New Jersey (LP).
	Teaches at Pratt Institute, NYC (1939–53).
1940	Daughter Jean born.
1942	*STRATOWARE* dinnerware, Universal Potteries, Cambridge, Ohio, for Sears, Roebuck & Co., Chicago, Illinois.
	UTILITY WARE (NP).
1944	Son John born.
1946	*MUSEUM* dinnerware, Castleton China, New Castle, Pennsylvania (LP 1946, full production 1949).
	New Shapes in Modern China: Designed by Eva Zeisel exhibition, Museum of Modern Art, NYC.
1947	*TOWN AND COUNTRY* dinnerware, Red Wing Potteries, Red Wing, Minnesota.
	Dinnerware and giftware, Riverside Ceramic Company, Riverside, California.
	Dinnerware, Butler Brothers, Chicago (NP).
	CLOVERWARE, Clover Box and Manufacturing Company, NYC.
	Perfume bottles, Charles of the Ritz and Richard Hudnut, NYC (NP).
	Picture frames, mail boxes, and tape dispensers, Metal-Craft, Chicago (NP).
	Glass jugs, Federal Tool Corporation, Chicago.
1948	Stainless-steel pot, pan, and kettle with plastic handles, General Mills, Minneapolis, Minnesota (NP).

Ohio Potteries Children's Toiletries utensils, 1949. Photo: EZA.

1949   *MUSEUM* dinnerware, Castleton China, full production begins.

Ohio Potteries Child Toiletries (NP)

This children's toiletries set consists of a shaker bottle with a cork in the bottom, which could be used for either oil or baby powder; a lidded jar for cotton balls; and two stoppered bottles that could be used for lotions, powders, or oils. Designed by Eva with the assistance of her student and model maker, Irving Achorn,[1] prototypes were produced by Ohio Potteries in 1949 in pink and blue glazes but were never manufactured.[2] While originally created as a baby set, the pieces could easily be converted to use as containers for personal toiletries as the child grew older (which may have been a consideration because Eva's own children were reaching their preteen years). *PM*

1949–50   *RESILIENT CHAIR* (LP).
1950   *RANCH HOUSE* tea set, Charm House, NYC (LP).
      NORLEANS CHINA dinnerware, Meito China, Japan, for United China and Glass, New Orleans, Louisiana.
1951   Rosewood, metal, and ceramic giftware, Salisbury Artisans, Salisbury, Connecticut (LP).
      EVA ZEISEL: INDUSTRIAL DESIGNER exhibition, Akron Art Institute, Ohio.

LOZA FINA

Eva designed a set of dinnerware that was manufactured by Loza Fina, S. A., in Guadalajara, Mexico. Little is known about the circumstances of this commission, the pieces from which were available at the Sears, Roebuck & Co. store in Mexico City and other retailers. A Sears advertisement in January 1951 entitled "Everything for the Modern Kitchen" included an illustration of Eva's design.[3] In late 1951, the shapes were also shown in advertisements from several other retailers.[4] Ads for the Loza Fina company in December 1951 promoted "Elegance and Distinction" and included an example of Eva's line.[5] The designs were also included in the exhibition *El Arte en la Vida Diaria*, curated by the designer-architect Clara Porset, opened in Mexico City in April 1952. Porset juxtaposed modern Mexican industrial products with traditional indigenous handcrafted objects.[6] Eva's Loza Fina design is shown in the exhibition catalogue. Porset had connections to MoMA in New York in the 1940s, and may have met Eva or been familiar with her work.[7]

    As of this writing, examples that have been found are decorated with decal patterns (several floral designs, "courting couples" tableaux, and Chinese-style imagery, some of which were also available on china produced in the U.S.). Additionally, Loza Fina used the same decals on shapes not designed by Eva. Sets with hand-painted designs have also been found. These may have been produced aftermarket, perhaps for the tourist trade. The line is marked with the acronym "LOFISA" and a symbol representing the twin spires of Guadalajara's cathedral. *JD*

Loza Fina pieces in aging cabinet at Eva's studio. Photograph: EZA.

1952   Hallcraft *TOMORROW'S CLASSIC* dinnerware, Hall China Company, East Liverpool, Ohio.
      SILHOUETTE glassware, Bryce Brothers, Mt. Pleasant, Pennsylvania.

1953   Glassware, A. H. Heisey and Co., Newark, Ohio.
EVA ZEISEL FINE STONEWARE dinnerware and kitchenware, Monmouth division, Western Stoneware Co., Monmouth, Illinois.
Moves to Chicago. Hans Zeisel takes position at University of Chicago.

Goss China: *WEE MODERN*

Eva designed what became the *WEE MODERN* children's ware for her own children in the late 1940s.[8] It consisted of a two-handled mug, porringer-style bowl, and loop-handled dish. Her then-assistant, Irving Achorn, recalled "working on a set of ceramic tableware for children and photographing it" in about 1949.[9] The whimsical decal pattern used on the pieces was not approved by Eva, who had selected solid pastel glaze colors.[10]

Goss China Company, WEE MODERN children's service: bowl with spoon rest, cup, and plate with handle and spoon rest, 1953. SVC.

The set was introduced at the 1953 Chicago China and Glass Market, where it was displayed on the Sun Glo Studios table along with other designs.[11] Her commission was to find a commercially attractive product that could be produced in large, but very low, kilns previously used for the production of ceramic spark plugs. Produced under the stamp of Goss China, neither the exact name of the manufacturer nor the location of the plant are known; it may well have been Chatham Potteries, a small plant in Chatham, New Jersey, which was owned by a family named Goss.[12] *RV/PM*

1954   *PRESTIGE GLASSWARE,* Federal Glass Co., Columbus, Ohio.
Reestablishes NYC studio.
1955   Kitchenware, Hall China Company, East Liverpool, Ohio.

Watt Pottery: *SOUTH MOUNTAIN STONEWARE* (NP)

Eva Zeisel's kitchenware design for Watt Pottery (Crooksville , Ohio), named *SOUTH MOUNTAIN STONEWARE* in honor of her New York country home, may be her most obscure. Eva first met with Iliif Watt in 1954 during one of his periodic trips to New York and she agreed to design a line of dinnerware. The set was to be offered on a trial basis, so Watt gave her full creative control.[13] According to Watt's records, four examples of each of the eighteen pieces (numbered 101 through 118) were made (excepting the no. 111 coffee cups).[14]

Watt Pottery, SOUTH MOUNTAIN STONEWARE creamer, small covered bowl, large covered bowl, salt and mug, 1955. EZA.

Watt's customers favored a simple country look, and Eva took her cue from the company's existing lines. Her "fit-the-hand" sensibilities are evident in the forms. Pattern designs by the French artist-designer Michel Cadoret, who created sketches of abstract animals called "Jungle Barnyard," are related to his tapestry designs such as that featured on the cover of *10 Tapisseries: Michel Cadoret.*[15] Cadoret's creatures were applied in black slip using rubber stamps on handsome cream, ivory, and speckled almond glaze backgrounds.[16]

When introduced in 1955 at the Glass and Pottery exhibit, *SOUTH MOUNTAIN STONEWARE* did not generate sufficient orders to merit full production.[17] Watt's son Bryce recalled that his father hated Cadoret's weird animals but liked Eva's modern shapes.[18] In 1959, Watt incorporated some of her *SOUTH MOUNTAIN STONEWARE* pieces into the company's *ORCHARD WARE* line, using decorative autumnal leaves or colorful glazes to adorn the surfaces. This modified set was introduced and marketed through the company that had registered the *ORCHARD WARE* name: Newland, Schneeloch, and Piek. *ORCHARD WARE* sold reasonably well, but was never as popular as other lines designed by Eva at about the same time , possibly because her original vision at Watt Pottery was diluted. *DT*

1956 Hallcraft *Century* dinnerware, Hall China Company, East Liverpool, Ohio.
1957 *Hi-Fi Stoneware* dinnerware, Hollydale Pottery, South Gate, California.
1958 *Eva* dinnerware, Thomas and Johann Haviland divisions, Rosenthal AG, Germany.
Dinnerware and space dividers, Mancioli Pottery, Montelupo, Italy (NP).
1960–61 Teaches at Rhode Island School of Design, Providence, Rhode Island.

The Tea Council, 1961

When Hans Zeisel was working with the Tea Council, an organization formed to promote the drinking of tea in America in preparation for the opening of the Tea Center in midtown Manhattan in April of 1961, Eva was the obvious choice to design the graphics.[19] The organization used the logo she created on its letterhead, literature, and cocktail napkins.[20] *PM*

1962 *Stockholm* glassware, Federal Glass Co., Columbus, Ohio.
1963 Dinnerware, Noritake China Inc., Nagoya, Japan (NP).
Dinnerware, Bengal Potteries, Calcutta, India (NP).
1964 *High Fashion* giftware & dinnerware, Hyalyn Porcelain, Hickory, North Carolina.
Schmid Ironstone dinnerware & giftware, Nihon Koshitsu Toki Co., Kanazawa, Japan, for Schmid International, Boston, Massachusetts.
Resilient Chair exhibited, Milan Triennale, Italy.
1965–84 Eva focuses on historical research, writing, and peace movement activism.
1978–82 Designs *Closet Furniture* (NP).
1983 Senior Fellowship, National Endowment for the Arts.
Dinnerware and giftware, Kispester-Granit, Budapest, Hungary (NP).
Giftware, Zsolnay Manufactory, Pécs, Hungary (LP).
1984 *Eva Zeisel: Designer for Industry* exhibition, Le Château Dufresne, Musée des Arts Décoratifs, Montreal, Canada (travels to Brooklyn Museum, NYC; Art Institute of Chicago, Illinois; New Jersey State Museum, Trenton; Everson Museum of Art, Syracuse, New York; St. Louis Art Museum, Missouri; Flint Institute of Art, Michigan).
1985 *Pinnacle* dinnerware, Yamaka Shoten, Japan, for International China Company, NYC.
1987 *Eva Zeisel: Designer for Industry* exhibition in Budapest, Hungary.
1988 Honorary Doctorate, Royal College of Art, London, England.
1991 Honorary Doctorate, Parsons School of Design, New School University, NYC.
1992 Hans Zeisel dies.
Eva Zeisel: Designer for Industry exhibition in St. Petersburg, Russia.
1993–97 Designs furniture.
1995 Officially "rehabilitated" by Russian government.
Receptacle for storing household recyclables (NP).

Original Leather Stores

Steve Rappaport, who rented Eva's guest house in Rockland County from 1990 to 1995, was well-acquainted with Eva and her design ideas before he commissioned her to design the interior of his Original Leather Store in New York City. Eva designed display systems and furnishings which included a curved counter space for sales transactions. Discussions went back and forth while Eva measured the length of jackets and coats, and the size of bags, briefcases, and luggage, considering each display area and making careful calculations.

She decided on a cherrywood flexible rack system, with "eagle" shelf supports that were echoed in the mirrors she placed behind the shelving. She located a craftsman in North Carolina to build the shelving and a company in New York City to install it. Eva supervised the fabrication and installation, visiting the store every two to three days, ensuring that her

Noritake, prototype cup and saucer, covered dish, and creamer, ca. 1963. Photograph from EZA.

work met her exacting standards.[21] Additional New York stores in Greenwich Village and at Madison and 82nd Street followed, with Eva again creating display areas for each interior.

"The practical response to her work was that my business increased phenomenally," commented Rappaport.[22] He also noted that his favorite part of the creation process was when it became necessary to go into the basement of the 1st Street store, which could only be reached by lifting a trap door in the floor and descending via a rather steeply inclined ladder. Eighty-eight-year-old Eva led the way, ahead of others who were many years her junior. It was for more than her designs that Steve Rappaport remains an Eva fan. *PM*

1996	Office furnishings, Brownstone Publishers, NYC (LP).
	Reissues selected earlier designs, World of Ceramics, Morganton, North Carolina.
1997	Personal Recognition Award, Industrial Designers Society of America.
	Reissues *TOWN AND COUNTRY* dinnerware, Metropolitan Museum of Art Store, NYC.
1997–2000	New designs, reissues/adaptations of earlier designs, the Orange Chicken, NYC.
1998	Binns Medal for Excellence in Ceramic Art, New York State College of Ceramics, Alfred University, New York.
1999	New designs and reissues exhibited, the Orange Chicken gallery, NYC.
	LOST MOLDS AND FOUND DINNERWARE: REDISCOVERING EVA ZEISEL'S HALLCRAFT exhibition, the Schein-Joseph International Museum of Ceramic Art, Alfred University.
	EVA vases, KleinReid, NYC.
	Eva Zeisel Collectors Club founded (becomes Eva Zeisel forum in 2003).
1999–2008	Metal and crystal giftware, lamps, and bowls, Nambé, Santa Fe, New Mexico.
2000	Delegation from Lomonosov Porcelain Factory visits Eva, NYC.
	Travels to Russia.
	Zeisel medallions, Lomonosov Porcelain Factory, St. Petersburg, Russia.
	REIGN martini glass, Bombay Sapphire Gin (advertising use only).
	Bronze Apple Award, Industrial Design Society of America.
	Reissues Schramberg tea set, Metropolitan Museum of Art Store, NYC.
2001	Honorary Member, American Ceramic Society.
	Street in Schramberg, Germany, renamed Eva-Zeisel-Straße.
2002	Tea set and pitchers, KleinReid, NYC.
	Living Legend Award, Pratt Institute, NYC.
	Russel Wright Award for Design Excellence, Manitoga: The Russel Wright Design Center, Garrison, New York.
	THROWING CURVES: EVA ZEISEL documentary, Canobie Films, director Jyll Johnstone.

Acme Studios, Kula, Hawaii

Acme Studios approached Eva in 2002 to design surface patterns for its collection of printed pens. Eva submitted several options and *Capital* was released in 2003. She also designed a white ceramic desk pen, *Talisman* (2004), followed by the *Spring* pen and card case (2006). The *Olivia* pen (2010), named for Eva's longtime design assistant, Olivia Barry, was part of Acme's very thin Stiletto series of objects designed by women for women. *PM*

Acme Studio, SPRING pen and business card holder, 2006. EZA.

2004   Vases and bowls, marinha grande mglass, Marinha Grande, Portugal.
        TALISMAN tea service, Lomonosov Porcelain Factory, St. Petersburg, Russia.
        Crystal wine glasses, Nambé, Santa Fe, New Mexico.
        Vases released in crystal, KleinReid, NYC.
        RAINDROP Table (cast resin), Dune, NYC.
        EVA ZEISEL: THE PLAYFUL SEARCH FOR BEAUTY exhibition, Knoxville Museum of
            Art, Tennessee (travels to Milwaukee Art Museum, Wisconsin; High
            Museum, Atlanta, Georgia; Hillwood Museum & Gardens,
            Washington, D.C.).
        Order of Merit of the Republic of Hungary.
        Honorary Doctorate, University of Craft and Design, Budapest.
        Honorary Royal Designer for Industry, Royal Society of Arts, London.
        Publishes ***EVA ZEISEL ON DESIGN: THE MAGIC LANGUAGE OF THINGS***.

2005   ***CLASSIC CENTURY*** dinnerware, Royal Stafford, England (distributed
            worldwide, by Crate & Barrel in U.S.).
        MAGIC LANGUAGE prints, KleinReid, NYC.
        Honorary Doctorate, Rhode Island School of Design, Providence, Rhode
            Island.
        Lifetime Achievement Award, National Design Awards Cooper-Hewitt,
            National Design Museum, Smithsonian Institution, NYC.
        EVA ZEISEL: THE SHAPE OF LIFE exhibition, Erie Art Museum, Erie,
            Pennsylvania.

2006   Reissues ***PINNACLE*** tea set with newly designed mug, Chantal, Houston, Texas.
        Tables, candlesticks, and jewelry trees, Eva Zeisel Originals.
        EVA ZEISEL: MY CENTURY exhibition, Bard Graduate Center at the
            International Art+Design Fair, Park Avenue Armory, NYC.
        EVA ZEISEL AT 100: A LIFETIME OF MASTERWORK IN DESIGN exhibition, Pratt
            Manhattan Gallery, NYC.
        EVA ZEISEL: EXTRAORDINARY DESIGNER AT 100 exhibition, Mingei International
            Museum, San Diego, California (travels to Craft and Folk Art Museum,
            Los Angeles, California).

*Chantal, EVA kettle in brushed aluminum, 2006.
EZA.*

Chantal: *EVA* Kettle

In March of 2006, Heida Thurlow, founder and CEO of the Texas cookware
company Chantal, contacted Eva Zeisel about a commission.[23] Having
designed many teapots during her long career, Eva was thrilled by the idea
of creating a tea kettle. They created a tea kettle by Eva's antique copper
one with a bent, mashed-in handle. They aimed at a retail price of about
one hundred dollars.

The final design with its beautiful silhouette and a comfortable grip
was introduced at the 2006 International Housewares Trade Show.[24] It has
a 1.8-quart capacity, a seam-free body with a wide base for quicker boiling,
a Hohner whistle, and silicone stay-cool grip handle that is tilted in the
manner of the one in Eva's kitchen.[25] Bloomingdale's department store
carried the *Eva* Kettle in a brushed stainless-steel finish in a limited edition
of 550, while Crate & Barrel brought it out in an exclusive mirrored polish.[26]
Other retailers sold a cheaper brushed stainless-steel version. In 2007,
Chantal added enamel coatings in onyx and chili red.[27] *DDT*

Neue Galerie, baby feeder with spoon,
2008. EZA.

Yamazaki Tableware,
Eva flatware,
2013. EZA.

2007   *GRAND DINING TABLE,* Eva Zeisel Originals, Boston, Massachusetts.
       EVA ZEISEL COFFEE TABLE offered by Design Within Reach, San Francisco, California.

2008   *ONE-O-ONE* dinnerware and vases, Royal Stafford, England, for Bloomingdale's, NYC.
       EDEN dinnerware and giftware, Nambé, Santa Fe, New Mexico.
       Rugs, the Rug Company, London, England.
       Hanging lamps, Tazza Mia Coffeeshop, Cincinnati, Ohio (LP).
       Reissues baby feeder (1940s) with added spoon and Hall Kitchenware refrigerator pitcher, Neue Galerie Design Shop, NYC.
       Brass candlestick, Eva Zeisel Originals, Boston, Massachusetts.

2009   Visionary Award, Museum of Arts and Design, NYC.
       Handblown glass bowls and vases, Vitreluxe, Portland, Oregon, for Gump's, San Francisco, California.
       Lounge chair, Eva Zeisel Originals, Boston, Massachusetts.
       GRANIT dinnerware, Design Within Reach, San Francisco, California.
       Glass Christmas ornaments, Museum of Modern Art Store, NYC.

2010   *LOVERS' SUITE* and *TREES* prints, KleinReid, NYC.
       Reissues bird salt and pepper shakers based on Schmid Ironstone design, Eva Zeisel Originals, Boston, Massachusetts.

2011   Plexiglas picture frames, Wexel Art, Austin, Texas.
       Dies December 30, Rockland County, New York.

2012   *EVA ZEISEL COLLECTION* glass lighting, made in Italy for Leucos U.S.A., Edison, New Jersey.

2013   *EVA* flatware, Yamazaki Tableware, Japan, for Crate & Barrel.

ROLF ACHILLES is an independent art historian living in Chicago. He publishes and consults on ceramics, stained-glass windows, and decorative arts and home interiors of the nineteenth and twentieth centuries.

ANTAY S. BILGUTAY, Associate Director of Development for Dallas Theatre Center in Dallas, Texas, has been collecting the work of Eva Zeisel since 1994 when he discovered his first piece of TOWN AND COUNTRY in Red Wing, Minnesota. He has a degree in English and Theatre Studies from Yale University and has written seven plays. He writes about mid-century design and other topics on his blog, Midmod Musings.

BRENT C. BROLIN has an MA in architecture and has written and illustrated seven books about architecture. He's currently working on an enhanced iBook: The Uses of Architectural Ornament.

JIM CORLETT has been a GM scholar, a Fulbright scholar to India, a Woodrow Wilson scholar, and associate professor at Bishop College and Bennett College, and he undertook doctoral studies at Exeter University, England. He collected his first Nambé while living in New Mexico in the summer of 1968, and met Eva Zeisel at both RISD and Pratt.

MARY WHITMAN DAVIS, an independent writer, recently received her MA from the University of Illinois, Chicago. Her thesis, "Let's Make a Deal: Using Alasitas to Bargain with the Pachamama," considered the significance of alasitas (miniature versions of human desires) during ritual deployments in Peru and Bolivia. She first encountered Eva Zeisel's work in a beat-up box of Town and Country at a cemetery garage sale; Eva's ability to imbue her physical creations with camay (spirit) has inspired her ever since.

JIM DROBKA is a senior book designer at Getty Publications in Los Angeles. His work has been recognized by the AIGA, Communication Arts, the American Association of Museums, Western Art Directors Club, and the Association of American University Presses. He is a graduate of the California Institute of the Arts.

DAN HOLDEN and COLETTE MORTON both graduated from the University of Missouri, Columbia. Collette currently teaches in the St. Louis Public Schools and Dan works for University City at the Alternative School Program for At-Risk Students. They are relative newcomers to Mid-Century Modern collecting, since Dan discovered Town and Country in 1998. The highlight of their collecting was meeting Eva at a promotional event in Chicago, about which they wrote in the Eva Zeisel Times.

KAREN L. KETTERING holds MA and PhD degrees in art history from Northwestern University. Her publications include Eva Zeisel: The Playful Search for Beauty (Knoxville Museum of Art) and Russian Glass at Hillwood (Hillwood Museum & Garden), and she has contributed an essay to Eva's recently published prison memoirs. Her interest in Eva's work was sparked by her discovery, during her research on the Lomonosov Porcelain Factory, that Eva Stricker, who was exiled from the USSR in 1937, had resurfaced as the world-renowned Eva Zeisel.

PAT KIRKHAM is an award-winning author and editor of several books on design, film, and gender, including Charles and Ray Eames: Designers of the Twentieth Century (MIT Press, 1995), Women Designers in the USA, 1900–2000: Diversity and Difference (Yale University Press, 2000), and Saul Bass: A Life in Design and Film (LKP, 2011). A Professor at the Bard Graduate Center: Decorative Arts, Design History, Material Culture in New York, her doctoral degree in history is from the University of London.

REY LEDDA and his life partner, Bradley Brechin, have been collecting Zeisel artifacts since 1996 and are currently working on a series of stories about their Zeisel obsession called Chasing Eva: A Love Story Told in Teapots (zeiselcollector.blogspot.com).

EARL MARTIN is associate curator at the Bard Graduate Center: Decorative Arts, Design History, Material Culture in New York and was the editor of Knoll Textiles, 1945–2010 (Yale University Press, 2011). He holds a master's degree in the History of Decorative Arts and Design (Parsons School of Design / Cooper-Hewitt Museum) and has been an admirer of Eva Zeisel's designs and extraordinary life for many years.

PAT MOORE became interested in Eva's work when she inherited the family dinnerware. She and her husband, Gene Grobman, started the Eva Zeisel Collectors Club (now the Eva Zeisel forum) in 1998. She is the author of Eva Zeisel's Schramberg Designs (Identification Guide). She holds an M.A. degree in cultural anthropology after attending California State University in Northridge and the University of Canturbury, England. She and Gene cherished their close friendship with Eva until her death, and continue to cherish their friendship with Eva's family.

DENNIS M. THOMPSON began collecting Watt pottery in 1991 and soon began researching the history of Watt Pottery. He is a graduate of Cleveland State University and the author, with W. Bryce Watt, of Watt Pottery: A Collector's Reference with Price Guide (Schiffer Publishing, Ltd., 1994), which contains a discussion of Eva's Watt Pottery designs.

DEBBIE DEAVER TOWNLEY teaches English literature and art in a middle/high school in Lubbock, Texas. She developed an immediate interest in Eva's life and works after watching a CBS Sunday Morning presentation on her. She is excited to participate in this book project and hopes that through this book Eva's work will touch others as it has touched her.

TOM TREDWAY has taught design history at Pratt Institute. He curated Mid-Century Modern: Designs for New Lifestyles (2011), a benefit auction for which Eva Zeisel was Honorary Design Chair. A doctoral candidate at the Bard Graduate Center, his dissertation examines the arts of the table produced by Tiffany & Company. He collects twentieth-century tableware and has a particular affection for Hallcraft Century in the Sunglow pattern.

HORST ULLRICH was born in Goslar, Germany. He studied fine arts, art history, and, social science in Kassel, Germany. He settled in New York in 1987. Within his collection of twentieth-century industrial design, modern dinnerware constitutes a substantial part with Eva Zeisel and Grete Marks as the most cherished. He met Eva Zeisel in 1997 and formed a continuing friendship. He has loaned pieces of his collection to many Zeisel exhibits, including the centenary exhibits at the Pratt Institute and the Bard Graduate Center.

SCOTT VERMILLION was a budding antique collector as a child, saving and displaying treasures found in the attic of his parents' house and at the old family farm. In the process, Scott learned to appreciate and study history, architecture, and design. He has a degree in Industrial Design from the Institute of Design at IIT, in Chicago, and is the Vice President of Design at High Sierra. He continues to collect designs by Russel Wright and Eva Zeisel.

MERI VILLANE is an enthusiast and collector of Mid-Century Modern design. It began with her first purchase of a Town and Country yawning pitcher in 1996 and has been a love affair ever since. During those years she has researched the Town and Country designs and been fortunate enough to have acquired several interesting and rare pieces.

CONTRIBUTORS

RAYMOND CALVET VLACH, a native Chicagoan, is an artist, educator, and collector of twentieth-century design, particularly on pottery, glass, textiles, and furniture. Besides being an avid Eva enthusiast, he also enjoys the work of May and Vieve Hamilton, Michael and Frances Higgins, Charles Murphy, Gale Turnbull, and Russel Wright.

BARBARA WEBER has acted as assistant project manager for this book. An executive coach, management consultant, and business owner, Barbara has a long-standing interest in design and finds creative outlets to "feed the soul" and replenish the energy she expends on business pursuits. She is a member of the Eva Zeisel forum, having amassed a small collection of Eva's pieces that includes the line that led her to Eva: the Lomonosov *Talisman* tea service.

TED WELLS is an author, designer, historian, and the Creative Director of Guardian Stewardship Editions. His books include *Casting Shadows: August Rodin*; *Romantic Modern: The California Architecture of Harwell Hamilton Harris*; *Greene & Greene: Wood, Proportion, and Pattern*; and *Eva Zeisel: Friendly Curves*. He has curated museum exhibitions on numerous subjects and held lecturing posts in the U.S. and internationally.

PIRCO WOLFFRAMM mostly works as a graphic designer and design educator. She grew up in Germany and came to the U.S. with a fellowship to obtain her MFA degree at CalArts. Besides her design practice, she teaches in the Pratt Graduate Communications Design program, New York, and occasionally at MICA, Baltimore. Her designs and writings on design have been exhibited and published in Europe and the U.S. She had been friends with Eva for over a decade and was her personal assistant for the last two years of her life.

INDEX OF COLLECTIONS

The abbreviations used in the captions denote the following collections that lent their items for the purpose of photography:

BBA	Brent C. Brolin Archive
EMC	Earl Martin Collection
EZA	Eva Zeisel Archive
EZO	Eva Zeisel Originals Archive
GNA	Greg Neumeier Archive
HUC	Horst Ullrich Collection
JSC	John Striker Collection
KRC	KleinReid Collection
LC	Leucos Collection
MGC	Moore-Grobman Collection
PWA	Pirco Wolfframm Archive
RLC	Ronald T. Labaco Collection
SVC	Scott Vermillion Collection
TPA	TalismanPhoto Archive
TRC	The Rug Company
VHC	Volker Hornbostel Collection

PHOTOGRAPHY & REPRODUCTION CREDITS

BRENT C. BROLIN:
If not stated otherwise, the photographs in this book were taken by Brent C. Brolin.

JIM CORLETT:
page 211

JIM DROBKA:
pages 189, 191

KAREN KETTERING:
page 219

REY LEDDA:
page 219

LEUCOS COMPANY/FDV GROUP:
page 159

EARL MARTIN:
pages 193, 199, 201

GREG NEUMEIER
page 153

THE RUG COMPANY
page 158

STADTMUSEUM SCHRAMBERG ARCHIVE:
pages 170 to 181

TALISMANPHOTO:
pages 13, 42

HORST ULLRICH:
pages 181, 203, 208

SCOTT VERMILLION:
pages 43, 191, 219, 224

PIRCO WOLFFRAMM:
page 11

EVA ZEISEL ARCHIVE:
pages 12, 13, 14, 15, 16, 17, 18, 19, 20, 21, 22, 23, 24, 25, 26, 27, 28, 31, 32, 33, 34, 35, 36, 37, 38, 39, 40, 41, 42, 43, 55, 58, 59, 60, 61, 62, 63, 70, 71, 82, 87, 94, 95, 106, 108, 144, 150, 154, 156, 157, 160, 162, 163, 164, 165, 166, 167, 223, 225

EVA ZEISEL ORIGINALS:
page 157

SECTION TITLE ILLUSTRATIONS FROM EZA
pages 44, 168, 220

ACKNOWLEDGMENTS

Thanks to all those who wrote the entries on individual commissions and companies for all their efforts and for their patience, to Earl Martin and Tom Tredway for sterling work during the final stages of bringing this volume to publication, and to Brent Brolin for his photography. Thanks also to our patient commissioning editor Bridget Watson Payne at Chronicle Books and her colleagues Caitlin Kirkpatrick and Brooke Johnson. Our very special thanks to Barbara Weber, without whom this book would not have come together as smoothly as it did, and to Jean Richards, who does so much to honor and keep alive her mother's spirit. Our final joint thanks are to Eva, who gave us access to her recollections and to her archive, and so much more besides.

—PK, PM, AND PW

All scholarship is collaborative in that it builds on what has gone before, and I would like to thank those involved in the seminal exhibition and publication *Eva Zeisel: Designer for Industry* (1984), especially Martin Eidelberg and Derek Ostergard. I would also like to thank: Judith Szapor, whose biography of Eva's mother enriches our understanding of one of the prime influences upon Eva; Karen Kettering, who writes with such insight and understanding about Eva's time in the USSR; Ron Labaco and Earl Martin, who are founts of knowledge about Eva's work; Juliet Kinchin and Paul Stirton, for a wonderful trip to Hungary (thanks also to Wendy Kaplan for that) and many talks about Hungarian design, women designers, and Eva; Cheryl Buckley, a friend and colleague who has helped transform the ways we think about ceramics and gender; Tom Tredway, who worked as a research assistant on this project; Sequoia Miller, a potter scholar who gave valuable feedback; Gabriella Vincze for help with Eva's Dadaist performances; and Brent Brolin and Eva's family members and friends who have helped. Last but by no means least, my thanks to Andy Hoogenboom and Jeannie Richards for reading drafts, and for much more besides. Thank you all.

PAT KIRKHAM

I owe my greatest thanks to the many contributors to this volume. After Pirco Wolfframm and I agreed to write and design a book on Eva's work, I realized, considering the extent of Eva's ouevre and my age at the time, that I had bitten off more than I could chew, so I sent out a bulletin to our EZf members, announcing our intent and our dilemma. Many of them jumped right in, saying they had had the same impulse and the same misgivings, so I gained many talented and dedicated confreres whose work has been awe-inspiring, and who have become close friends. Scott Vermillion and Jim Drobka were the first to sign on, quickly followed by Antay Bilgutay, Mary Davis, Rey Ledda, and Karen Kettering. Earl Martin and Horst Ullrich came soon after, and as the scope of the book expanded (and Eva designed new lines), others volunteered to take on additional tasks, or to take over chapters when, during this long hegira, some early writers' lives took them elsewhere—Jim Corlett, Ted Wells, and many others. I owe special thanks to Rolf Achilles for taking over an ailing chapter which I had attemped to write when a long-promised chapter failed to arrive. Pat Kirkham became an exemplar of effective writing and editing, when it was decided to add Eva's history to the book. I owe much to Pirco, whose deep knowledge of Eva and her designs has been the backbone of the development of this book, and whose knowledge of the requirements of publishing has guided me through this long process. I am also grateful to her for her strong friendship and support when my spirits flagged, as well as to my husband, Gene Grobman (Mr. Computer Guy), who is just as committed to the Eva project, and who loved and was loved by Eva as much as I. And finally, my great thanks to my parents, Irene and Wesley Moore, who kick-started this whole project by buying Eva's dishes, and by instilling in me a love of learning about any subject which interests me.

PAT MOORE

From concocting various proposals of this book with Pat Moore to seeing the book take shape has been an adventure in itself, and it is blissfully gratifying to sense arrival. Like many participants in this project, I met Pat Moore through eBay, and I cannot thank her enough for having been such a loyal, persistent, and cheerful collaborator in this venture. Along the same lines I wish to thank my other collaborator, Pat Kirkham, for her complementary and vast knowledge, her supreme editorial advisement, and her tireless dedication, which are invaluable to this project. Though Barbara Weber is not mentioned on the cover, her stealth above and beyond support on this project has earned her my deepest respect.

Special thanks to Camila Burbano, who has been an indispensable help in drafting many of the illustrations for the Taxonomy section, to Olivia Barry for supplying technical drawings for many of the newer designs, and to Grace Ho, Melissa Garnwell, and Samira Gagne for offering their help even though life took its turns for each of them, and to Jim Drobka and Scott Vermillion for their respective support and kind encouragement from afar. I am indebted to the collectors who have opened their homes to show their enviable collections, offered valuable information, and have supplied a lot of their gems for the photography in this book: Leslie and Grace Ho, Ron Labaco, Earl Martin, and Horst Ullrich. Others who helped include Josie Anthony, Danilo DeRossi, Talisman Brolin, Gene Grobman, Susanna Joicey-Cecil, Luciano and Sabrina Mancioli, Greg Neumeier, Gary and Laura Maurer, and Adam Zeisel. Eva's caretakers were also mine. Thank you, Anya Boryka, Margaret Czukker, and Elena Uzhul for your dedication to Eva and for your wonderful cooking. Lastly, I want to express my deepest gratitude to Eva and her daughter, Jean Richards, for their immense generosity and their embrace.

PIRCO WOLFFRAMM

ACKNOWLEDGMENTS

The contributing authors wish to thank those who helped them with their individual chapters: Rolf Achilles, Irvin Achorn, Lynn Allen, Lidia Andreeva, Gary and Barbara Barneby, Olivia Barry, Franz Bauman, Katherine Bennett, Anne Bergsman, Antay Bilgutay, Antje Bilgutay, Buzz Blodgett, Wally Blodgett, Joe and Michelle Boeckholt, Georgy Bogdevich, David Bowen, Brent C. Brolin, Talisman Brolin, Steven Brown, Cheryl Buckley, John Boyd Cahoon III, Margaret Carney, Pam Carroll, Marion Church, Irene Haas Clark, Mary Coates, Elizabeth Colenaty, Laura Cox, Karen L. Crocker, Ellen Crouch, Jo Cunningham, Brad Davis, Ron Dinell, Tom Dinell, Jim Drobka, Ekaterina Eristavi, Rainer Etzrodt (dec.), Marion Fama, Inge Feltrinelli, Gerhard Franz, Horst Gladic, Barbara Glauber, Linda Gober, Marc Grobman, Steve Guarnaccia, Nancy Gustafson, Judy Nan Hacohen, Everson Hall, Helen Harrison, Jeffrey Head, Pam Forsee Hogue, Andy Hoogenboom, Volker Hornbostel, Randy Houts, Joyce Ilson, Elena Ivanova, Shawn Johnson, Jyll Johnstone, Don Joint, Michael Kaplan, Bill Katavalos, Douglas Kelley, James Kenny, Karen Kettering, Juliet Kinchin, Pat Kirkham, Susan Kowalczyk, Heath Krieger, Lex Krieger, Lois Krieger, Scott Kruger, Bhumi Kundra, Ronald T. Labaco, Ed Lebow, Craig Lee, Gisela Lixfeld, Ellen MacNeille, Earl Martin, Natasha McRee, Christian Mehl, Annette Melvin-Meyer, Sequoia Miller, Pat Moore, Marie Morehead, Dan November, Maureen O'Gorman, Megan Parry, John A. Paschal, Natalia Petrova, Kari Polanyi-Levitt, Michael Pratt, Richard Rachater, Steve Rappaport, Ray Reiss, Jean Richards, Jaime Robinson, Judy Rudoe, Evan Schoninger, Sharon Schroeder, Charles Seliger (dec.), Steve Slusarski, Todd D. Smith, Douglas Stanton, Bill Stern, Paul Stirton, David Stoelting, Mary Kay Stoelting York, Stephanie Storz, Bill Straus, John Striker, Norman Tempest, John Thompson, Bill Townley, Tom Tredway, Ruthann Uithol, Horst Ullrich, Mary Jane and Joe Vermillion, Scott Vermillion, Joe Villane, Ellie Ward, Amanda Washburn, Bryce Watt, Barbara Weber, Petra Werner, Bruce and Doris Wilson, Pirco Wolfframm, Annie Wright, Norm Yamamoto, Eva Zeisel (dec.), John Zeisel, and Beverly Zona (dec.).

SUPPORT

The publication of this book was supported by:
Anne Bergsman,
Diane Childs,
Virginia Croce,
Ellen Delehanty,
Design on Screen (H. Kirk Brown III & Jill A. Wiltse),
Jean Harris,
Nancy LaPaglia,
Dionysia Palmer,
Stephen Slusarski.

The following abbreviations are used:

PK Pat Kirkham
RL Ronald T. Labaco
PM Pat Moore
JR Jean Richards
TT Tom Tredway
PW Pirco Wolfframm
EZ Eva Zeisel
EZA Eva Zeisel Archive (in the care of Jean Richards)
Interviews are signaled by / (e.g. EZ/PK); conversations by "to" (e.g. JR to PK).
Memoirs: There is not a single formal memoir written by Eva but there are many short recollections (written, filmed, and audio-recorded) in the EZA.

Part One

1   Koestler also drew on his experience of being imprisoned by Nationalist forces in 1937 during the Spanish Civil War; he too was kept in solitary confinement and expected to be executed. See Arthur Koestler, *Dialogue with Death*, originally published as Part II of Arthur Koestler, *Spanish Testament* (London: Victor Gollancz, 1937); EZ, "Memories of Arthur Koestler (revision 3)," EZA.

2   Alexander Weissberg, *The Accused* (New York: Simon and Schuster, 1951).

3   EZ, "Early Autobiography," EZA.

4   Juliet Kinchin, "Hide and Seek: Remapping Modern Design and Childhood," in Juliet Kinchin and Aidan O'Connor, *Century of the Child: Growing by Design 1900–2000* (New York: Museum of Modern Art, 2012), 10–27; Kinchin and O'Connor, "New Century, New Child, New Art: Introduction," in *Century of the Child*, 29.

5   EZ, "Early Autobiography," EZA.

6   EZ to PK and RL, February 18, 1999.

7   See also Christopher Wilk, ed., *Modernism: Designing a New World, 1914–1939* (London: V&A Publications; New York: Distributed in North America by H. N. Abrams, 2006). 8 EZ to PK and RL, February 18, 1999.

9   EZ to PK and RL, February 18, 1999.

10 Eva Zeisel, "On Being a Designer," in Martin Eidelberg et al., *Eva Zeisel: Designer for Industry*. Montreal: Le Château Dufresne, Musée des Arts Décoratifs de Montréal (Chicago: University of Chicago Press, 1984), 78.

11 EZ, "Eva's Taped Dictation (6.17.00): Schramberg," EZA.

12 Ronald T. Labaco, "'The Playful Search for Beauty': Eva Zeisel's Life in Design," *Studies in the Decorative Arts* 8, no. 1 (Fall–Winter 2000–2001), Special Issue, Pat Kirkham and Ella Howard, eds., *Women Designers in the USA, 1900–2000*, 127–128.

13 Pat Kirkham, *Charles and Ray Eames: Designers of the Twentieth Century* (Cambridge, MA: MIT Press, 1995); Pat Kirkham, "Humanizing Modernism: The Crafts, 'Functioning Decoration' and the Eameses," *Journal of Design History* 11 no. 1, (1998): 15–29.

14 EZ, "About Design," EZA.

15 EZ to PK, February 13, 2000.

16 It was for one of Eva's many lectures about design (she gave them throughout her life and they formed the basis of *Eva Zeisel on Design: The Magic Language of Things, 2004*). In 2000, her sight was not quite good enough to read typed notes from a podium for a whole hour, so I read short sections, and then Eva spoke to images on a screen and I asked prepared questions.

17 NB: If Eva's recollections have a heading or date, then I cite it; if not, I note when I received a copy and from whom. Wherever possible I used multiple sources for citations and fact checking, and always compared Eva's "memoirs" against what she told me and what she told others over the years (both informally and in published interviews). Generally, if Eva remembered something, her recall was good until near the very end of her life. If she did not remember something or someone, then

she always said so. She may have gotten odd dates or numbers mixed up, but not very often. In my 45 years of conducting oral histories, I found that she had far more precise recollections than many much younger people. Eva's versions of her prison years, for example, check out against all the documents recently unearthed in Russia. Similarly her accounts of the Schramberer factory check out against other records.

18 EZ to PK and RL, February 18, 1999; EZ, "Eva's Taped Dictation (6.17.00): Schramberg," EZA.

19 EZ, "Resume of History Projects, December 1984," EZA; "1741" file, EZA.

20 They are in production as I write.

21 EZ, "About Berlin 1930–1931," EZA. Eva's concept of design as the giving of gifts, a social practice closely associated with women, adds to our understanding of the reasons why decorative arts production was considered appropriate for women of her class.

22 JR to PK, January 14, 2012.

23 EZ, "Eva's Taped Dictation (6 17.00): Schramberg," EZA.

24 EZ, "I Design Things in Groups . . ." Scrapbook file, EZA.

25 EZ, "I Design Things in Groups . . ." Scrapbook file, EZA.

26 EZ, "I Design Things in Groups . . ." Scrapbook file, EZA.

27 Jed Perls, Bill's Design Talks: A Tribute to Eva Zeisel event and online video (New York: Cooper-Hewitt National Design Museum, February 11, 2012), http://www.cooperhewitt.org/videos/bills-design-talks-tribute-eva-zeisel.

28 For Cecile see Judith Szapor, *The Hungarian Pocahontas: The Life and Times of Laura Polanyi Stricker, 1882–1959* (Boulder, CO: East European Monographs; New York: Distributed by Columbia University Press, 2005). Unless noted otherwise, information about Eva's family is taken from Szapor and from discussions with Eva and with her daughter, Jean Richards.

29 Labaco, 130; Szapor, *The Hungarian Pocahontas*, 12.

30 Szapor, *The Hungarian Pocahontas*, 12–13.

31 Szapor, *The Hungarian Pocahontas*, 11.

32 Szapor gives the date as both 1892 and the late 1880s (Szapor, *The Hungarian Pocahontas*, 15 and 46); Keri Polanyi-Levitt as the late 1880s (Keri Polanyi-Levitt, *The Life and Work of Karl Polanyi: A Celebration* (Montreal; New York: Black Rose Books, 1990). A son, Paul, died young.

33 Szapor, *The Hungarian Pocahontas*, 9, 18.

34 Szapor, *The Hungarian Pocahontas*, 17.

35 Szapor, *The Hungarian Pocahontas*, 126, 192. Dates vary from 1904 to 1912.

36 Szapor, *The Hungarian Pocahontas*, 126, 192; JR to PK, May 2, 2011.

37 JR to PK, January 14, 2012.

38 Walter Gulick, "Letters about Polyani, Koestler, and Eva Zeisel," *Tradition & Discovery: The Polanyi Society Periodical* 30, no. 2 (2003–2004): 6–10, http://www.missouriwestern.edu/orgs/polanyi/TAD%20WEB%20ARCHIVE/TAD30-2/TAD30-2-pg6-10-pdf.pdf; Szapor notes that most educated Hungarians at that time knew German (*The Hungarian Pocahontas*, 50).

39 Szapor, *The Hungarian Pocahontas*, 19–20.

40 Szapor, *The Hungarian Pocahontas*, 20.

41 Szapor, *The Hungarian Pocahontas*, 20–21, 52–53.

42 Labaco, 130.

43 Labaco, 130.

44 Szapor, *The Hungarian Pocahontas*, 23, 123, 126–127; EZ and JR to PK, October 31, 2006.

45 EZ to PK and Juliet Kinchin, February 18, 2003.

46 Young, *Eva Zeisel* (San Francisco: Chronicle Books, 2003), 9; Szapor, *The Hungarian Pocahontas* 23, 27; EZ to PK and Juliet Kinchin, February 18, 2003.

47 Kari Polanyi-Levitt to PK, June 3, 2012; Szapor, *The Hungarian Pocahontas* 27–28.

48 Kari Polanyi-Levitt to PK, June 3, 2012.

49 Kari Polanyi-Levitt to PK, June 3, 2012.

50 Szapor, *The Hungarian Pocahontas*, 30.

51 Szapor, *The Hungarian Pocahontas*, 30; Kari Polanyi-Levitt to PK, June 3, 2012; and EZ to PK and Juliet Kinchin, February 18, 2003.

52 Szapor, *The Hungarian Pocahontas*, 33.

53 See Kinchin and O'Connor, "New Century, New Child, New Art," in *Century of the Child*, especially 30–36; Wilhelm Viola, *Child Art and Franz Cizek* (New York: Reynal and Hitchcock, 1936); see also Friedrich Froebel, *Die Menschenerziehung* (Keilhau, Germany: Verlag der allgemeinen deutschen Erziehungsanstalt, 1826); James Liberty Tadd, *New Methods in Education: Art, Real Manual Training, Nature Study* (New York: Orange Judd, 1899); Norman Brosterman, *Inventing Kindergarten* (New York: Harry N. Abrams, 1997); and Jonathan Fineberg, ed., *Discovering Child Art: Essays on Childhood, Primitivism and Modernism* (Princeton, NJ: Princeton University Press, 1998).

54 See "Eva Zeisel, About 1950–55," EZA; EZ to PK and RL, February 18, 1999.

55 EZ, "Eva Zeisel—Biography," EZA.

56 For photographs of outdoor classes at Laura's kindergarten and drawings by the children, see EZA. For photograph (c. 1910) of children at the Gödöllő Arts and Crafts colony, see Kinchin and O'Connor, *Century of the Child*, 52.

57 Cited in Szapor, *The Hungarian Pocahontas*, 33 (Polanyi Collection at the Szechenyi National Library).

58 EZ to PK, May 1, 2000; Young, 9.

59 EZ, "Memories of Arthur Koestler (revision 3)," EZA.

60 I recall Eva telling me this, and an EZA document suggests that this may have been the case but Eva could have been referring to her school in Budapest. Family members do not know if she attended a school in Vienna. What is clear is that, for the most part, she was educated at home with tutors during that period (JR to PK and TT, September 4, 2012). See also EZ, "Early Autobiography," EZA.

61 EZ, "Early Autobiography," EZA.

62 EZ, "Early Autobiography," EZA.

63 EZ, "Early Autobiography," EZA.

64 For this progressive political culture see Szapor, *The Hungarian Pocahontas*; Judith Szapor, "From Budapest to New York: The Odyssey of the Polanyis," *Hungarian Studies Review* 30, no. 1–2 (2003), 29–60; Paul Stirton, "Frederick Antal and Peter Peri: Art, Scholarship and Social Purpose," *Visual Culture in Britain* 13, no. 2 (2012): 207–225.

65 Szapor, *The Hungarian Pocahontas* 35, 61–66; EZ to PK, May 1, 2000.

66 Lukács in the People's Commissariat for Education; Antal as Director of Museums in Budapest. A Polanyi cousin, Erno Seidler, a founding member of the Hungarian Communist Party, was a minister during the Republic.

67 Szapor, *The Hungarian Pocahontas*, 72–73.

68 EZ to PK and RL, February 18, 1999.

69 Labaco, 130.

70 I am grateful to Karen Kettering for this information. For Kati's mother, see JR to PK and TT, September 4, 2012.

71 Sandra Alfoldy, "Laura Nagy: Magyar Muse," in Bridget Elliott and Janice Helland, eds., *Women Artists and the Decorative Arts 1880–1935: The Gender of Ornament* (Burlington, VT: Ashgate, 2003), 143; and Juliet Kinchin, "Hungary: Shaping a National Consciousness," in Wendy Kaplan, ed., *The Arts & Crafts Movement in Europe & America: Design for the Modern World* (New York: Thames & Hudson in association with the Los Angeles County Museum of Art, 2004), 142–179.

72 Kinchin, "Hungary: Shaping a National Consciousness," 142–179.

73 This was probably Eva's aunt married to artist Karoly Kernstock (or possibly Laura's cousin, Matild Pollacsek, married to avant-garde sculptor Mark Vedres). The collection was of Hungarian hand-painted plates (JR to PK and TT, September 4, 2012).

74 Marlyn R. Musicant, "Maria Kipp: Autobiography of a Hand Weaver," in Pat Kirkham and Ella Howard, eds., *Studies in the Decorative Arts* 8, no. 1 (Fall–Winter 2000–2001), Special Issue, *Women Designers in the USA, 1900–2000* 94–95.

75 Eidelberg et al., "Eva Zeisel: Ceramist in an Industrial Age," 67, note 3.

76 Eva described Czigany and Márffy as early art teachers to Eidelberg (Eidelberg et al., 67, note 3); and Márffy as before art school in Labaco, 130. She mentioned both of them as her teachers around the time she studied at the academy when I visited with Juliet Kinchin in 2003 (neither of us recall the exact date).

77 Labaco, 130; and EZ to PK and RL, February 18, 1999.

78 Eva lived for three months in Paris with Koestler on one occasion in the late 1920s in Rue d'Aragon; JR to PK, January 12, 2012, and JR to PK and TT, September 4, 2012.

79 I am grateful to Karen Kettering for the information about Laurencin. For Zarraga, see EZ, "Eva's Taped Dictation (6.17.00): Schramberg," EZA.

80 EZ, "Eva's Taped Dictation (6.17.00): Schramberg," EZA.

81 "Eva autobiography"(memoirs on CD, EZA; JR to PK, May 1, 2010.

82 Labaco, 131.

83 Labaco, 131.

84 Eidelberg et al., 13–14.

85 JR to PK, January 14, 2012.

86 Tanya Harrod, "Eva Zeisel Obituary: Industrial Designer Known for Her Ceramic Tableware," *The Guardian*, January 18, 2012, http://www.guardian.co.uk/artanddesign/2012/jan/15/eva-zeisel.

87 Labaco, 131; Eidelberg et al., 14.

88 EZ, "Eva Zeisel: (typed)," 3, EZA.

89 Labaco, 131; *Throwing Curves: Eva Zeisel*, directed by Jyll Johnstone (San Francisco: Canobie Films, 2002), DVD.

90 Eidelberg et al., 14–17. This observation seems to have been based mainly upon pieces of Eva's work for Kispester-Granit rather than work from her own studio.

91 See Leslie Hayward, *Poole Pottery: Carter & Company and Their Successors 1873–1995* (Somerset, England: Richard Dennis, 1995).

92 For the DIA, Werkbund, and Carter Stabler Adams, see Pat Kirkham, *Harry Peach, Dryad, and the DIA* (London: Design Council, 1986), 47–70. See also Hayward, *Poole Pottery*, Frederic J. Schwartz, *The Werkbund: Design Theory and Mass Culture Before the First World War* (New Haven, CT: Yale University Press, 1996); Lucius Burckhardt, ed., *The Werkbund: Studies in the History and Ideology of the Deutscher Werkbund, 1907–1933* (London: Design Council, 1980).

93 The pottery was sold in Peach's *Dryad* store in Leicester, England, and shown to DIA members and students as examples of good form and decoration. See Kirkham, *Harry Peach, Dryad, and the DIA*, 61.

94 Labaco, 131; Eidelberg et al., 14. I have tried (so far unsuccessfully) to trace a catalogue of exhibits for the Hungarian section of the exhibition.

95 For quotation and other information about Kispester, see Labaco 131.

96 Labaco, 131; EZ to PK and RL, February 18, 1999; Eva Zeisel and Thomas Connors, "Conversation," *Glass Magazine* 42 (1990): 12.

97 Zeisel and Connors, 12.

98 Labaco, 131; Zeisel and Connors, 12.

99 Eidelberg et al., 14–15.

100 EZ, "Eva Zeisel: (typed)," 4, EZA. Eva also thought that her "sticking on" of pieces of clay to vases and other objects at that time was possibly related to her love of the "spontaneous thumbmarks in clay of Rodin's sculpture." It seems just as likely that she followed the flow of popular designs and influences in ceramics.

101 EZ to PK, November 8, 2000; *Throwing Curves*.

102 The pieces illustrated here and in Eidelberg et al. (14–15) were hand-painted by Eva. JR to PK, April 29, 2012.

103 Zeisel and Connors, 12; Labaco, 131.

104 EZ, "About Berlin 1930–1931," EZA.

105 For farthest from home, see Labaco, 131; Zeisel and Connors, 12; *Throwing Curves*.

106 I am grateful to PW for information about Altona.

107 EZ to PK, November 8, 2000. See also *Throwing Curves*.

108 There were about 3 or 4 such wheels (*Throwing Curves*).

109 Zeisel and Connors, 12; EZ to PK, May 1, 2000 (for couples).

110 I am grateful for this and other information on Eva's involvement with Dada theater to Gabriella Vincze of the Institute of Art History, Research Center for the Humanities, Hungarian Academy of Sciences. She curated the exhibition *The History and Connections of Hungarian Art Movement in the period 1902–1950*, Budapest, 2012.

111 EZ, "Early Autobiography," EZA.

112 EZ, "Early Autobiography," EZA.

113 EZ, "Memories of Arthur Koestler" (revision 3): 10, EZA.

114 According to Eva, even from Vienna it took 3 trains to reach Schilltach, from whence a single-line track ran through a narrow valley to Schramberg. EZ, "Eva's Taped Dictation (6.17.00): Schramberg," EZA.

115 EZ, "Eva's Taped Dictation (6.17.00): Schramberg," EZA.; Eidelberg et. al., 17.

116 EZ, "Eva's Taped Dictation (6.17.00): Schramberg," EZA.

117 For Eva and the factory, see EZ, "Eva's Taped Dictation (6.17.00): Schramberg," EZA. Gisela Lixfeld, of the Stadtmuseum Schramberg, confirmed documentary evidence that 320 people were employed there in 1922.

118 EZ, "Eva's Taped Dictation (6.17.00): Schramberg," EZA.

119 EZ, "Eva's Taped Dictation (6.17.00): Schramberg," EZA.

120 EZ, "Eva's Taped Dictation (6.17.00): Schramberg," EZA.

121 EZ, "Eva's Taped Dictation (6.17.00): Schramberg," EZA.

122 When I showed Eva the marks of the paintresses alongside the company mark on pieces of Carter Stabler Adams pottery, she was far more interested in finding out who designed the form and pattern form than the painters. For women pottery painters, see Cheryl Buckley, *Potters and Paintresses: Women Designers in the Pottery Industry, 1870–1955* (London: Women's Press, 1990).

123 See Young, 11; EZ, "Eva's Taped Dictation (6.17.00): Schramberg," EZA; EZ to PK and RL, February 18,1999.

124 EZ, "Eva's Taped Dictation (6.17.00): Schramberg," EZA.

125 Pat Moore, *Eva Zeisel's Schramberg Designs: Identification Guide* (San Francisco: Labor of Love Press, 2010), 13.

126 EZ, "Eva's Taped Dictation (6.17.00): Schramberg," EZA; EZ, "I Design Things in Groups . . ." Scrapbook file, EVA.; EZ to PK and Andy Hoogenboom, November 12, 2010.

127 EZ, "Eva's Taped Dictation (6.17.00): Schramberg," EZA.

128 Where similar company archives exist, I have found this to be the case.

129 Eidelberg gives no reference, but he was probably told this by Eva, as I was once.

130 For Cliff, see Greg Slater and Jonathan Brough, *Comprehensively Clarice Cliff* (New York: Thames & Hudson, 2005).

131 Pat Moore, *Eva Zeisel's Schramberg Designs*, 13; for Frankl, see Christopher Long, *Paul T. Frankl and Modern American Design* (New Haven, CT: Yale University Press, 2007).

132 EZ, "Eva Zeisel [About 1950–1955]," EZA. When Ron Labaco and I asked her about Delaunay's work at the 1925 Exposition in 1999, she said she knew Delaunay's work but could not recall having seen it in Paris in 1925.

133 Moore, 13.

134 For Breuer, see "Memories of Arthur Koestler," 11–12, EZA.

135 EZ to Cyril Smith, March 25, 1999; EZ, "Early Autobiography," EZA.

136 EZ, "Eva's Taped Dictation (6.17.00): Schramberg," EZA.

137 The Bauhaus only had a ceramics workshop between 1919 and 1925. From 1920 it was staffed by Max Krehan, *Lehrmeister* (craft or technical master), and Gerhard Marcks, *Formmeister* (form master), and located in a working pottery in Dornburg, a town near to the Bauhaus at Weimar. Strong vernacular hand traditions are evident in salt-glazed stoneware jugs by Marguerite Friedländer (later Wildenhain) that referenced traditional German forms, materials, and techniques. In 1924, a year after the Bauhaus turn toward "Art and Technology: A New Unity," Lindig and fellow Bauhaus student Theodor Bogler headed an experimental workshop where they developed slip-cast molds for mass-producing containers. When, in 1925, the Bauhaus moved to Dessau and closed its ceramics section, Lindig continued to manage the workshop (as the Ceramics Department of the State Building School, Weimar) until 1930, and as a private concern until 1947. For Bauhaus ceramics, see Juliette Desorgues et al., *Bauhaus: Art as Life* (London: Koenig Books in association with Barbican Art Gallery, 2012); and Barry Bergdoll and Leah Dickerman, *Bauhaus 1919–1933: Workshops for Modernity* (New York: The Museum of Modern Art, 2009).

138 EZ, "Eva's Taped Dictation (6.17.00): Schramberg," EZA; EZ, "Early Autobiography," EZA; EZ, "I Design Things in Groups . . ." Scrapbook file, EZA.

139 See Eva Zeisel, "Die Künstlerin hat das Wort," *Die Schaulade*, 8 (February 1932), 173–174.

140 EZ to PK and RL, February 18, 1999.

141 EZ, "My Work [at] Schramberg," EZA.

142 EZ, "Eva's Taped Dictation (6.17.00): Schramberg," EZA.

143 EZ, "Eva's Taped Dictation (6.17.00): Schramberg," EZA. The full name of the party to which Eva referred is *Deutschnationale Volkspartei* (DNVP, German National People's Party).

144 EZ, "Eva's Taped Dictation (6.17.00): Schramberg," EZA.

145 EZ, "Eva's Taped Dictation (6.17.00): Schramberg," EZA; JR to PK and TT, September 4, 2012.

146 EZ, "Eva's Taped Dictation (6.17.00): Schramberg," EZA.

147 EZ, "Eva's Taped Dictation (6.17.00): Schramberg," EZA.

148 For these aspects of her time in Schramberg, see EZ, "Eva's Taped Dictation (6.17.00): Schramberg," EZA. Eva usually called the SPD the German Socialist Party.

149 EZ to PK, date uncertain (c. 2006). Eva told me that Seghers, a Communist, once tore up Eva's SPD membership card, implying that it was through frustration at both Eva and that party; in EZ, "Memories of Arthur Koestler" (revision 3), 12, she only mentioned Seghers' attitude towards the SPD.

150 EZ, "Eva's Taped Dictation (6.17.00): Schramberg," EZA.

151 For the address (Tauentzien Straße) see EZ, "Memories of Arthur Koestler" (revision 3), 12, EZA.

152 EZ, "About Berlin, 1930–1931," EZA.

153 EZ, "About Berlin, 1930–1931," EZA.

154 "Memories of Arthur Koestler" (revision 3), 13, EZA.

155 EZ to PK, November 8, 2000.

156 EZ, "About Berlin, 1930–1931," EZA; EZ to PK, November 8, 2000.

157 Labaco, 133.

158 List compiled with assistance of JR from information given to her by Eva, family members, and from Szapor, *The Hungarian Pocahontas*.

159 EZ, "Memories of Arthur Koestler" (revision 3), 11, EZA.

160 JR to PK, January 14, 2012.

161 Eidelberg et al., 24; Young, 12–13; EZ, "About Berlin, 1930–1931," EZA.

162 EZ to RL and PK, February 18, 1999.

163 For Marguerite Friedländer (later Wildenhain), see Dean Schwarz and Geraldine Schwarz, eds., *Marguerite Wildenhain and the Bauhaus: An Eyewitness Anthology* (Decorah, IA: South Bear Press, 2007); and Marguerite Wildenhain, *The Invisible Core: A Potter's Life and Thoughts* (Palo Alto, CA: Pacific Books, 1973). For Friedländer and Petri, see Bobbye Tigerman, "Fusing Old and New: Emigre Designers in California," in Wendy Kaplan, ed., *Living in a Modern Way: California Design, 1930–1965* (Los Angeles: Los Angeles County Museum of Art; Cambridge, MA: MIT Press, 2011), 91–116. For Petri, who also studied at the Bauhaus, see Eidleberg et al., 35, illustration 48.

164 EZ to PK, November 8, 2000; EZ, "Eva's Taped Dictation (6.17.00): Schramberg," EZA.

165 Eva Zeisel, "Die Künstlerin hat das Wort," 172–173.

166 EZ to Hans Zeisel, letter, 1931, EZA; EZ, "About Berlin, 1930–1931," EZA. Eva often used this phrase when talking about Berlin in general, but in this letter it applied only to Koestler.

167 EZ, "Memories of Arthur Koestler" (revision 3), 12, EZA.

168 EZ, "Memories of Arthur Koestler" (revision 3), 12, EZA.

169 EZ, "About Berlin, 1930–1931," EVA; EZ; "Memories of Arthur Koestler" (revision 3), 10–13, EZA.

170 EZ, "Memories of Arthur Koestler" (revision 3), 12, EZA.

171 EZ, "About Berlin, 1930–1931," EVA; EZ to PK, November 8, 2000; Karen Kettering to PK, November 28, 2006.

172 For his appointment, see Arthur Koestler, Preface, Alexander Weissberg, The *Accused* (New York: Simon and Schuster, 1951), ix. For Eva's description, see EZ, "Memories of Arthur Koestler" (revision 3), 13, EZA. See also chapter 3.

173 Koestler, Preface, Weissberg, ix.

174 Koestler, Preface, Weissberg, ix. Koestler stayed with Weissberg on an extended visit to the USSR; Eva was working in Leningrad by then. Eva's mother made lengthy visits to the USSR when Eva lived there; see Szapor, *The Hungarian Pocahontas*, 67–99. JR's impression of Eva's relationship with Weissberg was that, if there had been a romance, it soon settled into close friendship. They probably married to please Eva's mother, who had quite conventional ideas about such things. JR to PK, Aug. 31, 2012.

175 Richards and Brolin, eds. *Eva Zeisel: A Soviet Prison Memoir.*

176 For Weissberg's intellect, see the testimony of German physicist Charlotte Riefenstahls, who knew him in both Berlin and the USSR (where her husband Fritz Houtermans worked at the Kharkov institute alongside Weissberg), in Eduardo Amaldi, "The Adventurous Life of Friedrich Georg Houtermans, Physicist (1903–1966)," in Giovanni Battimelli and Giovanni Paoloni, eds., *20th Century Physics: Essays and Recollections. A Selection of Historical Writings by Eduardo Amaldi* (River Edge, NJ: World Scientific, 1998), 610. Koestler described Weissberg thus: "My first impression of Alex was that of a prosperous and jovial businessman with a round face, rounded gestures, and a great gusto for telling funny stories, and a curious liking for sweets. . . . I failed to see what E. found so remarkable about this character until the other guests were gone and we became involved in an argument on some finer points of Marxist theory. . . . he made dialectical mincemeat of me." Koestler, Preface, Weissberg, ix.

177 EZ to PK and RL, February 18, 1999.

178 EZ to PK and RL, February 18, 1999; Szapor, *The Hungarian Pocahontas*, 85–86.

179 For Weissberg, see Koestler, Preface, Weissberg, ix; for Eva, see Eidelberg et al., 24; Young, 13.

180 For Tatlin, see Eva Zeisel, "On Being a Designer," 92.

181 See, for example, I.T. Rodin, ed., *Khudozhestvennyi farfor: katalog,* (Moscow-Leningrad: Iskusstvo, 1938), and B.N. Emme, *Russkii khudozhestvennyi farfor* (Moscow: Iskusstvo, 1950). I am grateful to Karen Kettering for this information.

182 See chapter 3.

183 Sarah Bodine, "Eva Zeisel: Humanistic Design for Mass Production," *Industrial Design* 30 (July–August 1983), 45, quoted in Eidelberg et al., 27.

184 Eidelberg et al., 24, figure 25.

185 Eva's memoirs refer only to gynecological furniture, the term Eva usually used when telling this story (EZ, "Eva's Taped Dictation (6.17.00): Schramberg," EZA). JR recalls Eva specifying the chaise longue, JR to PK and TT, September 4, 2012.

186 Zeisel, "On Being a Designer," 92. Eva told this story many times.

187 I am grateful to Karen Kettering for this and other information about Eva at this factory.

188 Eva used to say it was the largest. For the Homer Loughlin Company's claim to that distinction, see Charles L. Venable et al., *China and Glass in America, 1880–1980: From Tabletop to TV Tray* (Dallas: Dallas Museum of Art, 2000), 14, and Young, *Eva Zeisel*, 14.

189 For the liqueur set, see chapter 3 and Eidelberg et al., 27 figure 333.

190 For Leonov, see "Leonov, Petr Vasil'evich," in *The Great Soviet Encyclopedia,* 3rd ed. (1970–1979), http://encyclopedia2.thefreedictionary.com/Leonov,+Petr+Vasilevich (accessed September 15, 2012); JR to PK and TT, September 4, 2012; see also chapter 3.

191 JR to PK and TT, September 4, 2012.

192 See Richards and Brolin, eds.

193 JR to PK, May 2, 2012. Jascha was the model for Ivanov, an investigator in Koestler's *Darkness at Noon.* Eva told Koestler about Jascha being an investigator in a case involving certain "Mensheviks" in 1931. Convinced of the innocence of a particular man under investigation (a former comrade whom he respected), Jascha reported that he had been unable to obtain a false confession. For refusing to torture the man, Jascha spent six months in prison and was demoted for a while. See Richards and Brolin, eds.

194 JR to PK, May 2, 2012.

195 I am grateful to Karen Kettering and JR for this information. The German modeler was arrested on the same day as Eva but released. He returned to Germany and until his death never spoke of his arrest to anyone, not even close family. See Richards and Brolin, eds.

196 EZ to PK and Andy Hoogenboom, November 12, 2010.

197 I am grateful to Karen Kettering for this information. See also Richards and Brolin, eds.

198 Karen Kettering, in *Throwing Curves.*

199 See *Throwing Curves.*

200 EZ to PK, September 30, 2001.

201 Richards and Brolin eds.

202 EZ to PK. I visited the USSR on 3 occasions and Eva liked to hear about what I did and saw there. It offered both of us a way into talking about her days there. She told her "Russian story" many times but the basic narrative remained the same. See also *Throwing Curves,* Young, 15–16; Richards and Brolin, eds. The main body of information that follows is from the latter publication.

203 EZ to PK, November 1, 2000; Young, 15.

204 EZ, "Memories of Arthur Koestler" (revision 3), 18, EZA.

205 Young, 15.

206 EZ and JR to PK, December 12, 2006.

207 EZ to PK and JR, January 2001.

208 Richards and Brolin, eds.

209 Richards and Brolin, eds.

210 Eva's mother worked ceaselessly for Eva's release, learning the intricacies of Soviet law and bureaucracy in her determination to do so. Consular officials tried too, as did Weissberg until he too was arrested a few months after Eva. Eva was always grateful to him for his efforts, including approaching highly-placed Russians for letters in support of Eva. He recalled that because Eva was well-liked, most of them obliged, adding that even 6 months later, after the Zinoviev–Kamenev trial, most ordinary citizens would have been too worried about their own safety to do such a thing (Weissberg, 103).

211 Eva told a story about a passenger on the train who, trying to flatter her, told her she looked not a day over 45; she was 30; Young, 16.

212 Eva stated that her interrogator had hinted that, if she stated that Bychowskii had accused her after she had repulsed sexual advances by him, the charges might be dropped. It now appears to have been a means of trying to secure her release, but in those dangerous times of accusations and counter-accusations, Eva felt it best to tell the truth, and insisted that, whatever else the man may have done, he had never made any such advances toward her. Richards and Brolin, eds.; JR to PK, January 12, 2012.

213 This story was related to me by JR on several occasions between 2002 and 2012. Orlov normally did not talk afterwards about any of the material covered in the debriefing sessions, See Richards and Brolin eds.

214 I am grateful to JR for this information. Eva never knew what happened to him after he left for Manchuria. She accompanied him as far as Venice, and he sent her messages (via a friend in Paris) en route from Shanghai. Recently Karen Kettering found official evidence that he and his brother were killed in The Purges in 1939.

215 Weissberg, 338.

216 EZ to Hans Zeisel, letter, 1931, EZA.

217 Kari Polanyi-Levitt to PK, June 3, 2012; For "Red Vienna," see Helmut Gruber, *Red Vienna: Experiment in Working-Class Culture, 1919–1934* (New York: Oxford University Press, 1991); and Hans Zeisel, "The Austromarxists in 'Red' Vienna, Recollections and Reflections,"EZA.

218 Marie Jahoda, Paul Lazarfeld, and Hans Zeisel, *Die Arbeitslosen von Marienthal: Ein soziographischer Versuch über die Wirkungen langdauernder Arbeitslosigkeit* (Leipzig: Hirzel, 1933).

219 *Throwing Curves*; Young, 15. Eva told this story many times, but the basic narrative remained the same.

220 *Throwing Curves*.

221 PW to PK, August 26, 2012.

222 See JR to PK and TT, September 4, 2012. Other people who spoke to me about Eva and Hans were happy to do so but did not want to be named.

223 Information given on condition name not mentioned.

224 *Throwing Curves*.

225 Koestler, Preface, Weissberg, xi–xviii; Weissberg, 13.

226 Weissberg, 13.

227 Weissberg, 13.

228 *Throwing Curves*.

229 See Szapor, "From Budapest to New York: The Odyssey of the Polanyis," 32–33, for information in this and the following paragraph. A month later Eva's brother Michael and his wife left for the U.S., from whence they worked to secure entry for other family members.

230 Laura's brother-in-law was killed in Dachau in 1941. Her sister Sophie refused to leave Austria without her young son but no country, including the U.S., would take a child with a "mental handicap." They did not survive the Holocaust. EZ to PK, February 13, 2001; Szapor, "From Budapest to New York,"37. When Laura packed up her belongings in Vienna, she also packed Eva's photographic equipment and bought her a new painting easel.

231 Szapor, "From Budapest to New York," 37. So extremely grateful was Eva to 2 British women who worked ceaselessly for her mother's release that she named her daughter Jean Richards (Zeisel) in honor of each of them; John was also given Richards as a second name. Laura arrived in the U.S. in 1939; Sandor in 1941.

232 Eidelberg et al., 28; *Throwing Curves* (Eva mentions "ten miniatures for 100 dollars.").

233 Eidelberg et al., 28–29, 35. Those pieces featured blue and gold on white and are reminiscent of Trudi Petri's *Urbino* dinnerware c. 1931 (see illustration 48 in Eidelberg et.al.).

234 Eidelberg et al., 29; Pat Kirkham and Lynne Walker, "Women Designers in the USA, 1900–2000: Diversity and Difference," in Pat Kirkham, ed., *Women Designers in the USA, 1900–2000: Diversity and Difference* (New York: Bard Graduate Center for Studies in the Decorative Arts; New Haven: Yale University Press, 2000), 58.

235 Eidelberg et al., 29; Eva Zeisel,"Ceramic Design at Pratt Institute," *China, Glass and Lamps* 59 (June 1940), 20–21; Eva Zeisel, "Dinnerware from Pratt Institute," *China, Glass and Lamps* 60 (June 1941), 58–59; Eva Zeisel, "Some Problems of Dinnerware Design," *Ceramic Age* 40 (July 1942), 3–10.

236 Eidelberg et al., 29–30; Eva Zeisel, *Eva Zeisel on Design: The Magic Language of Things* (Woodstock, NY: Overlook Press,2004).

237 Eidelberg et al., 30.

238 Eidelberg et al., 30.

239 Among the better-known streamlined ceramics was Susie Cooper's *Kestral* line (1932) and Frederick Hurten Rhead's Fiesta line (1936). See Bryn Youds, *Susie Cooper: An Elegant Affair* (New York: Thames & Hudson, 1996); Ann Eatwell, *Susie Cooper Productions* (London: Victoria and Albert Museum, 1987); Sharon Dale, *Frederick Hurten Rhead: An English Potter in America* (Erie, PA: Erie Art Museum, 1986). NB: Cooper was presented with the Royal Designer for Industry award in 1940, the first time that it had been given to a woman and the first time it was awarded for pottery design. Eva received that same award many years later.

240 One result of which was the *Golden Curls* dinner service designed by Pratt student Ilse Meissener. See Eidelberg et al., 30, 32.

241 Eva told her daughter that Hans apologized for this shortly before he died. JR to PK and TT, September 4, 2012.

242 JR to PK and TT, September 4, 2012.

243 JR to PK and TT, September 4, 2012.

244 JR and John Zeisel to PK, June 2, 2012. The children also attended Sunday School there (encouraged by their grandmother, they recall).

245 Eidelberg et al., 43.

246 Szapor, *The Hungarian Pocahontas*, 147.

247 During World War II, Hans was a consultant to the U.S. War Department, the U.S. Department of Justice, the Rand Corporation, and the American Bar Association.

248 British wartime restrictions on materials and manpower, known as the "Utility" scheme, applied to some ceramics. Eva's *Utility Ware* (1943) designs may have been inspired by it.

249 For Noyes, see Gordon Bruce, *Eliot Noyes: A Pioneer of Design and Architecture in the Age of American Modernism* (London; New York: Phaidon, 2006).

250 Young, 17; Eidelberg et al., 69, note 40.

251 "Eva Zeisel Sees End of Schism Between Hand, Machine," *Retailing Home Furnishings* 14 (February 16, 1942), 24; Eidelberg et al., 32, 69, notes 33, 34, and 40.

252 Eidelberg et al., 32; Young, 17.

253 Eidelberg et al., 36; Young, 18.

254 See Kirkham, *Charles and Ray Eames*, 219–228.

255 For "Good Design," see Juliet Kinchin, "What Was Good Design? MoMA's Message, 1944–56," http://www.moma.org/visit/calendar/exhibitions/958.

256 Labaco, 127.

257 See Kirkham, *Charles and Ray Eames*, and Kirkham, "Humanizing Modernism."

258 EZ to Andy Hoogenboom, November 12, 2010; he to EZ re: "design police."

259 Eidelberg et al., 36–38; Young, 19.

260 See Venable et al., 99, 376, 429.

261 For "human quality," see Kirkham, *Eames*, 6.

262 EZ, "Memories of Arthur Koestler" (revision 3), 15, EZA.

263 EZ, "Memories of Arthur Koestler" (revision 3), 15–16, EZA.

264 EZ, "Memories of Arthur Koestler" (revision 3), 17, EZA.

265 EZ, "Memories of Arthur Koestler" (revision 3), 16, EZA.

266 EZ, "Memories of Arthur Koestler" (revision 3), 16, EZA; Koestler to EZ, March 31, 1948, EZA.

267 EZ, "Memories of Arthur Koestler" (revision 3), 16, EZA; Koestler to EZ, March 31, 1948, EZA.

268 EZ, "Memories of Arthur Koestler" (revision 3), 18, EZA.

269 EZ, "Memories of Arthur Koestler" (revision 3), 20, EZA.

270 EZ, "Memories of Arthur Koestler" (revision 3), 20, EZA.

271 EZ, "Memories of Arthur Koestler" (revision 3), 20, EZA.

272 EZ to Koestler, letter, March 29, 1948, EZA.

273 JR to PK and TT, September 4, 2012.

274 EZ to PK, March 1, 2004; JR to PK, January 14, 2012; EZ to Koestler, letter, 1948, EZA.

275 Eidelberg et al., 43. Lightweight wire chairs (not designed by Eva) were hung on the walls whenever additional space was needed.

276 Eidelberg et al., 43.

277 Eidelberg et al., 43.

278 For Japan, see Venable et al., 245–264, particularly 254.

279 For the fruit bowls, see Eidelberg et al., 8; for Eva's Mexican work, *La Vida Diaria*, catalogue (Instituto Nacional de Bellas Artes in Mexico City, 1952), 27–29. The caption reads "fabricacion de LOZA FINA, S.A."

280 Young, 20 (royalties); JR to PK and TT, September 4, 2012 (Hans).

281 EZ to Andy Hoogenboom, November 12, 2010.

282 Young, 20.

283 JR to PK, January 14, 2012.

284 For Noritake and Bengal Potteries, see Eidelberg et al., 62; for Thailand, JR to PK, October 18, 2012.

285 Pat Kirkham and Jennifer Bass, *Saul Bass: A Life in Film and Design* (London: Laurence King Publishing, 2011), 389.

286 EZ to PK, January 21, 2006.

287 EZ to PK, January 21, 2006.

288 EZ to PK, January 21, 2006.

289 EZ to PK, January 21, 2006.

290 I am grateful to JR for information about this *house*.

291 See Ira Berlin, *Slavery in New York* (New York: The New Press, 2005); Peter Charles Hoffer, *The Great New York Conspiracy of 1741* (Lawrence: University of Kansas Press, 2003); and Claudia E. Sutherland, "New York Slave Conspiracy (1741)," BlackPast.org, http://blackpast.org/?q=aah/new-york-slave-conspiracy-1741.

292 JR to PK, August 28, 2012.

293 He also wrote *Russia Through Foreign Eyes* and a biography of Alfred Nobel.

294 For "popularized history," see review by William D. Rodgers, *The Yale Law Journal* 65, no. 2 (Dec. 1955): 276–279.

295 See Ira Berlin, *Slavery in New York* (New York: The New Press, 2005); Peter Charles Hoffer, *The Great New York Conspiracy of 1741* (Lawrence: University of Kansas Press, 2003); and Claudia E. Sutherland, "New York Slave Conspiracy (1741)," BlackPast.org, http://blackpast.org/?q=aah/new-york-slave-conspiracy-1741.

296 JR to PK and TT, September 4, 2012.

297 EZ, "Typed draft of book: 2 [large print version]," EZA. Eva asked me how long I worked on particular projects, and seemed relieved when I said sometimes a decade or more.

298 JR to PK, January 14, 2012; Young, 22.

299 Eva Zeisel, *Eva Zeisel on Design: The Magic Language of Things*.

300 See Szapor, *The Hungarian Pocahontas*, 138.

301 Some people recall it was Koestler's publisher, others that it was Koestler's biographer, Michael Scammell (PW to PK, August 28, 2012).

302 JR to PK, January 14, 2012.

303 EZ to PK, September 30, 2000.

304 JR to PK, May 30, 2012.

305 Eidelberg et al., 64.

306 I am grateful to Karen Kettering for this information.

307 Young, 8–9.

308 James Klein and David Reid to PK, February 11, 2012.

309 Gyorgy Bogdevich to PK, August 28 2002.

310 JR to PK, February 21, 2012; PW to PK, August 1, 2011.

311 *Eva Zeisel: Extraordinary Designer Craftsman at 100* was at the Mingei Museum, California. *Eva Zeisel at 100: A Lifetime of Masterwork in Design* was held at the Pratt Institute while Ron Labaco curated *Eva Zeisel: My Century* for the Bard Graduate Center (both NYC).

312 EZ to PK, Caroline Maniaque, Tim Benton, December 10, 2008.

313 Olivia Barry to PK at 100th birthday party for Eva hosted by Maureen O'Gorman.

314 PW to PK, August 11, 2012.

315 JR to PK, January 4, 2012, citing telephone call with Christopher Sharp, cofounder of the company.

316 All three were made in Nepal (the first two from wool; the third from wool and raised silk) as part of GoodWeave, a project that seeks to improve the rug-making process in that area, both ethically and environmentally.

317 Olivia Barry to PK, November 20, 2012.

Part Two
Chapter 1

1 Brent Brolin to PM, e-mail, May 18, 2003.

2 Ronald T. Labaco, "The Playful Search for Beauty: Eva Zeisel's Life in Design," *Studies in the Decorative Arts* 8, no. 1 (Fall–Winter 2000–2001), 132.

3 Annette Melvin (relative of Schramberger owners) to PM, e-mail, October 12, 2005.

4 Gisela Lixfeld to PM, e-mail, October 29, 2012; EZA, typed sheet (no date), "Schramberg" (handwritten), EZA.

5 Melvin to PM, e-mail, October 12, 2005.

6 Melvin to PM, e-mail, October 12, 2005.

7 Melvin to PM, e-mail, October 12, 2005.

8 Martin Eidelberg et al., *Eva Zeisel: Designer for Industry*, Montreal: Le Château Dufresne, Musée des Arts Décoratifs de Montréal (Chicago: University of Chicago Press, 1984), 17.

9 Eva Zeisel, "On Designing for Industry," *Interiors* 105 (July 1984), 130.

10 Sarah Bodine, "Eva Zeisel: Humanistic Design for Mass Production," *Industrial Design* 30 (July–August 1983), 45.

11 Isabel Grüner, "Keramik-Museum Mettlach," in Werner Endres ed., *Steingut: Geschirr aus der Oberpfalz* (Munich: Deutscher Kunstverlag, 2004), 162–163. Thanks to Rolf Achilles for the translation.

12 JR to PM, e-mail, August 17, 2012. Eva's interest in promoting products is demonstrated in some of her later work at Carstens (she photographed products and arranged displays at trade fairs), Hall China, Western Stoneware, and the Orange Chicken.

13 Howard Kissel, "Zeisel Looks Back: The Eventful Journey of a Design Engineer," *Women's Wear Daily*, September 27, 1984: 8.

14 Schramberger Majolikafabrik GmbH, 1931 (catalogue).

15 Eidelberg et al., 19.

16 Brent Brolin to PM, e-mail, February 11, 2007.

17 Bodine, 44.

18 EZ/PM, June 12, 2003.

19 Volker Hornbostel to PM, e-mails November 18, 2005–March 4, 2006; Pat Moore, *Eva Zeisel's Schramberg Designs: Identification Guide* (San Francisco: Labor of Love Press), 2010.

Chapter 2

1 JR to PM, telephone conversation, December 5, 2005.

2 Michael Popp and Klaus Haußmann, *Hirschauer Steingut: Die Geschichte der Fabriken und Produkte* (Nuremberg: Popp, 2011): 83; Werner Endres, "Renomierte Designer in der Oberpfalzer Steingutproduktion: Möller, Stricker-Zeisel, Krause, Löffelhardt," in Werner Endres ed., *Steingut: Geschirr aus der Oberpfalz* (Munich: Deutscher Kunstverlag, 2004), 159–166.

3 Obituary. Christian Carstens, *Keramos*, August 1929, 581.

4 Joanna Flawia Figiel, ed., *Revolution der Muster: Sprtizdekor-Keramik um 1930* (Karlsruhe, Germany: Badisches Landesmuseum, 2006), 230.

5   JR to PM, e-mail, May 30, 2008.

6   Between 1923 and 1926, Siegfried Möller (1896–1970) worked for 4 Carstens subsidiaries and modernized production at each. He became artistic director of the Hirschauer Steingutfabriken in 1923, leaving there in 1926 to become artistic director of another Carstens subsidiary, Rheinsberg Keramik. In 1930 he organized Carstens Elsterwerda's art ceramics workshop and later joined Elmshorner Steingutfabrik as artistic director. For Möller, see Hans-Georg Bluhm, *Stationen: Der Keramiker Siegfried Möller 1896–1970* (Kellinghusen, Germany: Museum Kellinghusen, 2003).

7   Karen Kettering, *Eva Zeisel: The Playful Search for Beauty* (Knoxville, TN.: Knoxville Museum of Art, 2004), catalogue, 4.

8   Eva Stricker, et al., Von Einer Steingutfabrik und Von Steingutkeramik," *Die Schaulade* 8, no. 3–4 (February 1932), 72–174. Thanks to Antje Bilgutay for translating this.

9   EZ to PW, March 10, 2008.

10 Stricker et al., "Von Einer Steingutfabrik und Von Steingutkeramik," 72–174; Endres, 161.

11 Volker Hornbostel to PM, e-mails December 2005 and July and August 2007; Hornbostel to Rolf Achilles, February 19, 2005 and June 10, 2007.

12 Ad in *Die Schaulade*, no. 5 (1932), 55; Popp & Haußmann, 100–101.

13 *Holland* is illustrated in Chr. Carstens Kom. Ges., Hirschau OPF, 1932 catalogue. Holland and Ceylon in Popp & Haußmann, 103; *Ceylon* in Popp & Haußmann, 102, with a floral decoration that entered production in 1935.

14 Popp & Haußmann, 105.

15 Popp & Haußmann, 102.

16 Popp & Haußmann, 110; Hornbostel, "C &E Carstens die neuter Linie: Bunt und Modern", in Figiel, ed., 47–57. Although the *Jubiläumsservice* shape (designer unknown) is reminiscent of some of Eva's designs, it was not produced until long after Eva had left Hirschau and therefore the link to it is a speculative stretch on the part of Hornbostel.

17 For *Kugelservice*, see Hornbostel, 47–57.

18 Popp & Haußmann, 105.

19 Popp & Haußmann, 104.

20 Popp & Haußmann, 104.

21 Endres, 159–166.

22 Popp & Haußmann, 111–129.

23 Popp & Haußmann, 102; JR to PM, e-mail, December 3, 2005. After Chr. Carstens KG sold Hirschau to Alois Luckscha, the facilities were known as Hirschau Keramik GmbH. The firm closed in 1956.

Chapter 3

1   See Jean Richards and Brent C. Brolin, eds., *Eva Zeisel: A Soviet Prison Memoir*. iBook, 2012. Inquiries to various archives in Ukraine produced no record of Eva's employment. NB: Many Ukrainian records were destroyed during World War II.

2   Lucie Young, *Eva Zeisel* (San Francisco: Chronicle Books, 2003), 14.

3   See Mark B. Tauger, *Natural Disaster and Human Actions in the Soviet Famine of 1932-1933*, Carl Beck Papers in Russian and East European Studies no. 1506 (Pittsburgh, PA: University of Pittsburgh, 2001). Far more disturbing was the fact that the majority of the factory's staff was malnourished. It was the beginning of the great famine of 1932–1933 that hit the Ukraine particularly hard: a catastrophe generally agreed to have been exacerbated, or caused, by Soviet agricultural policies. Eva recalled the factories could feed only two-thirds of their workers each day; she witnessed hungry workers standing near canteen tables, hoping for a chance to find some remaining buckwheat gruel at the bottom of a dish. An even worse sight for her was children with abdomens grotesquely swollen from long-term starvation, some too weak even to beg for a handout. EZ/author, June 21, 2002.

4   EZ to author, 2002; Karen L. Kettering, *Eva Zeisel: The Playful Search for Beauty* (Knoxville: The Knoxville Museum of Art, 2003). See also Karen L. Kettering, "'Ever More Cosy and Comfortable': The Soviet Domestic Interior in the Stalin Period (1928–1938)," *Journal of Design History* 10, no. 2 (March 1997), 119–135.

5   R. E. F. Smith and David Christian, *Bread and Salt: A Social and Economic History of Food and Drink in Russia* (Cambridge, UK, and New York: Cambridge University Press, 1984), 228–247.

6   Ironically, the government that had commissioned standardized wares for mass-production, in the late 1930s reconfigured them as tea sets for important individuals. The wide expanse of the cylindrical form was particularly convenient as a backdrop for grandiose decorative schemes. The service remained in production until the USSR was invaded during World War II. Pieces should be marked on the underside with the Lomonosov factory mark (introduced in the mid-1930s).

7   L.V. Andreeva, *Sovetskii farfor, 1920–1930-e gody* (Moscow: Sovetskii khudozhnik, 1975), 261.

8   Examples with decoration by Nikolai Suetin and Ivan Riznich are reproduced in N. Sobolevskii, "Puti sovetskogo farfora," *Iskusstvo* 1934, no. 5: 162.

9   N. Bam, "Slovo za promyshlennost'iu," *Legkaia industriia* (Moscow), April 25, 1934, 1; clipping of a review by A. Kut, in a May 1934 issue of *Rabochaia Moskva* in EZA. For the vase, see Tamara Kudryavtseva, *Circling the Square: Avant-Garde Porcelain from Revolutionary Russia* (London: Fontanka, 2004), 103, 118.

10 [E.] Stricker and [H.] Fuhlbrügge, "Unsere Initiative wird nicht beachtet: Spezialistenbrief," *Rote Zeitung: Organ des Leningrader Gebietesrates der Gewerkschaften*, March 9, 1934, 4.

11 In the image, the tall windows of the eighteenth-century portion of the factory in which the artists still work are visible in the background.

12 This was revealed during Eva's interrogation during his imprisonment when Soviet officials were attempting to establish her movements since she had entered the Soviet Union. See NKVD interrogation file, 97a verso, EZA.

13 N. Sobolevskii, "Puti sovetskogo farfora," Iskusstvo 1934, no. 5: 169–171; R. K., "O dushe khudozhnikov i maslenitse," *Komsomol'skaia Pravda*, April 22, 1934, 1; and Bam, 1.

14 This list was compiled from critical essays of the period as well as the catalogue of a retrospective exhibition of Eva's work (held at the State Russian Museum in 1992) which drew on the collections of the State Russian Museum and the Museum of the Dulevo Porcelain Factory. It included many previously unknown works. See *Eva Zeisel—Eva Tsaizel. Farfor i keramika Evy Tsaizel'-Shtriker* (St. Petersburg: Titul, 1992).

15 While Eva did not recall this, Andreeva wrote that the designs were called S-1, S-2, and so on, because S was the first letter of her then-surname, Stricker. However, in Russian the surname was rendered as Shtriker or Shtrikker and the initial letter is the Russian 'Sh'(Ш) rather than 'S' (or C in Cyrillic). It is possible that these titles were assigned after Eva's departure. See Andreeva, 273.

16 Examples of Eva's service are illustrated in the 1978 catalogue of Dulevo's production. See *Katalog Dulevskogo Zavoda imeni Gazety* (Moscow: Ministerstvo legkoi promyshlennosti RSFSR ROSPROMFARFOR, 1978, with introductory essay by Petr Leonov), 197, 203.

17 For Eva's S-1 teapot and covered sugar bowl with Leonov's *Krasavitsa* Decoration, see Martin Eidelberg et al., *Eva Zeisel: Designer for Industry*, Montreal: Le Château Dufresne, Musée des Arts Décoratifs de Montréal (Chicago: University of Chicago Press, 1984), illustration 35, 28.

18 Bam, 1.

19 An example of the unpainted form appears in Eidelberg etal., illustration 34, 27. See also Young, 33.

20 EZ to author, 2000–2005. Eva considered Leonov's designs to be so important that she donated several of her personal pieces with Leonov's decorative designs hand-painted on them to the collection of The Metropolitan Museum of Art, New York, so that they would be preserved for future study. See Cup and Saucer (1987.291.1ab), Cup and Saucer (1987.391.2ab).

21 Lidia Andreeva, "Raspisnoi farfor Petra Leonova," *Dekorativnoe iskusstvo SSSR* 1969, no. 8, 35–37.

22 See Lidia Andreeva, *Sovetskii farfor: Fond Sandretti russkogo iskusstva XX veka* [*Soviet Ceramics: The Sandretti Collection of 20th Century Russian Art*] (Bad Breisig: Palace Editions, 2004), cat. 80, 52.

23 Alfred Durus (pseudo. Kemeny), "Sowjetisches Porzellan: Austellung im Mostorg," in *Deutsche Zentrale-Zeitung*, May 14, 1935. Copy in EZA. NB: No copies have been found outside Russia. The International Institute of Social History in Amsterdam lists the newspaper in its holdings but this issue is missing.

24 See Likörkrug 3366 with short, handleless cups (3367) and a circular tray (3387) in a Schramberger catalogue from the Leipzig Fair (1931), opp, 42 and 48, EZA.

25 The tea caddies are on a shelf directly above Eva's head. See Eidelberg et al., illustration 26, 24.

Chapter 4

1 Nancy Gustafson to author, e-mail, April 20, 2006; Dan November to author, e-mail, February 18, 2006; EZ/author, June 19, 2004. Of the 16 students in Eva's class, Blod was older and had more design experience. A native of Spokane, WA, he moved to New York in 1934 to study interior design at the Parsons School of Design, transferring after a year to study industrial design at the Pratt Institute. By the time Sears accepted Eva's proposition, Blod had graduated from Pratt. After much negotiation between Eva and representatives of Sears and Pratt, it was agreed Blod would develop the line, including models, and prepare the molds under Eva's guidance and using Pratt's ceramic facilities. For his efforts, Blod received a one-time fee of $25 (Nancy Gustafson/author, telephone interview, January 7, 2007). Eva confirmed that Blod received a small payment, and that she did not receive any compensation from Sears. Blod went on to have a successful design career, opening Francis Blod Associates in 1944, specializing in product, packaging, graphics, game, and exhibition design.

2 Sears, Roebuck & Co., *Spring and Summer 1942* catalogue (Sears, Roebuck and Co., Chicago, IL, 1942), 697J.

3 EZ/author, June 19, 2004.

4 Sears, Roebuck and Co., *Spring and Summer 1942* catalogue, 697J.

5 Sears, Roebuck and Co., *Spring and Summer 1942* catalogue, 697J.

6 Sears, Roebuck and Co., *Spring and Summer 1943* catalogue, 538. The 35-piece set included rimmed soup plates instead of the sauce dishes that were standard in the 23– and 32–piece sets.

Chapter 5

1 Martin Eidelberg et al., "Eva Zeisel: Ceramist in an Industrial Age," *Eva Zeisel: Designer for Industry*. Montreal: Le Château Dufresne, Musée des Arts Décoratifs de Montréal (Chicago: University of Chicago Press, 1984), 32.

2 Suzannah Lessard, "Profiles: The Present Moment," *The New Yorker*, April 17, 1987, 57.

3 Lucie Young, *Eva Zeisel* (San Francisco: Chronicle, 2003), 18.

4 EZ at Milwaukee Art Museum, November 7, 2004 (author's notes).

5 Ronald T. Labaco, "'The Playful Search for Beauty': Eva Zeisel's Life in Design," *Studies in the Decorative Arts*, Fall/Winter 2000-01, 126.

6 Eidelberg et al., 35.

7 Eugenia Sheppard, "China Service Is Displayed in Modern Shapes," *New York Herald Tribune*, April 17, 1946, 20.

8 Jennifer M. Downs and Judith A. Barter, *Shaping the Modern: American Decorative Arts at The Art Institute 1917–65* (Chicago: Art Institute of Chicago, 2001), 65.

9 Sheppard, 20.

10 Sheppard, 20.

11 Eidelberg et al., 36.

12 Sheppard, 20.

13 EZ and JR to author, e-mail, February 23, 2005.

14 Sheppard, 20.

15 EZ, "Ask Eva," *Eva Zeisel Times* no. 7, September 2001, 6.

16 Sheppard, 20.

17 "Modern Chinaware at the Modern Museum," *Art News of America*, May 1946, 13.

18 Lessard, 57.

19 Lessard, 57.

20 Sheppard, 20.

21 Mary Roche, "25 Pieces of Fine China in Modern Design To Be Shown at Museum Beginning Today," *New York Times*, April 17, 1946, 30.

22 *Retailing Home Furnishings*, April 18, 1946, 36.

23 Things you should know about China, brochure (Castleton), 1946.

24 James Love to Carlton Atherton, letter, February 17, 1947: "Mrs. Zeisel's 'wares' were scheduled for production in 1948 and would only be made using an Ivory Body, but 'we are now working on special types of decorations to use on it.'"

25 A Castleton ad (1950) implies that the name *Museum* was eventually used to specify the undecorated dinnerware, while "Mandalay," "Lyana," and so forth were used to identify the decorated versions.

26 Castleton ad: "As canvas takes on splendor from the touch of their brush, so their paintings enhance the inherent beauty of this translucent, pearl-toned ware."; *New York Times*, September 18, 1949. Artists featured in the advertisement were Modigliani, Vertes, John Marin, and Stuart Davis. Decorated plates were illustrated and plain *Museum* was represented by silhouettes (coffee pot, handleless creamer, covered bowl, and cup and saucer with revised upright handle).

27 Reproductions of Thomas Nason's *The Farm* were mechanically reproduced on a set of plates priced at $90 for a dozen. Other plate decorations came from Picasso's *Vin Rose*, Stuart Davis' *Town with Boats*, Marcel Vertes' *Plenty*, and Modigliani's *Caryatid*. Square salad plates with Arnold Blanche's *Green Thumb* pattern sold for $60 per dozen, while the large salad bowl (also with decoration designed by Blanche) cost $30 per dozen.

28 EZ, "Ask Eva," *Eva Zeisel Times*, no. 7, September 2001, 6.

29 "Useful Objects," *Everyday Art Quarterly*, Walker Art Center, Spring 1950, 6.

30 EZ, "Ask Eva," 2001, 6.

31 EZ and JR to author, e-mail, April 2, 2005.

32 EZ applied for patents for certain designs in 1946 (see US Patent no. 148,901 for "coffeepot or the like"; no. 148,900 for "teapot or the like"). NB: The teapot was not produced as shown in patent drawing. See *Eva Zeisel Times*, no. 9, March 2002.

33 PM and Beverly Zona/Harold Freed (interview, unpublished, July 16, 2003).

34 PM and Zona/Freed, 2003.

35 Young, 19.

36 The Shenango no. 9 parent company was purchased by the Syracuse company in 1988. The Susquehanna-Pfaltzgraff company bought Syracuse in 1989. The New Castle Shenango plant closed in 1991.

37 Marion Church, "I Worked at Castleton," *Eva Zeisel Times*, no. 7, September 2001.

38 Beverly Zona was told by a former Shenango employee that the company stopped stamping the Museum plates with the Castleton logo and began grinding the bottom stamps off the pieces in the closeout store because people were buying pieces there cheaply and returning them to regular retail stores as unwanted gifts for full retail refunds. See also PM to Mike Pratt, e-mail, November 12, 2002.

Chapter 6

1 Ronald T. Labaco, "'The Playful Search for Beauty': Eva Zeisel's Life in Design," *Studies in the Decorative Arts*, 8 no. 1 (Fall–Winter 2000–2001), 125.

2 Steven Brown to author, August 5, 2004.

3 Lucie Young, *Eva Zeisel* (San Francisco: Chronicle, 2003), 19.

4   *Town and Country* brochures, list prices, and color charts, January 1947–March 1955, Red Wing Potteries, Inc., Red Wing, Minnesota.

5   "New Dinnerware by Eva Zeisel Features Assymetrical Shapes," *China, Glass and Decorative Accessories*, March 1947, 50.

6   EZ/ Margot and Steve Brown (transcript), July 6, 2000.

7   Martin Eidelberg et al., *Eva Zeisel: Designer for Industry*, Montreal: Le Château Dufresne, Musée des Arts Décoratifs de Montréal (Chicago: University of Chicago Press, 1984), 93.

8   Eva Zeisel, "Schmoo Antedates Al Capp," *Interiors*, March 1950, Letters to the Editor, 8.

9   *Interiors*, March 1950, 8. According to Karen E. Steen, "*The Playful Search for Beauty*," Metropolismag. com, January 2001: Some observers interpret their holes as eyes or noses, and there is most definitely a "pettability" to the curves of the Town and Country line. *Eva Zeisel Times*, no. 10, June 2002, noted that the salt and pepper shakers have between 3 and 5 holes, each made by hand after the pieces came out of the mold and before they were fired.

10 "Ask Eva" column, *Eva Zeisel Times*, no. 13, July 2003 (attributed to *The Collectors' Encyclopedia of Fiesta* by Bob and Sharon Huxford, forwarded by Susan Hartwell).

11 *China, Glass and Decorative Accessories*, March 1947, 50.

12 The bowls appeared in *Goldilocks and the Three Bears: A Tale Moderne*, retold and illustrated by Steven Guarnaccia., 1999; EZ, *Eva Zeisel on Design, The Magic Language of Things* (Woodstock, NY and New York; Overlook Press, 2004), 128.

13 A brochure by the Orange Chicken noted 20 colors, specifying yellow, white, light green, chartreuse, red, orange, tan, black lustre, pink, black, beige, brown sand, blue mottled, brown mottled, plum, mauve, rust, and peach.

14 Don Joint to author, e-mail, April 8, 2008.

15 The Metropolitan Museum of Art mail-order catalogues, 1999–2000.

16 PM to author, e-mail, April 7, 2008.

Chapter 7

1   Lois Krieger to author, September 18, 2004.

2   "Work Starts on Ceramic Plant," *Riverside Enterprise*, April 8, 1947, 3. Investors included Howard Boylan, W. Ruel Johnson, Robert Shelor, and Arthur A. Culver of Riverside, together with Francis Crocker of Palm Springs and Thad A. Kay of Ontario.

3   Krieger to author, September 18, 2004.

4   That spring, Small's Seed Company and House of Charm also opened new locations nearby; "Business Goes Eastward," *Riverside Enterprise*, Wednesday, May 7, 1947, 5. This expansion was not long-lived. By 1956, the University of California at Riverside acquired the land to improve the campus entrance; today, a freeway passes over the site. See "Small's Nursery: Oldtime Business to Close Doors," *Riverside Daily Press*, June 22, 1956, B-4.

5   "Work Starts on Ceramic Plant,"3.

6   Krieger to author, September 18, 2004.

7   Karen Kettering to author, June 19, 2004.

8   Mary Roche, "Utility Exhibition Will Start Today," *New York Times*, September 17, 1947, 29.

9   EZ to author, November 7, 2004.

10 For Ferdinand, see "Work Starts on Ceramic Plant,"3; for Wilson, *Riverside City Directory 1947* (Los Angeles, CA: Los Angeles Directory Co., 1947), 502; for Parry, *Riverside City Directory 1947*, 353. The information about Cahoon Jr. is from his federal government security questionnaire, c. 1960

11 "A Ceramic Connection: From TVA Norris to the Art Center Oak Ridge. Some Molds, A Man, A Museum Collection," exhibition brochure, Art Center Oak Ridge, Tennessee, 1986.

12 Bruce Wilson to author, June 18, 2004.

13 "'Riverside China' to Have National Sales," *Riverside Enterprise*, August 10, 1947, 7.

14 Bruce Wilson to author, June 18, 2004.

15 Bill Stern, *California Pottery: From Missions to Modernism* (San Francisco: Chronicle Books, 2001), 96. JR recalls Eva telling her that this task was carried out on a donkey (JR to author, April 2, 2003).

16 Bruce Wilson to author, June 18, 2004.

17 Nell Parry, correspondence, October 6, 1947.

18 Bruce Wilson to author, June 18, 2004.

19 "'Riverside China' to Have National Sales," 7; "Riverside: New Fine China," *Giftwares and Housewares Magazine*, August 1947, 34. The company planned to exhibit its products in a month-long exhibition of California industries at Exposition Park, Los Angeles. See "Local Ceramics Company To Display Dinnerware," *Riverside Enterprise*, Wednesday, September 24, 1947, 5. NB: One of the main reasons that the plant closed when and as it did is that investors came to distrust Ferdinand.

20 *House Beautiful*, December 1947, 122; *House and Garden*, June 1948, 116; *American Home*, December 1947, 102.

21 *100 Useful Objects of Fine Design 1947: Available Under $100*, The Museum of Modern Art, New York, exhibition catalogue, September 16–November 23, 1947.

22 *Useful Objects for the Home: A National Survey and Exhibition, Presenting a Guide to Well Designed Objects for Everyday Use*, Akron Art Institute, Ohio, exhibition catalogue, November 2–December 2, 1947.

23 Ed Lebow/William Parry, November 21, 1993, and late 1990s.

24 "Personal News Items," *Ceramic Industry*, October 1947, 48–49. After the closure, Wilson returned to Tennessee and with his son-in-law Douglas Ferguson, founded the Pigeon Forge Pottery (closed 2000 after death of Ferguson), which used some of Eva's Riverside shapes. In 1951, Cahoon and a partner founded the Loma Manufacturing Co. in Phoenix, Arizona, which issued forms adapted from the *Riverside* line but decorated with Southwest Indian–themed imagery. In June 2004, 57 years after working on the molds for Eva's designs, Bruce Wilson finally met Eva. He and his wife Doris took a rare *Riverside* cruet to the Knoxville Museum of Art to show Eva, whose work was on display there. Running her fingers along the undulating lip of the cruet, Eva commented, "You did a good job on this." Bruce, proud of his connection to this history, spoke with admiration for the special "eye appeal" of the *Riverside* designs.

Chapter 8

1   The Walker Art Center's exhibition *What Are Plastics?* (November 25, 1947–January 11, 1948) sought to counteract prejudice against plastics and to promote them. See "What Are Plastics?," *Everyday Art Quarterly*, Winter 1947/48, 1; Rohm & Haas advertisement, *Everyday Art Quarterly*, Winter 1947/48, 16.

2   Tom Dinell to PM, e-mail, June 9, 2008. Monroe Dinell married an artist, and their son Tom feels that his mother's artistic sensibilities contributed to his father's desire to make objects that were both useful and beautiful.

3   Helen Henley, "Improved Plastic Table Accessories Bid for Social Regard: Eva Zeisel Uses New Approach in Her Designs for Cloverware," *The Christian Science Monitor* (Boston, MA), October 21, 1947: 10.

4   Henley, 10.

5   Henley, 10.

6   Tom Dinell to PM, e-mail, June 9, 2008: "The term I recall describing the process, used with the canopies and subsequently Cloverware, was extrusion. The plastic sheet, again as best I recall, was heated and placed on a plywood form and then shaped. I'll be darned if I remember whether air or a vacuum was used to give shape to the sheet or some other means." Extrusion was defined in *What Are Plastics?* as a method by which "the heated compound in viscous state is forced through a die of desired shape, is air cooled, and cut into sections." This may well have been a process with which Dinell and Eva experimented. Contemporary sources, including *Everyday Art Quarterly* and *The Christian Science Monitor*, described Cloverware as being "blown."

NB: "In blowing, thermoplastic sheets are placed inside closed molds and forced into shape by air or steam pressure."; "What Are Plastics?", *Everyday Art Quarterly*, Winter 1947/48, 5.

7   Eva would strive for this effect again in 1954 when experimenting with pressed glass for Heisey's *Town and Country* line.

8   "What Are Plastics?,"5.

9   Henley, 10.

10   Monroe Dinell to Charles Val Clear, letter, October 16, 1947.

11   "New Wonders for House Vie with Old Favorites," in supplement to Riverside enterprise, November 26, 1947, B15.

12   "New Wonders for House Vie with Old Favorites," B15.

13   Tom Dinell to author, e-mail, June 9, 2008; "What Are Plastics?" , exhibition brochure, Walker Art Center, 1947.

14   Other items included a pot by Red Wing Potteries, and pieces by Winfield Pottery and Kensington Aluminum, all available for purchase at Anderson's, Minneapolis. See *Everyday Art Quarterly*, Spring 1948, Where to Buy Well Designed Objects section. New Design, Inc. of New York was named as a place to buy Cloverware.

15   Monroe Dinell to Charles Val Clear (letter), October 16, 1947. He described these items as the no. 4711 salad bowl, no. 4712 servers, no. 4710 serving dish (white), and no. 4701 serving dish (amber).

16   Armour Research Foundation, Illinois Institute of Technology to James Prestini, letter, January 22, 1948.

17   Art Association of Indianapolis to Robert O. Parks, John Herron Institute, letter, January 23, 1948.

18   *Everyday Art Quarterly*, Spring 1948.

19   Cloverware Museum Pieces, brochure, Clover Box and Manufacturing Co. Inc., c. 1948.

20   Martin Eidelberg, ed., *Design 1935–1965: What Modern Was* (New York: Harry N. Abrams, 1995), 111.

Chapter 9

1   Charles L. Venable et al., *China and Glass in America 1880–1980: From Tabletop to TV Tray* (New York: Harry N. Abrams, 2000), 246.

2   Venable et al., 250.

3   Venable et al., 250.

4   EZ/author, September 20, 2002.

5   Martin Eidelberg, et al., *Eva Zeisel: Designer for Industry,* Montreal: Le Château Dufresne, Musée des Arts Décoratifs de Montréal (Chicago: University of Chicago Press, 1984), 43.

6   "Dinnerware among New Items Planned for United's 100th Anniversary," *China, Glass and Decorative Accessories*, December 1949, 94.

7   *Crockery and Glass Journal,*United China and Glass Company advertisement, 15.

8   *Crockery and Glass Journal,*United China and Glass Company advertisement, 15.

9   Shirley Howard, "Japanese Dinnerware: A Two-Sided Story," *Crockery & Glass Journal,* June 1954, 21.

10   *China, Glass and Decorative Accessories*, February 1954, 26–27. Early advertising for *Norleans China* cites 12 patterns. At least 29 have been identified. Pieces produced before 1952 bear the stamp "Made in Occupied Japan."

11   *China, Glass and Decorative Accessories*, February 1954, 26–27.

Chapter 10

1   It is not known how the relationship between Eva and Salisbury Artisans began. There is a tenous connection: Eva had an exhibition at the Museum of Modern Art in 1946 and in 1948 the company's rosewood muddlers (drink stirrers) made the museum's 100 "best-gifts" list.

2   EZ/author, August 4, 2004.

3   "Rosewood and Ceramic Combined in New Zeisel Line Shown in Akron," *Retailing Daily*, October 22, 1951, 51.

Chapter 11

1   "Midhurst Named Representative for New Line by Hall China," *China, Glass and Decorative Accessories*, November 1951, 27. Other reports support this. See "Eva Zeisel to Design Dinnerware for Hall," *Crockery and Glass Journal*, November 1951, 68; "What's New in Dinnerware & Glassware," *Gift and Art Buyer*, December 1951, 82.

2   "Eva Zeisel to Design Dinnerware for Hall," *Crockery and Glass Journal*, November 1951, 68. The article refers to this material as "semi-porcelain," an earthenware body; the term is meant to evoke the idea of porcelain with its characteristic fine translucent body, which is nonporous (impervious to liquids and resists staining) and resistant to chipping and cracking. These characteristics are not found in earthenware, including semi-porcelain bodies, which tend to be opaque, thicker, and more prone to staining, chipping, and cracking. John Thompson of Hall China noted that the Hallcraft body was very good quality and allowed for thinner potting and a whiter, more brilliant appearance. John Thompson/author, telephone interview, December 19, 2007. Thompson, who was president of Hall China Co. at the time of this interview, was the son of the president of Hall at the time of *Tomorrow's Classic's* manufacture. He worked at the company in the 1950s and interacted with Eva to a limited extent. Surviving Hallcraft pieces support this idea; they tend not to have crazing and are more resistant to cracking and chipping than other earthenware bodies of the period.

3   Charles Seliger/author, December 8, 2007, Mount Vernon, NY. A noted painter, Seliger (1926–2009) was formerly head of design at Commercial Decal, having been hired as a staff designer in 1949. Seliger was not part of this initial meeting between Eva and Durhssen but recalled her visit (c. 1950).

4   Seliger/author. Duhrssen, who emphasized the importance of design and designers to the dinnerware field, established an innovative design division within his company to offer customers easy access to both designers and a large variety of designs. See Alfred Duhrssen, "Are Today's Design-Standards Slipping?" *Crockery and Glass Journal*, December 1952, 96–97; Alfred Duhrssen, "A Quarter-Century of Dinnerware Design," *China, Glass and Decorative Accessories*, June 1953, 49–50.

5   Thompson/author, 2007.

6   Seliger/author, 2007. Seliger thought it likely that Duhrssen connected Hall China with his friend Higgins. Thompson recalled that Hall China was interested in engaging an outside marketing and distribution firm.

7   Thompson/author, 2007. Eva's contract to create the first Hallcraft line was with Midhurst China and Higgins.

8   Eva donated a *Tomorrow's Classic* blueprint drawing for a "marmite" to the Cooper-Hewitt, National Design Museum. It is dated June 18, 1951.

9   EZ quoted in "What Can Consumers Expect in Dinnerware Design?" *Crockery and Glass Journal*, December 1951, 146. Not every piece shared these commonalities: the cups are round, not oval, and the plates are not footed. The short foot, or "English foot," was Eva's idea and part of the original design (Thompson/author, 2007).

10   Eva Zeisel, "The Coming Era of Dinnerware Design," *China, Glass and Decorative Accessories*, December 1951, 59.

11   Information in this section comes from Seliger/author, 2007, unless stated otherwise.

12   Zeisel, "The Coming Era of Dinnerware Design," 59. This statement almost certainly applied only to those patterns initially offered on *Tomorrow's Classic* that had been overseen and approved by Eva.

13   Seliger/author, 2007.

14   "Paragraphs About Persons," *China, Glass and Decorative Accessories*, November 1951, 38. Dorflinger had previously worked for Steuben Glass and the Cleveland Museum of Art and left Midhurst in 1955 for Fostoria Glass and later Orrefors of Sweden. See "K.

Dorflinger Joins Fostoria," *Crockery and Glass Journal*, January 1955, 61; and "Katheryn Manchee: Historian, 86," *New York Times*, August 24, 1991, 36.

15 In April 1952, when Dorflinger appeared in the "American Design Show" at Miller and Rhoads, the leading department store of Richmond, Virginia, the store promoted her in the local press as a "well-known authority and lecturer on glass and china." See "Here's How Miller and Rhoads Sell American Design," *Crockery and Glass Journal*, May 1952, 28. In the spring and summer of 1953, Dorflinger traveled to the west coast, to department stores such as Gump's, Sloan's, Dorman's, and Macy's in San Francisco, and Barker Brothers and the Broadway Stores in Los Angeles. See "New in New York," *China, Glass and Decorative Accessories*, July 1953, 39; "Trade Tidings," *Crockery and Glass Journal*, July 1954, 92; "Hallcraft Makes Friends in Detroit," *Crockery and Glass Journal*, December 1954, 128.

16 "Trade Tidings," 92. Dorflinger's appearance at the leading department store J. L. Hudson Co., Detroit, for example, was accompanied by an appearance on a local television program. She emphasized the versatility and multiple uses of the line and presented Eva as well-suited to designing dinnerware that met the needs of other mothers and homemakers. See "Hallcraft Makes Friends in Detroit," *Crockery and Glass Journal*, December 1954, 128.

17 For showroom preview, see Ann Ruggles, "China Plates That Snuggle In Your Lap," *New York World-Telegram and Sun*, December 19, 1951, 18. The showroom, like the ware, was designed by Eva. See "New in New York," *China, Glass and Decorative Accessories*, January 1952, 33, which noted: "Curved walls finished in soft gray and yellow and punctuated by brightly lighted niches serve as dramatic display background for the dinnerware." The national trade preview was at the Pittsburgh show, January 3–11, 1952.

18 "Eva Zeisel to Design Dinnerware for Hall," 68; "What's New in Dinnerware & Glassware," 82.

19 "Echoes from Chicagoland," *China, Glass and Decorative Accessories*, February 1952, 38.

20 Ruggles, 18; Harriet Morrison, "Today's Living: Dinnerware Has Delicate Airs," *New York Herald Tribune*, March 11, 1952, 22.

21 Marion Gough, "Are You Aware of the Increasing High Style of Durability?" *House Beautiful*, April 1952, 118–119; Gertrude Bassard, "Place and Show," *American Home*, August 1952, 54. *Family Circle* called the dinnerware "serene" and "equally good from all angles"; see "New Shape in Dinnerware," *Family Circle*, October 1952, 108–109. *Pathfinder* noted its "dignity, restraint and a certain amount of elegance," as well as its practicality and "budget price." See Carol Brown, "What Makes a Set of Dishes Both Pleasant to Look at and Practical?" *Pathfinder*, April 23, 1952, 36–37.

22 "Interesting Curves to New Dinnerware," *New York Times*, March 11, 1952, 24.

23 Barker Bros. ad., *Los Angeles Times*, June 15, 1952, 2. The store stocked undecorated White and the Bouquet pattern.

24 Midhurst China Co. ad, *China, Glass and Tablewares*, December 1954, 22. The slogan "America's fastest selling modern dinnerware" (first used in an ad in *Jeweler's Circular Keystone*, October 1952) was used by Midhurst in most ads related to this line.

25 Unless otherwise noted, this section references "Hall China/Midhurst China, Hallcraft Tomorrow's Classic by Eva Zeisel," brochure, c. late 1951. Thanks to Michael Pratt for sharing a photocopy of this brochure, and to early Hall China researcher Harvey Duke, from whom he received it. The shapes listed on the flyer are: dinner, salad and bread and butter plates; teacup, saucer; teapot; cream; sugar; after-dinner cup, saucer, cream and sugar; fruit, cereal and soup bowls; baker; platter; gravy boat; celery dish; jug; covered onion soup; covered dish; open vegetable dish; salad bowl; ladle; marmite; ashtray; and vinegar.

26 The handleless creamer (Eva had an example in her own collection) was exhibited at the Pittsburgh china and glass trade show (January 1952). "Exhibits at the Pittsburgh Shows Sparkle with Retail Display Ideas," *Crockery and Glass Journal*, February 1952, 30.

27 Patterns not produced were Autumn, Burbank, Festive, Chantilly, and Dusty Rose. Another pattern, Beaux Arts, may have been produced in very limited quantities: 9 patterns were noted in an early article (Harriet Morrison, "Today's Living: Dinnerware Has Delicate Airs," *New York Herald Tribune*, March 11, 1952, 22) and the pattern was featured in a trade journal's new products section ("Illustrating the Market," *China, Glass and Decorative Accessories*, May 1952, 21). Some of the patterns that did not come into full commercial production were shown at the New York showroom preview; see Ruggles, "China Plates That Snuggle In Your Lap."

28 "Midhurst Features Hallcraft Zeisel-Designed Dinnerware," *Crockery and Glass Journal*, July 1952, 81; Midhurst China Co. ad, *Crockery and Glass Journal*, December 1952, 39. The completely new shape, the coffee pot, was called "a symphony of line—from its graceful lid to its well-rounded base"("Midhurst Shows Hallcraft's New Accessory Pieces," *Crockery and Glass Journal*, December 1952, 92). It cost $3.75 undecorated; $4.25 and $5.50 with decal decoration.

29 "Sun Glo Studios Introduce Eva Zeisel's Silhouette,"*Crockery and Glass Journal*, August 1952, 62: "The theme of the glass is the same as the Hallcraft dinnerware, and Mrs. Zeisel believes the combination represents the first coordination of [the] shape of dinnerware and glassware."NB: It could be argued that the shapes of *Tomorrow's Classic* and *Silhouette* were not that well coordinated.

30 This section references Hall China/Midhurst China, *Hallcraft Tomorrow's Classic* brochure, December 1, 1953. Thanks to Michael Pratt for sharing a photocopy of this brochure and Harvey Duke, who sent it to him.

31 "Informal-but-elegant," *Crockery and Glass Journal*, September 1953, 32. Satin Black was probably introduced at the July 1953 china and glass trade show in New York City. Undecorated items were the cheapest, at $9.95 for a starter set for 4 people. "Group A" pattern (Arizona, Bouquet, Caprice, Fantasy, Frost Flowers, Holiday) starter sets cost $10.95; "Group B" pattern sets (Buckingham, Dawn, Lyric, Mulberry, Peach Blossom) $12.95. The Satin Black glaze, available only on certain shapes, fell into Group A.

32 Previous to this, Robinson Clay Products Company, a Canadian company that distributed various American dinnerware lines, offered *Tomorrow's Classic*. See "Where to Buy It," *Gift Buyer*, April 1953, 34.

33 "Where to Buy It," *Gift Buyer*, November 1953, 26. While styled "Moderncraft" in this feature, subsequent features and advertisements used "Modern Craft."

34 Canadian China & Glass emphasized "the multiple uses of the various pieces" just as Midhurst had done in the United States. See "Modern Craft Leads a Double Life," *Gift Buyer*, December 1953, 29.

35 There are noticeable imperfections in many Modern Craft pieces, especially the plates. Modern Craft likely utilized seconds (Thompson/author). Modern Craft ads stated that the line was exclusively distributed by Canadian China & Glass and that its distribution was "limited in Canada." See *Gift Buyer*, December 1953, back cover.

36 Of the 4 Modern Craft patterns, only Sweet Grass was used on *Tomorrow's Classic* in the U.S., where it was known as Prairie Grass. Cloverdale was originally created for the Salem China Company and Bittersweet for Crooksville China Company (see Commercial Decal Inc. Collection, 1993-107-1, Smithsonian Institution, National Museum of American History: Archives Center). Seliger indicated that Commercial Decal patterns were created exclusively for certain potteries (Seliger/author) but this arrangement probably did not apply outside the U.S. Salem marketed its pattern as Peach and Clover (ad in *Crockery and Glass Journal*, February 1951, 11), and Modern Crafts Queen's Rose was known as Betsy Rose on a U.S. line under Sears' Harmony House brand (produced by one or two unknown American companies, possibly Crooksville China and Universal Potteries).

37 For Cloverdale, see Canadian China & Glass ad, *Gift Buyer*, November 1954, back cover. For more on Canadian China & Glass, see "Out of the Dust—Modern Merchandising Decor," *Gift Buyer*, October 1951, 28–29.

38 The featuring of Modern Craft in the 1956 model home ("Giveaway Home") was a publicity coup for the distributor. See *Gift Buyer*, July 1956, back cover; Moyra Otterson, "A Show House for Canadian Living," *Canadian Home and Gardens*, September 1956, 33–45.

39 The last known mention of Modern Craft is in "Patterns, Brands and Lines," *Gift Buyer*, July 1958, 85.

40 Dorflinger left Midhurst for Fostoria Glass Co.; see "K. Dorflinger Joins Fostoria," *Crockery and Glass Journal*, January 1955, 61.

41 "Top Ten Patterns in Tablewares Registered by Brides," *Crockery and Glass Journal*, July 1958, 56–58.

42 "Tested: They're Staples and They've Proven Their Value," *Crockery and Glass Journal*, September 1960, 30–31.

43 Production of both Hallcraft lines was discontinued about 1962 (Thompson/author). Just before that happened, *Tomorrow's Classic* was due to receive a new group of patterns designed by Eva which, it was hoped, would reinvigorate the Hallcraft brand; "Debut New Zeisel Patterns," *Gift and Tableware Reporter*, March 1962, 98. The patterns appear to have got to the prototype stage since they were featured in a few trade publications; see "Here's a Wide Range of Styles for the Bride," *Gift and Tableware Reporter*, April 1962, 18; "Design Review: Tableware," *Industrial Design*, February 1962, 84. The last known retail ad for *Tomorrow's Classic* was placed by the May Company; see *Los Angeles Times*, March 24, 1963, F9.

44 See Margaret Carney, *Lost Molds and Found Dinnerware: Rediscovering Eva Zeisel's Hallcraft* (Alfred, New York: International Museum of Ceramic Art, 1999).

45 The line includes both *Century* and *Tomorrow's Classic* shapes but the majority are from *Tomorrow's Classic*. The mug was developed specially for *Classic Century* based on *Tomorrow's Classic* shapes.

Chapter 12

1 Eva Zeisel Fine Stoneware from Monmouth, brochure, 1953.

2 Eva Zeisel Fine Stoneware from Monmouth, brochure, 1953.

3 Eva Zeisel Fine Stoneware from Monmouth, brochure, 1953.

4 Pat Moore, *Eva Zeisel Times*, no. 11, September 2002.

5 Mary Coates to author, e-mails, 2006–2007.

6 Jim Martin and Bette Cooper, Monmouth-Western Stoneware (Des Moines, Iowa: Wallace-Homestead Book Co., 1983), 44–47.

7 Mildred Warner to Mary Coates, e-mail, July 2007.

8 Gertrude Brassard, "Place and Show," *The American Home*, August 1954; justamodernguy.com/?p=133.

9 Mary Coates, e-mail to author, 2006.

10 Moore, *Eva Zeisel Times*, no. 11.

11 Moore, *Eva Zeisel Times*, no. 11.

12 PM to author, e-mail, September 2007, referring to e-mail from Mary Coates: "Summer days in Monmouth were brutally hot, especially inside the factory, where the kilns and stoneware dust intensified the stifling heat and humidity. Sometimes, it was more comfortable and productive for Eva to work in the evening. It was not unusual for a manager or model maker to get a call from Eva asking them to join her in her late night creative sessions—and she was very disappointed if they did not accept her invitation!"

13 16-piece starter sets in "Pals" pattern cost $20.95; solid glaze and other patterns cost from $9.95 to $19.95; Moore, *Eva Zeisel Times*, no.11.

14 Eva Zeisel Associates, Eva Zeisel Fine Stoneware, brochure. The basic dinnerware line could be sold with casseroles, French casseroles, a tea set, a coffee set, chop plate, and salad and other serving bowls. Another dinnerware set included various covered marmites, and a teapot, creamer, and sugar bowl. Casseroles, pitchers, sets of bowls, and an ice bucket made up a kitchenware line.

15 Eva Zeisel Associates, Eva Zeisel Fine Stoneware, brochure.

16 Mary Coates to author, e-mail, 2006.

17 Eva Zeisel Fine Stoneware from Monmouth, brochure. Wally L. Blodgett, at the Brack Shops in Los Angeles, represented the line in the West; Alvin Rosenthal of New York in the East.

18 Pat Moore, *Eva Zeisel Times*, no.11.

19 Mary Coates to author, e-mail, 2006.

20 Otto and Jessie Hupp established a pottery in 1935.When high demand for their colored dinnerware led to larger production facilities in Hollydale, California, the company took the name *Hollydale*; *West Coast Ceramic News*, February 1988. According to Michael Pratt (A Brief History of Hollydale Pottery and Malibu Modern" 2007, http://www.modish.net), the firm moved to another facility in South Gate in 1943 but retained the name. It had two periodic kilns for bisque-firing and a tunnel kiln for glaze-firing with a rated production capacity of 1.3 million pieces per year; *Los Angeles Times*, May 11, 1952. When fire destroyed the main production facility in May 1953, a new concrete and steel building was built and new kilns installed that allowed for higher firing temperatures.

21 *West Coast Ceramic News*, February 1955.

22 Giftwares, February 1954. Blodgett's showroom was on the twelfth floor of the Brack Shops building in Los Angeles. There he represented various dinnerware, pottery, and decorative art companies. Full of energy and ideas, he turned several surplus wartime ambulances into traveling showrooms to better serve the retail customers in his eleven-state territory; Buzz Blodgett to author, e-mail, January 14, 2008.

23 *Crockery and Glass Journal*, May 1957, 60.

24 Broadway ad, *Los Angeles Times*, May 17, 1957.

25 *Crockery and Glass Journal, May 1957, 60.*

26 *China, Glass & Tablewares*, April 1957.

27 *Crockery and Glass Journal, May 1957, 60.*

28 Anne Norman, *Los Angeles Times*, March 23, 1957.

29 *China, Glass & Tablewares*, April 1957.

30 Broadway ad, May 17, 1957.

31 Photograph: Gump's display window, 1957.

32 Nikko Ceramic, Inc., NikkoCeramics.com (2010), www.nikkoceramics.com/NKhistory.htm.

33 Norm Yamamoto to author, e-mail, February 7, 2006. Mr. Yamamoto is employed by Nikko Ceramics, Inc.

34 Schmid Ironstone brochure, 1964.

35 The foot on the bottom of the bird bowl was revised for better stability; the curve on the scoop of its bird-head ladle was revised for a better transition to the handle. The covered casserole was slightly bigger than its Monmouth and Hollydale counterparts. Like the non-bird casseroles, the bottom edge of its lid was redesigned for greater durability. Eva redesigned the salt and peppers with an accentuated tail and the ability to rock back and forth (see her Riverside line). A bird-shaped container, with an open tail and beak, was designed for oil and vinegar, along with a charming bird sauceboat with a delicate tail-shaped ladle.

36 Schmid Ironstone brochure, 1964.

37 Schmid Ironstone brochure, 1964.

Chapter 13

1 EZ/author, September 25, 2007; John Thompson/author, telephone interview, December 19, 2007. Both confirmed that Eva was given this commission because of the success of *Tomorrow's Classic*. President of Hall China Company when interviewed, Thompson worked at the company in the 1950s and interacted with Eva to a limited extent.

2 "Market Preview," *Crockery and Glass Journal*, December 1954, 22.

3 See "Hall's Casual Living China designed by Eva Zeisel," Hall China Co., brochure, c. 1955. I am grateful to Michael Pratt for sharing a photocopy of this brochure with me and to Harvey Duke, who sent it to him. The remainder of this section is based on Michael Pratt, "The Hall China Company: 104 Years of Exceptional Design and Production," http://modish. net/hall-china; and Catherine S. Vodrey, *A Centennial History of The Hall China Company* (Cleveland, OH: Stevens Barons Communications Inc. and Hall China Company, 2002), 6–24.

4 Hall first introduced products for the home market in 1920; see company ads in *Pottery, Glass and Brass Salesman*, February 19, 1920, 52, and July 8, 1920, 10; Jeffrey B.Snyder, *Hall China* (Atglen, PA: Schiffer Publishing, 2002), 17–19.

5 Information in this section is based on a study of trade journals, newspapers, and department store ads. See "Casual Ware: It's a Big Business!," *Crockery and Glass Journal*, March 5, 1951, 25–27; "Casual Living, Third Annual Report," *Giftwares*, March 1954, 33. Many stores, including Chicago-based retailer Marshall Field and Company, established departments of Casual Living accessories. See "Shopping the Market: Chicago," *Giftwares*, March 1956, 58.

6 "Hall's Casual Living China designed by Eva Zeisel," c. 1955, illustrates 23 items and lists their Hall numbers, names, capacities, and dimensions.

7 EZ/author, September 25, 2007.

8 EZ/author, September 25, 2007. The manufacturer designated the glaze as "Seal Brown"; see "Hall's Casual Living China designed by Eva Zeisel," c.1955.

9 This contrasts with Eva's dinnerware lines which Midhurst China marketed and distributed for Hall.10 For an example see "We Sell What We Like," *Gift and Art Buyer*, March 1958, 47.

11 Thompson/author, 2007. He indicated Eva probably would have demanded a higher level of compensation if her name had appeared on each piece.

12 Hall introduced the new decoration in January at the major annual china and glass trade show; "1956 Pittsburgh Show Best Since Before the War," *Crockery and Glass Journal*, February 1956, 45.

13 EZ/author, 2007; Thompson/author, 2007. It is not clear to me which recollection is correct, but Hall did not produce decorations similar to Tri-Tone in its other kitchenware lines.

14 This section is based on Hall China Co., "Tri-Tone Hall China" line sheet, March 1956. I thank Michael Pratt for sharing a photocopy of this sheet, which he received from Harvey Duke. Outside of the cookie jar, bean jar, and the mixing bowls, the shapes with Tri-Tone decoration carried the same Hall item numbers as in Casual Living. The Hall item numbers for the Tri-Tone cookie jar and bean jar were 1566 and 1565, respectively, versus 1576 and 1575 in Casual Living. For cookie jars in different sizes, see Taxonomy.

15 EZ/ author, March 18, 2008. Eva confirmed the salad bowls in the kitchenware line were her design. Similar mixing bowl sets were part of Hall's other kitchenware lines of the time.

16 See Midhurst China Company ad, *Crockery and Glass Journal*, December 1957, 80; *China, Glass and Tablewares*, June 1957, 18; "Feature These for Christmas," *Crockery and Glass Journal*, September 1957, 38.

17 For pattern names, see Midhurst ad, *Crockery and Glass Journal*, December 1957, 80. At the same time, Midhurst introduced Flight pattern on Eva's *Century* dinnerware line (likely not put into full production). For illustrations of many of the pieces in Exotic Bird, see Margaret and Ken Whitmyer, *Collector's Encyclopedia of Hall China*, 3rd ed. (Paducah, KY: Collector's Books, 2001), 190–191 (pieces illustrated there that were not designed by Eva include three sizes of oval "shirred egg" dishes, a straight-sided mug, and a straight-sided bowl).

18 Described as "brightly colored cookery motifs" in "Feature These for Christmas," *Crockery and Glass Journal*, September 1957, 38.

19 I have yet to discover anything about Elena.

20 Companies often tried out new decorations at trade shows and if orders resulted, then the patterns were put into production. For images of Flight-decorated salt and peppers, water pitcher, and large salad bowl, see Pratt, *Mid-Century Modern Dinnerware: A Pictorial Guide, Ak-Sar-Ben to Pope-Gosser* (Atglen, PA: Schiffer Publishing, 2003), 96–97. No other examples of this pattern are known. I am aware of only a few examples of Eva Zeisel kitchenware in Gold and White (a white glaze accented with gold).

21 "Patterns for 1957—New Dinnerware, Glassware & Accessories," *Crockery and Glass Journal*, February 1957, 48. The magazine featured Hall's "coordinated line of oven ware" including the cookie jar in "pastel shades" with "lots of gold trimming." Eva did not design other shapes in the later Hall kitchenware lines.

22 PM to author, e-mails, April 4 and 7, 2008.

23 See Neue Gallerie, https://www.neuegalerie.org/product/zeisel-icebox-pitcher.

Chapter 14

1 John Thompson/author, telephone interview, December 19, 2007. President of Hall China Co. at the time of the interview, Thompson's father was company president in the 1950s when Thompson worked there and interacted with Eva on a limited basis.

2 "Candid Camera Highlights of New York Market," *China, Glass and Tablewares*, August 1956, 30; "Midhurst Holds Party to Introduce New Design," *Gift and Art Buyer*, September 1956, 80. The reception was July 16, 1956. Georg Jensen's was an upscale design-focused retailer with a shop on Fifth Avenue, New York. It featured artistic modern goods, many of them Scandinavian, including Danish silver by another firm named Georg Jensen.

3 "Distinctive Petal Shape Sparks Dinnerware Line," *Retailing Daily*, July 16, 1956. NB: This article mentions a coffee pot but there was only a teapot in the *Century* line.

4 It has been suggested that Eva's *Century* design was influenced by the stop-action photography of Harold Edgerton, especially a milk drop splashing; Virginia Postrel, "How Modernism Got Its Curves: A Look at the Extraordinary Career of Designer Eva Zeisel," Slate, September 1, 2005, *http://www.slate.com*.

5 See chapter 11 for *Tomorrow's Classic* line and decal patterns.

6 This section is based on a *Hallcraft Century by Eva Zeisel* brochure, c.1956. 41 *Tomorrow's Classic* shapes were available when *Century* was introduced (chapter 11).

7 The snack plate was added shortly after the line debuted; "What's New in Tableware and Drinkware," *Crockery and Glass Journal*, March 1957, 30.

8 *Hallcraft Century by Eva Zeisel*, c. 1956.

9 A significant number of *Century* items have no decal decoration but have lids/interiors glazed blue or yellow. Such examples seem to be unmarked but it is not clear if these were sold as seconds by Hall.

10 This section is based on Seliger/ author, December 8, 2007. Well-known as an abstract painter, Seliger worked for Commercial Decal for over forty years.

11 *Hallcraft Century by Eva Zeisel*, c.1956.

12 The only known popular press article featuring *Century* was Lois Maxon, "White China Best to Start," *New York World Telegram and Sun*, May 16, 1957, 20.

13 Thompson recalled the manufacturing problems and breakages (Thompson/author); Eva redesigned the plate shape at the request of Hall/Midhurst (EZ/author). See also "Tableware Fashions For Fall," *China, Glass and Tablewares*, August 1957, 24. No examples of round *Century* plates appear to have been produced other than prototypes, and Flight, quite a rare pattern introduced at the same time as the round plate, has been found only on plates with petal tips.

14 "Tableware Fashions for Fall," *China, Glass and Tablewares*, August 1957, 24. This article mentions the Dolly Madison pattern (a floral border) but there is no evidence that it was produced. For Flight-pattern *Century* ware, see Michael Pratt, *Mid-Century Modern Dinnerware: A Pictorial Guide, Ak-Sar-Ben to Paden City Pottery* (Atglen, PA: Schiffer Publishing, 2007), 92.

15 This section is based on Thompson/author, and a study of trade journals and popular press.

16 Thompson thought the greater diversity of contemporary modern dinnerware was likely a factor in *Century*'s lack of success (Thompson/author).

17 These include Crooksville China Co., Crooksville, OH; Pope-Gosser China Co., Coshocton, OH; Santa Anita Potteries, Los Angeles, CA; Southern Potteries, Inc., Erwin, TN; Steubenville Pottery Co., Steubenville, OH; Vernon Kilns, Los Angeles, CA; and several others. The ceramic bodies of "casual china" were similar to the restaurant wares made by many of the same manufacturers. Among the best-selling "casual china" were three lines from Iroquois China: Russel Wright's *Casual China* (considered the first line of this type, it was in production from 1946 to 1967), and *Impromptu* and *Informal* by Ben Seibel (introduced 1956 and 1958, respectively, and manufactured through the mid-1960s). For a history of Iroquois and these lines, see Michael Pratt, *Mid-Century Modern Dinnerware: Ak-Sar-Ben Pottery, Denwar Ceramics, Iroquois China Company, Laurel Potteries of California, Royal China Company, Stetson China Company* (Atglen, PA: Schiffer Publishing, 2002), 40–86. Marketed as more practical versions of the fine china ideal, casual china became increasingly popular as the 1950s progressed. By the end of the decade, stores around the country made it a main focus of their dinnerware departments and sales of earthenware dropped. See "Profits with Casual China," *Crockery and Glass Journal*, August 1959, 23–29.

18 Hallcraft dinnerware lines were discontinued about 1962 (Thompson/author). The last known advertisement for *Century* at the retail level was for "Burdines Bargain Bee" (see *Palm Beach Post*, June 19, 1964, 11).

19 See Martin Eidelberg et al., *Eva Zeisel: Designer for Industry*, catalogue of the exhibition organized by Le Château Dufresne, Musée des Arts Décoratifs de Montréal and the Smithsonian Institution Traveling Exhibition Service (Chicago: University of Chicago Press, 1984).

20 Margaret Carney, *Lost Molds and Found Dinnerware: Rediscovering Eva Zeisel's Hallcraft* (Alfred, New York: International Museum of Ceramic Art, 1999). *Century* jugs sold by the Orange Chicken were in white, yellow, gray, black, blue, green, and purple. PM to author, e-mails, April 4 and 7, 2008.

21 The other serving items and place-setting dishes in *Classic Century* by Royal Stafford reproduce, or are based upon, Eva's *Tomorrow's Classic* designs.

Chapter 15

1 "When your original sketch evolves into a tangible, three-dimensional object, your heart is anxiously following the process of your work. And the love in making it is conveyed to those for whom you made it." *Eva Zeisel, Eva Zeisel on Design: The Magic Language of Things* (Woodstock, NY: Overlook Press, 2004), 210.

2 Suzannah Lessard, "Profiles: The Present Moment," *The New Yorker*, April 13, 1987, 40. See also Lucy Young, *Eva Zeisel* (San Francisco: Chronicle Books, 2003), 22.

3 The 22 year-old had just earned her first $50 by selling her photograph of Greta Garbo to Life magazine. See Natalia Aspesi, *Inge Fotoreporter*, (Milan: Seniorservice Books, 2000), 104. In 1958 she met Giangiacomo Feltrinelli at one of Rowohlt's parties, married him in 1960 and moved to Italy. She took over his publishing empire after his death in 1972 and in 2011 she was awarded the "Karlsmedaille" for European media.

4 Inge Feltrinelli to author, telephone conversation, January 8, 2008.

5 Her photograph of Hemingway, the boatman Gregorio Fuentes, and herself with a 33-kilogram marlin was published around the world in magazines like *Paris Match* and *Picture Post*; Aspesi, 100.

6 Inge became very good friends with Philip Rosenthal. Peynet worked for Rosenthal AG from 1955 to 1966.

7 Charles Venable et al., *China and Glass in America: 1880-1980: From Tabletop to TV Tray*, (Dallas: Dallas Museum of Art, New York: Harry N. Abrams, Inc., 2001), 239.

8 Rosenthal AG, which had invested very heavily in *Form 2000*, advertised it as "the form of the second half of the twentieth century"; Angela Schönberger and Raymond Loewy: *Pioneer of American Industrial Design* (Munich: Prestel, 1990), 140 ff.

9 The Rosenthal Block China Corporation was established in 1952.

10 For Latham see, *Rosenthal Verkaufsdienst* 55, January 1955, in Schönberger, 141.

11 Both were still present in the 1962 price list; Bernd Fritz, *Die Porzellangeschirre des Rosenthal Konzerns 1891–1979* (Stuttgart: Union Verlag, 1989), 76.

12 Fritz, 77.

13 This unique design for holding the lid in place was already implemented in *Form E* by Latham/Loewy.

14 Fritz, 75.

15 *Finlandia* was very likely already designed by Wirkkala when he worked with Loewy in New York (1956).

16 *Exquisit* offered vases in 7 sizes, a candlestick, and a cigarette holder.

17 Dietrich Müller, "Rosenthal AG," in Fritz, 139.

18 Fritz, 27.

19 *2000* was constantly promoted by the company and advertised as "the form of the second half of the twentieth century." Schönberger, 1990: 140 ff. In 1962, 5 artist-designers, Wiinblad, Wirkkala, Day, Schröder, and Fischer, selected *Form 2000* for their designs for (20) new decorations; Fritz, 141.

20 Fritz, 80–83.

21 Both *Constanze* and *Eva* were produced at the same time in the same facilities, a situation which led to a number of items receiving Eva's signature in error.

22 A feature of this set, the mushroom knob, would become quite fashionable in the years to come. Though lacking grace and sculptured elegance in comparison, it appeared in a variety of Rosenthal lines: from Jensen's *Rheinland* (1962) and Scharrer's *Medallion* (1962) to Wirkkala's *Composition* (1963), *Rotunda* (1966), and *Grosshandelsform* (1970). Eva, it seems, was once again ahead of the curve and very well in tune with the pulse of the time.

Chapter 16

1 Christine and Jamie Boone, "Hyalyn," paper presented to Wisconsin Pottery Association, February 9, 1999.

2 Lynn Allen to PM, April 27, 2006.

3 Martin Eidelberg et al., *Eva Zeisel: Designer for Industry*, Le Château Dufresne, Musée des Arts Décoratifs de Montréal (Chicago: University of Chicago Press, 1984), 14.

4 "High Fashion 1964," Hyalyn brochure. Distributed by Raymor, NY.

5 Boone, "Hyalyn" paper 1999.

6 Eidelberg et al., 62.

7 Scott Vermillion to PM, e-mail, June 6, 2007.

8 Suzannah Lessard, "Profiles—The Present Moment," *The New Yorker*, April 13, 1987, 40.

Chapter 17

1 Wendy Clark to JR, June 12, 2012.

2 Martin Eidelberg et al., "Eva Zeisel: Ceramist in an Industrial Age," in *Eva Zeisel: Designer for Industry*, Montreal: Le Château Dufresne, Musée des Arts Décoratifs de Montréal (Chicago: University of Chicago Press, 1984), 64.

3 Eidelberg et al., 64; Agnes Kovacs, "The State of the Art: Hungary," ARTMargins Online, January 2000, http://www.artmargins.com/index.php/2-articles/426--the-state-of-the-arthungary.

4 EZ to PK, July 16, 2002.

5 *The History of the Zsolnay Factory*, http://www.zsolnay.hu/2011/eng/gyartortenet.html; Jan Adam, "The Hungarian Economic Reform of the 1980s," *Soviet Studies* 39, no. 4 (October 1987), 610–627; Éva Csenkey and Ágota Steinert eds., *Hungarian Ceramics from the Zsolnay Manufactory 1853–2001* (New Haven, CT: Yale University Press, 2002), 155.

6   *The History of the Zsolnay Factory* http://www.zsolnay.hu/2011/eng/gyartortenet. html.

7   Csenkey and Steinert, 155.

8   EZ to Ibolya Kabok, May 9, 2001; JR/Shawn Johnson, November 24, 2008.

9   Csenkey and Steinert, 159.

10 Csenkey and Steinert, 159.

11 Csenkey and Steinert, 235; Joyce Corbett to JR, e-mail, October 20, 2008.

12 EZ to Ibolya Kabok, May 9, 2001.

13 David Shearer, "Mission," Totem Designs, http://www.totemdesign.com/about/index. html; Karen E. Klages, "Eva Does It," *Chicago Tribune*, July 26, 1998, http://articles. chicagotribune.com/1998-07-26/news/9807260382_1_eva-zeisel-recyclers-tin-cans.

14 Don Joint/Shawn Johnson, October 2, 2008; Don Joint/TT, August 13, 2012; James Pearson, "Eva Zeisel at the Orange Chicken," in *Eva Zeisel: The Shape of Life* (Erie, PA: Erie Art Museum, 2009), 8.

15 Joint/TT, 2012. Many of Eva's other iconic designs were included (none were in production at the time) as well as new designs for furniture and lamps. Alterations to the original designs ranged from slight changes to translating them into entirely different materials, as for example in the hammered sterling silver adaptation of the *Hallcraft Century* stacking platters and bowls. Other items included Hyalyn belly button plates carved out of cherrywood, "Salisbury Artisans" candlesticks and stacking trays, "Mancioli" room dividers, "Schramberg" pitchers, and numerous objects based on designs for the *Town and Country*, *Century*, *Tomorrow's Classic*, and *Museum* lines.

16 Joint/TT, 2012.

17 Joint/TT, 2012.

18 Joint to PM, e-mail, March 28, 2012.

19 Joint/TT, 2012.

20 Joint to Shawn Johnson, e-mail, October 3, 2008.

21 Pearson, 9.

Chapter 18

1   JR/Maureen O'Gorman, August 15, 2011.

2   Toki City, May 4, 2012, http://www.city.toki.lg.jp/wcore/English/Toki.html.

3   JR to author, e-mail, May 4, 2012.

4   JR to author, e-mail, August 4, 2012.

5   JR to author, e-mail, August 4, 2012.

6   JR to author, e-mail, October 5, 2012.

7   JR to author, e-mail, August 4, 2012.

8   Housewares and china departments had different marketing strategies. Housewares suppliers did not offer many accessory pieces, partly because of high inventory costs. The strategy was to keep prices low and to move in and out of different fashionable patterns and shapes. Suppliers to china departments sought to get customers to return year after year to buy accessory pieces for established lines and patterns. This line may have fared better had it been sold in china departments rather than housewares sections but heavier opaque stoneware, including *Pinnacle* with its more casual look, was not considered appropriate for "fine china" departments.

9   Ellen Crouch to PM, e-mail, May 10, 2011.

Chapter 19

1   Their master's degrees are from New York State College of Ceramics at Alfred University and the Cranbrook Academy of Art, respectively.

2   Gregory Garry, *Flaunt no. 44*, 2003, 110. Their work is sold in the U.S., Canada, England, France, Switzerland, Turkey, Hungary, the UAE, Korea, Taiwan, and Japan.

3   William L. Hamilton, "House Proud; In Williamsburg, Streetwise Style and Indie Spirit," *New York Times*, January 20, 2000.

4   The exhibition was in 1999 at the Schein-Joseph International Museum of Ceramic Art, Alfred University.

5   James Klein and David Reid/author, October 21, 2008.

6   They remembered Eva's love for "family" relationships within her dinnerware designs.

7   See chapter 24.

8   Reid/author, October 21, 2008.

9   Klein/author, October 21, 2008.

10 "I think, Eva thought of it as kind of simple at first, like a big gold shape that would go on the wall like an object."; Klein/author, October 21,2008.

11 Klein and Reid/author, 2008.

12 *Lover's Suite* was about the perfect "lover." Created in 2009/2010, it mirrored shapes: Wings, Tulips, Swans, Sprouts. *Lover's Suite 2* came out in 2010 and 2012 saw an edition of the first suite in new colors.

Chapter 20

1   See Nambé website, "History: 1953," http://www.nambe.com/ctl10101/sitecontent/ History. Santa Fe sculptor Richard K.Thomas helped raise the company profile when 3 pieces he designed were shown in the 1953 *Good Design* exhibits in Chicago and New York (organized by MoMA and the Chicago Merchandizing Mart); 2 were included in the exhibition *Creative Skills Today* (1956).

2   Nambé site, "History: 1956," http://www.nambe.com/ctl10101/sitecontent/History; Bob Borden to author, e-mails and telephone conversations, August and September 2008.

3   Caroline Barry, "Eva Zeisel, Mother of Modern," Pure Contemporary, May 27, 2005, http://www.purecontemporary.com/Article/eva-zeisel-mother-of-modern; Borden to author, 2008

4   Stephanie Sawyer, "Eva Zeisel at Nambé", *Eva Zeisel Times*, no. 9, March 2002; Borden to author, 2008.

5   Margaret Carney, "Eva Zeisel—All About Relationships," *Eva Zeisel Times*, no. 9, March 2002; Borden to author, 2008.

6   Eva Zeisel, *Eva Zeisel On Design: The Magic Language of Things* (Woodstock, NY: The Overlook Press, 2004), 209.

Chapter 21

1   After the Soviet period, the factory was known as the Lomonosov Porcelain Factory; in 2006 it reverted to its pre-1917 name, the Imperial Porcelain Factory (*Imperatorskii farforovyi zavod*).

2   John Varoli, "Darkness at Noon Dispelled," *The Art Newspaper*, November 2000, no. 108, 44–45; "Revolutions Come and Go, but a Porcelain Factory Endures," *New York* Times, December 21, 2000, D6.

3   For the introduction of this new material at the factory see T. Astrakhantseva, "Leningradskii kostianoi farfor," in *Sovetskoe dekorativnoe iskusstvo 7*, 1984, 5–12. See also *Kostianoi farfor Imperatorskogo farforovogo zavoda: K 40-letiiu sozdaniia kostianogo farfora v Rossii* (St. Petersburg: Imperatorskii farforovyi zavod, 2009); http://ipm.ru/upload/ file/quick-folder/kostyanoy_farfor_(1).pdf.

4   EZ and JR to author, 2001–2002.

5   It was still available in 2012 in the factory's most elite shop at 6 Petrovka Street in Moscow's fashionable Kuznetskii district.

Chapter 22

1   Olivia Barry/author, October 28, 2011.

2   Barry/author, 2011.

3   Company Production log. Royal Stafford's managing director, A.N. (Norman) Tempest, provided me with material from the company's production log (May 2006–February 2008) in which meetings, samples, and the completion of specific dishes were noted.

4   JR wrote about Bloomingdale's request for the shape change in an unpublished version of this chapter ("1 Oh 1", EZA).

5   JR noted that the oval shape was too extreme ("1 Oh 1," EZA.); both Royal Stafford lines by Eva were made from the same clay (Barry/author, 2011).

6   JR noted this in a full list of One-o-One pieces (1 Oh 1 file, EZA).

7   Tempest/author, telephone interview, October 27, 2011.

8   JR to author, e-mail, April 21, 2012.

9   Tempest/author, 2011.

10 JR, "1 Oh 1," EZA.

11 Barry/author, 2011.

Chapter 23

1   Martin Eidelberg et al., "Eva Zeisel: Ceramist in an Industrial Age," in *Eva Zeisel: Designer for Industry*, Montreal: Le Château Dufresne, Musée des Arts Décoratifs de Montréal (Chicago: University of Chicago Press, 1984), 64.

2   Eva Zeisel, "On Being a Designer," in Eidelberg, et al., 103.

3   Zeisel, "On Being a Designer," 77.

4   Zeisel, "On Being a Designer," 81.

5   The effect of the mottled, semi-matte brown-black glaze on the *Ufo* line may have alluded to her early smoke-fired earthenware but there were major difference in materials and techniques.

6   JR to author, e-mail, July 17, 2012.

7   EZ to Luciano Mancioli, July 25, 1996, EZA; JR to PW, e-mail, 2012.

8   EZ to Luciano Mancioli, 1996, EZA.

9   JR to author, e-mail, 2012.

10 JR to author, e-mail, 2012.

11 Design Within Reach (DWR), "Granit Salt + Pepper Shakers," http://www.dwr.com/product/granit-salt---pepper-shakers.do.

12 JR to author, e-mail, 2012.

13 Metropolis 29: 8 (March 2010), 1 (DWR ad).

14 JR to author, e-mail, 2012; DWR, "Granit Salt + Pepper Shakers."

Chapter 24

1   JR to author, e-mail, March 13, 2005: "Just spoke to Eva. She did not have direct glass experience in Russia or Hungary. However, in Montelupo, Italy, she worked closely with the glass blowers at Mancioli's."

2   Martin Eidelberg et al., "Eva Zeisel: Ceramist in an Industrial Age," in *Eva Zeisel: Designer for Industry*, Montreal: Le Château Dufresne, Musée des Arts Décoratifs de Montréal (Chicago: University of Chicago Press, 1984), 44.

3   Federal Tool Corporation to EZ, letter, May 9, 1947. Only a fragment of the letter exists.

4   JR to author, e-mail, 2005.

5   Michael J. Goldberg, *Collected Plastic Kitchenware & Dinnerware 1935–1965* (Atglen, PA: Schiffer Publishing, 1995), 102. A photograph (102 top) shows 3 dispensers but does not credit the Federal Tool Company.

6   "Sun Glo Studios introduce Eva Zeisel's Silhouette, *Crockery and Glass Journal*, December 3, 1953, 62.

7   "Good Design Selections for January 1953," *Crockery and Glass Journal*, March 2, 1953, 63. A caption reads: "Silhouette glassware, designed by Eva Zeisel . . . Distributed by Sun Glo Studios, 225 Fifth Avenue, NYC"; see also "Sparkle of Glass Heralds New Social Season," *New York World-Telegram and Sun*, October 11, 1952, 9; Corning Price List, 1961.

8   Ad in *Crockery and Glass Journal*, December 3 1953, 53 (reprinted: Heisey Collectors Association News [HCA News], October 1998, 9.) In later interviews, Eva noted that the simplicity of the forms was an economical solution to the company's financial problems.

9   Walter Ludwig, "Convention Banquet Speakers: Ken Dalzell and Eva Zeisel," *HCA News* 22, July 1993, 10.

10 JR to author, 2005.

11 Eva Zeisel, "Notes from a Designer's Diary", *China, Glass and Decorative Accessories*, March 1954, 38.

12 Pattern no. 1637A.

13 Louise Ream, "Imperial Glass Corp. Sold," *HCA News*, February 1973, 7.

14 Pattern no. 6006.

15 "New Products from the Pittsburg Market," *Crockery and Glass Journal*, February 1954, 12; Pattern no. 6007A; Zeisel, "Notes from a Designer's Diary," 1954, 12.

16 Pattern no. 6009A.

17 "New Products from the Pittsburg Market," 12.

18 Pattern no. 520B; EZ, "Notes from a Designer's Diary,"12.

19 Pattern no. 521B.

20 Pattern no. 522B.

21 Zeisel, "Notes from a Designer's Diary," 12.

22 Zeisel, "Notes from a Designer's Diary," 38.

23 Other known variants include a cocktail shaker (the Iced Tea design with a metal cover) and a creamer (the old-fashioned design with an indented spout).

24 Urban Glass, http://www.urbanglass.org.

25 United Nations, *Women in Glass* exhibition, http://www.un.int/portugal/mglassfotos.htm.

26 www.gumps.com/decor/artists...designers/eva-zeisel/...Vitreluxe.

Chapter 25

1   John Zeisel/Rich Cronin, telephone interview, January 23, 2012.

2   William Katavalos, notes (via e-mail from JR), March 25, 2012.

3   Zeisel/Cronin, 2012.

4   Katavalos, 2012.

5   Jonathan Thayer/Rich Cronin, telephone interview, March 23, 2012.

6   Thayer/Cronin, 2012.

7   Steve Slusarski/Ted Wells, telephone interview, December 12, 2011.

8   JR/Rich Cronin, telephone interview, January 10, 2012.

9   Zeisel/Cronin, January 23, 2012.

10 Zeisel/Cronin, 2012.

Chapter 26

1   EZ to PW, August 20, 2003: "Novelty is a commercial term. Novelty has the purpose to consciously search for something different in order to attract attention. Variety is a different aspect of things. It makes life less monotonous and more colorful. It is part of the playful search for beauty."

2   Scott Baldinger, "Looking Forward," *House Beautiful* 138, no. 111, November 1996, 142.

3   Rex Newcomb, Ceramics Consultant, Conservation and Substitution Branch, War Production Board, to EZ, letter, March 16, 1943, EZA: "Inasmuch as the molds used in the Pottery Industry are made of non-critical materials, the standardization will not save any critical materials, but I do believe this program is to be commended because of the manpower saving it can accomplish."

4   Reprint from *Retailing*, May 10, 1943, EZA; reprint of Donald R. Dohner, "Design Techniques for War-Ware," *Interiors*, July 1943, EZA; MoMA, Art in Progress 1944 (Fifteenth Anniversary Exhibition and Catalogue), 236; clipping from *Popular Science*, January 25, 1944, EZA.

5   R. E. Imhoff, General Mills, Inc., home appliance department, to EZ, letter, September 28, 1948: "We wish to express our appreciation of your cooperation throughout this arrangement. The designs are proving satisfactory to us and should be a definite source of professional satisfaction to you." EZA

6   See Kirkham. Part One; Eva Zeisel, *Eva Zeisel On Design: The Magic Language of Things* (Woodstock, NY: The Overlook Press, 2004), 117.

7   Brochure, no date, EZA.

8   EZ to PW, May 15, 2005.

9   Luciano and Andrea Mancioli, Marina Vignozzi, *Dedicato Eva Zeisel*, catalogue (Mancioli Porcellane, Altopascio, Italy 1995).

Select Chronology

1   Irving Achorn to author, e-mail, July 24, 2005.

2   JR to author, June 28, 2008. See also Eva Zeisel, *Eva Zeisel on Design: The Magic Language of Things* (Woodstock, NY: Overlook Press, 2004), 177.

3   "Todo para Su Cocina Moderna," *El Excelsior*, Mexico City, Friday, January 26, 1951, 13.

4   Four retailers showed Eva's design (unidentified) in ads in *El Excelsior*, namely El Centro Mercantil, S.A. (September 19, 1951, 7-B), La Ciudad de Mexico (October 6, 1951, 24-A), Ferreteria de San Juan (October 20, 1951, 16-A), and Salinas y Rocha (Sunday, January 6,1952, 6-C).

5   Loza Fina, S.A., ad "Elegancia y Distinción," in *El Excelsior*, Friday, November 16, 1951, 22-A.

6   Ana Elena Mallet, Clara Porset et al., *El diseño de Clara Porset: Inventando un México moderno / Clara Porset's Design: Creating a Modern Mexico*, Franz Meyer Museum, Mexico City, 45. See also Mallet's essay in the same publication.

7   For MoMA, see Mallet, Porset et al., *El diseño de Clara Porset*, 22.

8   Martin Eidelberg et al., "Eva Zeisel: Ceramist in an Industrial Age," in *Eva Zeisel: Designer for Industry*, Montreal: Le Château Dufresne, Musée des Arts Décoratifs de Montréal (Chicago: University of Chicago Press, 1984), 44.

9   Achorn to Ray Vlach, e-mail, July 13, 2005.

10 EZ/Ray Vlach, September 20, 2000.

11 *China, Glass and Decorative Accessories*, March 1953, 30.

12 See Ronald T. Labaco, "The Playful Search for Beauty: Eva Zeisel's Life in Design," in *Studies in the Decorative Arts*, vol. 8 (New York: Bard Graduate Center): 137. For Goss, see Jaime Robinson to PM, e-mail, August 9, 2009.

13 Zeisel/ author, August 28, 1993.

14 Iliif Watt's annotated "Jungle Barnyard" listing, January 10, 1955.

15 Michel Cadoret, 10 Tapisseries (Paris: Paris Editions, 1955).

16 Zeisel/author, 1993.

17 Bryce Watt (Iliif Watt's son)/author, mid-1993.

18 Bryce Watt/author, mid-1993.

19 The Tea Center, brochure, 1961.

20 JR to PM, e-mail, October 25, 2011.

21 Steve Rappaport/PM, telephone interview, November 7, 2011.

22 Lucie Young "At 90, a Designer Still Ahead of the Curve," *New York Times*, Living Arts section, August 14, 1997, C1.

23 Natasha McRee to PM, e-mail , July 15, 2008.

24 McRee to PM, July 15, 2008.

25 Corp.www/Chantal.com/usecare_classicteakettle.asp.2007.

26 McRee to PM, e-mail, November 4, 2006.

27 McRee to PM, e-mail, July 15, 2008.

BIBLIOGRAPHY

Earl Martin

Abrams, Jane. "Leisure Theme of Italian Show." *New York Daily News*, August 9, 1964, 88.

Adam, Jan. "The Hungarian Economic Reform of the 1980s." *Soviet Studies* 39, no. 4 (October 1987): 610–627.

Agarkova, G. D., and Nataliia Petrova. *250 Years of Lomonosov Porcelain Manufacture, St. Petersburg: 1744–1994*. Desertina, Switzerland: Lomonosov Porcelain Manufacture, 1994.

Andreeva, L. "Raspisnoi farfor Petra Leonova." *Dekorativnoe iskusstvo SSSR*, no.8 (1969): 35–37.

Andreeva, L. V. *Sovetskii farfor, 1920–1930-e gody*. Moscow: Sovetskii khudozhnik, 1975.

Andreeva, Lidia. *Sovetskii farfor: Fond Sandretti russkogo iskusstva XX veka / Soviet Ceramics: The Sandretti Collection of 20th Century Russian Art*. Bad Breisig, Germany: Palace Editions, 2004.

Art in Progress, A Survey Prepared for the Fifteenth Anniversary of the Museum of Modern Art. New York: Plantin Press, 1944.

Aspesi, Natalia. *Inge Fotoreporter*. Milan: Seniorservice Books, 2000.

Astrakhantseva, T. "Leningradskii kostianoi farfor." *Sovetskoe dekorativnoe iskusstvo* 7 (1984): 5–12.

Baldinger, Scott. "Looking Forward." *House Beautiful* 138, no. 11 (November 1996): 142.

Bam, N. "Slovo za promyshlennost'iu." *Legkaia industriia* (Moscow), April 25, 1934, 1.

Barter, Judith A., and Jennifer M. Downs. *Shaping the Modern: American Decorative Arts at The Art Institute 1917–65*. Chicago: Art Institute of Chicago, 2001.

Bee, Harriet, and Michelle Elligott. *Art in Our Time: A Chronicle of The Museum of Modern Art*. New York: The Museum of Modern Art, 2004.

Bergdoll, Barry, and Leah Dickerman. *Bauhaus 1919–1933: Workshops for Modernity*. New York: The Museum of Modern Art, 2009.

Berlin, Ira. *Slavery in New York*. New York: The New Press, 2005.

Blauvelt, Andrew. *Ideas for Modern Living: The Idea House Project / Everyday Art Gallery*. Minneapolis: Walker Art Center, 2000.

Bluhm, Hans-Georg. *Stationen: Der Keramiker Siegfried Moller 1896–1970*. Kellinghusen, Germany: Museum Kellinghusen, 2003.

Bodine, Sarah. "Eva Zeisel: Humanistic Design for Mass Production." *Industrial Design* 30 (July–August 1983): 42–49.

Boram-Hays, Carol Sue. *Bringing Modernism Home: Ohio Decorative Arts, 1890–1960*. Athens, OH: Ohio University Press in association with the Columbus Museum of Art, 2005.

Brassard, Gertrude. "Place and Show." *American Home*, August 1954, 54.

Bredehoft, Neila, and Thomas Bredehoft. *Handbook of Heisey Production Cuttings*. St. Louisville, OH: Cherry Hill Publications, 1991.

Bredehoft, Neila, and Thomas Bredehoft. *Heisey Glass, 1896–1957*. Paducah, KY: Collector Books, 2001.

Bröhan, Torsten, and Thomas Berg. *Design Classics, 1880–1930*. Cologne; London; New York: Taschen, 2001.

Brosterman, Norman. *Inventing Kindergarten*. New York: Harry N. Abrams, 1997.

Browder, Walter. "Eva Zeisel's New Stoneware." *Crockery and Glass Journal* 153 (October 1953): 116.

Brown, Carol. "What Makes a Set of Dishes Both Pleasant to Look at and Practical?" *Pathfinder*, April 23, 1952, 36–37.

Bruce, Gordon. *Eliot Noyes: A Pioneer of Design and Architecture in the Age of American Modernism*. London and New York: Phaidon, 2006.

Buckley, Cheryl. *Potters and Paintresses: Women Designers in the Pottery Industry, 1870–1955*. London: Women's Press, 1990.

Burckhardt, Lucius, ed. *The Werkbund: Studies in the History and Ideology of the Deutscher Werkbund, 1907–1933*. London: Design Council, 1980.

Cadoret, Michel. *10 tapisseries*. Paris: Éditions Printel Paris, 1955.

Carney, Margaret. *Lost Molds and Found Dinnerware: Rediscovering Eva Zeisel's Hallcraft*. Alfred, NY: International Museum of Ceramic Art, 1999.

"Casual Ware: It's a Big Business!" *Crockery and Glass Journal* (March 5, 1951): 25–27.

Chipman, Jack. *California Pottery Scrapbook*. Paducah, KY: Collector Books, 2005.

Csenkey, Éva, and Ágota Steinert, eds. *Hungarian Ceramics from the Zsolnay Manufactory, 1853–2001*. New Haven and London: Yale University Press for Bard Graduate Center, 2002.

Cummings, Keith. *A History of Glassforming*. Philadelphia: University of Pennsylvania Press, 2002.

Cunningham, Jo. *Homer Laughlin China 1940s & 1950s*. Atglen, PA: Schiffer Publishing, 2000.

Cunningham, Jo. *The Best of Collectible Dinnerware*. Atglen, PA: Schiffer Publishing, 1995.

Cunningham, Jo. *The Collector's Encyclopedia of American Dinnerware*. Paducah, KY: Collector Books, 1982.

"Debut New Zeisel Patterns." *Gift and Tableware Reporter* (March 1962): 98.

DeCaro, Frank. "Collecting." *Martha Stewart Living*, June 1996.

"Decoration Topic: Tea." *Living for Young Homemakers* (September 1952): 63.

Desorgues, Juliette, et al. *Bauhaus: Art as Life*. London: Koenig Books in association with Barbican Art Gallery, 2012.

"Dinnerware Adorned." *Interiors* 111 (February 1952): 114.

"Dinnerware Among New Items Planned for United's 100th Anniversary." *China, Glass and Decorative Accessories*, December 1949: 94.

"Distinctive Petal Shape Sparks Dinnerware Line." *Retailing Daily*, July 16, 1956.

Doering, Erika, Rachel Switzky, and Rebecca Welz. *Goddess in the Details: Product Design by Women*. New York: Association of Women Industrial Designers and Pratt Institute Department of Exhibitions, 1994.

Dohner, Donald R. "Design Techniques for War-Ware." *Interiors* 102 (July 1943): 36–39.

Drexler, Arthur, and Greta Daniel. *Introduction to Twentieth Century Design, From the Collection of the Museum of Modern Art, New York*. Garden City, NY: Doubleday, 1959.

Duhrssen, Alfred. "A Quarter-Century of Dinnerware Design." *China, Glass and Decorative Accessories* (June 1953): 49–50.

Duhrssen, Alfred. "Are Today's Design-Standards Slipping?" *Crockery and Glass Journal*, (December 1952): 96–97.

Duke, Harvey. *Hall 2*. Brooklyn, NY: ELO Books, 1985.

Durus, Alfred (pseudo. Kemeny). "Sowjetisches Porzellan: Austellung im Mostorg." *Deutsche Zentrale-Zeitung*, May 14, 1935.

Eatwell, Ann. *Susie Cooper Productions*. London: Victoria and Albert Museum, 1987.

Eidelberg, Martin (ed.). *Design 1935–1965: What Modern Was*. New York: Harry N. Abrams, 1991.

Eidelberg, Martin et al. *Eva Zeisel: Designer for Industry*. Montreal: Le Château Dufresne, Musée des Arts Décoratifs de Montréal (Chicago: University of Chicago Press, 1984).

"1850–1950: A Century of Progress in Both Domestic and Import Fields Is Being Marked by United China & Glass Co." *Crockery and Glass Journal* 145, no. 6 (December 1949): 122.

El Arte en La Vida Diaria: Exposición de Objetos de Buen Diseño Hechos en México. Mexico City: Instituto Nacional de Bellas Artes, 1952.

Emme, B. N. *Russkii khudozhestvennyi farfor*. Moscow: Iskusstvo, 1950.

Endres, Werner. "Renommierte Designer in der Oberpfälzer Steingutproduktion: Möller, Stricker-Zeisel, Krause, Löffelhardt." In *Steingut: Geschirr aus der Oberpfalz*, edited by Werner Endres, 159–166. Munich: Deutscher Kunstverlag, 2004.

Endres, Werner, ed. *Steingut: Geschirr aus der Oberpfalz*. Munich: Deutscher Kunstverlag, 2004.

Eva Zeisel—Eva Tsaizel: Farfor i keramika Evy Tsaizel'-Shtriker. St. Petersburg: Titul, 1992.

"Eva Zeisel: Potter." *The Art of Living* series, (dir. Chip Cronkite). Retirement Living Television Network (RLTV). Web video. October 29, 2011. http://www.davidheidelberger.com/player.php?name=aol/2036_zeisel&rexte=mov&title=Eva%20Zeisel&xdim=384&ydim=288.

Eva Zeisel: The Shape of Life. Erie, PA: Erie Art Museum, 2009.

"Eva Zeisel to Design Dinnerware for Hall." *Crockery and Glass Journal*, (November 1951): 68.

"Eva Zeisel, 1906–2011." *Modernism* 15, no. 1 (April 2012): 24.

Figiel, Joanna Flawia, ed. *Revolution der Muster: Sprtizdekor-Keramik um 1930*. Karlsruhe, Germany: Badisches Landesmuseum, 2006.

"Fine China in Modern Design by Eva Zeisel." *Arts & Architecture* 63 (June 1946): 28.

"Fine China, U.S.A." *Newsweek*, April 29, 1946, 90.

Fineberg, Jonathan, ed. *Discovering Child Art: Essays on Childhood, Primitivism and Modernism.* Princeton, NJ: Princeton University Press, 1998.

Franklin, Paul B. "Eva Zeisel." *Nest: A Magazine of Interiors* (April 2001): 104–113.

Frauen im Design: Berufsbilder und Lebenswege seit 1900 / Women in Design: Careers and Life Histories Since 1900. Stuttgart: Landesgewerbeamt Baden-Wurttemberg, 1989.

Fritz, Bernd. *Die Porzellangeschirre des Rosenthal Konzerns 1891–1979.* Stuttgart: Union Verlag, 1989.

Fritz, Bernd, and Helga Hilschenz. *Rosenthal, Hundert Jahre Porzellan: Ausstellung, Kestner-Museum Hannover.* Stuttgart: Union Verlag, 1982.

Froebel, Friedrich. *Die Menschenerziehung.* Keilhau, Germany: Verlag der allgemeinen deutschen Erziehungsanstalt, 1826.

Hiesinger, Kathryn B. *Design Since 1945.* Philadelphia: Philadelphia Museum of Art, 1983.

Goldberg, Michael J. *Collectible Plastic Kitchenware and Dinnerware 1935–1965.* Atglen, PA: Schiffer Publishing, 1995.

Gough, Marion. "Are You Aware of the Increasing High Style of Durability?" *House Beautiful* (April 1952): 118–119.

Gruber, Helmut. *Red Vienna: Experiment in Working-Class Culture, 1919–1934.* New York: Oxford University Press, 1991.

Guarnaccia, Steven. *Goldilocks and the Three Bears, A Tale Moderne.* New York: Abrams Books, 2000.

Gulick, Walter. "Letters about Polyani, Koestler, and Eva Zeisel." *Tradition & Discovery: The Polanyi Society Periodical* 30, no. 2 (2003–2004): 6–10.

Harrod, Tanya, ed. "Craft, Modernism and Modernity." Special issue, *Journal of Design History* 11, no. 1 (1998).

Harrod, Tanya. "Eva Zeisel Obituary: Industrial Designer Known for Her Ceramic Tableware." *The Guardian*, January 15, 2012, http://www.guardian.co.uk/artanddesign/2012/jan/15/eva-zeisel.

Hauschild, Joachim. *Philip Rosenthal.* Berlin: Ullstein, 1999.

Hayward, Leslie. *Poole Pottery: Carter & Company and Their Successors 1873–1995.* Somerset, England: Richard Dennis, 1995.

Heard, Frances. "For a Successful Wardrobe of Tableware Spend More Thought Than Money." *House and Garden* (June 1952): 108–109.

Henley, Helen. "Improved Plastic Table Accessories Bid for Social Regard: Eva Zeisel Uses New Approach in Her Designs for Cloverware." *Christian Science Monitor*, October 21, 1947, 10.

Hoffer, Peter Charles. *The Great New York Conspiracy of 1741.* Lawrence: University of Kansas Press, 2003.

Hornbostel, Volker. "C. & E. Carstens die neue linie: Bunt und Modern." In *Revolution der Muster: Spritzdekor Keramik um 1930*, edited by Joanna Flawia Figiel, 47–57. Karlsruhe, Germany: Badisches Landesmuseum, 2006.

"Important People." *China, Glass and Decorative Accessories* 65 (May 1965): 20.

"In the Showrooms: New Furniture Designs." *Interiors* 109 (March 1950): 125.

"Interesting Curves to New Dinnerware." *New York Times*, March 11, 1952, 24.

Jahoda, Marie, Lazarfeld, Paul, and Hans Zeisel, *Die Arbeitslosen von Marienthal: Ein soziographischer Versuch über die Wirkungen langdauernder Arbeitslosigkeit.* Leipzig: Hirzel, 1933.

Jenkins, Steven. *Midwinter Pottery: A Revolution in British Tableware.* London: Richard Dennis, 1997.

Johnson, J. Stewart. *American Modern, 1925–1940: Design for a New Age.* New York: The Metropolitan Museum of Art and Harry N. Abrams, 2000.

Johnstone, Jyll. *Throwing Curves: Eva Zeisel.* San Francisco: Canobie Films, 2003, DVD.

Kahn, Eve M. "All about Eva." *Interiors* 158, no. 9 (September 1999): 78–81.

Kaufman, Edgar. *What Is Modern Design?* New York: Museum of Modern Art, 1950.

Kerr, Ann. *Rosenthal: Excellence for All Times.* Atglen, PA: Schiffer Publishing, 1998.

Kettering, Karen L. *Eva Zeisel: The Playful Search for Beauty.* Knoxville, TN: Knoxville Museum of Art, 2004.

Kettering, Karen L. "'Ever More Cosy and Comfortable:' Stalinism and the Soviet Domestic Interior, 1928–1938." *Journal of Design History* 10, no. 2 (March 1997): 119–135.

Kinchin, Juliet. "Hide and Seek: Remapping Modern Design and Childhood." In *Century of the Child: Growing by Design, 1900–2000*, edited by Juliet Kinchin and Aidan O'Connor, 10–27. New York: Museum of Modern Art, 2012.

Kinchin, Juliet. "Hungary: Shaping a National Consciousness." In *The Arts & Crafts Movement in Europe & America: Design for the Modern World*, edited by Wendy Kaplan, New York: Thames & Hudson in association with the Los Angeles County Museum of Art, 2004.

Kinchin, Juliet, and Aidan O'Connor, eds. *Century of the Child: Growing By Design, 1900–2000.* New York: Museum of Modern Art, 2012.

Kirkham, Pat. *Charles and Ray Eames: Designers of the Twentieth Century.* Cambridge, MA: MIT Press, 1995.

Kirkham, Pat. *Harry Peach, Dryad, and the DIA.* London: Design Council, 1986.

Kirkham, Pat. "Humanizing Modernism: The Crafts, 'Functioning Decoration' and the Eameses." In "Craft, Modernism and Modernity," edited by Tanya Harrod. Special issue, *Journal of Design History* 11, no. 1 (1998): 15–29.

Kirkham, Pat, ed. *Women Designers in the USA, 1900–2000: Diversity and Difference.* New Haven and London: Yale University Press for Bard Graduate Center, 2000.

Kirkham, Pat, and Jennifer Bass. *Saul Bass: A Life in Film and Design.* London: Laurence King Publishing, 2011.

Kirkham, Pat, and Ella Howard, eds. "Women Designers in the USA, 1900–2000." Special issue, *Studies in the Decorative Arts* 8, no. 1 (Fall–Winter 2000–2001).

Kissel, Howard. "Zeisel Looks Back: The Eventful Journey of a Design Engineer." *Women's Wear Daily*, September 27, 1984.

Koestler, Arthur. *Darkness at Noon.* London: Jonathan Cape, 1940.

Koestler, Arthur. *Spanish Testament.* London: Victor Gollancz, 1937.

Kudryavtseva, Tamara. *Circling the Square: Avant-Garde Porcelain from Revolutionary Russia.* London: Fontanka, 2004.

Labaco, Ronald T, "'The Playful Search for Beauty': Eva Zeisel's Life in Design," in "Women Designers in the USA, 1900–2000," edited by Pat Kirkham and Ella Howard. Special issue, *Studies in the Decorative Arts* 8, no. 1 (Fall–Winter 2000–2001): 125–138.

Lehner, Lois. *Lehner's Encyclopedia of U.S. Marks on Pottery, Porcelain & Clay.* Paducah, KY: Collector Books, 1988.

Lessard, Suzannah. "Profiles: The Present Moment." *The New Yorker* (April 13, 1987): 36–40, 43–46, 49–52, 56–59.

Levitt, Kari. *The Life and Work of Karl Polanyi: A Celebration.* Montreal; New York: Black Rose Books, 1990.

"Local Ceramics Company to Display Dinnerware." *Riverside Enterprise*, September 24, 1947, 5.

Loesch, Anette, and Wolfgang Hennig. *Rosenthal-Porzellan vom Jugendstil zur Studiolinie.* Dresden: Staatliche Kunstsammlungen, 1991.

Loewy, Raymond. *Industrial Design.* Woodstock, NY: Overlook Press, 1979.

Loewy, Raymond. *Never Leave Well Enough Alone.* New York: Simon & Schuster, 1951.

Long, Christopher. *Paul T. Frankl and Modern American Design.* New Haven and London: Yale University Press, 2007.

Makovsky, Paul. "A Maker of Things: The Legendary Eva Zeisel Reflects on Some of Her Iconic Designs." *Metropolis* 31, no. 3 (October 2011): 50.

Mallet, Ana Elena, Clara Porset, and Oscar Salinas Flores. *El diseño de Clara Porset: Inventando un Mexico moderno / Clara Porset's Design: Creating a Modern Mexico.* Mexico City: Museo Franz Meyer, 2006.

"Market Preview." *Crockery and Glass Journal* (December 1954): 22.

Martin, Jim, and Bette Cooper. *Monmouth-Western Stoneware.* Des Moines, IA: Wallace-Homestead Book Co., 1983.

Maxon, Lois. "White China Best to Start." *New York World Telegram and Sun*, May 16, 1957, 20.

McCready, Karen. *Art Deco and Modernist Ceramics*. London: Thames and Hudson, 1995.

Meikle, Jeffrey L. *Design in the USA*. Oxford and New York: Oxford University Press, 2005.

Meisenbach, J. A. "Der neue Stil des praktischen Gebrauchsgeräts." *Die Schaulade* 6 (February 1930): 177–179.

"Merchandise Cues: More Zeisel Serving Pieces." *Interiors* 111 (November 1951): 124.

"Midhurst Features Hallcraft Zeisel-Designed Dinnerware." *Crockery and Glass Journal* (July 1952): 81.

"Midhurst Holds Party to Introduce New Design." *Gift and Art Buyer* (September 1956): 80.

"Midhurst Named Representative for New Line by Hall China." *China, Glass and Decorative Accessories* (November 1951): 27.

"Modern China Shown at Museum." *Retailing Home Furnishings* (April 18, 1946): 36.

"Modern Chinaware Designed by Eva Zeisel at the Modern Museum." *Art News* (May 1946): 12.

"Moderne Steingutkeramik." *Die Schaulade* 7 (February 1931): 238–239.

Moore, Pat. *Eva Zeisel's Schramberg Designs*. San Francisco: Labor of Love Press, 2010.

Morrison, Harriet. "Today's Living: Dinnerware Has Delicate Airs." *New York Herald Tribune* (March 11, 1952), 22.

"Museum Honors New Castleton Line." *Crockery and Glass Journal* 138, no. 5 (May 1946): 39.

"Museum Pieces Belong at Home." *House Beautiful* (December 1947): 122.

Musicant, Marlyn R. "Maria Kipp: Autobiography of a Hand Weaver." In "Women Designers in the USA, 1900–2000," edited by Pat Kirkham and Ella Howard. Special issue, *Studies in the Decorative Arts* 8, no. 1 (Fall–Winter 2000–2001): 92–107.

"New Dinnerware by Eva Zeisel Features Asymmetrical Shapes." *China, Glass and Decorative Accessories* (March 1947): 50.

"New in New York." *China, Glass and Decorative Accessories* (January 1952): 33.

"New Profits with Casual China." *Crockery and Glass Journal* (August 1959): 23–29.

"New Shape in Dinnerware." *Family Circle* (October 1952): 108–109.

Norman, Anne. "Ceramist Doesn't Call Kettle Black." *Los Angeles Times*, May 23, 1957, B7.

100 Useful Objects of Fine Design 1947: Available Under $100. New York: The Museum of Modern Art, 1947.

Paszkowski, Marina Vignozzi. *Manifattura Mancioli: dalla maiolica alla porcellana*. Milano: Electa, 1999.

Philipp Rosenthal, sein Leben und sein Porzellan. Leipzig: Klinkhardt & Biermann Verlag, 1929.

Popp, Michael, and Klaus Haußmann. *Hirschauer Steingut: Die Geschichte der Fabriken und Produkte*. Nuremberg: Popp, 2011.

Postrel, Virginia. "How Modernism Got Its Curves: A Look at the Extraordinary Career of Designer Eva Zeisel." *Slate*, September 1, 2005, http://www.slate.com.

Pratt, Michael. *Mid-Century Modern Dinnerware: Ak-Sar-Ben Pottery, Denwar Ceramics, Iroquois China Company, Laurel Potteries of California, Royal China Company, Stetson China Company*. Atglen, PA: Schiffer Publishing, 2002.

Pratt, Michael. *Mid-Century Modern Dinnerware, A Pictorial Guide: Ak-Sar-Ben to Paden City Pottery*. Atglen, PA: Schiffer Publishing, 2003.

Pratt, Michael. *Mid-Century Modern Dinnerware, A Pictorial Guide: Redwing to Winfield*. Atglen, PA: Schiffer Publishing, 2003.

Pratt, Michael. "The Hall China Company: 104 Years of Exceptional Design and Production." http://modish.net/hall-china.

Prisant, Carol. "In the Firing Line: Eva Zeisel." *World of Interiors* 26, no. 1 (January 2006): 80–87.

R. K. "O dushe khudozhnikov i maslenitse." *Komsomol'skaia Pravda*, April 22, 1934, 1.

Raizman, David. *History of Modern Design*. Upper Saddle River, NJ: Pearson Prentice Hall, 2004.

Rapaport, Brooke Kamin, and Kevin L. Stayton. *Vital Forms, American Art and Design in the Atomic Age, 1940–1960*. New York: Brooklyn Museum and Harry N. Abrams, 2001.

Ream, Louise, Neila Bredehoft, and Thomas Bredehoft. *Addendum to Encyclopedia of Heisey Glassware, vol. 1: Etchings and Carvings*. Newark, OH: Heisey Collectors of America, 1981.

Reiss, Ray. *Red Wing Dinnerware: Price and Identification Guide*. Chicago, IL: Property Publishing, 1997.

"Red Wing is 75 years old." *Crockery and Glass Journal* (November 1952): 64.

Richards, Jean, and Brent C. Brolin, eds. *Eva Zeisel: A Soviet Prison Memoir*. iBook, 2012.

"'Riverside China' to Have National Sales." *Riverside Enterprise* (August 10, 1947): 7.

"Riverside: New Fine China." *Giftwares and Housewares* (August 1947): 34.

Roche, Mary. "25 Pieces of Fine China in Modern Design to Be Shown at Museum Beginning Today." *New York Times*, April 17, 1946, 30.

Roche, Mary. "Utility Exhibition Will Start Today." *New York Times*, September 17, 1947, 29.

Rodin, I. T., ed. *Khudozhestvennyi farfor: katalog*. Moscow-Leningrad: Iskusstvo, 1938.

Rosenthal, Philip. *Einmal Legionär*. Hamburg: Knaus, 1980.

"Rosewood and Ceramic Combined in New Zeisel Line Shown in Akron." *Retailing Daily*, October 22, 1951.

Rudoe, Judy. *Decorative Arts 1850–1950: A Catalogue of the British Museum Collection*. London: British Museum Press, 1991.

Ruggles, Ann. "China Plates that Snuggle in Your Lap." *New York World-Telegram and Sun*, December 19, 1951, 18.

Sardar, Zahid. "Doyenne of Design: Eva Zeisel's Curvy, Organic Shapes Changed the Look of the American Table." *San Francisco Chronicle*, April 23, 2003, http://www.sfgate.com/homeandgarden/article/Doyenne-of-design-Eva-Zeisel-s-curvy-organic-2620995.php.

Schönberger, Angela, ed. *Raymond Loewy: Pioneer of American Industrial Design*. Munich: Prestel, 1990.

Schreiber, Hermann, Dieter Honisch, and Ferdinand Simoneit. *Die Rosenthal Story, 1879–1979*. Düsseldorf: Econ Verlag, 1980.

Schwartz, Frederic J. *The Werkbund: Design Theory and Mass Culture Before the First World War*. New Haven and London: Yale University Press, 1996.

Schwarz, Dean, and Geraldine Sawyer , eds. *Marguerite Wildenhain and the Bauhaus: An Eyewitness Anthology*. Decorah, IA: South Bear Press, 2007.

"Sees the End of Schism Between Hand, Machine." *Retailing Home Furnishings* 14 (February 16, 1942): 24.

Sheppard, Eugenia. "China Service Is Displayed in Modern Shapes." *New York Herald Tribune*, April 17, 1946, 20.

Sheppard, Eugenia. "New Shapes for Old." *New York Herald Tribune*, May 25, 1947, 42–43.

Shinn, Deborah Sampson. *Revolution, Life, and Labor: Soviet Porcelains (1918–1985)*. New York: Cooper-Hewitt, National Museum of Design, Smithsonian Institution, 1992.

Slater, Greg, and Jonathan Brough. *Comprehensively Clarice Cliff*. London: Thames & Hudson, 2005.

Smith, R. E. F., and David Christian. *Bread and Salt: A Social and Economic History of Food and Drink in Russia*. Cambridge, UK, and New York: Cambridge University Press, 1984.

Snyder, Jeffrey B. *Hall China*. Atglen, PA: Schiffer Publishing, 2002.

Sobolevskii, N. "Puti sovetskogo farfora." *Iskusstvo* 1934, no. 5: 169–171.

Steen, Karen E. "The Playful Search for Beauty: Eva Zeisel, Industrial Designer." *Metropolis* (January 2001): 84–88. http://www.metropolismag.com/html/content_0101/ez.htm.

Stern, Bill. *California Pottery: From Missions to Modernism*. San Francisco: Chronicle Books, 2001.

Stirton, Paul. "Frederick Antal and Lazlo Peri: Art, Scholarship and Social Purpose." *Visual Culture in Britain* 13, no. 2 (2012): 207–225.

Stoneware Designed by Eva Zeisel Is Launched in Los Angeles." *Crockery and Glass Journal* (May 1957): 60.

Stricker, Eva. "Die Künstlerin hat das Wort." *Die Schaulade* 8, no. 3–4 (February 1932): 173–174.

Stricker, Eva. "Grimasy Bezvkusitsy na Farfore." *Legkaia Industriia*, April 4, 1936.

Stricker, Eva, et al. "Von Einer Steingutfabrik und Von Steingutkeramik." *Die Schaulade* 8, no. 3–4 (February 1932): 172–174.

Stricker, [E.], and [H.] Fuhlbrügge. "Unsere Initiative wird nicht beachtet: Spezialistenbrief." *Rote Zeitung: Organ des Leningrader Gebietsrates der Gewerkschaften*, March 9, 1934, 4.

Struss, Dieter. *Rosenthal Dining Services, Figurines, Ornaments, and Art Objects*. Atglen, PA: Schiffer Publishing, 1997.

"Sun Glo Studios Introduce Eva Zeisel's Silhouette." *Crockery and Glass Journal* (August 1952): 62.

Szapor, Judith. "From Budapest to New York: The Odyssey of the Polanyis." *Hungarian Studies Review* 30, no. 1–2 (Spring–Fall 2003): 29–60.

Szapor, Judith. *The Hungarian Pocahontas: The Life and Times of Laura Polanyi Stricker, 1882–1959*. Boulder, CO: East European Monographs; New York: Distributed by Columbia University Press, 2005.

Szarkowski, John, et al. *The Museum of Modern Art at Mid-century at Home and Abroad*. New York: The Museum of Modern Art, distributed by H. N. Abrams, 1994.

Szenasy, Susan S. "An Appreciation: The Long and Prolific Life of Eva Zeisel." *Metropolis* 31, no. 7 (February 2012): 14.

"Table Fashions '65: Earthenware Is Prettier Than Ever." *China, Glass & Tablewares*, December 1964.

Tadd, James Liberty. *New Methods in Education: Art, Real Manual Training, Nature Study*. New York: Orange Judd, 1899.

Tauger, Mark B. *Natural Disaster and Human Actions in the Soviet Famine of 1931–1933*, Carl Beck Papers in Russian and East European Studies, no. 1506. Pittsburgh, PA: University of Pittsburgh, 2001.

"There's Harmony in Contrast." *Crockery and Glass Journal* (November 1951): 56.

Thompson, Dennis, and W Bryce Watt. *Watt Pottery: A Collector's Reference with Price Guide*. Atglen, PA: Schiffer Publishing, 1994.

"Ungarische Kunstler in Philadelphia." *Pester Lloyd*, December 31, 1926.

Useful Objects for the Home: A National Survey and Exhibition, Presenting a Guide to Well Designed Objects for Everyday Use. Akron, Ohio: Akron Art Institute, 1947.

Varoli, John. "Darkness at Noon Dispelled." *The Art Newspaper*, no. 108 (November 2000): 44–45.

Varoli, John. "Revolutions Come and Go, but a Porcelain Factory Endures." *New York Times*, December 21, 2000, D6.

Venable, Charles, Katherine C. Grier, Ellen Denker, and Stephen G. Harrison. *China and Glass in America, 1880–1980: From Tabletop to TV Tray*. Dallas: Dallas Museum of Art; New York: Harry N. Abrams, 2000.

Viola, Wilhelm. *Child Art and Franz Cizek*. New York: Reynal and Hitchcock, 1936.

Vodrey, Catherine S. *A Centennial History of the Hall China Company*. Cleveland, OH: Stevens Barons Communications and Hall China Company, 2002.

Weissberg-Cybulski, Alexander. *The Accused*. New York: Simon & Schuster, 1951.

"What Are Plastics?" *Everyday Art Quarterly* (Winter 1947/48): 1.

"What Can Consumers Expect in Dinnerware Design?" *Crockery and Glass Journal* (December 1951): 146.

"What's New in Dinnerware & Glassware." *Gift and Art Buyer* (December 1951): 82.

Whitmyer, Margaret and Ken. *Collector's Encyclopedia of Hall China*, 3rd ed. Paducah, KY: Collector Books, 2001.

Wildenhain, Marguerite. *The Invisible Core: A Potter's Life and Thoughts*. Palo Alto, CA: Pacific Books, 1973.

Wilk, Christopher, ed. *Modernism: Designing a New World, 1914–1939*. London: V&A Publications; New York: Distributed in North America by H. N. Abrams, 2006.

"Work Starts on Ceramic Plant." *Riverside Enterprise*, April 8, 1947, 3.

Youds, Bryn. *Susie Cooper: An Elegant Affair*. New York: Thames and Hudson, 1996.

Young, Lucie. "At 90, a Designer Still Ahead of the Curve." *New York Times*, August 14, 1997, C1.

Young, Lucie. *Eva Zeisel*. San Francisco: Chronicle Books, 2003.

"Zeisel Designs Stoneware Line." *Crockery and Glass Journal* 153 (July 1953): 116.

Zeisel, Eva. "Are Handles Necessary?" *Department Store Economist* 8 (July 1945): 97, 112.

Zeisel, Eva. "Can Dun's Rate the Designer?" *Retailing Home Furnishings* 18 (May 30, 1946): 24.

Zeisel, Eva. "Ceramic Design at Pratt Institute." *China, Glass and Lamps* 59 (June 1940): 20–21.

Zeisel, Eva. "Ceramic Design for Replacement." *China, Glass and Lamps* 61 (May 1942): 12, 24.

Zeisel, Eva. "Decorations Grow to Fine Arts Level." *Crockery and Glass Journal* 162 (February 1958): 40.

Zeisel, Eva. "Dinnerware from Pratt Institute." *China, Glass and Lamps* 60 (June 1941): 58–59.

Zeisel, Eva. *Eva Zeisel on Design: The Magic Language of Things*. Woodstock, NY: Overlook Press, 2004.

Zeisel, Eva. "Eva Zeisel on the Playful Search for Beauty." Filmed February 2001. TED2001 video. Posted December 2008. http://www.ted.com/talks/eva_zeisel_on_the_ playful_search_for_beauty.html.

Zeisel, Eva. "Foreword." In *Sourcebook of Architectural Ornament* by Brent C. Brolin and Jean Richards. New York: Van Nostrand Reinhold Co., 1982, 6–7.

Zeisel, Eva. "How to Make Designs 'Different.'" *Crockery and Glass Journal* 137 (September 1945): 36–37.

Zeisel, Eva. "Notes from a Designer's Diary." *China, Glass and Decorative Accessories* (March 1954): 12, 37–38.

Zeisel, Eva. "On Being a Designer." In *Eva Zeisel: Designer for Industry*, by Martin Eidelberg et al. *Eva Zeisel: Designer for Industry*. Montreal: Le Château Dufresne, Musée des Arts Décoratifs de Montréal (Chicago: University of Chicago Press, 1984): 73–104.

Zeisel, Eva. "On Designing for Industry." *Interiors* 105 (July 1946): 76, 130–132.

Zeisel, Eva. "Registering a New Trend." *Everyday Art Quarterly* (Fall 1946): 1–2.

Zeisel, Eva. "Sees End of Schism Between Hand, Machine." *Retailing Home Furnishings* 14 (February 16, 1942): 24.

Zeisel, Eva. "Some Problems of Dinnerware Design." *Ceramic Age* 40 (July 1942): 3–10.

Zeisel, Eva. "The Coming Era of Dinnerware Design." *China, Glass and Decorative Accessories* (December 1951): 59.

Zeisel, Eva. "Subtleties of Plastic Design in Ceramics." *Interiors* 101 (November 1941): 53–55, 68–71.

Zeisel, Eva, and Thomas Connors. "Conversation." *Glass Magazine* 42 (1990).

INDEX

Library of Congress Cataloging-in-Publication Data available.

ISBN: 978-1-4521-0852-0

Manufactured in China.

EDITOR: Pat Kirkham

EXECUTIVE DIRECTOR: Pat Moore

CONCEPT AND DESIGN DIRECTION: Pirco Wolfframm

TAXONOMY ILLUSTRATIONS: Camila Burbano and Pirco Wolfframm

PHOTOGRAPHY: Brent Brolin

ASSISTANT PROJECT MANAGER: Barbara Weber

10 9 8 7 6 5 4 3 2 1

Chronicle Books LLC
680 Second Street
San Francisco, CA 94107

www.chroniclebooks.com